The Lancashire Witch Conspiracy

A History Of Pendle Forest
And The
Pendle Witch Trials

JOHN A CLAYTON

The Lancashire Witch Conspiracy

A History Of Pendle Forest
And The
Pendle Witch Trials

Second Edition

BARROWFORD
PRESS

August 2007

Copyright © 2007 John A Clayton

ISBN 978-0-9553821-2-3

Plans, diagrams and maps are intended for illustrative purposes only

Photographs and illustrations by the author unless otherwise stated

COVER DESIGN: Barrowford Press

VERSO IMAGE: Pendle Hill from the Middop Valley

OTHER TITLES BY THE SAME AUTHOR

Internet Ancestry (out of print)

ISBN 0-9538364-0-1 *Published 2000*

Valley of the Drawn Sword:
Early History of Burnley, Pendle and West Craven

ISBN 0-9553821-0-6 *Published 2006*

First published in paperback April 2007
ISBN 978-0-9553821-1-6

Revised and published in Second Edition August 2007

Printed in the UK

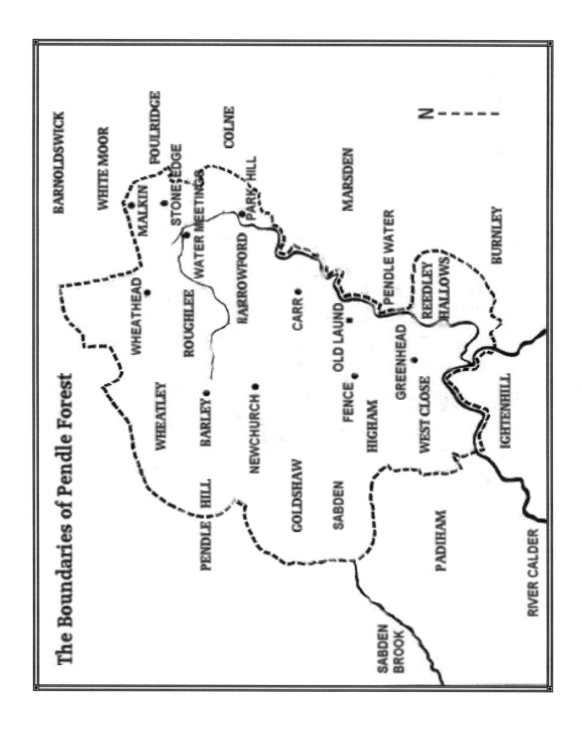

The Boundaries of Pendle Forest

Contents: Part One

Part Two

Preface

The prior publication to this book, *'Valley of the Drawn Sword,'* covered the early history of the East Lancashire region of Burnley and Pendle and also 'washed over' into the neighbouring West Cravenshire district of Yorkshire. *The Lancashire Witch Conspiracy* takes up the story where the previous volume left off, namely at the Norman Invasion of 1066. This text is not intended to be a dedicated sequel to the earlier publication as the area of this present research is centred firmly upon the historical formation, people and places of the Forest of Pendle. There is, however, a continuity between the two works that can be seen to cover the history of a corner of Lancashire that has long been famous for events at the very end of our earlier formative history – the Lancashire Witch Trials.

To understand the events that were to unfold in that fateful year of 1612 a study of the formation of the Pendle Forest will prove invaluable. This is an area whose very soul has been exposed to public view for many years. Living and working in the Forest of Pendle I have met with many people from the outlying farming areas, these are the very places mentioned within the available texts covering the witch legend. Fifty years ago the country people of Pendle were living and working in very much the same way as their predecessors of four-hundred years earlier. They had the same dry sense of humour, dressed similarly and spoke virtually the same localised language; this broad country dialect would seem to be a foreign language today but I now realise that, as Pendle youngsters, my generation were to be the last to be exposed to a culture that would soon clash with the age of television and pay the price.

Through a lateral study of the available records it has been possible to trace the real people behind the Pendle Witch legend and to extend our knowledge of them significantly. The main characters of the story, and their family roots, are placed in a fresh context; who would have thought, for example, that Old Demdike was possibly from a relatively wealthy family?

Alongside these new insights into the characters behind the story we also have surviving sites that were closely connected to those accused of practising the art of witchcraft; West Close, Newchurch, Greenhead, Roughlee, Barley, Blacko, Higham, Fence, Wheatley *et al* still proudly wear their country roots firmly upon their sleeves.

As a native of Barrowford I have long been fascinated by the mystery of Malkin Tower and the stories of Old Demdike who lived there. We have to this day, on the southern Blacko Hillside, the Malkin Tower Farm and I hope to show, through the results of long research, that this site is where Elizabeth Southern (Old Demdike) spent the last years of her life. Due to the fact that Blacko was, at the time, a part of Over Barrowford I view Old Demdike as an adopted fellow Barrowfordian and, were she to be alive today, I hope that she would see at least some value in the text that follows!

The *conspiracy* within the title of this book reflects the extremely complex cousinhood between the land-owning gentry families who were responsible for pressing the case against the Pendle Forest poor-folk in 1612; and to a lesser degree, in 1633. There is a great deal of new evidence to show that this alliance of the powerful was ultimately responsible for the Witch Trials and that the pursuit of their cause ran much deeper than we have previously realised.

Acknowledgements

As always I extend my gratitude to my wife, Sylvia, for her inexhaustible patience. Her support in this project has been invaluable, as has the additional research that she has so ably carried out.

No project of this kind can possibly come to fruition without the aid of the information stored within our Local District Libraries. The staff within the local studies departments of these establishments have been ever-helpful and for this I must thank them; especially the staff at Colne, Nelson, Burnley and Clitheroe Libraries. Lancashire Records Office also merits a large thank you for the efficient way in which invaluable records are so efficiently and quickly produced.

Along with a wealth of surviving historical records the people of the Forest of Pendle have also been fortunate in that we have had a wealth of dedicated local historians to chart the historical course of our area. Gladys Whittaker, in the concise way of all good local historians, has shown in her research within *Roughlee Hall - Fact and Fiction* that the accepted story of the 1612 trials is not always accurate and that research can, and does, pay dividends. I hope that I have taken up this mantle in some acceptable fashion.

Mary Brigg has done much to increase our knowledge of the history of Pendle Forest, her publications upon the subject have been providing an accurate analysis for many years and I make no apologies for drawing upon her knowledge wherever necessary.

Doreen Crowther, a fellow Barrowfordian, has provided a wealth of hand-written source material for the local historian to study. The local libraries hold these invaluable texts covering the whole spectrum of our local interest.

The loan of photographs and postcards is much appreciated. Some of the early photographs are not of as good a quality as might be desired but, of course, this is by virtue of their age.

Last, but certainly not least, I must mention our landowners upon whose property the local history of our area can still be found. Sites, such as Malkin Tower Farm, would not have given over their available secrets without the cooperation and enthusiasm of the owners and for this I thank them.

Glossary

AMERCEMENT:
A fine in respect of breaking the law.

AGISTMENT:
The rental paid to a landlord for grazing stock upon his land.

ASSIGN:
One to whom property (or rights) were legally transferred.

BAILIFF:
An official responsible for two or three manors.

BOOTH:
Originally from the Norse word for *'farmhouse'* the term eventually described the hamlets within the forest.

CAPITAL MESSUAGE:
A large house

CLOSE:
An enclosure taken from open fields in which deer or farm-stock were kept.

COPYHOLDER:
Holder of land or property from the overlord by written deed.

DEMESNE:
Land and property retained by the lord of the manor for his own use. In the Honour of Clitheroe this also applied to the main property of a large estate.

DOWER:
The portion of a widow's right - usually one-third of the estate of the deceased.

ENFEOFFMENT (FEOFF): The act of placing someone legally in charge of property - a Trustee.

GREAVE:
Also known as a reeve - a person elected by his fellow boothsmen, or tenants of the manor. As chief officer he was responsible for the running of his community.

HALMOTE:
The local court of the lord of the manor.

HONOUR:
As in the Honour of Clitheroe - a large co-division of land including many separate manors and estates under the administration of a single overlord.

INSTAURATOR:
From the Latin *'taurus = bull'* - chief officer of the vaccaries.

LAUND:
An open clearing or enclosure for deer within the forest.

MANOR:
The landed estate of the lord of the manor. Strictly speaking there were no official *'manors'* within the Pendle Forest area although many areas were given the title to facilitate administration.

MESSUAGE:
A house along with the outbuildings and yard.

OXGANG:
A land measure - variable throughout different areas - related to the amount of land that a team of oxen could plough within one year. Also known as a bovate.

PINFOLD - POUNDER:
A pinfold was an enclosed area in which stray cattle were impounded. The owner could not release his stray stock until he paid a fine to the pounder.

RODELAND:
Land cleared from former waste lands - related to the land measure of a ROD.

SUIT:
Labour provided by an under-tenant in lieu of payment to the lord - also to be obliged to attend the manorial court.

SOKE:
Usually applied to the rights of the lord, or king, to receive payment for the grinding of his tenant's corn. The manorial tenants were obligated to use the manorial mill.

TURBARY:
The right to take peat (or turf) from the commons to burn for fuel.

VACCARY:
A cow farm within the forest areas.

VILL:
A commonly-organised settlement under the feudal system - village.

Dedicated to the memory of my father

Following the publication of the first edition of this book a number of people have expressed their wish to see the Part One (A History of Pendle Forest) extended and, therefore, I have taken the opportunity to do so in this Second Edition.

The material in Part Two (The Lancashire Witch Conspiracy) has also been re-organised; this has provided the opportunity to include findings that have come to light in the short space between editions.

I have also taken the opportunity to add an extra thirty-six pages, additional photographs, maps, a glossary and footnotes; all of which, it is hoped, will provide additional aid to the researcher and casual reader alike.

John A Clayton
Barrowford
August 2007

Part One

A History of the Forest of Pendle

Chapter One

To the Norman Conquest

The Norman shall tread on the Saxon's heel,
And the stranger shall rule o'er England's weal

The Danish-born Cnut was Crowned in the year AD 1017 and turned out to be a relatively successful king of England, he used the wealth of the English treasury to reward his followers from the Scandinavian homelands and, as an act of political astuteness, he married Emma, the widow of former king Aethelred. In 1018 Cnut signed an agreement with the English people and paid off the Danish forces, at land and at sea, with a Danegeld tribute of some £72,000. Unlike Aethelred's previous attempts to pay off the invaders, Cnut's actions worked a treat and all but forty Danish ships sailed home. As time passed Cnut found that, by necessity, he was spending an increasing amount of time abroad and to address this problem he appointed close allies to run things in his absence. He partitioned England into four main parts, Wessex, East Anglia, Mercia and Northumbria – he kept Wessex for himself and appointed ealdormen, or earls, to rule over the other three. One of these earls was an Englishman called Godwin whom Cnut appointed as earl of Wessex, Godwin married Cnut's sister-in-law (or possibly his sister) and created for himself huge estates.

Cnut died at around the age of fifty in November 1035 and again the succession was disputed, on the one side was Harold Harefoot, who was Cnut's son by Aelfgifu, and on the other was Emma's son, Harthacnut. The solution to this problem was for both men to rule in a joint regency, a protracted period of political intrigue followed, mainly instigated by Emma, but earl Godwin finally had his way and Harold Harefoot was generally accepted as sole king of England in 1037. Harefoot died in March 1040 and the absent Harthacnut, along with his mother Emma, arrived back in England with a great fleet and took over what they had always considered to be their rights of kingship. Unfortunately the line of Harthacnut was programmed genetically to live a short life and Emma, realising this, brought Edward, a son by her earlier marriage to Aethelred, to England to rule with Harthacnut in joint kingship – to prove Emma right Harthacnut duly died in June 1042!

Edward was Crowned king and one of his first steps was to strip his formerly powerful mother of her estates because she *'had been formerly very hard'* on him, although they were to be partially reconciled, the good times for Emma were over and she died at Winchester in 1052.[1] In

---

[1] David Starkey, *The Monarchy of England*, (Chatto & Windus, 2004)

15

1045 Edward married Edith, the domineering daughter of earl Godwin, Edith had two elder brothers who had already risen to the ranks of earldom, Swein of Wessex and Mercia and Harold of East Anglia. Gradually king Edward came to despise the powerful house of Godwin and things eventually came to a head with a military stand-off, the eventual consequence of which was that Godwin and his family were outlawed and fled to Flanders. In the meantime, Edward had been cultivating his contacts in France, where he had lived for so long in exile, he invited his nephew, William, Duke of Normandy, to England and it is possible that on this visit Edward made a political gesture and promised William the succession to the English Crown.

The people of England, however, were not best pleased at this apparent move to hand control of England over to the French, the aristocracy began to show their allegiance to the exiled Godwin and he was not slow to take advantage. He returned to England with his son, Harold, and eventually effected a pardon before the *witan* council, the fact that Edward had to co-exist with his enemy appears to have played upon Edward's mind and he went into a major sulk. He turned his back on the perceived ingrates of the English people and threw himself into his religious project of the Westminster Abbey foundation. In April 1053 Godwin died and gradually Edward became closer to Godwin's sons, Tostig and Harold, in fact Harold became the king's confidante and Tostig became earl of Northumbria in 1055 – two of his other brothers, Gyrth and Leofwin (the husband of Lady Godiva) were also given earldoms. In 1063 Harold and Tostig attacked Wales for the king and sent him the severed head of one Gruffud ap Llwelyn.

The later period of Edward's reign was relatively successful, things bumped along as they had a tendency to do but trouble arose in 1065 when earl Tostig alienated the Northumbrians. As a southerner his ways were somewhat alien to the northerners who accused him of false taxation, perversion of the law and robbing of churches. The Northumbrian leaders moved against Tostig and stripped him of his power and marched south, eventually Harold, acting as mediator, persuaded Edward to accept the northerners' choice of leader, Morkere, as earl of Northumbria. The Domesday Book refers to much of the area of Pennine Lancashire as *'wastes'* and it has been suggested that this might have been as a result of the northern uprising. [1]

Edward was sixty years of age at this time and it would appear that the northern uprising affected him badly, by late December 1065 he had taken to his deathbed. Surrounded by his close court, Edward, in one of his more lucid moments, said to Harold *"I commend this woman* (his wife, Edith) *and all the kingdom to your protection."* This was taken to be a formal declaration of the succession of Harold on Edward's part, he died on the 5th January, 1066. Harold was duly Crowned king and was soon at loggerheads with his brother, Tostig, who attacked the coast from his base in the Isle of Wight and progressed to Lincolnshire. Harold, with a massive show of force, booted Tostig out of England causing him to flee into exile in Scotland, Harold then positioned his forces along the south coast in readiness to combat the expected threat from William in France.

During much of Edward's reign the old Viking enemy were too busy fighting amongst themselves to trouble England but this was to end when king Harold Hardrada of Norway brought an armada of some three-hundred ships and landed in the Tyne where Tostig joined forces with him - despite a valiant defence by the earls Edwin and Morkere, the invaders took York. Harold arrived on the scene, having marched his southern-based troops north, and both Tostig and Hardrada were slain at the ensuing Battle of Stamford Bridge – the English all but annihilated the Vikings. Meanwhile, William had been amassing his troops in France and now

---

[1] Denise Kenyon, *The Origins of Lancashire* (Manchester University Press, 1991)

only required favourable weather to mount his campaign to capture the English throne to which, as far as he was concerned, he had a God-given right. By a cruel stroke of fate the wind turned in William's favour immediately following Harold's victory at Stamford bridge, the Norman invasion of England was now underway.

On hearing the unwelcome news Harold started straight for the south, he consolidated in London for around a week and then set out, possibly before he was fully prepared, to meet the newly-arrived William. Harold's hoped for element of surprise did not materialise as the Normans had advanced notice of their coming and were prepared. The ensuing Battle of Hastings commenced on the 14th October, the English foot soldiers facing mounted French knights, Harold's brothers Leofwin and Gyrth, were killed but then it appeared that a number of the Norman army were attempting to flee the field; it is thought that the English broke ranks to pursue them and were cut down by the troops of William's half-brother, Bishop Odo. The constant volleys of arrows began to take their toll upon the English positions and eventually Harold's close entourage were slain, the king himself was disabled by an arrow (traditionally to the eye) and then killed by a heavy sword blow to the thigh. The English, seeing their leader had fallen, fled into history.

William of Normandy, not so fondly known as William the Bastard, now had his prize of the English Crown and he brought with him a hegemony that was to change the face of the nation. No longer would rich and poor share a common language and no longer would the poor man or woman enjoy the relatively even-handed Saxon laws. The diverse former Saxon estates of Lancashire would become the single lordship of William's favourites, it would not be long before the powerful new religious orders would appear on the scene and the lord's hunting forests of Pendle, Trawden, Rossendale and Bowland would be created. These forest areas gradually gave way to new farming operations but the culture of the Forest of Pendle, by and large, remained firmly rooted in its ancient past.

Duke William's Legacy

The Domesday Book, commissioned by William The Conqueror and finalised in 1086, is a survey which, in reality, indicated the state of the nation's land-holdings and possessions at the end of the Saxon era; the boundaries of most of the nation's estates had been carried over from this period. It shows that tenth and eleventh century Lancashire as a whole consisted chiefly of large multi-settlement estates whose origins were in the society not long anterior to the Conquest; the centre of these estates shifted within the Scandinavian era so as to accommodate changing defensive requirements. In our particular area of east Blackburnshire these estates had been held largely as royal demesne (for the use of the king, or lord), possibly since the pre-Norman time of Cnut. We did not warrant many listings in the Domesday Survey as the area tended to have many small settlements within the larger estates.

The Survey indicates that the national population at that time was around two million, perhaps one-tenth of these lived within towns; this is a marked change to the early Saxon period when no towns appear to have existed. There were 13,418 named vills, these were areas of feudal land, with buildings, that were organised so as to benefit the vill community. Within these named vills were some 268,984 recorded individuals, some of these people would live within vills that had expanded to become true villages. The topography of our area, however, meant that we tended to retain the small hamlet settlements, and scattered farmsteads of the Anglo-Saxon period. A local example of this is the cluster of farmsteads on the heights above Barrowford where Pasture Lane climbs over to Roughlee. From Higher Ridge Farm across to West Pasture Farm, Spitalfield Head, Fulshaw on to Ridgaling and Noggarth, the farmsteads hug the ridge top. Buildings have been lost within this area over time, notably a possible early one at Spitalfield Head. The ridge-top settlement lay on the cross-roads of a section of the important early ridgeway from Ribchester to Elslack (here passing along the ridge to Utherstone and beyond) and the route from Ridgaling down to Higherford.

The ancient ridgeway route from Pasture Lane to Utherstone

Shortly before the Norman Conquest Anglo-Saxon England had developed an agricultural system that would change little for hundreds of years. Earlier methods saw the vill inhabitants sharing the available common land, each year the villeins cultivated different strips of land, often scattered around the common to ensure that no one person had the advantage of continually using the best land. The strips were cultivated with different crops over two years and left fallow on the third year.

The open-field method of farming became established within other parts of the country, this meant that two or three fields were cultivated as one plot, the use of manure ensured continuity of crops. Instead of the scattered individual strips the fields were cultivated using larger communal lengths. These were a furrow's length, or furlong, other land measures were perches, poles, rods and chains; it is thought that these relate to the pre-historic *megalithic yard*. The furlong is still used today in horse-racing and represented the distance that a pair of oxen could pull the plough before they required resting. This also related to the common medieval land measure of an *oxgang* used to describe larger areas, this measure was based on the area that teams of oxen could cultivate and varied according to the heaviness of the soil. Study of early estate records shows that the two/three infield type of cultivation was beneficial to the larger farming community.

Charters of field and estate boundaries dating to the tenth century begin to mention a feature called *headlands* – at the head of each plough length (where the ox team turned around) a strip of land was left unploughed, this meant that a passable trackway remained to enable the cultivators to access the whole of the land, this was the *headland* and it was illegal to spoil it with the plough. An interesting example of this is provided by the Clitheroe court rolls of the sixteenth century.[1] The ancestors of the Smiths (who founded the cotton manufacturing firm of Smith and Nephew at Brierfield) owned copyhold land at Hill Farm in the hamlet of Lane Bottom, Briercliffe.[2] A surrender (where the property had to be released in court back to the sovereign, or lord, before being re-granted) of 1530 states that:

To this Halmote (Ightenhill Court) *comes John Smith of Briercliffe upon Hill and surrenders 1 messuage* (farm buildings) *and 10 acres of land called Dodgefield and 6 acres in Le Townfield*

---

[1] W. Farrar, *Clitheroe Court Rolls,* (Volumes 1 & 2 , 1912)

[2] Roger Frost, *A Lancashire Township,* (The Rieve Edge press, 1982)

(common) *and 1 acre called Marlecroft lying between Dodgefield and Holthill and 1 acre called Battiehole to the use of Stephen Smith chaplain..............*

Then in 1565: *Nicholas Hargher and Richard Woodruff, Queen's tenants, surrender 1 house, 1 parcel of a barn with garden now in the tenure of Alice Smith of Hill widow: and a close of land called Dodgefield, another field called Headlands adjacent to Dodgefield and also 8 ridges or seliones of land abutting upon said headland, which ridges, called "landes," be in Le Townefield of Burnley containing 5 acres of land: which the said Alice Smith delivered to Nicholas and Richard, to the use of William Halstead of Ridehalgh and his assigns during her life, in consideration of a marriage to be solemnised between the said William Halstead and Margaret Smith daughter of the said Alice Smith. Admittance granted at 20d.*

The house, barn, garden and land mentioned here were all parcel of Hill Farm. The house was replaced by a later building in the early nineteenth century and still stands on Halifax Road as it heads out of Lane Bottom towards Boulsworth Hill. The barn, directly opposite the farm house, was a rare example of a sixteenth century aisled barn but has now been converted into a dwelling. The Dodge Field, Headlands, Townfield and Ridges still exist exactly as they were except for the later enclosure walls. A group of crofts behind the barn were still known as *Eight Lands* on the 1843 tithe map, these are the *8 ridges* or *seliones*.

A selion was a strip of arable land in the common fields, normally about twenty-two yards (twenty metres) in length. The team of oxen ploughing the strip kept going in the same direction, round and around the strip in narrowing turns, so that each furrow turned the soil inwards, eventually making a ridge along the centre of the selion. The lowest furrow around the outside acted as a drain.

The name of *Dodgefield* almost certainly has its roots within the old English *dodge* for a description of a *'nose-like protuberance'* [1]– this is an exact description of the land as it dips into the valley where the Ice Age waters of the Burnley Basin burst through into the Walverden Valley. To this day Dodgefield is a single, open field of some fifteen acres, never having been divided. The *Townfield* adjoins the *8 Lands* and was the common land for the use of the community. The modern field wall boundaries of this area incorporate gate-posts of millstone grit whose style and extreme wear suggests that they pre-date the 'modern' enclosure walls by many centuries. [2]

The Ownership of Lands

The ecclesiastical parishes of pre-Norman times were generally made up of a number of townships, often there was a detached portion of the parish showing that the land-use requirements had changed. A good example of this within our area is Brogden, a detached portion of the parish of Barnoldswick adjoining the old Lancashire and Yorkshire county boundary. The hamlet of Admergill within Brogden, whilst falling within the Lancashire parish of Colne, was part of the Yorkshire constabulary. The former township of Brogden was actively depopulated by the Cistercians in the post-Norman period and can no longer be referred to as a township, it consists of a few scattered farms within a superb area of open moorland.

---

[1] Eilert Ekwall, *The Place-Names of Lancashire* (1922)
[2] John A Clayton, *Valley of the Drawn Sword - Early History of Burnley, Pendle & West Craven,* (Barrowford Press, 2006)

The larger parishes, such as Blackburn and Whalley, were well defined by natural boundaries such as rivers, and can be seen to conform to the areas covered by secular estates when the tithe system became accepted as the norm during the tenth century. The hundred of Blackburnshire was made up of two large parishes; the forty-five townships within Whalley parish and the twenty-four townships within the parish of Blackburn.[1]

Following the Norman Conquest events began to unfurl that would culminate in the creation of the historic county of Lancashire. William Ist was faced with problems of insurrection from his noblemen in the North and regularly had need to march on York to reassert his authority. On the 20th September 1069 a faction of the army of Swein, king of Denmark, joined forces with a group of English rebels, amongst whom was Earl Waltheof, and the coalition captured the city of York. They demolished William's castle there and slaughtered the resident French garrison. William understandably took umbrage at this and for the third time that year found himself on the long march north. He was determined to stamp out the insurrection once-and-for-all, having bought off the Danes he set about wreaking a destruction that must have been horrendous to behold. Everything within his path to York was ravaged, villages were burnt, crops destroyed and livestock killed. An eleventh century writer stated that:

'Never did William such cruelty; to his lasting disgrace, he yielded to his worst impulse, and set no bounds to his fury, condemning the innocent and the guilty to a common fate.'

This *Harrying of the North* was truly shocking, never again did the north think to oppose William. It is known that his destruction was carried north of York but it is not clear as to what extent he ravaged Lancashire. The Domesday Book mentions that of the fifty-nine vills dependant upon Preston *'16 of them have a few inhabitants....The rest are waste.'* There are a number of possible explanations for this however; other than destruction at the hands of William it is possible that the area had not recovered following the ousting of earl Tostig in 1065.

The upshot of all this was that William decided that he needed a hard man to take charge of his naughty northern subjects and he decided upon Roger de Poitou, the third son of William's cousin Roger de Montgomery. Thus in 1071 Roger de Poitou was entrusted with the huge north-west estates of lands between the Ribble and Mersey (Lancashire *south of the sands*) and large holdings in the Craven district of Yorkshire. However, by the year 1086 the king had reclaimed these holdings for the Crown; the reason for this is unclear but was possibly due to a rebellion or a land exchange. By the 1090s Roger de Poitou again held the Lancashire estates along with the lands north of the sands. In 1102 Roger again lost the estates when he joined with his brothers in a rebellion against Henry Ist. The lands were then kept together as a unit and granted to Henry's nephew Stephen, Count of Bologne (later to become King Stephen) between 1114 and 1116. In 1138 the Scots army occupied the areas north of the Ribble and Ranulf II, Earl of Chester, annexed the lands between Ribble and Mersey, eventually holding them legally between 1141 and 1149.

The 1153 treaty of Wallingford saw Stephen's son, William de Warrene, hold the Lancashire estates until his death in 1159, the honour reverted to the Crown in 1164. Following the accession of Richard the Lionheart, John (Richard's brother) was granted the honour in 1189. The honour of Lancaster was not exactly the same as the shire of Lancaster; the honour was a

[1] T.D.Whitaker, *History of Whalley*, (1st Edition, 1881)

feudal lordship of castles and dues and covered other parts of the country such as Derby, Nottinghamshire and Suffolk.

Under the early rule of Henry III the honour of Lancaster was run by a sheriff on behalf of the Crown; after his restoration in 1266 Henry bestowed the honour of Lancaster, and all the royal demesne of Lancashire, upon his son Edmund – this effectively established the Duchy of Lancaster. Edmund died in 1296 and his son Thomas became the third Earl of Lancaster, he married Alice de Lacy, the daughter and heir of Henry de Lacy, third Earl of Lincoln. On the death of Henry de Lacy in 1310 at Lincolns Inn, Thomas succeeded to the earldoms of Pontefract, Bollingbroke, Clitheroe and Halton.

Forty years later Henry, the fourth earl of Lancaster, was made up into a duke and Edward III created the County Palatine of Lancaster. This was largely because of Lancashire's strategic position in the war against the Scots who had carried out many violent incursions into our area in the fourteenth century. Palatine powers only ran within the county boundaries, the king's writ did not take effect within the palatine although he had the final say within the Duke's court. The king's writ was effective elsewhere within the Duchy of Lancaster (outside the palatine bounds). The Queen is, of course, the present Duke of Lancaster.

Roger de Poitou built the castle at Lancaster and also endowed a priory there, this was a daughter house of St. Martin of Seez in France. Roger had his knight's services to the king to consider and so he *enfeoffed* sub-tenants to his Lancashire holdings. Blackburn was granted to Albert de Greslet and Roger de Busli, the latter also had large land holdings in Yorkshire which became the Barony of Tickhill.

An early photograph of Clitheroe Castle

It is thought that many of the pre-Conquest Saxon land holders were allowed to retain their holdings, albeit under the new Norman jurisdiction; this meant that the existing pattern of Saxon farmsteads and settlements survived within our area.

Ilbert de Lacy had acquired the honour of Clitheroe by 1102, having been placed as a reliable *Overlooker in the North* by Roger de Poitou, and the family retained it for over a century until, as we have seen, the estates passed into the Duchy of Lancaster. It has been suggested that Robert de Lacy built the stone castle at Clitheroe in 1186, probably as a replacement for an earlier structure.[1] There were many castles within the area of east Blackburnshire following the Conquest, these structures often replaced later Saxon defensive *burhs* and early Norman earthwork defences of the eleventh century.

The new Norman overlords took the vills and estates with the best defensive advantages, gave them borough status and erected their new castles. As time progressed these structures were often abandoned in favour of other sites as the importance of certain areas increased; this can be seen where the lord's manor house at Ightenhill gradually relinquished its importance to the administrative centre of Clitheroe. Castle sites locally included Burnley, Colne, Castle Haugh near Gisburn (known locally as Cromwell's Basin), Ellenthorpe (Gisburn), Briercliffe and Extwistle although it is unclear as to the role that these played within the local defensive structure of the Normans. [2]

The impressive Castle Haugh earthwork, Gisburn

[1] D. J. C. King, *Castellarium Anglicanum* (New York, Vol 1, 1983)
[2] John A Clayton, *Valley of the Drawn Sword,* (Barrowford Press, 2006)

Chapter Two

The Honour of Clitheroe

The earliest reference to Clitheroe by name appears to be a charter of 1122 when Hugh de Laval, lord of Clitheroe, granted the castle chapel there, together with the other churches of Whalley, Colne and Burnley, to the monks of Pontefract Priory. This grant never actually came to fruition.

In the year 1311, following the death of Henry de Lacy, one Robert de Woodhouse, the king's *Escheator Beyond Trent,* came to Clitheroe to carry out an enquiry (*Inquisitio post mortem*) into Henry's possessions. It was stated that the earl had held the honour of Clitheroe, the lordships of Rochdale and Tottington, the barony of Penwortham and lands in the Widnes area. A detailed survey of Henry's holdings was carried out and these lands then passed to the earl's son-in-law, Thomas, earl of Lancaster. The survey is a valuable account of the state of Blackburnshire at this time with the caveat that there are two important omissions. The lands held by the church in free alms are not included and the dower lands held by the earl's mother are hardly covered. [1]

The honour of Clitheroe appears to follow the normal pattern of a feudal estate whereby land was either held within demesne manors by the lord for his own use, or leased to tenants. Sometimes the term *Manerium (manor)* is used as being synonymous with the term *hundred* as in *'Manerium vel Hundretum de Blackburnshire'* whilst in the early *'Status de Blackburnshire'* it is used simply as a settlement, or separate holding.

Outside of the forest areas the lord's main manorial sites were the domanial establishments of Ightenhill Stud and the granges of Standen and Accrington. These were estates that the lord exploited for his own use and the people of the peripheral vills probably performed *suit* at these three places.[2] At the time of the 1311 inquisition most of the demesne vills (a commune of the lord's workers) within Blackburnshire were located to the east of the River Calder. Places such as Colne, Great and Little Marsden, Briercliffe, Burnley, Ightenhill, Padiham, Pendleton, Standen and Downham were all noted as not having been officially granted out. This is complicated, however, by the fact that some of these places were of dual tenure – Colne, for instance, appears to have been largely demesne on the west side.[3] The smaller villages that we know today, such as Foulridge, Worsthorne, Simonstone, Read, Twiston etc, were homage vills whereby the inhabitants owed suit to the lord. The hamlets of Great and Little Mearley, to the east of Pendleton, were in this category but have now disappeared. In 1326 an inquisition reported that Adam Noel (Nowell) had a right to the woods in the chase of Great Mearley, his father before him held the area of a knight's service and rent of twenty pence. Adam's service consisted of:

'20d to the ward of Lancaster Castle, and by finding a plough-team, ploughing one day a year

---

[1] T. D. Whitaker, *History of Whalley,* (1st edition, 1881)

[2] *Suit* was a form of homage where those dependant upon the lord worked his land in lieu of payment of rent - it also describes the obligation to attend the manorial court

[3] Denise Kenyon, *The Origins of Lancashire, (*Manchester University Press, 1991)

in Lent in the demesnes of Standen, receiving fourpence for the ploughman's food from the said demesnes; and by finding a reaper to reap one day a year in harvest time, receiving three halfpence for his food.'

The whole of the area constituting the honour of Clitheroe had changed hands following the Norman Conquest and the changes in its administration, estates and social structure was marked. New laws were brought into being, communities had new overseers and the business of the honour was to be documented as never before.

The lord's developed certain areas of their estates out of all recognition, Walton-le-Dale, for instance, grew to become one of the most affluent places in this part of Lancashire. Other vills were not so lucky, as we have seen at Mearley, over time they were to dwindle in importance to such an extent that they became none-existent.

An engraving of Clitheroe in the 18th century

The area within the honour of Clitheroe kept by the lord was organised as a single unit rather, than a series of individual manors, with their own administration. This meant that the lord carried out his jurisdiction through separate halmote courts, each one serving the wider community of vills within its area. During the fourteenth century the two main estate centres of the honour were Clitheroe Castle and the manor house at Ightenhill. Colne had its own *'Hall of Pleas'* and there were probably similar establishments at Accrington and Standen. The Pendle area was served by the halmote at Higham Hall from 1522; Burnley was served by a court held at Saint Peter's church as the Ightenhill establishment had, by this time, deteriorated to such an extent that it had become unusable. The castle at Clitheroe was garrisoned but it is not clear as to the date that this practice ceased; the records do show, however, that the castle church of St. Michael was an important establishment with its own parish encompassing the forests of Clitheroe, Standen Grange and the castle complex itself.

The constable of the castle shared the responsibility for the running of the estates with the steward of Blackburnshire, he was responsible for the garrison armaments, supplies and general logistics, this was a particularly important post in those times of frequent conflict. Beneath the constable was the porter who was responsible for the general maintenance of the castle. An early account of the Duchy of Lancaster shows the fees due to the officers of the honour of Clitheroe:

Officer	£	s	d
Receiver to the honour	*15*	*13*	*4*
Master forester of	*15*	*13*	*4*
Master forester of Bowland	*6*	*13*	*4*
Steward of Blackburnshire	*3*	*6*	*8*
Const. of Clitheroe castle	*10*	*0*	*0*
Porter of the castle	*3*	*0*	*8*
Keeper of Radholme Park	*1*	*10*	*4*

Radholme Park, shown in the list of officer's fees as providing the least income for estate officers, was one of two great deer parks within the forest of Bowland and was allied closely to the Parker families. Peter de Alcancotes, of the Alkincoats estate in Colne, was born around the year 1230, he had a son Adam de Alcancotes who was living at the Colne estate in 1311. A Richard le Parker, of the Forest of Trawden, inherited Alkincoats Hall and his son, Edmund Parker, became the park keeper at Radholme. Edmund inherited Alkincoats Hall and his two sons, Richard and John, became joint park keepers at Radholme.

From 1380 the brothers held the lease of the vaccary of Radholme, this was renewed in 1400 and Richard Parker went on to build the first house at what is now Browsholme Hall. The Parker families continued at Browsholme and Alkincoats, the latter becoming freehold in 1570 when it combined several estates.

In 1534 Jamys Parker and Xpofer Parker were paying a subsidy on their goods at Alkincoats and by 1534 we see Xpofer Parker paying in goods, Lawrence Parker paying in lands, Alexander Parker paying in goods and Ellen Parker was also paying in goods.[1] By the 39th year of the reign of Queen Elizabeth I (1597) the *Subsidy Lists* show that less people were paying but the amount they contributed was higher than in the previous lists. Here we see Gerrarde Parker paying a subsidy of over twenty shillings for his land at Alkincoats and Henrye Parker paid the same for his lands. By the middle of the seventeenth century the lists had lengthened again but the solitary member of the Parker family met with here is one Alexandre Parker who paid twenty-four shillings on land. By the year 1673 the Parkers have all-but disappeared from the official Colne lists as we have for that year;

'*An Account and Returne of the Fire hearths and Stoves chargable with the Dutcy of Hearth Money within the County Palatine of Lancr. for the Halfe yeare beggininge at our Ladey Day and ending at Michelmas in the year 1673.*'[2]

---

[1] The *Lay Subsidy Rolls* show the local people who owned land and how much tax they paid on it. The *Subsidy Lists* allow for a calculation of population extent and land values at a particular time.

[2] The *Hearth Tax* was a tax levied on the number of fireplaces and is a good indicator of house size

Table: A relates to the stewards of the honour of Clitheroe; these officials were elected from leading families of the time, they had an important role in liasing between the common people, tenants, land holders and the lords. This particular list of the stewards is taken from records at Browsholme Hall to the seventeenth century. Those shown as having been *armigers* were entitled to bear their own arms.

Table: A   Seneschalli (Stewards) de Blackburnshire

Adam de Dutton	1178-	Ric.de Towneley	1366-
Alan de Clericus	to 1240	Joh de Poole	
Nich. de Burton		Tho .Radcliffe	
Willi. de Burch		Robertus	1393
Gilbert de Hocton		Hen. Hoghton	
Henric de Torboc		Joh. Stanley	
Gilbert de Clifton		Ric. Tunstal	
Ada.de Blckburn		Tho. Dns.	
Henric.de Kighley		Tho.Comes	
Robert de Hepple		Petrus Legh	
Simo. Balderston		Ric. Tempest	1537
Edmundus Talbot		Tho. Clifford	
Rob. Sherburne		Arthur D'Arcy	
Joha de Midhope	1318	Tho. Talbot	
Will.de Tatham	1325	Tho. Talbot	
Rich. de Radcliffe	1333	Joh Towneley	Armiger
Willi. de Tatham	1340	Joh. Towneley,	Armiger
Joha.de Radcliffe	1349	Ric. Molineaux,	Armiger
Willi. Laurence	1354	Will. Assheton	Armiger
Ric. de Radcliffe		Ric. Molineaux	
Rob.de Singleton		Jacobus Strange	
Gilb.de la Legh		Nich. Assheton,	Armr
Thos. Radcliffe		Andrew Holden	Gent
John Lawe,	Gent	Car.Molineaux	
Johnn.Baynes.	Armiger	Tho. Coulthurst	Armiger
Thos. Stringer		Ant. Parker	Armiger

Table: B shows the rental value and type of tenure enjoyed by the tenants of Blackburnshire. **A** = a *knight's service* was the grant of lands and property by the overlord, or sovereign, in return for the knight being willing to take up arms on behalf of his master whenever necessary. In the later medieval period the knight's service was often reduced to a cash payment towards the sovereign's war chest. **B** = *Thegnage* is where lands were held of the lord by one who was of noble birth but inferior to the lord. **C** = *Frankalmoigne* was the tenure in which religious houses held lands in exchange for praying for the lord's soul. Religious houses, such as Whalley Abbey, obtained large tracts of land in return for very little money in this way. **D** = Homage where allegiance is sworn to the lord in return for a grant of land.

Table: B   Holders of vills within the hundred of Blackburnshire:

Vill		1334	Holder 1311	Tenur
Altham	1	12s 6d	Sim.de Alvetham	A
Briercliffe	?	20s 0d	Demesne	--
Burnley	2	26s 0d	Demesne	--
Chatburn	2	12s 0d	Dower	--
Clitheroe	?	47s 0d	Borough & Castle	--
Cliviger	1	20s 0d	Demesne	--
Colne	2	26s 8d	Demesne	--
Downham	3	20s 0d	Demesne	--
Extwistle	1	with	Kirkstall & Newbo	--
Foulridge	1	23s 0d	Wm. de. Poitou	--
Huncoat	1	11s 2d	Demesne	--
Ightenhill	---	------	Demesne grange	--
Marsden	2	26s 8d	Demesne	--
Marsden	1	included	Demesne	--
Mearley	2	------	Roger Noel	A
Mearley	1	7s 0d	W. de Heriz	A
Padiham	3	13s 4d	Demesne	--
Read	?	9s 6d	Four tenants	B
Simonston	2	12s 0d	Five tenants	B
Twiston	1	6s 8d	Hugh de Twiston	B
Whalley	2	6s 0d	Abbot of Whalley	C
Wiswell	2	12s 0d	Ric. Shireburne	A
Worsthor	?	12s 0d	O. de Stansfield	D
Worston	3	11s 6d	Demesne	--

Chapter Three

The Lot of the Common Man

The evolution of Lancashire is convoluted to say the least; in short, the story to the fifteenth century is that the Normans took the established Anglo-Saxon estates and moulded them to their own use. Their tenants-in-chief, such as Roger de Poitou, were granted vast estates by William Ist, but this grant came at a price. The earls were responsible for the defence of their holdings and it was therefore necessary for them to provide fighting men for the king's army. As a result of this they granted smaller estates within their territories to knights who would perform this service and, in turn, the knights granted smaller units to thegnes who acted as overseers of the vills.

Thegnes who held land post-Conquest *'had to render by custom two ores of pence for each caracute of land and by custom used to make the king's houses and (that) which pertained thereto..... and the fisheries and the enclosures in the wood and the deer-hays: and who were not to these when he ought paid a fine of two shillings and afterwards came to the work and laboured until it was done.'*[1] The thegnes subsequently employed villeins to cultivate the lands in return for a small share of them.

Each village had a common group of oxen and the hardware to plough the lands, the workers helped each other to cultivate the fields. The villages also had their own greave or reeve who was charged with overseeing the villeins, ensuring that they carried out the necessary work on behalf of the thegne. If a villein did not perform his tasks then he was liable to a fine of four shillings. The villein was virtually tied to his master's holding unless he was able to buy his freedom upon payment of a forty-shilling fine.

This amount also applied to a member of the family of a deceased landholder wishing to take over the deceased's tenancy. If the heir could not pay an entrance fine of forty-shillings the land and goods would revert to the king. This was the custom of *heriotship* and was felt most keenly by poor widows who, in many cases, had lost their only means of subsistence.

The following offers a scathing indictment of the role that the Crown, and the church, played when they demanded fees and fines from a dead man's family:

> *And also the vicar, as I know,*
> *Will not fail to take a cow,*
> *And uppermost clothes, though babes belong,*
> *From a poor and sickly husbandman,*
> *When he lies ready to die,*
> *Having small children two or three;*
>
> *And his three cows who have no more,*
> *The vicar must have one of those,*
> *With the grey cloak that covers the bed,*
> *How are they so poorly cled;*

---

[1] T.D.Whittaker, *History of Whalley,* (First edition, 1881)

And if the wife dies on the morn,
And all the babes should be forlorn,
The other cow he takes away,
With her poor coat and petticoat grey;

And if within two days or three,
The eldest child shall happen to die,
Of the third cow he shall be sure,
When he hath under his cure;

And father and mother both dead be,
Beg must the babes without remedy,
They hold the corpse at the church style,
And there it must remain awhile,
Til they get sufficient surety
for the church right and duty;

Then comes the landlord perforce,
And takes to him the fattest horse;
Poor labourers would that law were down,
Which never was founded by reason,
I heard them say, under confession,
That this law was brother to oppression [1]

Inhabitants of demesne vills paid suit to the lord by serving in his courts and also owed the homage (*boon work*) of working the lord's fields for a certain number of days, the rent would be paid by supplying food, services and fuel for the lord's household.

In true nucleated dominical manors the community radiated out from the central manor house - the lord's fields were always the best in the area. Our area of Pendle, however, was largely a scattering of disjointed hamlets inhabited by copyhold tenants with an absentee landlord.[2] Villages changed slowly over the centuries, some prospered under the patronage of their lord, some remained dormant and some were abandoned altogether leaving us nothing but their poignant memory in a few earthen ditches and banks. The Sites and Monuments Record for Lancashire contains entries for forty-two deserted or shrunken medieval villages. Stock, at Bracewell outside Barnoldswick, is one of these deserted villages although records show it to have been inhabited to the nineteenth century.[3] The adjacent Forest of Bowland was also a part of the Clitheroe estates and, earlier, was a part of the lands of the deans of Whalley. A thirteenth century inquisition shows the villages within the forest, amongst these were *Bogworthe, Sotlie* and *Radun*. The latter referred to Radholme, known in the centuries following the inquisition only as a park. *Bogworthe* and *Sotlie* appear to be former villages that have left no trace of their existence – a good example of early depopulation.[4] Some villages appear to have been abandoned following outbreaks of disease and famine, others were de-populated by the abbeys

---

[1] Sir David Lindsay, *The Monarch*
[2] Denise Kenyon, *The origins of Lancashire,* (Manchester University Press, 1991)
[3] Richard Newman (Ed), *The Archaeology of Lancashire,* (Lancaster University, 1996)
[4] W.R.Mitchell, *Bowland and Pendle Hill,* (Phillimore and Co; 2004)

whilst yet others disappeared when the later land enclosures took place. The extended area around Pendle Forest can show examples of all these types of lost village; Great and Little Mearley, Stock, Brogden etc; there are, no doubt, many more that have gone unrecognised.

An illustration of the life of the poor *cottars* during the fourteenth century was given in Bouchot's *Exposition des Primitifs Francais;* this related to the French peasantry of the time but equally applied to their English counterparts:

And as I went by the way weeping for sorrow
I saw a poor man by me on the plough hanging
His coat was of a clout that cary was called

His hood was full of holes and his hair cut
With his knobby shoes patched full thick
His tongue peeped out as he the earth trod
His hosen overhung his gaiters on every side

All beslobbered in mire as he the plough followed
Two mittens so scanty made all of patches
The fingers were worn and full of mud hung
This fellow wallowed in the muck almost to the ankle

Four heifers before him that weak had become
You could count all their ribs so wretched they were
His wife walked by him with a long goad
In a coat cut short, cut full high

Wrapped in a winnowing sheet to cover her from the weather
Barefoot on the bare ice that the blood flowed
And at the field end lay a little bowl
And on it lay a little child wrapped in rags

And two of two years old on another side
And they all sang a song that was sad to hear
They all cried a cry, a note full of care
The poor man sighed sore and said "children be still"

The Gentry

In the 1530s Henry VIII severed his kingdom from the religious hegemony of Rome and a new age of Protestantism was ushered in. This sea-change within the religious practices of a whole nation was not universally accepted, in fact the county of Lancashire held on tightly to the traditional Catholic religion.

Many of the second generation of Catholics to be born into the new Protestant authority were not able to compromise between their allegiance to the old ways and conformation to the new; these people, unwilling to attend church service as many of their fathers had done, were forced to declare their allegiance openly and they were consequently subjected to *recusancy* fines.[1]

The Spanish Armada of 1588 had caused a crisis, it was feared that the Spanish might well land on the Lancashire coast where they would have been welcomed by Catholic sympathisers wishing to overthrow the Protestant Crown. This overlooked the fact that most Catholics were still staunchly loyal to their country and would never have countenanced such a treacherous act. A report of 1590 informed the Privy Council that there were definitely seven-hundred indicted recusants in Lancashire and probably many more. It was widely acknowledged that the more secluded areas of the county, such as the Pendle Forest, held many priests who were baptising babies and celebrating marriages, Catholic schoolmasters were 'corrupting' their young charges, popish festivals were being openly observed and the required attendance at parish churches was being ignored.

Within the circles of true Lancashire gentry one family loomed large and that was the Stanleys, earls of Derby. This family dominated the county thanks to their support of Thomas Cromwell during the *Pilgrimage of Grace,* this support led to the family being granted full governmental powers within the county, this meant that the earls of Derby had effectively more power locally than the distant authorities in London. Below the all-powerful Stanleys within Lancashire were a wider elite of knights and esquires who provided the manpower for officialdom such as deputy lieutenants, sheriffs, forest officials and Justices of the Peace. Around a dozen of these families were particularly active within the county and below these were a number of lesser, parochial gentry who brushed against the class of upper yeomanry. Lancashire could boast only a low number of true gentry families below which milled a large number of middling landowners poised between the minor parish gentry and the upper farming classes.

The sole aim of many of the minor gentry, as it seems fair to entitle the families central to our Forest of Pendle area, was to improve their standing through the acquisition of lands and wealth. The most common method of gaining lands was that of marriage between landowners and this created a close, inter-related cousinhood of families. As we shall see, it is difficult to find a middling landowning family from the Early Modern period within our area that could be said to be independent of any other family of equal standing. Every branch of the Pendle minor gentry, along with the yeoman classes, appear to have been related by the early seventeenth century. The acquisition of wealth meant that many of these people were bred into a ruthless mindset, if land could be gained by doing a disservice to a neighbour then so be it, popularity was not the name of the game. An example here is that of the Towneley family of Towneley Hall in Burnley. Sir John Towneley (1482-1541) took it upon himself to enclose 194 acres of common land at Horelaw and Hollin Hey Clough in the area around Clowbridge reservoir. The Burnley tenants of this common land were outraged and attempted to have their rights restored, unfortunately, through the intransigence of Sir John and later Richard Towneley this was unsuccessful and a number of evictions followed.

Following this period the local farmers despised the Towneleys and a legend grew that Sir John was unable to rest in his grave through his greed – as we saw earlier every seventh year (according to the legend) Sir John's ghost was doomed to restlessly wander the area crying:

"Be warned! Lay out! Be warned! Lay out!
Around Horelaw and Hollin Clout . . .

---

[1] M. Mullett & L. Warren, *Martyrs of the Diocese of Lancaster,* (Rome, 1987)

The term *'Lay out'* was a reference to the fact that the farmers pleaded with the Towneleys to throw open the land to them once again. Additionally, it was said that the appearance of the ghost would be a portent of the death of a member of the Towneley family and any member of the family from the hall who died was said to have been cursed.[1]

Towneley Hall, Burnley

The Towneley act of enclosure was deemed to be illegal in 1556 and the Crown seized the land, James I leased it to the earl of Devon who sold it back to Richard Towneley in 1612. The Towneleys remained dedicated Catholics throughout the new Protestant order and as a consequence suffered loss of lands and wealth. Many other local members of the minor gentry had seen the political advantages of following the Crown party-line and had become fervent Puritans over the space of a generation or so.

Plague

The lord of the manor kept an iron grip upon his workers, especially those at the lower end of the hierarchy who required his permission before they could move house, visit other areas or marry. The lot of the labouring classes was to change in their favour, however. The overlords had enjoyed a period of relative prosperity following the Conquest; sustained population growth meant that there was an adequate supply of labour, both to tend the land and to develop former waste lands. A severe blow was dealt to communities both rich and poor when, in the fourteenth century, a series of outbreaks of the plague pandemic known as the *Black Death* reduced the available workforce dramatically. The population growth reversed and the labouring classes found that they now held a certain amount of bargaining power with their masters - they were

---

[1] W. Bennett, *History of Burnley,* (Vols 1 & 2, Burnley Corporation, 1946)

able to dictate more favourable terms of employment as (to a certain extent at least) their heavy feudal bonds were beginning to loosen. This, of course, was contrary to the master's advantage and a law was passed in 1349 in an attempt to ensure that labourers were paid no more than their pre-plague rates.

Wages did rise, however, and as a consequence Parliament fixed a minimum wage in 1388. This was reassessed in 1444 so that a *'common servant'* was paid fifteen shillings per year along with a clothing allowance of three shillings and four pence: a woman servant earned ten shillings with clothing at four shillings. It was illegal for workers to demand, or employers to pay, over the official rate. The Clitheroe court rolls of 1392 show that a mower, Richard Wilson Wilcockson, received excessive payment of one shilling and three pence from Richard Mankinholes of Roughlee. The penalty for this offence was that both the farmer and the labourer were fined the amount of the excess in direct increment: equal for the first offence, for a second offence the fine was double the excess, a third offence was fined at treble the excess and so on. None-payment of the fine saw the labourer imprisoned for a period of forty days.

The workers could now move much more freely between estates and command an increase in their food allowance whilst wage rates slowly increased. They were also in a position to take on better quality small-holdings; this meant that the poor land they formerly worked often became abandoned.

This period saw the first real economic migration within England since the Anglo-Saxons spread throughout the land; there are two arguments relating to this point. Some historians are of the opinion that the new wave of migration had the advantage of introducing new blood into formerly isolated communities and therefore helped to strengthen the peasant stock. In turn this helped to ensure that infant mortality fell and the longevity of the land-worker increased. The opposite camp quote the relatively new findings whereby DNA sampling of the modern population shows that the majority of the indigenous peoples of England are of Anglo-Saxon descent alone. This suggests that the Saxons did not inter-breed with the native British but rather they exercised a high degree of apartheid. The pioneers on the front-lines of the Saxon migration brought their own families along with them. The early forest people, then, could well have been seen as two distinct racial groups - the majority would have been of Anglo-Saxon descent whilst others were of a definite British/Celtic origin.

It is not clear as to exactly how much the plague affected the population within our area, being a relatively sparsely populated backwater we may have escaped the worst of the effects of the pandemic. It is thought that famine could have played a more important role in premature fatality within the forest areas, for example, a seven-year period in the late fourteenth century saw major crop failures.[1]

The early forest dwellers were certainly no strangers to the constant threat of the Grim Reaper. The de Lacy overlords had set up a number of leper hospitals during the thirteenth and fourteenth centuries, a major one being at Eddisford Bridge on the outskirts of Clitheroe. Some twenty acres of land were granted at the Colne estate of Alkincoats to the Knights of St. John of Jerusalem in order for this order to provide the constant hospital treatment required by both the local sick and those who travelled through the area.[2] Spittalfields, to the east of Pasture Lane in Barrowford, was probably either the site of a local hospital or this was possibly the land granted by the de Lacys to the order of St. John on the Alkincoats estate.

---

[1] H. H. Lamb, *Climate, Present, Past and Future,* (Methuen, 1977)
[2] James Carr, *Annals and Stories of Colne,* (Colne 1878)

The incidence of plague did not die down following the major outbreak of 1348-9; on numerous occasions, over the coming centuries, the disease would rear its ugly head. Manchester, for instance, suffered an outbreak in 1581 and this was seen as a direct consequence of a poor harvest the previous year. Again in 1586 and 1590 the town suffered more outbreaks and, in 1604-5, the disease struck with such severity that six acres of waste land at Collyhurst, outside the town, were set aside. This area housed the many wooden cabins occupied by the plague sufferers and the plague-pits in which some 2,000 victims were buried.[1]

To this day we find boundary stones and market cross bases whose carved hollows were filled with vinegar in which the plague sufferer (or leper) would place their coins when purchasing goods. One such upright, possibly a plague-stone, can be seen on the ancient trackway above Ball House in the Foulridge area.

Boundary Stones such as this one between Roughlee and Goldshaw were sometimes adapted for use as 'plague-stones'

[1] P. J. Gooderson, *A History of Lancashire,* (Batsford, London, 1980)

Chapter Four

Land Holding

Justice was provided through the local halmote courts where a jury of local men would be summoned to sit in judgement on their peers. This system was particularly useful when matters of land tenure were to be heard. The elders of the community would be required to give a deposition as to the occupancy, boundaries, tenure and the earliest time when a tenant held the land where a land dispute arose. These matters occupied much of the time of local halmotes, especially as more *assart* (clearance of the wastelands) came into use. Court rolls were written to record the operations of the various courts, William Farrer transcribed and published many of these – they date from the fourteenth century and are an invaluable source of information for the local historian.[1] The details of these records for the sixteenth and seventeenth centuries will be met with later.

Besides the court records there are numerous other vital tools in the local historian's armoury, amongst these are subsidy lists, hearth tax and window tax records, estate records, probate and inventories, inquisitions, family papers, trade records and many others.[2]

Major stone-built houses began to appear throughout Blackburnshire in the sixteenth century; the study of the development of housing is interesting as it provides an indicator of the growth of wealth within different areas. It appears that most of the earlier large houses were built towards the western edge of Blackburnshire – as only men of considerable standing erected these houses it seems likely that there were fewer of these around the Pendle Forest area. [3]

As we have seen, the post-Norman structure of the honour of Clitheroe saw more of the lord's demesne lands retained in the east of the hundred whereas the west had much more land granted out to tenants. These tenants, who rented their lands from the de Lacy overlords in the fourteenth century, had the opportunity to turn their enterprise into substantial holdings, their successors built on this and in the fifteenth and sixteenth centuries many of them became minor gentry. These people built the higher-status houses within Blackburnshire that have survived to this day.

Few major families developed within the eastern area due to the fact that the estates were mainly demesne. In relation to the high number of gentry houses to the west of the Blackburn hundred, the east could only really boast two families (with holdings in 1311) having houses of this type, the Towneleys of Towneley and the Stansfields of Heasandford.[4] However, the eastern part of the hundred began to see a rise in the minor gentry and wealthy yeomanry by the later sixteenth century.

There is a definite concentration of the minor gentry houses to be found around Burnley, (including Worsthorne and Hurstwood) and in parts of Pendle Forest. This could be directly related to the tenurial system of the east where the lord's under-tenants eventually came good.

---

[1] W. Farrar, Clitheroe Court Rolls, (Volumes 1, 2 and 3, 1912)
[2] The Lancashire Records Office at Preston holds a wealth of these primary source documents
[3] Sarah Pearson, *Rural Houses of the Lancashire Pennines - 1560-1760,* (HM Stationery Office, 1985)
[4] Denise Kenyon, *Origins of Lancashire,* (Manchester University press, 1991)

In the township of Colne, along its border with Barrowford (Malkin, Sandhole, Wanless, Swinden etc,) it is thought that substantial houses may have existed but have now completely disappeared.

As a rule the surviving yeoman-class houses are situated around the periphery of the gentry estates and are most commonly found in Pendle and Worsthorne, they are less common around the Burnley and Padiham areas where large gentry houses are thicker on the ground.

A major reason for the rise of the yeoman class was the official *deforestation* of Pendle Forest; in 1507 the kings *escheators* arrived at a lodge within the Forest of Trawden and, from this base, they toured the courts of the three forests of Trawden, Pendle and Rossendale with the remit of rationing out lands to the existing tenants. This was the period whereby the old forest areas were to be let out as copyhold and a virtual 'land-grab' ensued. At this time the tenants of the *Old Hold* (prior to 1507) were granted new leases on their holdings which gave them rights of succession and fixed rents – this transformed the local farming system by giving the tenants good reason to improve their farms for future generations to come. Increasing areas of waste lands were cleared and drained so as to provide new pasture. Throughout this century the acquisition of land was high on many people's agenda; Henry VIII's *Dissolution of the Monasteries* began slowly in 1538 but soon gathered momentum, this created a scramble for land on an unprecedented scale.

Upon the death of a tenant under the *Old Hold* his lands legally reverted to the highest relevant authority (the lords of Clitheroe or the Crown) but the *New Hold* gave the holder the right to pass on his holding to his family, to this end wills were of vital importance. The sovereign's authorities proved these documents but in some cases of land *surrender* (where land was sold or transferred amongst parties) it
became the duty of the local halmote courts to determine the legality of the issue. In either case it was a legal prerequisite that the holding in question reverted to the relevant authority (in the Pendle area this was usually the lords of Clitheroe/Pendle Forest) and then it was granted to the new tenant when the court was satisfied with his credentials.

The steward to the lords of the forest was responsible for accepting the claim of the presenting heir and, if he was satisfied with their claim, they were admitted to the property on payment of a fine equal to the value of one year's rent. Upon payment of this admittance fine the transaction was recorded on a court roll and this, along with the other documents from that
particular court assembly, was deposited at Clitheroe Castle. For a fee of two shillings the copyholder would be supplied with an official copy (hence the term *'copyholder'*) of this document – a number of these copies relating to land and property in Pendle Forest survive and they make fascinating reading.

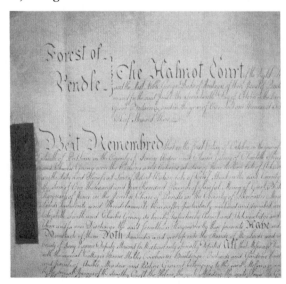

This copy of a court roll dates from 1780 and relates the purchase of a number of farms in Roughlee by James Hargreaves

Local families and their seats up to around 1600: [1]

Name	Status	Holding	Township
Bannister	gent.	Park Hill	Barrowford
Bulcock	yeoman	Whitehough	Barley
Parker	gent.	Extwistle Hall	Briercliffe
Folds	yeoman	Danes House	Burnley
Haydock	gent.	Heasandford House	Burnley
Barcroft	gent.	Barcroft Hall	Cliviger
Whitaker	gent/y	The Holme	Cliviger
Shaw	yeoman	Langroyd Hall	Colne
Shttlewth	esquire	Gawthorpe Hall	Habergham
Towneley	esquire	Royle Hall	Habergham
Towneley	esquire	Towneley Hall	Habergham
Ryley	gent.	The Green	Hapton
More	yeoman	Dean Farm	Higham
Hancock	gent.	Pendle Hall	Higham
Robinson	gent/y	Old Laund Hall	Old Laund
Sagar	yeoman	Catlow Hall	Marsden
Webster	yeoman	Hargrove Farm	Padiham
Whitaker	gent.	High Whitaker	Padiham
Smith	yeoman	Roughlee Old Hall	Roughlee
Smith	yeoman	Hill End/Hill Farm	Briercliffe
Starkie	gent.	Huntroyde Hall	Simonstone
Halstead	yeoman	High Halstead	Hurstwood
Towneley	gent.	Hurstwood Hall	Hurstwood
Jackson	yeoman	Jackson's Farm	Hurstwood
Halstead	gent	Rowley Hall	Hurstwood
Spenser	yeoman	Spenser's House	Hurstwood

It had been more convenient for the landlords to accept their estate rents by cash payment, rather than in *suit,* for many years; this was also beneficial to the tenants who could concentrate upon developing their own holdings. The lords of the honour of Clitheroe eventually began to lose interest in the day-to-day running of their estates; providing they received their income

---

[1] Based upon evidence shown by Sarah Pearson, *Rural Houses of the Lancashire Pennines*

regularly they were happy for their officers to oversee the estates and for their tenants to expand their own holdings.

By the sixteenth century a firm system of land exchange was in place whereby the land-holding tenants could freely exchange, and acquire, holdings throughout the area. As an example the land-holders of Blacko, who also owned small plots in other parts of Barrowford, traded these plots with land-holders of Barrowford who held small plots in Blacko etc; thus scattered plots became more viable as they were added to the tenant's larger holding.

The original land tenancies of the fourteenth century were organised in such a way that they remained stable – they did not account for inflation and, over the centuries, this worked decidedly in the favour of the tenant. Henry VII increased this advantage to the tenants by providing for a fixed rent with security of tenure. Enterprising tenants, with the wherewithal to acquire and develop estates, were richly rewarded as the Rental Lists of the sixteenth century record.

Copyholders were able to demand rents from their sub-tenants that were many times higher than the amount they themselves paid to the overlord. This was as a direct result of the copyhold rights within the honour of Clitheroe being almost the same as freehold rights; low rents and admittance fees to inherited property, along with the right to sell a tenancy and the enjoyment of rights of inheritance, led to a reduction in the dichotomy between important families and the rising yeoman class. On the east-west extremities of Blackburnshire the gap between minor gentry and the farming classes was narrowing.

Many of the gentry built up substantial estates of several hundred acres; Bannister of Park Hill, in Barrowford, held some 120 freehold Lancashire acres in Barrowford and 130 in Foulridge totalling 250 acres.[1] The Lancashire acre was a larger land measure than the statutory acre; there were approximately 1.62 Lancashire acres to 1 statutory measure. This meant that Bannister actually owned 405 statutory acres; he also leased copyhold land in Pendle. Although the Bannister family of Park Hill had their ups and downs over the centuries the Park Hill estate flourished. In the later nineteenth century the following properties were attached to the Park Hill estate:[2]

Park Hill Estate Property

Trawden Forest:
Lumb Laithe Farm*
Boulsworth Dyke*
Lodge Moss
Two cottages

Foulridge:
Spen Farm*

Barrowford and Blacko:
Trough Laithe Farm*
Grove House (two crofts)*
Clough Farm*
Wood Croft
Fulshaw Farm

---

[1] Sarah Pearson, *Rural Houses of the Lancashire Pennines,* (HM Stationery Office, 1985)
[2] Jesse Blakey, *Annals and Stories of Barrowford,* (SP, Nelson, 1929)

Barrowford and Blacko (cont.)

> Higher Park Hill*
> Cross Gaits Farm & Inn*
> Malkin Tower Farm*
> Lower Park Hill Farm*
> Clough Garden

Water rents:

> Albert Mills
> Victoria Mills
> Hodge Bank Canal Co,

Tenanted by Mrs. Holt:

> Mosley Farm, Chipping
> Higher Fence Gate Farm
> Buttack Farm, Barley

* denotes properties still attached to Park Hill in 1921 when Earby Council published a sales catalogue, with plans, of a list of properties; also included at this time were Lower Laithe, Lower Fulshaw, Lodge Moss and Frigham Chapel Cottages.

Inevitably the sixteenth century land-grab caused friction amongst neighbours and inquisitions into legal ownership of land were to become commonplace. An illustration of this is the following interrogatory statement by local elders on behalf of Lawrence Towneley, of Stone Edge and Henry Blakey, of Blakey Hall, both in Blacko. In 1582/3 these landowners were taken to court by one William Tusser who, acting on behalf of the Queen, disputed their rightful claim to certain lands within Blacko. These two closes, known as Sym Pasture and More Hey, were areas of improved waste that Simon Blakey, of Blakey Hall, had enclosed. The land lies to the east of Barnoldswick Road as it climbs from Barrowford to the Cross Gates Inn. The area was formerly known as *Flaight Moor*, then *Flawed Moor* (it was still shown as this on the first OS survey maps) and is now commonly known as Flax Moor. The term *Flawed* is an Old English term describing the meandering motion of a stream and this would apply to the stream bisecting the two closes; this ancient feature is the eastern boundary of the Forest of Pendle. [1]

The name *Sym Pasture* would refer to Simon Blakey's pasture and More Hey meant *The Moor on the Boundary* – it is not clear, however, if the latter was a part of the Sym Pasture or if it appertains to the Hoarestones Moor (now Greystones Moor) on the lower western slopes of Weets Hill as will be seen in Bernard Blakey's deposition. Witnesses for the defence answered twelve questions as follows:

The deposition of James Robinson, husbandman of the Pendle Forest, aged 80: [2]

He did know the Forest of Pendle and Blacko and had done so for 70 years:

That Blacko is a parcel of 2 vaccaries and has been so used for 70 years:

---

[1] David Mills, *The Place-Names of Lancashire,* (Batsford, 1976)
[2] James Robinson was probably of the Stone Edge (Blacko) or Foothouse Gate (Barley) families

That part of the said two vaccaries was divided by the tenants sixty years ago and the other part since then and further that some parcel of Blacko was divided by the tenants of Over Barrowford and Nether Barrowford as parcel of the said vaccaries and that some tenants had part of their portions in Blacko and some in Barrowford:

The said two vaccaries are bounded from other grounds as follows:- beginning at a place called Whiteyate adjoining Henry Bannester's land, from there to the water of Wandless, then following the said water to the outside of Fowlerig, from there to Driecloughe, from there to Haiestack Thorne, from there by an old dike to Hanson Dike Newke from there after a dike and a wall over the top of Blackowhill, from there to Whiteheadfote and so to Smithiehole from there to Whitelee, from there over the water to Ridgende, from there to Rudgall Inge and so to Knogworthend, to the Carmill Deemhead, from there to Colne Waterfote and following Barrowford Water joining the lands of Henry Bannester to the said Whiteyate. That Blackow lies within the said boundaries:

The Blackow in Barrowford joins another parcel of land called Blacko lying in Admergill and that a ditch divides the said grounds:

That he knew that the tenants of Blacko exchanged lands with the tenants of Barrowford. Lawrence Hartlaie of Nether Barrowford exchanged with James Hartley of Blacko and others of like manner:

To his judgement the tenants of Blacko had spent £1000 and more in buildings etc, since gaining the copyholds:

The Blacko vaccaries are as dearly rented as any other in the Pendle Forest: Certain lands attached to certain vaccaries are known by other names such as The Lower Pasture, The Ridge, Fulsha and divers others all parcels of the said vaccaries and that Blackowe is known to be part of these.

Others who gave depositions were:
Nicholas Robinson of Roughlee: husbandman aged 70
John Manckenowles of Marsden: husbandman aged 86
Laurence Shuttleworth of Winewall: husbandman aged 67
William Hyggin of Lymeroid: husbandman aged 40
William Edmondson of Midopp: husbandman aged 70

The deposition of John Hartlaye of Cotes-in-Craven, aged 76 : [1]

After the grant was made to the tenants, Over Barrowford was divided into 4 parts:

Nether and Over Barrowford were not in his memory divided, this was done by agreement of the tenants for their profit:
His own father Bernard Hartlaie was one of the first to take the said vaccaries from the King's

---

[1] John Hartley was originally of Pendle Forest - his family were related by marriage to Henry Shaw of Langroyd Hall, Colne

Commissioners by copy of a Court Roll – he had heard that the Commissioners were Sir Henry Halsall and Sir Peter Lee, knights:

That he hath known Blacko all the time of his remembrance and that it is bounded by a place called Whitemore of the east side, of the water of Wandles of the south side and joins the freehold land of one Bernard Blakey of another side, and of the freehold land of the Parkhill of another side, and some part of the same land joins to the Newbrigg of Barrowford and to the Whitelee, from there to Blackofootyate, from there to Smithihole, from there to the dike of Admergill and to the top of Blackowmount and so to Hestackthorn. And have all been used and occupied by the tenants of Barrowford during his remembrance, except one enclosure now in the occupation of Bernard Blakey:

That about sixty-six years ago a house was built upon Blackow where one Henry Blakey now dwells: [1]

That he hath not known Blackow to have been occupied as a common ground to the copyholders of Pendle Forest, but as a parcel of Barrowfordes:

There is a pasture in Blacko called Sym Pasture containing thirty acres enclosed, but knows not if it is the same as More Hay, but that it has been enclosed for sixty years or more and that it is within Blackow:

That the ground called The Fence hath been enclosed within the time of his remembrance, but is not part of the said two vaccaries, and before was a vacant ground and not part of Barrowford and Blackow: [2]

The plot now thickens as Bernard Blakey, of the same Blakey Hall family as the Henry of the above inquisition, finds himself (at a later date) before the court of the Duchy of Lancaster pleading the case again. From his evidence it appears that his ancestor, Simon Blakey, was awarded lands around Blacko in the thirteenth century. A parcel of these grants was possibly part of the White Moor and, because of its inferior quality, Simon was given compensatory land at Greystones (above the Moorcock Inn on the Blacko to Gisburn road) and Flawed Moor:

The answer of Bernard Blakey, gent, defendant, to the Attorney General

The defendant pleas with regard to certain property in Barrowford, in the Manor of Ightenhill, called Sympasture and Horestones. A messuage and divers lands called Blakey were granted by Letters Patent in 1277 to Simon Blakey, ancestor of this defendant, with sufficient pastures in the pasture in Barrowford for him and his heirs forever, yeilding to the said late King at 11s 5d. This defendant has the common pasture and premises as heir lineally descended from the said Simon.

The defendant said that he and all his ancestors had used and enjoyed the common of pasture

---

[1] Blakey Hall stands adjacent to the Leeds Liverpool Canal, to the south of Blacko
[2] This indicates that the area now occupied by the village of Fence was, in the early 16th century, uncultivated land - probably due to it having been an enclosure for the lord's deer

granted by reason of inclosures made in ancient times by the Queen's Progenitors and the same piece of ground being marsh and barren, the ground called Sym Pasture and Horestones were alloted to the ancestor of the said defendant to hold in recompense of the said common of pasture originally granted. Thus the defendant proves his title to the premises.

The deposition of John Hargreaves, of Nether Barrowford, husbandman aged 73:

That he hath known the said pasture since he was six and that Pendle Forest was divided into certain booths, and one was called Barrowford Booth which containeth Nether Barrowford, Over Barrowford and Blackowe, but why the Barrowfords were called vaccaries was, he supposed, that they were granted by the King's Commissioners by the name of vaccaries:

He cannot bound Nether Barrowford by itself but he knoweth how to bound Nether Barrowford and Over Barroeford and Blackowe together because they are all one:

He hath heard that the said forest was destroyed seventy-five years ago – that the King's Commissioners did sit at a lodge in Trawden and did grant the said vaccaries to the tenants of the same, by Copy Court Roll:

That Henry Towneley and the tenants of Nether Barrowford do occupy the Rushton Thornes:

A tenant of Under Barrowford called Christopher Blakey built one of the first houses upon ground called Blackowe about sixty years ago, wherein one Henry Blakey now dwells, that same was taken by Copy of Court Roll:

That parcel of ground called More Hey was enclosed before the time of his remembrance by Simon Blakey or his elders, and hath heard that 3 shillings rent is yearly paid to Her Majesty for the same together with Barrowford, and the same lieth within Blackowe and within Barrowford.

These records provide us with a nice contemporary description of the boundaries dividing the two booths of Barrowford from their neighbours of Colne, Roughlee, Wheatley, Foulridge and Marsden. Known as Over Barrowford and Nether Barrowford the area was divided at the Whiteyate, this refers to the present Whittycroft area of Higherford. The northern portion of the area included part of the modern Higherford but was largely the area of Blakey, now covered by Blacko, although this was sub-divided. A study of sixteenth century [1] and early OS maps [2] shows that the upper portion was contained within a boundary running from the present site of the weir at Grimshaw's Wood on Pendle Water, at the Holme (Water Meetings). The boundary ran eastwards up the hill and across the modern Gisburn Road (a modern boundary stone by the roadside marks this point) to the Towneley's property of Stone Edge. Continuing across to Flax (Flawed) Moor Farm the line then carried on straight past Lower Slipper Hill and on to the Foulridge boundary. This latter was a line taken from Wanless Water and up the hill slightly to the west of Sand Hole, the present Holly Bush Farm (formerly Moss Farm) and on to Pasture

---

[1] The 1581 *Map of Whitemoor* covers a boundary dispute between the townships of Foulridge and Barnoldswick. A copy can be seen at Colne Library.
[2] 1840s Ordnance Survey

Head where it picked up the old County boundary. The lower portion of Over Barrowford ran from the same weir, along the northern edge of the modern Stone Edge housing estate and down to the road passing Blakey Hall. Here it joined an old track from the present Grange Avenue, past Ralph Laithe Farm and straight through the fields to Higher Wanless Farm where it followed the ancient road (now a footpath) towards the Cross Gates Inn before heading along the stream to Hollin Hall. This is the point where the limit crosses a clough, this has the appearance of a dyke, road or dry stream bed, and runs parallel with the Barnoldswick Road from Hollin Hall to White Moor.

The boundary then proceeded to Pasture Head where it met with the Foulridge boundary. The whole of this eastern boundary also formed the Pendle Forest limits. From Hollin Hall, on Slipper Hill, the boundary keeps to the stream towards Pasture Head Farm where it turns sharply westward at a mark-stone. Heading up towards Blacko Tower the boundary meets the old county boundary that ran parallel with Standing Stone Lane, a standing boundary-stone shown on the 1581 Whitemoor Map as *The Stone on Slipper Hill* marks this spot. [1]

The Stone on Slipper Hill

This stone marks the exact north-eastern tip of the Pendle Forest

Edward the Second (around 1324) issued an order that all forests should be properly bounded. This stone possibly dates from this period

Moving on, the stream passes through the hollow feature known as Heynslack or Mawkin Hole, this is where the *Hestacke Thorn* of John Hartley's deposition is situated. The stream turns sharply to the north when it reaches the Black Dyke Nook but the boundary carries on over the Blacko Hill ridge where it takes the form of a ditch. Descending Blacko Hill the boundary follows a deep clough, known here as the Dry Clough, to the marker stone of the old Blacko Cross at Blacko Bar. Following the clough down into the *Whitehead Fote* that we now call The Hole, the bridge here, now called The 1914 Bridge, crosses Admergill Water at what was once a ford on the main Clitheroe to Colne road. The stream flows south-west beneath the bridge, through Bell Wood (once known as Smithie Hole) where local folklore has it that a battle once took place. Admergill Water is known as Blacko Water at this point and the boundary follows this across the Blacko Foot road towards the Water Meetings where the Over Barrowford boundary follows the river to its starting point at the weir.

The Nether Barrowford boundary leaves the stream slightly to the north of the spot where Blacko Water meets with Pendle Water and heads westwards up through Utherstone Woods.

---

[1] With a great deal of difficulty, and numerous thorn-scratches, the author has located this extant stone

The ancient route from Utherstone to Pasture Lane top, and along by Ridgaling Farm, forms the Barrowford and Roughlee boundary – above Higher Fulshaw the boundary line takes a ninety-degree turn to the south before heading west along the line of an ancient dyke below Ridgaling Farm (and parallel to the top edge of the Noggarth quarry) this means that this latter property is firmly placed within the parish of Roughlee. Following the Noggarth Top trackway, past the small shop of Noggarth Top Cottage, the boundary follows the modern road for a short distance before turning south through a style to Marles Hill and The Old Sparrow Hawk Inn. It then follows the modern road towards Barrowford before turning south at The Clough from where it passes through Carr Laund, through the Carr Hall estate, past the site of Carr Mill and down into the valley bottom where it meets Pendle Water at Whitefield. The river then carries the limit eastwards into Barrowford once more where it picks up Colne Water at the Bull Holme, following the river through Swinden the boundary picks up Wanless Water to the Foulridge boundary at which point it heads north once again, past Sandy Hole and up to Pasture Head.

Dicky Nook, Higherford

In general terms Over Barrowford was the area of Blakey, above Whitegate, as we have seen this is now Whittycroft. The modern Whittycroft would be named after a parcel, or croft, of land owned by the Blakey and Marsden families and this was separated from neighbouring lands by a dyke. The spot where the Barrowford to Gisburn road forks to Barnoldswick has long been known locally as *Dicky Nook*, this is commonly thought to have been named in memory of Dicky Stansfield who lived in the farm cottages that once stood here. However, the name Dicky Nook (*nook = corner*) could well have applied to this area for many centuries before old Dicky came along because this was where the Whittycroft dyke turned down to Pendle Water. *Dyke Nook* is a description often applied in the fourteenth and fifteenth centuries to places where the boundary ditches turned. [1]

The actual area of Nether Barrowford straddled the area from Bank Hall (now the Lamb Working Men's Club) past Charles Farm (now the White Bear Inn) up to Crow Trees Farm by the Old Roman Bridge. The western-most area of Barrowford, now known as New Bridge, was Lower Clough and Reedyford, this was an area of boggy waste land to the south of Lower Clough Farm and in the Reedyford area this adjoined the area of Whitefield, an area once largely owned by the Bannisters of Park Hill. [2]

---

[1] A number of examples of the term *Dyke Nook* occur locally at Blacko Hill, Wheatley Booth and at Sabden Fold
[2] *A Bannister Family History,* (Heritage Trust for the North West, 2006)

Chapter Five

Rebellion

The dawning of the fourteenth century held much hope for the people, the long reign of Edward I was drawing to a close and his foreign policies had resulted in relatively settled conditions for the common man. Unfortunately the new century was to be far from settled, miserable times were ahead, both nationally and locally. King Edward (Longshanks) was also known as the *Hammer of the Scots* because of his campaigning over the border; by 1297 these campaigns had resulted in crisis for Edward as he found that his resources were not able to support his commitments. Furthermore, the clergy were refusing to pay into the royal coffers, Parliament was unhappy with the spiralling costs of the foreign policies and the barons were grumbling loudly – the Earls of Hereford and Norfolk refused point blank to serve the king in Gascony.[1]

King Edward died in 1307 and, as we have seen, the local overlord, Henry de Lacy, died 1310/11. Edward II succeeded to the throne and Henry de Lacy's successor was Thomas, earl of Lancaster and steward of all England. In 1314 Edward II was defeated by the Scots at the battle of Bannockburn and this was to be the beginning of an intensive period of southern incursions by Sots raiders. A contributing factor here was that the Scottish system of inheritance differed from the English in that all male offspring had equal rights of inheritance. The southern system of the eldest inheriting, and the younger siblings having to make their own way in life, meant that large estates were kept together under a single master. The Scottish inheritance laws meant that farms and estates were divided many times to a point where the area of land held by families would hardly sustain them. As a result of this landless young men grouped together in gangs in order to eke out a living the best way they could – this usually meant robbery and the pillaging of property. Some of these gangs could be numbered in their thousands, especially in the border regions.[2] These were the people who regularly came over the borders into England to take the easy pickings from largely defenceless farmers. Our area was certainly not immune from these brigands as the defensive towers in Bowland, Paythorne, Hellifield and possibly Rimington Moor, Admergill and Malkin testify.

There was a great deal of unrest amongst the earls, this had been rumbling on since the late thirteenth century and came to a head when Thomas, earl of Lancaster, led a revolt of the northern barons against the king. Thomas had refused to serve Edward (who was actually his cousin) in Scotland and needless to say the king was not best pleased. In 1322 the king met the barons in battle at Boroughbridge and having defeated them had Thomas tried for treason in his own castle at Pontefract; on the 22nd of March Thomas was executed there. Following this all the estates formerly belonging to the Duchy of Lancaster were confiscated by the Crown.

Thus began a period of social unrest within Lancashire as, being effectively rudderless, the county descended into a state that bordered upon anarchy. The officers of the honour of Clitheroe, rather than exercising their power to sustain order, were actually implicated in extortion and corruption.

---

[1] David Starkey, *The Monarchy of England* (Vol 1, Chatto and Windus, 2004)
[2] Douglas Huntingdon, *The Solway Plainsmen,* (Helmwind Books, 1995)

The area of Over and Nether Barrowford within Pendle Forest

Villagers entered the forests and helped themselves to the lord's game and robbers from other regions roamed the countryside in search of plunder. The chief *instaurator* at this time was Gilbert de la Legh of Hapton who was unable to act against this unlawfulness as he had been kidnapped and held to ransom at Holbeck, near Leeds. A mob of forty-seven men came out of Yorkshire to take advantage of the situation, they were led by Nicholas de Maulverer who happened to be the constable of Skipton Castle. His men had been gathered from Craven and Airedale and they descended upon the king's stud farm at Ightenhill from where they stole three stallions, eighteen mares, nine three-year olds, five fillies, eighteen foals and three oxen. They also raided vaccaries within the Forest of Pendle (including Swinden Old Hall in Marsden) from where they took some fifty-three cows, two bulls, four oxen, two steers and six calves. [1]

This situation could not be allowed to continue and, wishing to restore some sense of normality, the king organised enquiries into the situation. As a result a special court was set up at Wigan to try the people who were accused of wrongdoing by the enquiry. The hearing was held on the 22nd of October 1323 and the king attended in person, he broke his journey from Skipton by staying at Ightenhill manor house from the 4th to the 12th of October. By no means all the perpetrators of civil disobedience were caught, of those tried and convicted some were fined and others imprisoned. Following the hearing at Wigan it appears that things were beginning to settle down in the forests although total order was not quickly restored, people still poached the game, stole the lord's timber and coal and generally got away with whatever they could – the forests were a large area to police.

Things tightened up somewhat when the dowager queen of Edward II, Queen Isabella, decided to clamp down on the indiscipline within her forests of Bowland, Pendle, Accrington, Trawden and Rossendale. In 1332 she ordered the arrest of those people who had entered her forests and killed or stolen her deer. Amongst these was Richard Merclesden, of Roughlee and Blacko, who had been the chief forester under king Edward III in 1330. Again, in 1337, the dowager queen was wielding her power over the naughty northern pilferers, seventy-six people were charged with entering her hunting grounds, taking deer and felling trees.

The fourteenth century was to cause further misery amongst the people as, not only was there the *Hundred Years War* from 1338 to 1453 (started by Edward III), we have seen that there was also the Black Death pandemic of 1348-1349 to contend with. All of these problems came on the back of a major famine that struck between 1314 and 1316, disastrously wet weather had destroyed the crops and much of the livestock died from disease. [2]

It would be many years before the poor could rebuild even their former subsistence level of existence, the people had (understandably) been unprepared to meet the looming problems. In the middle of the fourteenth century William Langland wrote in his *Piers the Plowman* of the problems faced by the labouring classes when awaiting the next harvest. There did not appear to be a satisfactory method of storing food in time of plenty and therefore there would not be much more corn grown than was necessary for that particular season.

The following only refers to a short period of drought, the effects of true famine would have been dreadful indeed:

I have no penny quoth Piers, pullets for to buy
Nor neither geese nor piglets, but two green cheeses
A few curds and cream, and an oaten cake
And two loaves of beans and bran, to bake for my little ones

And besides I say by my soul, I have no salt bacon
Nor no little eggs, by Christ, collops for to make
But I have parsley and leeks, and many cabbages
And besides a cow and a calf, and a cart mare
To draw afield my dung, the while the drought lasteth

---

[1] Mary Brigg, *The Early History of the Forest of Pendle,* (Pendle Heritage Centre, 1989)
[2] H. H. Lamb, *Climate, Present, Past and Future,* (Methuen, 1977)

And by this livelihood we must live until next lammas time
And by that I hope to have harvest in my croft

And then may I prepare the dinner as I dearly like
All the poor people those, peascods fatten
Beans and baked apples they brought in their laps
Chalots and chervils and ripe cherries many

And proferred pears these present, to please with hunger
All hunger eat in haste, and asked after more
Then poor folk for fear, fed hunger eagerly
With great leeks and peas, to poison hunger me thought

But then it came near harvest, new corn came to market
Then were folk glad and fed hunger with the best
With good ale as glutton taught, and got hunger to sleep
And when wasters wouldn't work, but wandered about

Nor no beggar eat bread, that beans within were
But two sorts of fine white, or else of clean wheat

Nor no half-penny ale, in nowise drink
But the best and the brownest that in town is to sell
Labourers that have no land to live on, only their hands
Designed not to dine each day on herbs not fresh gathered
Have no penny ale given them, nor no piece of bacon
But if it be fresh flesh or fish, fried or baked
And that warm or hot, to avoid chilling their bellies.

Weaving

The Norman vaccaries can be seen as having formed our present-day settlement pattern of both tenanted and owner-occupied individual farmsteads and hamlets. However, most of these farming operations did not generate sufficient income to support entire families. It was necessary for farming folk to have a number of children in order to provide labour on the land; sons would help to develop waste lands and expand the holding whilst daughters were, generally, employed in the dairy produce and domestic side of the farm. The constant threat of disease meant that many families lost children on a regular basis, to offset this there would be a steady stream of new life being brought into households – where the offspring did survive a family might number in the region of ten to fifteen people.

The boom in sheep production within the medieval period meant that there was a constant supply of wool, almost everyone within the Pendle Forest turned their hand to the production of woollen cloth, from the carding and spinning of the fibres to the weaving, fulling and dying of the finished fabric. Up to the beginning of the eighteenth century woollen cloth manufacture had developed in many countries, some 86% of all garments were made from wool or linen at this time.

The cotton that would prove to be the mainstay of industry throughout our area was slow in coming. It is thought that the first known cotton cloths originated in India around 1100 BC, following the invasion of Alexander the Great in 300 BC the barriers between Asia and Europe began to break down, this allowed the Indian textile skills to slowly spread westwards. It was not until the ninth century that this knowledge reached Spain when the Spanish Moors introduced the advanced textile arts. By the sixteenth century other European countries had adopted cotton goods, in 1560 Venice was known for its variety of quality cotton fabrics. By 1601 traders from Antwerp were importing cottons from Sicily, the Levant and Lisbon although this did not affect the woollen producer as cotton goods at this time were rated as luxury goods on a par with Chinese silks. [1]

As early as the beginning of the sixteenth century the towns of South Lancashire had a reputation for making so-called cotton goods, these stuffs, however, were not actually made of cotton but were wool mixed with a little flax. The real turning point in our becoming genuine cotton cloth producers was the revocation of the *Edict of Nantes* in 1685 when the Huguenots (French Protestants) began to settle in England. They moved to the Protestant countries of Europe in their hundreds of thousands, it is estimated that 70,000 of the best silk weaver in France settled in England, many of them initially in Manchester and Bolton. These skilled artisans were encouraged to prosper by the English Government, they were allowed to cut as much wood as they required for firing and for making their looms on a payment of four pence per year. It was probably these newcomers who introduced cotton to Lancashire, cotton-wool was imported from India and Asia Minor and mixed with wool, or more often linen, to be made up into various materials. Of these fustian and what was called 'Manchester ticking' were the best known. Cotton yarn, at this time, was used for the weft only as it was not possible to spin a thread strong enough be used as warp, it would not be until the eighteenth century that an invention by Richard Arkwright allowed for cotton to be spun with sufficient strength to be used for this purpose.

About 1750 the woollen trade was still an important source of income to the country weavers but in the neighbourhood of Manchester and Bolton some £600,000 worth of cotton goods were being produced annually. For the county of Lancashire this showed that the 'writing was on the wall,' as the Lancashire cotton trade increased the manufacture of woollen goods was gradually pushed over the border into Yorkshire.

It is often said that our area of Pendle prospered in the production of cotton because our damp climate lends itself to the practice of weaving as the threads did not break as often as those in a dryer climate. In actual fact one of the main reasons for the growth of the Lancashire textile industry was the freedom of trade enjoyed by the area within the Elizabethan and Stuart periods. In other areas the Guilds within incorporated towns acted to restrict the development of industry within country districts. The Weaver's Act of 1558, and the Statute of Apprenticeship of 1563, were aimed at restricting the number of looms that a country weaver could own. The period of apprenticeship, and apprenticeship qualifications, was legislated for in such a manner as to restrict the growth of country operations. The towns of Manchester and Bolton, however, were not Guild incorporated and so the Acts did not apply to them, neither did they apply to Lancashire or the West Riding of Yorkshire – this of course meant that there was an advantage to be gained here over other areas, especially when the coming of the canals and railways opened up our area. Guest's *History of the Cotton Manufacturer* states that:

---

[1] Edwin Hopwood, *A History of the Lancashire Cotton Industry,* (Amalgamated Weavers Association, 1969)

'In 1740 the Manchester cloth merchants began to give out warps, and raw cotton, to the weavers and receiving them back in cloth and paying for the carding, roving, spinning and weaving. After the fustians were manufactured, the merchants dyed them, and then carried them to the principal towns in the kingdom on pack-horse, opening their packs, and selling to shopkeepers as they went along.'

This practice of 'putting out' cotton spread rapidly into the far-flung corners of Lancashire where, out of a population total of 6,000,000 for all England, there were approximately 43,000 cottage workers engaged in the production of cloth.[1] Putting out was not exactly a new method, however, from at least the sixteenth century clothiers in the rural areas had been supplying cottagers with the raw materials to weave woollen kersey pieces which were then supplied to markets both locally and abroad.

Handloom weaving

A contemporary account of the handloom weaver is given in the writings of William Radcliffe; an improver of the later power loom here he looks back from 1775

'The land (in Mellor, Blackburn) was occupied by between 50 and 60 farmers and out of these there were only six or seven who raised their rents directly from the produce of the farms; all the rest got their rents partly in some branch of trade, such as spinning, weaving woollen, linen or cotton. The cottagers were employed entirely in this manner, except for a few weeks in harvest. Cottage rents at that time, with convenient loom-shop and a small garden attached, were from one-and-a-half to two guineas per annum. The father would earn from 8s to half a guinea, and his sons, if he had any, two or three alongside of him, 6s or 8s a week........and when it is considered that it required six or eight hands to prepare and spin yarn, sufficient for the consumption of one weaver, this shows clearly the call there was for labour for every person, from the age of seven to eighty years (who retained their sight and could move their hands) to earn their bread, say from 1s to 3d per week, without going to the parish.'

The established system of clothiers putting out cloth pieces from the cottage producers was to change dramatically within a relatively short period. The Enclosures Acts ensured that in excess of 5½ million acres of previously unenclosed lands were 'privatised' between 1760 and 1840, this meant that the poor subsistence farmer and handloom weaver lost their independence. At

---

[1] Edwin Hopwood, *A History of the Lancashire Cotton Industry*, (Amalgamated Weavers Association, 1969)

the same time the textile industry was undergoing rapid change, improvements to the manufacturing process were constantly being made by men such as Arkwright, Kay, Hargreaves and Crompton.

To meet the increasing demand for cotton goods the wealthier landlords and entrepreneurs were erecting new spinning and weaving mills wherever they could. These new factories absorbed the disaffected, now landless, workers who had little alternative but to supply their labour. The increase in demand for cottons in the later eighteenth century meant a greater supply of yarns, this saw whole families concentrating their efforts in cloth production.

It would be easy to assume that the weavers earned more money from the factory than they did in their former cottage enterprises but this was not the case. It is said that the period between 1788 and 1800 saw the peak of handloom weaving when a combined family income could be from 40 shillings up to 120 shillings per week. By around 1808 a handloom weaver in a factory could expect to be paid around 15 shillings per week, by 1833 a good weaver in Colne would only expect 5 shillings and 4 pence per week. In 1829 it is recorded that one-hundred and three weavers in Higham earned an average of 2 shillings per week, this was at a time when a 4lb loaf of bread cost 1 shilling and 2½ pence. At this time the average weekly income per head in Burnley was 1 shilling and 8½ pence. [1]

One of the earliest factories in Burnley was the Dandy Shop in Massey Street, this was built in 1787. [2] The name 'Dandy Shop' was commonly applied to what we now know as mills, the dandy was an improved loom where the frame was made of cast-iron, rather than the heavy wooden structure of the earlier looms.

Over the years the weavers of Pendle Forest were as affected by the vagaries of cotton imports as were the weavers in any other area. The operation of the textile industry was subject to foreign wars, fluctuations in the price of raw materials and industrial unrest, all of which led to periods of 'boom and bust.' The mainstay for our area throughout the poorer times was a cloth known as delaine, this was a lightweight, plain-weave cloth made from wool originating from mousse line delaine which means wool muslin.

The main woollen cloth market for the Pendle Forest had always been that of Heptonstall and Halifax, even through the cotton boom these close ties were maintained, the handloom weaving of woollens was carried on to a relatively late period within the rural areas. As an example of this the 1851 census for Blacko Hillside, which appears to cover three farms, shows that out of forty-four adults, four were farmers, three were farmer's wives and the remaining thirty seven people were all delaine handloom weavers.

Clothiers in rural areas did not always feel that it was necessary to set up their new operations within the larger villages or small towns, for example William Smith of Lane Bottom, Briercliffe, attracted former agricultural workers from the outlying areas to work at his Hill End factory. The erection of another factory in Hill Lane was accompanied by the building of cottages to house the workers and the hamlet of Lane Bottom came into existence where originally only two farms existed. The family would go on to found the still extant cotton mill enterprise of Smith and Nephew at Brierfield.

Neighbours of the Smiths, from higher up the Thursden Valley, were the Ecroyd family of Foulds House and Edge End who founded the first real mill enterprise in Nelson. This small woollen mill, at Lomeshaye, employed whole families and it is recorded that children as young as three and four were earning their own living here.

---

[1] Walter Bennett, *The History of Marsden and Nelson,* (Nelson Corporation, 1957)
[2] Walter Bennett, *The History of Burnley,* (Burnley Corporation, Parts 1 & 2, 1946)

As the erection of mills accelerated they clustered around certain areas, a good supply of running water was an obvious requirement for the water-powered factories and as steam-power became the norm a good supply of local coal was also needed - there was certainly no shortage of water within the Pendle area and coal was readily available within the coal fields of the Burnley Basin. These basic requirements saw the burgeoning factories follow the valley bottoms, as can be seen in our area from Colne through to Blackburn, Bolton and Manchester. Fortunately our rural Forest of Pendle region, to the north of the industrialised valley, has remained untouched to such an extent that many of the people whose names are a legacy of the early forest vaccaries of Barrowford, Roughlee, Newchurch, Barley etc, still farm those lands today. Old Pendle Forest names such as Nutter, Hartley, Hargreaves, Robinson and Marsden can be traced straight back to the creation of the forest in the post-Conquest period.

Many of the extant early farmstead sites still retain fascinating clues to their past. The area of Blacko Hillside, particularly around Malkin, for instance, still shows its history in the many surviving ancient dykes, ditches, holly 'ringyard' fences, mark-stones and trackways.

To a large extent the weaving community of the Pendle area survived the vagaries of the trade – many of them had at least a small patch of land to help sustain then through periods of depression. This was not the case when the large mills became established, however; people had migrated into the towns to follow the cotton and they no longer had anything other than back-yards (if they were lucky). Periods of instability within the textile trades hit the new mill workers hard; taking Barrowford as an example there was hardly a settled period for the weavers between 1820 and 1880. The worst of these bleak times was the decade of the 1860s when the American Civil War all but strangled the supply of raw materials to the northern factories. The Local Board supplied a certain amount of *subsistance* to the unemployed mill workers in the form of 'dole' whereby the men had to toil on public works in order to earn a few coppers. Christopher Grimshaw, who owned Higherford Mill, was the overseer of a gang of men who replaced the whole of the river wall through Barrowford at this time.[1]

Further to this the Barrowford Congregationalist minister, Reverend E. Gough, wrote in reference to his ministry in *dole time*: [2]

'During the cotton famine those who owned houses were said not to need help whilst those without were given relief. It was forgotten that the house-owners could only sell their houses at a substantial loss – they cannot eat stones! People would attend church and then ask for charity, after the famine was over they were never seen in church again.'

> *God help the poor, who in lone vallies dwell,*
> *Or by far hills, where whin and heather grow!*
> *Theirs is a story sad indeed to tell;*
>
> *Yet little cares the world, nor seeks to know*
> *The toil and want poor weavers undergo.*
> *The irksome loom must have them up at morn;*
>
> *They work till worn-out nature will have sleep;*

---

[1] Jesse Blakey, *Annals and Stories of Barrowford,* (SP, Nelson, 1929)
[2] *Barrowford Directory,* Nelson Local Studies Library

They taste, but are not fed. Cold snow drifts deep
Around the fireless cot, and blocks the door;
The night-storm howls a dirge o'er moss and moor.

And shall they perish thus, oppress'd and lorn?
Shall toil and famine hopeless, still be borne?

No! GOD will yet arise and HELP THE POOR!

Barrowford Mill in the Park

The Old Barrowford Mill stood in the western corner of what is now Barrowford park. This is thought to have been the site of one of the earliest factories in North-east Lancashire and the building, as shown in the photograph left (early 20th century), illustrates the evolution of different stages of industry.

The weir on Pendle Water, below the George and Dragon Inn, (see photograph below) was built to allow water to sluice off to what is now the park lake. The banked footpath now running to the children's play area from the pond was the mill-leat and supplied water from the lodge to the original water-wheel. The pen-trough outlet (used water from the wheel) emptied into Pendle Water opposite the children's swings and the outlet can still be made out.

The mill was used variously as a corn mill and a fulling mill and was converted to a twist spinning mill by Abraham Hargreaves who bought the premises for £233 in 1783. The mill was provided with a steam engine to run in tandem with the water-wheel around 1830 and then passed through a number of hands, including the Stowe and Stansfield families of Barrowford. This important example of our industrial heritage ended its days as a dye-works and motor-cycle repair shop before suffering demolition at the hands of the council who purchased the mill and cottages for £1,000.[1] Only the corner of the engine house still remains of the mill.

---

[1] Jesse Blakey, *Annals and Stories of Barrowford,* (SP, Nelson, 1929)

The Barrowford Mill weir, or caul; c. 1910

Jesse Blakey gave the words to a song sung by the 'doffers' working at the Old Mill in the later nineteenth century:[1]

> *At half-past five the bell does ring,*
> *At six o'clock we all flock in*
> *To see Tom Procter just how he stands*
> *With the strap all ready in his hands.*
>
> *He whips the poor 'doffers' until they cry,*
> *But the Devil will fetch him by and by.* [2]

---

[1] *Annals and Stories of Barrowford,* (SP, Nelson, 1929)
[2] To *'doff'* was *'to take off'* - 'Doffers' were involved at the end of the weaving process

Chapter Six

The Forests

> *'We give no law to wolves and foxes,*
> *but knock them on the head wherever we find them.'*

The Norman hunting forests of the honour of Clitheroe were set up shortly after the Conquest. The four forest areas were **Pendle,** between Pendle Hill and Ightenhill; **Trawden,** between Colne and Boulsworth; **Rossendale**, between Haslingden and Cliviger and **Accrington** to the south of the Grange of Accrington. Overall these areas covered almost a quarter of Blackburnshire (35,000 statute acres), it is thought that the forests were larger at their earliest period but this is the area covered when they were officially deforested in 1507.

In the fifteenth century the Forest of Trawden contained the five vaccaries of Over and Nether Wycoller, Wynewall and Over and Nether Beardshaw. By this time the yearly value of the farming operations had increased from £2: 8s: 0d in 1323 to £21: 13s: 4d.

The vaccaries of Pendle Forest at the 1507 Inquisition

West Close and Hunterholme
Heigham Boothe
Newelawnde
Bareley Boothe
Heigham Close olim Nether-Heighham
Overgouldhey and Netherhouldhey
Feelie Close
Old Lawnde
Whitley Carre
Over Barrowforde and Nether Barrowforde
Over Roughney and Nether Roughney
Haweboothe and Whitley in Haboothe
Redhalowes
Admergill not now within the Forest bounds

When the post-Norman Forest of Pendle was first created it was known as the Chase of Pendle, this was because the appellation of *forest* applied only to the king's hunting grounds; any hunting area assigned to a noble was known as a *chase*. Pendle was owned by a subject of

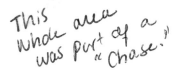

This whole area was part of a "Chase"?

the king and was therefore an official *chase*, this situation changed for a period in 1399 when the king became the lord of the manor and the title Forest of Pendle and Pendle Chase were both equally applied to the area in official documents.

The village of Higham was an obvious Saxon settlement (the *ham* suffix denotes this), and by the time of the creation of the new chase it was the only recognised village within the area. Unfortunately for the inhabitants no occupied village was allowed to exist in a forest or chase and so the people were uprooted and moved to a vill outside the area. The Chase of Pendle consisted of Pendle Hill, Barley, Newchurch-in-Pendle, Sabden, Higham, Reedley Hallows, New Laund, Old Laund, Filly Close, Hamston Cliffe, Wheatley Lane, Over Barrowford (including Blacko), Nether Barrowford and Roughlee. Hunting lodges were built throughout the chase, these included one near to the Inghamite Chapel at Fence, probably one on the site of Berry's Mill at Barrowford, Padiham Moor, Hamston Cliffe (Quaker Bridge or Pendle Waterside at Brierfield) and Trawden.[1]

T. D. Whitaker, in his *History of Whalley* (1801), had much to say on the subject of the ancient forest of which the following is an extract:

The word forest, in its original and most extended sense, implied a tract of land lying out, (foras) that is rejected, as of no value in the first distribution of property. There is no clear evidence that the Saxons reserved their deer hunting areas for the peculiar recreation of their monarchs, and still less, that they were placed under a distinct code of laws, before the reign of Canute, who, in AD 1016, promulgated the first 'constitutions de foresta'.

In these constitutions, therefore, we have the first outline of that singular system, which from the anxiety of the first Norman princes to secure to themselves the envied pleasures of the chase, afterwards became very artificial, which is now very picturesque and amusing indeed to us to view the apparatus at a distance, but was oppressive and cruel in a high degree to those who had the misfortune to live within its grasp.

By these laws, the supreme jurisdiction over the forests of England, was committed to four Thegenes (thegnes or principal barons), an inferior authority delegated to four Lesthegenes, (homines mediocres or lesser barons), and the immediate custody of each entrusted to two Tinemen (minuti homines), whose office it was to guard by nightly watches against offences of vert and venison.

The sanctions of this code were chiefly pecuniary, saving that in two cases, first of having offered violence to one of the four great thanes, and secondly of having slain a staggon or royal beast, a free man forfeited his liberty and a slave his life.

The supreme administration of the forests, however, fell by degrees into the hands of one chief judiciary, 'til in the year 1184 Henry II divided the forests of England into two jurisdictions, north and south of the Trent, which gave rise to the two itinera or eyres, still nominally subsisting. Over each of these he place four justices, viz. two clerks and two knights, together with two servants of his own household, as wardens, over all the other forests. Each of these itinera gradually fell back under the jurisdiction of one.

---

[1] Jesse Blakey, *Annals and Stories of Barrowford*, (SP, Nelson, 1929)

Henry II (1154-1189) fixed the forest constitution and we find their officers, under chief justices, to have consisted of the wardens, now first introduced, of foresters, verdurers, regarders, agisters, woodwards (sometimes called woodreves and bedels) whose respective offices are ascertained with great exactness in the old writers on this subject.

After the Conquest a much more material alteration took place in the internal government of the forests by which even a free man trespassing against the king's venison was condemned to a punishment worse than death, namely mutilation and loss of eyes, a penalty which, from the assizes of Henry I (1100-1135) and Richard I (1189-1199), appears to have been inflicted with no sparing hand.

Forests were generally exempt from the operation of both civil and ecclesiastical law; they belonged in strictness to no parish, hundred, county or diocese; and accordingly they had pleas of their own, greater and less; the former held every third year by the chief justice or his deputy; the latter, that of Swainmote, which carries its inferior rank and rustic character, in the name, summoned thrice in every year. Beside these was a court of attachment, subordinate to both the former.

The pervading principal of forest law was essentially different either from humanity or general policy - justice absolute under the sole discretion of the king - we may, therefore, cease to wonder that under a system like this it was equally criminal to lop a holly and to fell an oak; or that it was even more penal to kill a stag than to murder a man.

In the 9th of Henry III (1125/26), under a second charter, orders were given that inquisitions should be held, and perambulations made, in order to distinguish the lands afforested by the late kings, from old and rightful forests. In the beginning of Edward I (1272) a commission was issued to cause all the true and ancient forests to be mered and bounded by certain landmarks;- all newly afforested lands to be severed from the former, and the boundaries of each to be returned into the court of chancery.

And these lands so afforested were called pouralles or purlieus, from the French pourallee, a perambulation; yet, notwithstanding all these steps, as lands of this peculiar description had never been completely afforested, so they were never considered by the lawyers as entirely restored to their original rights; but, as partaking of a middle nature and constitution between free and forest land, and were therefore placed under certain laws and regulations peculiar to themselves.

This wise and excellent prince (Edward I) rendered an essential service to English liberty by abolishing the old code, it was expressly declared that no English subject shall henceforward lose life or limb for any trespass for vert or venison; but if any one be convicted of killing the king's deer he shall be sentenced to pay a heavy mulct which, if he cannot discharge, he shall lie in prison one year, after which, if he be unable to find pledges, he shall abjure the realm.

Verdurers were judicial officers sworn to keep the assizes of the forest and to receive and enrol all presentment of trespass against vert and venison. He was also a kind of coroner who, with ridiculous solemnity, held an inquisition 'super visum corporis' over the slain deer. The regarder was to view and enquire of similar trespass.

Foresters were sworn to preserve the vert and venison, to attend the wild beasts, to attach and present offenders. These were of two kinds, ordinary foresters holding their office during pleasure, though under great seal, or foresters of fee who held the office to them and their heirs, paying a fee-farm to the king. These were the real efficient guardians of the forest and they had under them inferior servants called underkeepers or walkers.

Next to the forester ranked the bedels of the forest, whose office was merely to execute process and to make garnishment to the courts of Swainmote and Attachment. The lowest office in this and vert, an object then deemed of no importance, excepting as it regarded the accommodation of the deer. The woodward was not allowed to bear a bow as this power belonged to his superiors.

Whitaker goes on to describe the hierarchy of the animals within the forest. Canute declared in AD 1016 that the stag alone was to be considered the true beast of the forest. At the trial of the earl of Strafford the Solicitor General stated that *'We give law to hares and deer, because they are beasts of chase; but we give no law to wolves and foxes, because they are beasts of prey, but knock them on the head wherever we find them.'*

In the mid-sixteenth century the prioress of Sopewell wrote:

> *Four maner Bestes of venery ther are,*
> *The first of hem is a Hart,*
> *The second is an Hare,*
> *The Boor is one of tho,*
> *The Wolf and no mo;*
>
> *And wherefo ye come in Playe or in Place,*
> *Nowe I shal tel you which be Bestes of Chace,*
> *On one of the' a Buck, another a Doo,*
> *The Fox and the Martyn, and the wilde Roo,*
> *And ye shal, my dere Sones, other Bestes all,*
> *Wherfo ye finde, Rascals hem call*

The *rascal tribe* or *'other beasts all'* category changed from period to period but over time it has included the otter, the badger, the weasel, the beaver, the squirrel, the martin and the wild cat. Some animals were not allowed within the confines of the forest, these were the goose, the goat, the hog and the sheep. For obvious reasons dogs were particularly legislated against, the greyhound and spaniel were absolutely prohibited from entering within forest bounds – people living within forest areas were barred from keeping these animals. Another type of dog, the mastiff, could be kept by forest dwellers on condition that they were either *hoxed*, which meant that their leg tendons were cut, or *lawed* where three toes were removed from the front paws. From the time of Canute it was deemed lawful to keep the *velter* or *langeran* (long-snout terrier) and the *ramhundt* (sheep dog). Surprisingly it was also legal to keep staghounds; Whitaker suggests that this was because people with the rights to hunt the king's forests travelled with their retinue of hounds and horses, chief amongst these were the peers and bishops. On their official travels to London, and back, these people were allowed to hunt within the king's forests en-route; in 1216 an archdeacon of Richmond, on a visitation to the priory of Bridlington, was accompanied by ninety-seven horses, twenty-one dogs and three hawks!

Theoretically only the king could own a forest, no subject was allowed to commission a seat of justice although there were exceptions. Attached to a forest, beside the seat of justice, were two inferior courts of *swainmote* and *attachment* with *foresters, verdurers, regarders* and *agisters*. A chase was the entitlement of the *keepers* and *woodwards* only. The period of fifteen days prior to midsummer, and the fifteen days following, were called the *fence month*, at this time all hunting was strictly forbidden as the hinds were either with calf or would have recently calved. A forest drive took place twice a year, this was carried out by the forest people forming a chain and beating noisily across the forest area. The idea was to coral the beasts of the forest into a pound and sort them for various purposes such as meat and breeding; the *agisters* with common rights of the forest had their rights of forest *gait* (entry to the forest) checked and took their cattle home. Any person who had let their stock into the forest without grazing rights either paid a fine or had his beasts confiscated.

By 1305 it is clear that the forests were no longer primarily reserved for the hunting of deer, by this time the game was largely, but not solely, confined to the two major parks of Ightenhill and Musbury in Rossendale. The reason for this was that the earls were realising that putting the forest lands out to farm would be far more profitable to them than retaining them purely as hunting grounds – like everyone else the lords had need of steady income to meet their burgeoning monetary outgoings. The creation of the forest vaccaries (cattle farms) can be seen as the beginning of the established farming settlements that we know today. Over time the lords of the honour took less interest in their cattle rearing operations and these were subsequently run by sub-tenants. In 1507 the Forest of Pendle was finally deforested and the vaccaries were let as copyhold tenancies. Some of the forest cow-keepers of earlier times now began to appear on the scene as tenants in their own right; the following is a list of thirteenth and fourteenth century cow-keepers in the vaccaries of Pendle Forest :[1]

1295 - 1296	1304 - 1305
Robert Attebrigge	Adam the Baker
William Gougge	Adam son of Nicholas
Adam son of Nicholas	Richard of Bradley
John del Barrowford	William son of Hawsia
Richard de Birchenlea	Robert de Merclesden
Richard son of Benedict	Richard son of Benedict
Henry son of Kitte	Henry son of Christiana
William de Penniltone	William de Wode
Benne de Holcombe	Benne de Holcombe
John del Hargreaves	John del Hargreaves
William son of Gryffrey	

Leland, the famous medieval historian, visited the Whalley area in the early part of the fourteenth century and mentioned that there were *bubuli*, or wild cattle, remaining *'not long before his time'* in the area. These were moved to the dean's park at Whalley Abbey and, upon

[1] Mary Brigg, *The Early History of the Forest of Pendle*, (Pendle Heritage, 1989)

The area had not that distantly seen major changes such as wide deforestation – once a noble-owned hunting forest – and the advent of the enclosure system

the *Dissolution of the Monasteries,* were transplanted to Gisburn Park. The story is that when the herd of beasts were driven from Whalley to Gisburn a flute player walked at their head whilst the cattle followed quietly along behind.[1] Each forest had its own *instaurator* (head cattle-man), the Pendle one at this time being Gilbert de la Legh of Hapton. A type of *head ranch* was the centre of operations and a *geldherd* was charged with the overseeing of the vaccaries. It was his task to visit all the farms within his area and account for the cattle, he would take cattle from one vaccary to another so as to maintain the quality of the breed and to ensure that each farm had an equal number of stock. He also dealt with the welfare of the stock and checked the *boothman's* accounts. To improve breeding standards certain cattle were taken to the central Accrington stock centre where beasts were sent to market, sold or transferred between the lord's estates.

Wood for the building of ships, houses and barns became the subject of legislation, new plantations were only previously allowed to be enclosed for a period of three years but a statute of 1483 encourage this period to be extended to seven years. In 1544 the *Act for the Preservation of Woods* decreed that plantation of two acres or more were not to be turned over to tillage or pasture – this also applied to any woods lying at a distance of two furlongs or more from a dwelling. In a complicated extension to the Act, timber owners were allowed to harvest one quarter of their wood provided that (amongst other things) other people had the rights of common over the area. This was a direct attempt to increase the amount of hard-woods available to the Navy and did not particularly affect our area; in fact the tenants of Pendle Forest petitioned James I in the early seventeenth century saying that there was no timber to be had for building purposes within the forest. This was no doubt an overstatement of the case to enforce their point that their land was not as valuable as the Crown said it was. However, the sentiments of the foresters would not be very far from the truth as the idea of Pendle Forest being an area of continuous woodland had not applied for many centuries. In the sixteenth century records show that timber for the erection of the new corn mill at Barrowford Carr was brought in from other areas; the Walk Mill at Colne Waterside was repaired using timber from Clitheroe and Barnoldswick.[2]

Enclosure

> We have shut away all cloisters,
> But still we keep extortioners,
> We have taken their land for their abuse,
> But we have converted them to a worse use

In the reign of Elizabeth I, Francis Bacon was a lawyer, Queen's Counsel and Member of Parliament – with reference to the fifteenth century events Bacon wrote; *'Enclosures began to be more frequent, whereby arable land, which could not be manured without people and families, was turned into pasture, which was easily rid by a few herdsmen; and tenancies for years, lives, and at will, whereupon much of the yeomanry lived, were turned into demesnes. This bred a decay of people.'*

---

[1] T.D.Whitaker, *History of Whalley,* (First edition, 1881)
[2] *Warner's History of Barnoldswick*

Henry VII deforestation

We have seen that the forests of Blackburnshire were deforested by grant of Henry VII – this was not the end of the matter for those people taking up the new copyholds, the small-holder in particular would be vulnerable to trouble emanating from more than one source. The established tenants who had prospered through their acquisition of common lands were, in certain cases, ruthless in their treatment of local small-holders.

The profits to be had from sheep and cattle meant that land could be more important than people and many of the subsistence-level cottagers were evicted from their meagre holdings and forced from the area. Even larger hamlets were not always safe from the grasping hands of the more ambitious land-holders. Much has been written of the *Clearances* that took place in Scotland, where crofters were ejected from their livelihoods to make way for the overlord's sheep, the equivalent of these *Clearances* happened in many other areas but this has not received the same measure of historical publicity. This is illustrated by the historian T. E. Scrutton who stated in a nineteenth century paper that:

Sir Anthony Fitzherbert in his 'Book of Surveying' in 1523, has told us how the action of the lords pressed on the poorer classes. 'It was,' says he, 'of old time that all the lands enclosures and pastures lay open and unenclosed. And then was their tenement much better chepe than they be now: for the most part the lords have enclosed a great part of their waste groundes and straitened their tenants of their commons therein; also they have enclosed their demesne lands and meadows and kept them in severalty, so that the tenants have no common with them therein. '

'They have also given license to divers of their tenants to enclose part of their arable land, and to take in new intakes or closes out of the commons, paying to their lords more rent therefore, so that the common pastures waxen less, and the rents of the tenants waxen more.'

As a result of the enclosures a General Act was passed by Parliament in 1487 commonly known by the name of *The Statute of Enclosures*. In fact this was one of two Acts, the other one was a *Local Act* effectively stating that no one person should own more than one farm. The *General Act* was against '*the pulling down of towns*' and stated that arable land should not be turned over to pasture and houses should not be removed. All houses having more than twenty acres of tillage land three years prior to the act were to be maintained and any such house being in a state of decay was to be restored. Two more Acts were passed in 1514 and 1515 to further emphasise the preservation of tillage land. *how much of Malkin was tillage land?*

It is unfortunate for the small man that these Acts were not enforced as becomes clear from yet another Act of 1536 stating that the earlier Acts had only been enforced to any degree on the lands owned by the king. The 1536 Act recited; *'but that the lords immediate and thoder mesne lords have not put the saide act into due execution, the houses yet remaining unedified, and the lands still remaining in pasture'* and went on to say that each house had to have thirty, forty or fifty acres of land and, until desolate houses were fully restored, the king was to have half of the profits of the land. Again this Act was toothless, derelict farm houses often had a single room made habitable and a shepherd, or other worker, was installed. Pasture land had a single furrow ploughed across it in order for it to qualify as tillage. To by-pass an order that sheep were to be limited in number many cattle farmers transferred their fields into the names of their sons. Another Act of 1588 stated that no house was to be without at least four acres of land and in 1597 Parliament was still struggling to address the matter of maintaining cultivated land.

> *The towns go down, the land decays;*
> *Of corn fieldes, plaine lays;*
> *Great men maketh now-a-days*
> *A sheepcot of the church*

[handwritten: Enclosure was happening all around here...]

The Acts of Parliament relating to enclosure did not effect the deer parks so favoured by the lords and gentry, even though they had long been a source of discontentment to the poorer people. They had seen the commons enclosed to their distinct disadvantage and were, understandably, not best pleased. This is nicely illustrated by enclosures that took place on and around the Towneley estate in Burnley. Sir John Towneley obtained a licence from the Crown in 1491 to enable him to enclose the old park at his seat of the Towneley Hall estate. This was repeated in 1497 when he turned a number of small enclosures in the neighbouring village of Hapton into parkland and in 1514, by means of yet another licence, he was able to *'impark and enclose with pales, ditches and hedges all his lands in Hapton and make a park into which no one might enter to hunt or chase without permission.'* In fact Towneley was so hungry for land that he regularly encroached upon areas that he did not own. As we have seen, it appears that this was the cause of the Crown confiscating 194 acres of land that he had illegally enclosed at Horelaw, near Towneley and Hapton. In 1603 the king granted these lands *'formerly inclosed in severalty by John Towneley Knight'* to the earl of Devon, in 1612 this land was sold back to the family when Richard Towneley purchased it for the sum of two shillings per acre. These were not the only lands affected by Towneley, he carried out much the same amount of enclosure on his other holdings throughout the parish of Whalley.

By the middle of the sixteenth century the Crown began to press the issue of payment for wastelands, in 1547 and 1553 an enquiry was directed into the encroachments of the wastes of Ightenhill and the surrounding forests and manors. Queen Elizabeth forced the issue in 1589 when a royal commission was appointed to visit the area and enquire as to which tenants had the right of common. The amount of unenclosed waste was ascertained and this was offered to the tenants on the understanding that they enclosed the new grounds and paid the customary rent of four pence per acre. Alternatively the Crown was willing to enclose the waste and lease it to the tenants at four pence per acre. The tenants realised that this would mean the loss of their traditional common and agreed to pay an annual rent for lands enclosed by the Crown provided that they could pay an extra lump sum to ensure that some of the land could be used as common.

Matters came to a head in 1607 when James I decided to quench his ever-raging thirst for funds by attempting to declare that the titles granted to tenants in 1507 were not actually legal. The king's lawyers stated that any clearance of forest areas, by necessity, turned the soil into tillage and this was anciently an offence. Also they argued that the holders of enclosed forest lands could not claim copyhold thereon because *'custom (tradition) never extended to anything newly created, custom of copyhold was, therefore, not legally possible.'*

This was a bombshell to the land owners within the honour of Clitheroe, many families relied upon the holdings that they had created under the 1507 grants, they were now being told that they were, in effect, tenants under sufferance. Much wrangling followed, the important land owners entered pleas and the small-holders flatly refused to pay. Eventually, in an inevitable victory for the Crown, an agreement was reached by means of an act called *'An Act for the perfect creation and confirmation of certain copyhold lands in the honour, castle, manor and lordship of Clitheroe.'* The upshot of this was that a sum of £3,763 was paid to the Crown, this was the equivalent to twelve-year's ancient rent.

[handwritten: The laws of land ownership in the area were certainly in flux — that much is clear]

Things quietened down for a while but, by 1611, the king was up to his old tricks. He commissioned another enquiry as to the doubtful holdings, and holdings taken from wastes. The Crown commissioners, Sir Richard Molyneux (earl of Sephton) and Sir Ralph Assheton (of the Downham family), stated that they would only recognise copyholds if they were purchased from the king for nine shillings and four pence per acre (twenty-eight year's rent at four pence per acre). A carrot was offered here in as much as any tenant wishing to pay this sum was offered extra waste land, the ordinary people were not happy with this state of affairs and said so. The gentry, however, were quick to spot an opportunity to acquire yet more land, this put them at variance with their smaller neighbours. In a letter to the Commission the gentry presented their case saying that they were only too willing to accept the king's proposals but were being held back by the naughty peasants. As they quaintly put it *'The friars should not be beaten for the nun's fault.'*[1] Again, the Crown won the case and the copyholders of the Manor of Ightenhill paid a settlement of £2,141: 10s: 10d – this ensured that the remaining waste lands were divided amongst them at a rental of six pence per acre.

As a result of the apportionment of the remaining wastes the commons were largely enclosed between 1617 and 1630. The newly acquired wastes were exchanged between copyholders, poorer holders were bought out of their holdings and so new farms appeared on the new intakes. At this time many of the familiar dry-stone walls surrounding the chequer-work fields that we are so familiar with were erected. The final phase of enclosure began under the *Enclosure Act* of 1801, this was largely to ensure that the remaining outlying commons, or moors, were officially apportioned and enclosed. Taking Trawden as an example the Act stated that the common lands within Trawden Forest should be valued, divided and allotted as soon as was convenient. As a result of this Boulsworth Hill, one of the last 'untamed' areas of the Trawden Forest, was enclosed under the auspices of a Parliamentary Commissioner in 1821.[2]

Many stone enclosure walls come from this period of the early to middle 17th century

Vaccary keepers within Pendle Forest 1324

Chief tenant	Holding	Rental
Richard de Whiteacre	West Close and Higham	40 shillings
John de Whiteacre	Part of Goldshaw	28 shillings
Richard de Merclesden	Part of Roughlee	28 shillings
Richard de Greenacre	Part of Roughlee	28 shillings
Robert de Penhille	Barley	28 shillings
Gilbert de la Legh	Whitehough	28 shillings
Simon de Blakey	Part of Barrowford	28 shillings
Richard de Merclesden	Close of Blakey	20 shillings
Richard de Whiteacre	Royle and Filly Close	20 shillings
John de Dyneley	Haigh (Wheatley, Barley)	18 shillings
John le Parker	Part of Barrowford	13 shillings 4 pence

[1] T.D.Whitaker, *History of Whalley,* (1st edition, 1881)
[2] Fred Bannister, *The Annals of Trawden Forest,* (Colne, 1922)

In the year AD1324 the halmote court at Ightenhill, the house of the lord of the honour of Clitheroe at Burnley, the people within the above list had the grant of the vaccaries within Pendle Forest (this is not to say that they actually worked the land, the farmsteads were sub-let to farmers for this purpose):

We have in the following list a snapshot of the more important people throughout much of the Forest of Pendle. They were in the enviable position of renting their holdings from the overlords of the honour of Clitheroe at very favourable rates and then sub-letting their holdings to farmers, in many cases for a substantial profit. Following their original grants of vaccaries many of these families played an important role within Pendle Forest society for many centuries. Some 119 years later we have the Clitheroe court roll record of the freeholders and tenants of the honour of Clitheroe, the following is the list for Pendle Forest 1443:

Pendle Forest: Freeholders and tenants 1443 [1]

Christ Banaster	*John Banaster*	*William del Foldes*
John Robinson	*Christopher*	*Robert Blakey*
James Banaster	*Henry*	*Robert Grymeshagh*
John del Legh	*Robert Balhole*	*Oliver Blakey*
Roger Tatersall	*John Crolilhagh*	*Thomas Haryngton, Chev.*
William de Carr	*Robert Bullcock*	*John Bullcock*
John Haliday	*John Nutter*	*Rrd Parker for Heghin*
Wm Ingham	*John Hargreaves,*	*William Mankinholes*

Here the same, familiar names of the minor gentry appear, along with the yeoman tenants who were beginning to assume an importance within the social hierarchy.

Many of these names can still be recognised locally; *Bullcock* of Whitehough: *Blakey* of Over Barrowford (Blacko) and Marsden: *Mancknowles* of Town House in Marsden and Roughlee: *Carr* of Langroyd: *Bannister* of Altham, Park Hill, Barnoldswick, Marsden and Foulridge: *Parker* of Alkincoats, Barrowford, Browsholme and Extwistle: *Foulds* of Trawden, Colne and Briercliffe: *Nutter* of Roughlee, Goldshaw, Reedley, Briercliffe, Colne and Blacko. These were the yeomanry, farmers who rented their lands from the minor gentry who, ultimately, leased them from the Duchy of Lancaster. *land – ultimately owned by AKA the crown Duchy of lancaster – DAKA the crown*

Many of today's local farmers descend directly from the forest stock-keepers of the post-Norman period when the vaccaries of Pendle Forest were first established. In the following century, as we see in the following list, some of the earlier tenants had disappeared but others (Robinson, Hartley, Hargreaves etc;) were consolidating their positions:

---

[1] Mary Brigg, *The Early History of the Forest of Pendle*, (Pendle Heritage, 1989)

Pendle Forest Tenants: 1527

Christ. Robynson	Christ. Baldwyn
Jones Sutclyff	Jones Hayke
Laurencius	Jacobus Hertley
Jones Smyth	Crist. Robynson
Jones Haregreves	Laur. Haregreves
Bernardus Hertleye	Crist. Blakey
Laurencius Hertley	Jacob Hertley
Henr. Mitton	Jacobus Michell
Jacobus Hertley	Laur. Hertleye
Jones Wylson	Duchy of Lancaster

Certain surnames within the forest lists can be seen to echo their early roots:-

Hartley *(Hart...deer: Ley...clearing in the woods)* described a person who looked after the forest deer.

Parker was the officer charged with overseeing the king's, or the lord's forest.

Nutter *(Neat...forage: Herd...stock-keeper)* is possibly the description of a person who was responsible for keeping the forest feeding grounds healthy.

Bullock would be the obvious name of a person who worked closely with the oxen bred within the forest for working the land.

Whittaker is the modern version of *Whiteacre* whereby the name described the land-holding – *white* could be *wheat,* or it could be related to a salt route, but their is also a case for this name being descriptive of *high* thus giving a possible derivation of Whittaker as '*of the high land.'* [1]

Merclesden is the early name for *Marsden* (Nelson). [2]

Marsden (see above).

Bradley *(broad clearing),* locally, is the area of Marsden near to the present Fire Station where the king's corn mill stood.

---

[1] Alfred Watkins, *The Old Straight Track,* (First published 1925, Reissued by Abacus, 1974)
[2] Walter Bennett, *The History of Marsden and Nelson,* (Nelson Corporation, 1957)

Wood and **Woodward** were names applied to the lowest office of the forest keepers, they were responsible for the protection of the wood and vert (small game).

Greaves, Constable and **Swain** were officials of the community.

Pinder relates to the keeper of the pinfolds where stray stock was held until it was claimed by the owner.

Pounder also relates to the keeping of impounded forest stock

Smith originates in the blacksmith and whitesmith trades. The latter smith worked with lighter metals than the blacksmith i.e., tin and lead.

Hargreaves possibly derived from *hare* or *hart* and *greave* thus giving an occupation of someone who had charge of the forest deer.

Booth and **Boothman** comes from the name given to cow-keepers within the vaccary areas. Over and Nether Barrowford, for instance, were divided into two *booths* which would be occupied by boothmen.

Driver was the person who rounded up the forest animals on certain days of the year in order to sort them.

Huddart was applied to a keeper of forest animals where *hudd* is woodland or forest. This is possibly the original derivation of the surname of *Robin Hood*.

Robinson was the son of Robert

[handwritten: Farming system is in flux during period.]

   By the middle of the seventeenth century it is fair to say that our present farming system had become firmly established, although by no means all of the farmsteads of today were in existence at that time. Some of the farm sites that we see scattered around the Pendle area are undoubtedly of Saxon origin whilst others were created during the later periods of enclosure within the forest.

Early enclosure walls at Spen above the settlement of Dimpenley

The village of Newchurch and Pendle Hill in the background

Chapter Seven

People and Places

Bannister, Towneley and Wilkinson of Barrowford

[handwritten: This is a major Boundary area.]

The area now encompassed within the parish of Blacko was, until the late nineteenth century, a part of the village of Barrowford. Blacko formed a booth (a designated farming area within the forest) in Over Barrowford. The name Blacko is commonly taken to mean the *Black Hill* from the Old English *blaec* + Old English *hoh* or Old Norse *haugr* - the name was given as *Blacho* in the twelfth century and *Blakhow* in 1329.[1] There is also an argument for the name having originated from its position on a major boundary (the old Lancashire/Yorkshire county boundary) and therefore the Old English *heigh* (fence, hedge, boundary) can be ascribed to the suffix within *Blak-ey*.[2]

The Blacko Hill stands at around 1,000 feet and is situated to the east of the relatively modern village of Blacko. The ancient boundary that splits the hill east-west along its ridge became the original county boundary of Lancashire and Yorkshire; the southern slopes of Blacko Hill fall just within the bounds of Pendle Forest. In this small area we find the farmsteads of Malkin Tower, Blacko Hillside, Burnt House and Brownley Park and, just metres beyond the forest boundary, Pasture Head. Further to the south is the Great Stone Edge estate, this comprised a number of properties held variously by the Towneleys, Hartleys, Bannisters and Robinsons.

Following the creation of Pendle Forest the lands around the Blacko Hillside were gradually improved and the area became known as Blacko Pasture. A filter-down of property occurred whereby Blacko Hillside fell largely within the ownership of a very small number of landowners and there is documentary evidence that the Marsden family were early tenants.[3] The estate of Stone Edge came to occupy the lands and properties of Blacko Hillside under the Towneley family. As we shall see shortly, the Bannister family of Park Hill will also enter the arena.

The fourth Laurence Towneley of Stone Edge emigrated to America where he founded a dynasty that would produce at least one of that country's presidents and also a number of leading military figures. The brother of Laurence, John Towneley, also emigrated to America and a third brother, Thomas, became the heir to the Stone Edge estate in 1674, he was buried from Slipper Hill Farm (below Malkin Tower Farm) in 1697.[4] Richard Towneley (1682-1727), a son of Thomas, moved his own family around the Blacko Hillside, they lived at Near White Moor Farm and Malkin Tower Farm from where Richard's son, also Richard, was baptised in 1719. It is probable that Richard (senior) built the present property of Malkin Tower farmhouse

---

[1] David Mills, *The Place-Names of Lancashire*, (Batsford, 1976)
[2] John A Clayton, *Valley of the Drawn Sword*, (Barrowford Press, 2007)
[3] Walter Bennett, *The History of Marsden and Nelson*, (Nelson Corporation, 1957)
[4] *Towneley MSS* (manuscripts and papers)

[handwritten: 1719 - ? might have built the oldest part of the present Malkin Tower farmhouse]

[handwritten: Richard Towneley]

(the earliest part of the extant buildings) to house his family in the early part of the eighteenth century. Richard's daughter, Grace, was baptised in 1722 at nearby White Moor and Richard himself was buried from Malkin in 1727. A court roll dated 24th July 1622 shows the brothers Robert (born around 1545) and Charles Towneley (born around 1547), the sons of Laurence of Barnside (Laneshawbridge near Colne), living at Lower Blacko (this probably refers to Stone Edge):

Lease for 31 years at 40 shillings rent: for £70: John Habergham of Habergham, gent., and Anne his wife, to Robert Townley of Lower Blacow, gent. . . . Fowlrigge Hall, barn, orchard, garden, toft, croft, Well Flatt, Calf Crofte, Sowerby, Cockerhill Field with cottage, Dearen Royd, in tenure of Charles Townley of Lower Blacowe, brother of Robert Townley . . . term to commence on the death of Charles.

Moving alongside, and intermarrying with the Towneleys at this time were the Bannisters of Park Hill (now the Pendle Heritage Centre) in Barrowford. The earliest documented evidence relating to the Bannisters at Park Hill is where, in 1461, Richard Bannister was granted dispensation by the church to marry Joan Walton of Marsden Hall, Great Marsden. The Bannisters prospered and, in 1475, Richard was renting the vaccary of Over Barrowford from the king for the sum of £4: 0s: 0d per annum. Richard's son, Robert, took over the *Old Hold* lease and by the time of the *New Hold*, in 1507, the family held lands in Ightenhill, Foulridge, Colne, Lomashaye (Marsden), Reedyford (Marsden) and Great and Little Marsden. This placed the family in the position of acquiring the copyhold of their lands at a fixed rental; they were then able to re-let at a substantial profit. [1]

Marsden Hall

Lomashaye House

---

[1] *A Bannister Family History,* (Heritage Trust for the North West, 2006)

Clitheroe court rolls are /seem to be primary historical documents here.

Robert's son, Henry, inherited Park Hill with rights also going to Robert's other sons James and Christopher. In 1563 the 'manor' of Parkhill was still in the possession of a Henry Bannister (probably the son of Henry) as he, along with his son Robert, made a settlement of a part of the manor of Foulridge. Henry died in 1602 and his son, Robert (who had married Ellen Towneley of Towneley Hall), died in 1616 when Park Hill, along with its lands, corn mill and fulling mill (Barrowford Mill in the Park) was said to have been *'held of the king in socage as of his castle at Clitheroe.'* [1]

Photograph: A. J. Morris Collection

The Bannister property of Park Hill, Barrowford

In reference to the Bannister land holdings in Over Barrowford a Clitheroe court roll shows:

1550: *The doors on the North side of the house built on land at Stony Edge, occupied by Hugh Wilkinson, Agnes Dawtrie and others, belonging to Henry Bannister, Gentleman, are to be closed up to stop the trespass on said land.*

This would relate to a house on the extended Stone Edge estate, as opposed to the Stone Edge properties themselves, and could have been situated anywhere around the lower Blacko area; the house referred to in the court roll did not have land attached to its northern aspect as this ground belonged to Henry Bannister. The Bannister holding terminated at Blacko Outgate (now Blacko Bar on the Barrowford to Gisburn Road); where the Stone Edge Farm sloped steeply into Pendle Water the Bannister lands met with those of the Hargreaves family at Water Meetings.

---

[1] In this context *Soke* was the right of the king to a percentage of the business done at Barrowford Mill through the central authority of the Honour of Clitheroe

Between Malkin Tower Farm and Pasture Head the Bannister holdings met with those of the manor of Foulridge. To the north of both the Blacko Hill ridge and the township of Foulridge the area became the property of the Lister family of Westby Hall (Gisburn).

Hugh Wilkinson, who was to have his door blocked up, appears in the records again in 1561 when:

John Hartley of Admergill surrenders one parcel of land in and upon Blacko at £0: 4s: 8d to the use of Hugh Wilkinson, Jennett his wife and Elizabeth his daughter, and survivor, . . . shall pay the Queen's rent and 14s to John Hartley, his heirs and assigns and 1 day of shearing, 1 day of turves drawing and 1 day of hay making.

The term 'upon Blacko' refers to the Blacko Hillside and would describe the location of the house occupied by Hugh Wilkinson as having been one of the farms ringing the southern flanks of Blacko Hill, or a worker's cottage in the same area. As these houses and farms all faced south it follows that Bannister's land to the north was to the rear of Wilkinson's house.

The southern Blacko Hillside; Malkin Tower farm is on the extreme top right of picture

In the above record of 1561 it appears that Hugh Wilkinson had either moved house or the '*Agnes Dawtry and others*' (who were shown in the earlier record of 1550) had moved out as there is no mention of them. Alternatively these people may have been servants or relatives in the Wilkinson household and would not have merited a mention in the land grant. It is clear from this record that John Hartley of Admergill (the valley at the northern foot of Blacko Hill) was in a position to allow Wilkinson the use of his land (around fourteen acres in extent) for an

Towneley or Wilkinson Malkin

How old is the Malkin name?

[handwritten: 1589 ACT IMPORTANT RE DEMDIKE!!]

[handwritten margin: not prosecuted]

entry fee of three year's rent and three day's boon work.[1] Hartley would have been a sub-tenant of the Bannister's Park Hill estate within the Blacko Hillside area.

We have the distinct possibility that the Wilkinson family lived at either Malkin or a close neighbouring property. They were probably tenants of both the Bannisters and the Hartleys, furthermore the Wilkinsons must have been trusted tenants as they had held their property for ten years at least. Often a sub-tenant would be granted a lease of less than a year-and-a-day as this was the limit above which land transactions had to be recorded in the court rolls at the halmote courts. Hugh Wilkinson's tenure appears to have been more secure than this, not only because of the length of his tenure, but he was also granted adjoining lands on long-term lease. There is a caveat here, however, as an Act of 1589 was designed to halt the spread of squatters and limit the amount of tiny hovels that were springing up on marginal land. The Act stated that no cottage should be built or occupied if it had less than four acres of land attached to it. Because of the attractively high rents available to the landlords for tiny cottages and small holdings they tended to ignore this Act. The local courts heard a number of cases relating to the breaking of this law in the 1590s but this type of case was not prosecuted again to any extent until the 1620s when thirty-one offences were reported. This means that either the courts were deciding to crack down on the problem in these periods of high conviction or (less likely) landlords were obeying the law in the interim. In either case it is not apparent that this was the kind of tenure enjoyed by Hugh Wilkinson.

[handwritten margin: This could have been a proper house or a hovel]

Malkin is firmly placed within the immediate area of the Bannister land discussed above and, interestingly enough, the oldest part of the Malkin Tower Farm property has a bricked-up doorway on its north-facing side. To have direct relevance to the matter this latter fact would need to assume that the present building dates from the time of the 1550 record where Wilkinson's house was ordered to have its northern doorway sealed – it is unlikely that this is the case as the present property is thought to date from the early eighteenth century. However, there are the remains of a much older property immediately to the rear of the present Malkin Tower Farm property and this appears to have had a single doorway facing south.

[handwritten margin: about this ASK]

The following writ shows John Wilkinson, a farmer of Barrowford, and others being thrown out of the church, probably for none-attendance. *[handwritten: ABOUT BRICKED-UP door way]*

April 1622: *Writ of excommunicato capiendo against Robert Bancrofte of Blakey, husbandman, Thomas Wittakers of Rudey Hallowes, husbandman, and John Wilkinson of Burrowsford, husbandman.* *[handwritten: — were they catholics??]*

There was also a Wilkinson presence within the extended area of Fence as shown in the following court roll record:

1569: *John Hartley and Isobel his wife surrender one messuage, other buildings, lands, tenements, meadows, pastures, grazing lands and mosses in le Fence; annual rent to the queen £0: 2s: 6d now or lately in the tenure of George Wylkinsone to the said George Wylkinsone and Jennet his wife and their assigns for the lives of the said John and Isobel Hartley. Admittance sought and granted. Annual rent payable at £0: 2s: 6d to John and Isobel Hartley if lawfully asked for. Fine £0: 2s: 6d by the pledge of Hugh Moore.*

---

[1] *Boon Work* was roughly equivalent to the feudal *Suit* whereby tenants worked for the lord or landlord - in this case work was carried out in lieu of rent

[handwritten: WILKINSONS first then Towneley were ??? owners of property at Malkin — Wilkinson was landlord..]

Here, again, we have John Hartley granting lands to a Wilkinson, was this Hugh Wilkinson's brother? Hugh Moore, who stood surety for the land surrender, was probably the Hugh Moore of Higham Dean who was allegedly bewitched to death in 1594/5 by Old Chattox.

The rear of Malkin Tower Farm. The house (extreme left) is the earliest building

The Wilkinsons of Blacko Hillside would later spread their branches throughout the area. My own ancestors hail from these people and eventually, in the nineteenth century, became a long line of journeyman (master-craftsmen) builders. In this capacity they erected many of the properties around the Foulridge area and within the town of Burnley, particularly around the Burnley Wood and Fulledge areas.

As a final word on the Wilkinsons; we have seen that, in 1561, Hugh was living in a property at Blacko with his wife, Jennett, and daughter Elizabeth. It has been suggested that the family dwelling could have been the property now known as Malkin Tower Farm - this leads to the natural question as to whether the daughter, Elizabeth, would eventually inherit the tenancy of the family dwelling upon the death of her parents. We know that Elizabeth Southern (Demdike) lived at Malkin Tower for many years preceding the 1612 Lancashire Witch Trials - is it possible that we have in Elizabeth Wilkinson the future Elizabeth Southern? Certainly the date of occupancy of the Wilkinsons (1561) would not preclude the idea, furthermore the Wilkinsons definitely lived within the Malkin area.

Before "Malkm", we have only references to Blacko Hillside

Could Elizabeth southern be Elizabeth Wilkinson??

*Blacko village; taken before Stansfield's Tower was erected on
Blacko Hill (background - right) in 1890*

The Cross Gates Inn at Blacko

*The name derives from the fact
that the inn is sited on the
crossing point of three former
forest trackways*

Blacko Hillside in the north-eastern corner of Pendle Forest

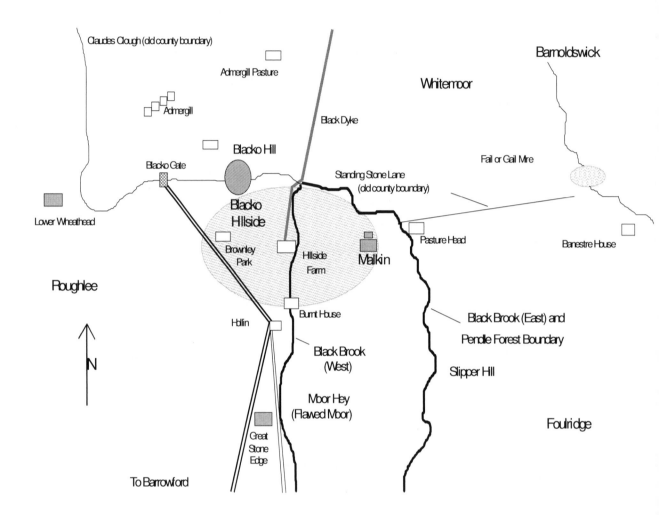

The area covered on this map corresponds roughly with the area shown to have been at variance, between Foulridge and Barnoldswick, on the 1581 map of Whitemoor

Chapter Eight

People and Places Continued

West Close, Goldshaw and New Laund

Possibly the strongest 'claim to fame' enjoyed by the small area of West Close was the fact that the family of Anne Whittle (Old Chattox) lived there at the time of the 1612 Pendle Witch Trials. The area around West Close has, of course, a far wider and interesting history than a single family might provide. The area of our interest lies in the very south-western corner of Pendle Forest and to the north of Pendle Water. The extended area of West Close is sandwiched between Ightenhill and Old Laund (east to west) and Higham and Burnley (north to south). Following the initial creation of the forest by the Normans this particular south-western corner of Pendle Forest was largely comprised of Reedley Hallows, Higham, Whitelee, West Close, Hamstone Cliffe, Filly Close, Hunterholme, Moor Isles and Old Laund. The area of Reedley Waterside is now known as Quakers-in-Pendle Bridge and, from its former name of Hamstone Cliffe, (*ham* denotes a Saxon settlement) appears to have been settled well before the Norman invasion. The site of the highest status here, within the medieval period, was The Lodge in Reedley, home of the Barcroft family. [1]

Small oxen-rearing sites were established on the best land within the forest for the breeding of draught animals. Clearings of open land within the deer hunting areas were known as *parks* or *launds* (from the Old French *laundes*) and these were often the sites of early cattle operations; in charge of these (beneath a central *geldherd*) were the first foresters of whom a John del Hargreaves appears as early as 1295.[2] This family retained an unbroken lineage within the forest to the present day whilst others, such as John del Barrowford and William Gougge, seem to have disappeared. The lord's of Clitheroe eventually saw the monetary benefit to be had from the increased breeding and supply of farm animals and turned over an increasing amount of forest land to vaccary and the growing of crops.

Booth (Old Danish *bōth = dairy farm*) was the name applied to the first vaccary sites and this becomes apparent in Goldshaw Booth (the area around Newchurch-in-Pendle). The somewhat peculiar name of *Goldshaw* is of complex origin but is thought to have its roots within the Old English (Anglo-Saxon) name of *Goldgeofu*. Originally this was a woman's name but the -*g* would become vocalised to an -*i* with the result of *di* sounding like *'judge.'* Therefore the second element of the name would be replaced by *shaw* (OE *sceaga - small wood*) as a description of the wooded area of Pendle. Eventually the word *bōth* was added to give the early spelling of

---

[1] Walter Bennett, *The History of Burnley,* (Burnley Corporation, 1946)

[2] Mary Brigg, *The Forest of Pendle in the Seventeenth Century - Part Two,* (Lancs / Cheshire History Society - Paper, 1963)

Goldiauebothis - now Goldshaw Booth.[1] Originally Goldshaw consisted of two separate booths, in 1324 John de Whiteacre farmed one of these at a rental of twenty shillings and Richard de Whiteacre farmed the other at the same annual rent. Richard de Whiteacre was obviously an enterprising type as, along with Goldshaw, he also had the farm vaccaries of West Close, Higham, Royle and Filly Close.

By the 1440s there were around two dozen tenants and freeholders within Pendle and the names with which we have become familiar were beginning to appear. Amongst these were *James, Christopher* and *John Banastere, John Hargraves* of Lomeshaye, *John Nuter, William del Foldes, John Robinsone, Christopher* and *Robert Blakey* and *John* and *Robert Bullcocke*.

Whiteley Hey Booth, (Wheatley Booth) not to be confused with Whitelee in Higham, is often found within references to the early forest and this was the area stretching from Wheathead Height, through the Black Mosses and on to the village of Barley. Fence, (now a village straddling the old Barrowford to Higham road) was originally of little consequence as it had no particular settlement and, as we saw earlier, the area was mostly waste land up to the later sixteenth century. The actual fence that gave the area its name was a wooden palisade animal enclosure that ran from Rishton Thornes (the area around the Old Sparrow Hawk Inn) to Higher New Laund. The reason for the area having been fenced, or enclosed, was to contain the forest deer as the new farming booths began to encroach ever-more widely upon the old forest areas.

Fence was included within the bounds of Goldshaw, Higham and West Close and was therefore let to the tenants of those areas. In 1526 the steward of Blackburnshire, at the direction of the king's auditors, attempted to separate the lands within Fence and rent them out to the highest bidders. The thirteen tenants who had long held the rights of these lands were quite peeved at this and took their case to court. Under oath they swore that *'King Henry VII did grant the said parcels, closes etc, to them as old tenants to enjoy and occupy without disturbance.'* The case rumbled on until finally, in 1545, the king's Commissioner granted the permanent copyhold to the tenants.[2]

Initially the amount of new lands granted out to vaccary within the forest amounted to some 13,000 acres, foresters saw their opportunity and took on as much new land as became available and that they were able to manage. In a 1258 survey of Blackburnshire estates it was stated that *'Respecting the Foreste of Pennal, it can sustain five vaccaries and the herbage is worth forty shillings and still sustains deer.'*[3] Some fifty years later there were eleven vaccaries within Pendle. By the time of the 1507 deforestation many of the modern farming names had become scattered throughout the whole of Pendle – Smith, Nutter, Hartley, Hargreaves, Robinson, Mitton *et al* were extremely common names. Added to this was the fact that these families used the same Christian names through the generations and this provides us with an almost impossible task when it comes to accurately ascertaining the genealogy of each family!

In 1539 John Towneley, knight, surrendered the whole of Filly Close, with all of its buildings, at £10: 13s: 8d to Thomas Hesketh, John Neville, Richard Sherburne and Robert Dalton. Forty-six shillings of the yearly income of Filly Close was to go towards the education of the Towneley sons in each college term. The above named were feoffes entrusted with the estate and were; *'Not to inquiet hurt vex or Trowble my Tenantes, fermers and occupyers of the said Filly Close*

[1] David Mills, *the Place-Names of Lancashire,* (Batsford, 1976)
[2] Mary Brigg, *The Forest of Pendle in the Seventeenth Century - Part Two,* (Lancs/Cheshire History Society - Paper, 1963)
[3] T. D. Whitaker, *History of the Parish of Whalley,* (First edition, 1801)

by eny Incores or Ingressomes takynge off them during their naturall lyves oneley.'

A good reason for the rapid spread of the original tenancy holders, apart from the general rise in population numbers, can be said to be the necessity for labour. Whether they were small-holders or middling farmers the early improvers required a supply of new land and a regular and cheap supply of labour. Labourers from the neighbouring villages and towns were available but were often unreliable and required regular wages. The answer was for the farmers to have as many children as possible, sons would provide the brawn to improve and maintain the land whilst daughters would provide labour for the weaving and dairy side of the farming operation. This often meant that people would marry in later life, it is often the case that a bachelor farmer, or one who married later in life, would have had a number of illegitimate children who carried an *alias* name. [1]

The fact that the eldest sons inherited the family property usually meant that they stayed upon the farm and this meant that more living space was required, more cottages were built on the farm site to house the new families and so the properties tended to expand. Younger sons, and most of the daughters, found it necessary to leave the family property; the sons would find work on neighbouring farms or start their own enterprise by improving waste lands wherever possible. Daughters, ideally, would marry the eldest son of another established farmer and thus the properties might eventually form a compound estate. Those not able to do this often worked in the dairy and weaving side of the family farm, they went into service with the gentry or worked for other farmers. Where two or more daughters were the surviving heirs to an estate the property was divided between them and, if the daughters were unmarried, or could not buy-out their siblings, this would often lead to the breaking up of their properties.

By 1527 there were ninety-eight forest copyhold tenants who were swelling the coffers of the Clitheroe overlord to the tune of £114: 6s: 8d. As the century progressed the 'land grab' became ever more competitive and this led to a large number of property surrenders and land disputes, these are readily apparent within the Clitheroe court rolls. By 1662 there were 230 copyhold farmers within Pendle and records indicate that this century was a period of prosperity for the yeomen and husbandmen of the forest. By the end of this century, however, a change swept through the area as it becomes apparent that land holdings, and the wealth generated by them, began to dwindle. [2]

Many Tudor and early Stuart buildings were of relatively high-status and were erected by the wealthier farming class. During the later seventeenth and early eighteenth centuries these larger properties had passed into the ownership of the more wealthy gentry who let them out to tenant farmers. This indicates an important change within the economy of the forest area and could very well be a consequence of the ever-increasing demand for land coupled with an ever-decreasing supply. This quickly led to the farming family occupying only a part of these large properties whilst the remainder of the buildings became semi-derelict. Examples here were Charles Farm, in Barrowford (the problem here was solved by the property being turned into the White Bear Inn), Old Laund Hall, Water Meetings Farm and Roughlee Old Hall – the Bannisters of Park Hill were not immune to the problem and were busy re-mortgaging their Park Hill estates, only to see them taken over and sold. [3] Many more substantial houses have

---

[1] It is extremely common to find *alias* names within the records. As a rule the *alias* was the surname of the person's father; however, in many instances where the father of an illegitimate child was of the gentry class then the mother would receive an income to support the child and to keep the father's name as *'unknown'*

[2] *Subsidy Rolls and Rental Lists* - Pendle

[3] *The Farrar Papers* - Manchester Central Library

been replaced by much smaller properties as at Whitelees (Higham), Reedley Lodge and Moor Isles. This state of affairs did not abate in the coming centuries when numerous other examples fell into ruin, not least amongst these were Extwistle Hall (outside the forest to the north of Burnley), Carr Hall (Barrowford) and Emmott Hall (Laneshawbridge). The long-established yeomanry family of the Nutters of Reedley Waterside had expanded and improved their land and property holdings over the centuries but, in 1742, Ellis Nutter left a will in which he requested that his two farms be sold to pay his debts and provide an income for his wife and children – within some 250 years things had turned full-circle. Many of the families who had gained from the *New Hold* in 1507 were now in decline. Generally, in the long-term, the survivors were to be the offspring of the established forest farmers who consolidated their lands through marriage and worked manageable (in terms of size) land.

The new intakes of south-west Pendle coincided with the parochial Reedley Hallows and the forest riverside site of Old Laund. The king's horse-breeding operation at nearby Ightenhill began to use this part of the forest for grazing their expanding herds and this became known as Filly Close. In 1502 a Commission for Henry VII said that:

'Feely Close always hath beene agifted to ye fume of IX/ XIs VIIId. . . and noe more, becaufe of ye recourfe yt ye deere of pendle hathe thereunto, an yt was thought by us that they fhould have the fame yt faveinge ye like courfe of deere as hath beene ufed afore.'

The area below the hamlet of Higham became the West Close (literally - *the field to the west*) of the Old Laund and the Laund itself, having been established alongside the earlier deer park of Old Laund, naturally became known as New Laund. The name of Hamstone Cliffe fell into disuse when the higher status property of Chamber-in-Pendle was established there whilst the riverside site of the new Nutter land holdings became Pendle Waterside (now Quakers-in-Pendle Bridge).

Old Laund Hall in the later 19th century

This area of the forest is somewhat unusual as its boundary reaches south over the river of Pendle Water, the river could have been expected to form a natural southern boundary of the forest at this point. It is very possible that the reason for this was for the forest to encompass the grange estate that existed (within the early forest period) in the Lodge area of Reedley Hallows. This latter area falls within the forest on both sides of Pendle Water.

The manor of Ightenhill falls just outsie the southern boundary of Pendle Forest and the jurisdiction of this major manorial centre included Burnley, Briercliffe, Little Marsden, Habergham, Cliviger, Padiham and the Pendle Forest. Nearby was the Gawthorpe estate, the seat of the Shuttleworth family who held the grant of much of the Padiham and West Close areas for many generations.

As the early Nutter families of Goldshaw spread their holdings towards the southern boundary of the forest they created the farmsteads with which we are now familiar. Robert Nutter, who expanded the New Laund holdings, found that he held enough land in the later sixteenth century to enable the creation of farms for each of his three sons, Henry, Christopher and Ellis. This saw the creation of Waterside Farm on the south-side, the Middle Piece was centred upon a sixteenth century house name *'Cock Robin'* (possibly after Robert) which was still standing in the mid-twentieth century and became one of the present Laund Farms. Land upon each side of Greenhead Lane became the property of Christopher and his son Robert, the farmhouse of Greenhead (now rebuilt as Greenhead Manor) being at the centre of this land. It would appear that Ellis's sons, Henry and John, had a dispute and Henry moved into a farm across the river at Reedley whilst John took the Waterside Farm.[1]

Reedley Waterside

Now
Quakers-in-Pendle Bridge

Also farming within the extended area of the southern forest were the Hartleys of New Laund and the Robinsons of the Old Laund. Reedley Waterside developed into a hamlet as more cottages were built to house the family, the site was closely linked to the settlement of nearby Chamber-in-Pendle. The high ground along the river behind Waterside was known as Hamstone Cliffe and there was a fulling mill within the area; the Barcroft family owned a small area here known as *Walker Hoile* and it is possible that this (from the motion of walking woollen pieces to full, or bind, them) was the site of the mill. For many years the Waterside male family name of Ellis was rotated with that of John and Robert, it is thought that the two men of this name who were executed (John in 1584 and Robert in 1600) for the Catholic cause were the sons of Ellis Nutter of Waterside. Another member of this family

---

[1] Doreen Crowther, unpublished papers on the *Nutter* genealogy held at Nelson Local Studies Library

The Nutters were famously Catholic & fought for the cause.

was of a noted ecclesiastical bent and that was Archbishop Tillotson who attended Colne Grammar school for a while. [1]

Thomas Tilson, of Woocliff in the parish of Carlton-in-Craven, changed his name to Tillotson and had a son, George, who married Eleanor, daughter of Ellis Nutter of Waterside. George and Eleanor Tillotson had a son, Robert, who married Mary Dobson of Sowerby to whose son the following memorial in Sowerby church survives:

The Most Reverend
JOHN TILLOTSON, D. D.
Born at Haugh End, in this township; 1630
Archbishop of Canterbury
In the reign of William and Mary
Died November 22 1694
In the 65th year of his age

Archbishop John Tillotson enjoyed a successful ecclesiastical career, he married the niece of Oliver Cromwell and could boast many influential friends. Not only did the Nutter family of Waterside own the lands around their own property but, by the sixteenth century, they also held the tenancies of lands in other areas such as Briercliffe, Burnley and Newchurch-in-Pendle. The Nutter families were scattered throughout the forest and were all interrelated, a study of the surviving local land deeds and court records illustrates this; furthermore, the major forest yeomanry families of Robinson, Smith, Hargreaves, Mitton and Hartley were also heavily interrelated. The family of Alice Nutter, of Roughlee (executed 1612), were no exception to the rule as they were related as second cousins to the Nutters of Greenhead and Reedley Waterside. Upon the death of Alice Nutter's grandson, Henry Nutter, alias Hartley (illegitimate), his share of the Nutter properties descended to the Nutters of Waterside. The other Nutter properties descend through Henry's sister, Ellen Nutter, who married James Robinson. Their share possibly passed to the Robinsons of Dam Head in Roughlee close to Alice Nutter's home at Crowtrees Farm. [2]

The village of Roughlee
in the later 19th century

---

[1] James Carr, *Annals and Stories of Colne*, (Colne, 1878)
[2] Gladys Whittaker, *Roughlee Hall - Fact and Fiction*, (Marsden Antiquarians, Nelson, 1982)

John and Robert Nutter

A local product of covert Catholic education system was Robert Nutter who was the son of Ellis Nutter of Waterside and New Laund within the Forest of Pendle. Robert accompanied his brother John to the Douai college and was ordained at Rheims in December 1581 – within a fortnight of this Robert, who assumed the surname of Rowley after the area near to his home in Reedley, was sent on the English mission where he concentrated on the areas of the South Midlands, London and the South Coast. Unfortunately for the English missionaries Elizabeth's government had a highly effective spy network that were adept at quickly apprehending the illegal priests. A surviving record of this spy network shows that Robert was an excellent missionary and this led to his being quickly caught in Oxford early in 1584; he was imprisoned in the Tower of London and tortured, whilst this was going on his brother John, also recently apprehended, was executed in February 1584. The case against Robert appears to have collapsed because he was put on a ship in January 1585 and, along with a number of other captured missionaries, was banished abroad under the threat of death if they were to attempt to return to England.

Before the year was out Robert was once again throwing himself at the English shores and was arrested even before he had reached dry land. The threat of execution was not carried out, instead he was subjected to a number of prison sentences culminating in a long stay at Wisbech Gaol where he enlisted as a Jesuit in the Saint Dominic's Order of Preachers. His second attempt at escape from Wisbech succeeded and by early 1600 Robert was making his way back to his native Lancashire. Probably because he was expected to return home by the government agents he was arrested in Lancashire in May 1600 and was imprisoned in Lancaster Castle and executed in July of that year for being a priest under the Act of 1585. This was seen as being a deterrent to the Catholic people of Lancashire; a hymn by the name of *'Nutter's Bould Constancie'* was composed in ballad form in honour of Robert Nutter. Ellis Nutter, the nephew of Robert and John, was ordained as a priest in 1601 and went on to train at the English College in Rome for the English mission. [1]

The Nutter family of Pendle Waterside held lands throughout the western Pendle Forest area and would continue to do so for many years to come. In 1507 Ellis Nutter devised his properties at New Laund to Robert Nutter for £6: 13s: 4d per annum and by 1527 the New Laund rent was held equally between Ellis Nutter of Waterside, John Haliday and John Nowell. In 1530 Henry Nutter complained that his younger brother had disputed his hereditary rights to tenements in New Laund and Reedley Hallows. In 1609 the rental of this tenement descended to John Nutter. John Nutter living in 1592 was the son of John Nutter who was the son of Ellis Nutter – Eleanor Nutter, the daughter of Ellis Nutter, was reputedly the grandmother of Archbishop Tillotson who attended Colne Grammar School for a period of time.

Henry Towneley of Dutton Hall (died 1645) married Alice who was the daughter of Abraham Colthurst of Burnley. Their daughter Anne Towneley is shown in Dugdale's visitations of 1644 as marrying Ellis Nutter of Waterside, Reedley Hallows. The Nutter estate of Roughlee passed down through the children of reputed witch Alice Nutter who was executed in 1612. Alice's grandson was Henry Nutter, alias Hartley (illegitimate), and his share of the Nutter properties descended to the Nutters of Waterside. The other Nutter properties within Roughlee descended

---

[1] M. Mullett and L. Warren, *Martyrs of the Diocese of Lancaster,* (Rome, 1987)

through Henry's sister, Ellen Nutter, who married James Robinson. Their share possibly passed to the Robinsons of Dam Head in Roughlee – this was probably where Alice Nutter's home of Crowtrees was.

Many branches of the Nutter families existed throughout the extended area, their property and land holdings stretched from Cheshire into Yorkshire, in fact it is safe to say that within the district of Burnley and Pendle almost every farm and hall will have been owned or tenanted by a member of the extended Nutter clan over the past six-hundred years. An example is shown within the Nutter records: *'In 1619 John Nutter, late of New Laund in Pendle died enfeoffed of the late Laurence Ormerod of..... a manor house at Fulledge; seven farms in Burnley and seventy-one parcels of common lands around Burnley.'*

The Nutter name was one of the very first to be recorded in connection with the creation of the new Pendle Forest. Originally forest keepers, and then vaccary keepers, the family took advantage of newly created tenancies as they arose and over the coming centuries were to play their part in the formation of the Pendleside area. The family will be covered in more detail in due course.

Greenhead Manor -built around 1630 on the site of the
West Close Nutter family's original house

Dean Nutter

Not content to be outdone in the supply of clerics the family of John Nutter of Newchurch (Goldshaw) could also boast of an important member of the church. John Nutter entered Brasenose College in 1575 where, in that same year, he took the degree of B.D; he became a royal chaplain and was characterised by Queen Elizabeth as a *'Golden Ass.'* He was probably the curate of Eccles in 1563, was rector of Aughton (Huyton in Liverpool) in 1577 and of Bebington in 1579. Nutter had appointments in Chester Cathedral and became dean there in 1589. He was also the rector of Sephton, (Sefton in Liverpool), and it was here that he was buried in 1602 following his sudden death. *'Though a preacher he seems to have been but a money-seeking pluralist who went with the times and joined, perhaps rather to procure favour than out of zeal, in the persecution of his recusant parishioners. In 1590 he had an assistant who was "no preacher".'* [1] . . . this latter assistant was one John Nutter, dean Nutter's cousin of Goldshaw.

From other evidence it would appear that John Nutter was initially well disposed towards the Catholics within his diocese, this is not surprising given his background; the Nutter families of the south-western forest were still refusing to attend the protestant church in the mid-seventeenth century. The dean had actually been reported to the relevant government agencies in respect of his Catholic leanings and it is likely that he was pressured into taking a firm pro-Protestant stance. It is clear that dean Nutter, during his thirteen year sojourn within the halls of ecclesiastical power, was not averse to feathering his own nest and there was nothing unusual in this given his position at that time. To illustrate this, his patron was Sir Richard Molyneaux, lord of Sefton, under whose auspices Nutter gained a surprising amount of land throughout the Cheshire and South Lancashire areas. Added to this were the lands granted to Nutter, probably by inheritance rights, in and around his homelands of the Pendle Forest; evidence of this is shown within a number of forest land surrenders, examples being:[2]

1568: Richard Nutter junior of Goldshaw, son of Richard Nutter, surrendered by John Nutter of New Laund a parcel of land containing a barn in Goldshaw Booth and also sufficient turf-land in Goldshaw Booth to sustain the burning in one house to (dean) John Nutter, clerk, for twenty years.[3] John Nutter of New Laund was John the clerk's attorney.

1569: Alice, the widow of John Nutter of Goldshaw remarried to Lawrence Butterfield and surrendered her rights to all farms, buildings, lands, tenements, meadows, grazing lands, pastures, moors and mosses of which her deceased husband John Nutter was tenant, to the use of John Nutter, clerk and rector of Sefton, for the lifetime of Alice. Pledge provided by John Nutter of New Laund.

The same wording applied to another surrender of that year in which Agnes, widow of Richard Nutter (father of Richard junior) of Goldshaw, transferred her rights to properties etc, in Pendle Forest to John Nutter, clerk, for the lifetime of Agnes. Both of these surrenders related to lands inherited by Alice and Agnes who were probably (Hargreaves?) sisters. Other records, held within the papers of the Earls of Sefton, show the extent to which Nutter acquired lands within the Molyneux patronage; [4]

1588: William Hargreaves of Higham Deane, yeoman, pays a sum of money to John Nutter, the rector of Sefton with regard to the surrender of a farm in Higham called Higham Dean. In the same year Richard Hargreaves, also of Higham, pays a £200 bond to John Nutter.

1591: Richard Browne of Sawley in Yorkshire, yeoman, pays the sum of £12: 0s: 0d to Henry

[1] Farrar, *Victoria County History,* (Liverpool)
[2] W. Farrar, *Clitheroe Court Rolls,* (1912)
[3] The Goldshaw 'turf-lands' and mosses were the *turbary* (peat-lands) still in evidence today. They ran along the valley bottom from Spen Brook to Sabden Fold - they are particularly evident below Tynedale Farm
[4] Lancashire Records Office

Nutter of Heyhhouses in Sabden for 12 oak trees to be supplied to Mr. Nutter Dean of Chester. Witnessed by were George Nutter, Thomas Crook, William Nutter, John Nutter of Bull Hole.

John Nutter, of Bull Hole Farm (Newchurch-in-Pendle), who witnessed the above record, would be of the same family as dean John Nutter; the Nutter family of Heyhouse (Sabden) were also of this branch. It would appear that dean Nutter was either the son of John of Bull Hole or the son of John senior's brother, Anthony.

Because of dean Nutter's sudden death in 1602 there was a rumour that there was a problem with his will and many people said that he had hidden his money. However, in 1602, the administration of the dean's will was granted to William Nutter of Pendle Forest and James Hartley of Haighton in Liverpool. Anthony Nutter, of Goldshaw, and his wife, sent a receipt for £40, in 1602, to Sir Richard Molyneux in respect of a part settlement of dean Nutter's will and this would strongly suggest that the William Nutter, co-heir of the will, was the brother or father of the dean.

From the beginning of the sixteenth century the Bull Hole property had been in the tenancy of the Nutter family; John and Alice (Hargreaves?) farmed there in the first part of the century and in 1551 William Nutter's widow, Alice, was fined for obstructing the road at Bull Hole so that Richard Nutter could not drive his beasts thereon. The names of John, William and Anthony follow through the Nutter families of Bull Hole to the early seventeenth century.

Both John and Anthony Nutter figure in the 1612 Pendle Witch Trials whereby the former had asked Demdike to cure a sick cow at his Bull Hole Farm; Anne Whittle of West Close (Old Chattox) for some reason declared that Anthony Nutter 'favoured' Elizabeth Southern (Old Demdike) over herself. Anthony Nutter's daughter, Anne, was allegedly killed by Chattox for showing disrespect to her. There is a point of interest here as to why Anthony Nutter favoured Demdike over Ann Whittle. [1]

1592: *Acquittance for; Hugh, the son of Richard Hargreaves of Higham Deyne, (deceased), paid £13: 68s: od to John Nutter, rector of Sefton and Dean of Chester (by James Hartley, clerk, his attorney) properties in Higham Dean called the Over Felds, Bent and Back Field in the tenure of Hugh Hargreaves and his mother Jennet. Witnesses; Edmund Starkie, Richarde Woodrough, John Nutter of Bull Hole, Henry Nutter.*

1593: *Blaze Hargreaves* of Higham, yeoman, and Hughe his son and heir surrender to John Nutter, Dean of Chester, (by Edmond Starkie of Huntroyde, gent) properties in Higham Dean called the Over Fields, Bent and Backe Field in the tenure of Hugh Hargreaves. *(Blaze Hargreaves of Higham, and his brother John, were allegedly bewitched to death by James Device).*

1600: *Ellize Robinson of Gouldshaiebooth, yeoman, payed £100 to Mr. John Nutter, Dean of Chester (by John Nutter his servant) to the use of Anne, the second daughter of Ellis Robinson, for her 'permanent' in marriage. Witnesses: Roger Nowell senior, Edmund Starkie of Huntroyde, Roger Nowell junior, Henry Nutter, Rychard Bawdine.*

The family of dean John Nutter were not slow to make advantageous marriages; a marriage

---

[1] Part Two of this book introduces evidence for this having been a consequence of Chattox being both a long-term enemy of the extended Nutter family and possibly a relative (by marriage) of Old Demdike

settlement of 1581 shows that dean Nutter's sister, Jennet, married a William Garrs of Belbroke in Yorkshire. Their daughter, Anne, married a Robert Houlme of Tranmore and Robert's father, Richard, was involved with property deals in Chester along with John Nutter.

Dean Nutter also acquired properties in Eccleston, Heskin, Ince Blundell and Sefton. Following his death his relative, John Nutter, gent, of Greenhead, became one of Sir Richard Molyneux's right-hand men. In this capacity John Nutter, gent, was elected as Steward of Blackburnshire and the manor of Tottington and, along with other notables such as the Asshetons of Downham, he fulfilled this position for a number of years. On 9th June 1613 Sir Richard Molyneux wrote an order *'To his servants Hugh Nelson and John Nutter'* that they were to oversee the halmotes and Wapentake courts within the hundred of Blackburnshire because his *'Cousin Assheton, assistant deputy to Richard Woodruffe,* was unable to carry out this duty as *"yt hath pleases God to visit him with an Imperfectione in his speech."'* [1]

Sir Richard Molyneux had a daughter, Elizabeth, who married Richard Sherburne of the Stoneyhurst family in 1629. Richard was the son of Richard Sherburne (grandson of Sir Richard and Jane Towneley, daughter of Sir John of Towneley Hall) and Dorothy, daughter of Richard Assheton of Downham. Richard junior was also the brother-in-law of Lord Towneley of Barnside whose relatives lived at Carr Hall (Barrowford). Richard Assheton was said to have been killed by Demdike whilst Anne, the wife of Henry Towneley of Carr Hall, was supposedly bewitched to death by Demdike's grandson, James Device. It is reasonable to assume, then, that both Sir Richard Molyneux and his servant, John Nutter of Pendle, would have been aware of the accusations of witchcraft that had been stirring for some time (prior to the 1612 trials) within the bounds of the Pendle Forest – in fact John Nutter had lost both his father (Christopher) and brother (Robert) to the supposed evil machinations of Chattox and her daughter, Ann Redfern. To what extent would this have effected John Nutter – enough for him to take the case up with his master Sir Richard Molyneux? It has to be remembered that Molyneux was one of the most powerful men in the country and effectively the boss of the two magistrates, Roger Nowell and Nicholas Bannister, who were directly responsible for rounding up Chattox and her co-accused and prosecuting them at Lancaster Castle in the August of 1612.

John Nutter of Greenhead had a younger brother, Robert, who was John's heir. Robert had a daughter named Elizabeth who became the wife of John Moore of the Higham family of yeomanry and, in the seventeenth century, this family resided at Greenhead (Elizabeth was shown there as a widow in 1636). It was probably this family who built the present property of Greenhead Manor which stands on the old Greenhead site near to the road (Greenhead Lane) from Wheatley Lane and Higham to Ightenhill - this property appears to date from around the middle of the seventeenth century. Robert Nutter also had a daughter, Eleanor, who married into the influential family of Crombock of Clerk Hill in Whalley. Robert's third daughter (and co-heiress) was Margaret who married a Robinson by whom she had a son, Henry Robinson who, in 1636, was farming at Chatburn.

Robert Nutter had died in 1593 and so his daughters inherited his brother John's estate upon his (John's) demise. John, whether through inheritance from dean Nutter, or by means of his own service to his Molyneux master, had been granted, along with Sir Thomas Walmsley and William Fazakerley, the town and lordship of Liverpool. By the time of John's death he was the sole remaining owner apart from the originator's family who was, at this time, one Caryll Molyneux. In 1636 the leases of these Liverpool properties were transferred by Caryll

---

[1] *The Molyneux Papers*, Preston Records Office

Molyneux and the Nutter descendants to Messrs. Ralphe Mercer of Edge Lane, John Tatlock of Cunscoe and Thomas Boulton of Kirkdale. It is clear that certain members of the Nutter families of Newchurch, Greenhead and Reedley Waterside had risen rapidly through the ecclesiastical ranks – quite an achievement for forest back-water farmers!

Jewel Mill

It is apparent that the Filly Close and Reedley Hallows area of the forest was once far more important than is now the case; the settlement around Waterside, the large number of farms in the area and the grange site of Monk Hey all suggest a former hive of activity. There is a single mention within the Clitheroe court rolls of a mill having stood within the area, sometime prior to the seventeenth century. This is no surprise given the riverside location of the area; a water-powered cloth-fulling mill is the most likely operation to have existed here although a corn mill is not out of the question.[1] The milling operation on the river here in antiquity could well have been attached to the monastic operation of Reedley Grange. Reference is made in the Towneley Papers to a *Walker Hoile* (as we saw earlier) in the possession of Henry Barcroft - the *Walker* name has a direct relationship to the fulling of cloth and a natural progression to the walking process would have been the provision of water-power - perhaps the Walker Hoile was indeed a small mill site?

Within living memory a large textile mill, by the name of Jewel Mill, stood on the riverside at Monk Hey (SD 836 360), this mill was built around 1790 and was owned by Julia Holden of Worcester and James Dickinson of London. The mill passed through various stages and ownerships, one of whom was Robert Shaw of Colne. The mill closed around 1972 and was demolished in 1978. [2]

As far as the name of *jewel* goes the etymology is (as usual) difficult; it is apparent that the name was taken from the area of land upon which the mill was built i.e., Jewel Holme. This allows us a flight of fancy in as much as we can delve much further back into the name than we could if it was of purely eighteenth century origin. The Norman-French word *jewel* has the same meaning as the one we now use and does not appear to have any sound credentials within the mill-site context - it is necessary then to look at the Norse and Saxon origins for the word.

This period did not employ the letter **J** as such and therefore, to appropriate the necessary inflection, we have to look at words beginning with **G**. First of all we have a couple of suggestions relating to textile operations; *gewind* is the Norse for *winding thing* or *wound thing* whilst *gewynde* means *weaving*. There is the Norse *gewrid* for *husk* and this would be a possible suggestion of a corn-milling operation. *Geweallod* means *walled* and this would therefore apply to a formal enclosure such as the land belonging to a farm within the Reedley Hallows area. Finally we have two appropriate names with reference to water whereby *geswell* describes a *whirlpool* or *turbulent water* and *gewealc* for tossing or rolling motion. These latter two examples appear to fit the bill in as much as they are clearly descriptive of the rushing nature of the river at this point; also, phonetically, they are very close to the modern pronunciation of *jewel*.

This former mill site is, then, a nice illustration of our modern urban development where the

---

[1] Most corn mills belonged to the lord of the manor; farmers from this area of the forest were meant to use the lord's mills at Bradley (Marsden / Nelson) and Burnley

[2] Geoff Shackleton, *The Textile Mills of Pendle,* (Landmark, 2006)

towns have absorbed the population of the countryside and what appear now to be insular farmsteads were once thriving places of industry. Hurrying along the M65 motorway, through the very centre of the lost Jewel Mill site, it is difficult to imagine that here was a place that probably supported many people over its communal lifetime of perhaps some 1200 years.

Before leaving the subject of the Jewel Mill it is worth mentioning that an Archbishop John Jewel lived in the middle of the sixteenth century (1522-1571). Jewel, a Devonian, became Bishop of Salisbury and was an advisor to Queen Elizabeth; he took a strongly Protestant line and, as such, was often to be seen preaching in areas known to be of a strong Catholic persuasion. We know that John Nutter, whose family lived in the riverside area of Jewel Holme, was the dean of Chester and that Pendle Forest was regarded by outsiders as having been somewhat of a Catholic stronghold in the later sixteenth century. Is it possible, therefore, that dean Nutter invited Archbishop Jewel to visit Pendle in order to spread the Protestant directives of the Crown - did Jewel baptise local foresters in the Pendle Water at Jewel Holme?

Filly Close

Within the extended area of West Close the Filly Close area runs from the village of Higham southwards through New Laund and down to Pendle Water. The name originated in the thirteenth century when the land was used as over-spill grazing for the young stock of the Ightenhill Stud Farm. In the fifteenth century the lands of Filly Close were let out to general agistment and the *New Hold* of 1507 saw Lawrence Towneley and Rauff Askue being granted the copyhold at a yearly rent of £10 13s 4d. By 1536 the lands were held by Sir John Towneley of Towneley and the rent rolls of that family show 9 tenants within Filly Close:[1]

Fely Close Tenants 1536	Towneley Tenants 1685
George Grymshay	For Morehiles -
Thomas Watmough	Rich. Stuttard
John Spenser	Jo; Ingham
Rycd. Claiton	Simeon Ingham
William Mychell	Tho. Addamson
Jamys Smith	Charles Duckworth
George Smyth	Widow Spenser
William Taiyler	Jo; Smyth
Henry Barcroft	Item for Duckpits -
	Mrs. Barcroft for
	Walker Hoile

The Church Survey of 1650 shows that there were some forty families living within New Laund, Filly Close and Reedley Hallows.[2]

---

[1] Filly Close tenancy lists from the *Towneley Rent Rolls* (Preston Records office)
[2] Held at Preston Records Office

Chapter Nine

More People and Places

The Mitton and
Hartley Families

The Mitton families were well-established as farmers within Pendle Forest, certainly by the dawning of the seventeenth century they were tenanting a number of farmsteads in Roughlee, Barrowford and Colne. Henry Mitton figures within the story of the Pendle Witches (1612) because he was said to have been bewitched to death by Old Demdike, her daughter, Elizabeth Device, and Alice Nutter of Roughlee. When interviewed by the magistrate, Roger Nowell of Read Hall, Demdike's grand-daughter, Alison Device, apparently stated that her mother . . . *'then said shee would haue him to kill one Mitton of the Rough Lee, whereupon the said Ball said, he would doe it, and so vanished away, and about three weekes after, the said Mitton likewise dyed.'*[1] This statement referred to the alleged killing of Henry Mitton following his refusal to give Demdike a penny when asked to do so. This, of course, is an extremely suspect excuse for the alleged crime, especially when the higher status of Alice Nutter (as a prominent local landowner) is taken into account. The general flavour of fantasy within the whole prosecution case against the accused within the Witch Trials becomes evident here as it is unlikely that Alice Nutter would have become embroiled in a dispute over such a trivial amount of money.

That a Henry Mitton had died at this time is not in doubt as the name relates to a burial at Newchurch (St.Mary's) in 1610 and this ties in well with his having been *'killed about a year agon'* as Alison Device stated. It is possible that at least one of the accused trio of 'witches' had an old score to settle with Henry Mitton (or his family) and this might become evident as we progress the story. The Mitton family had long been landholders within the area of Roughlee, amongst their properties were Dole House, Whitehough and Dam head. The King's Commissioner's list of 1527 shows a Henry Mitton as one of the *'Tenants of the Lorde the Kynge in Penhull.'* The Pendle Forest Rental List of 1608/9 names Roger Mitton as tenant for the Roughlee vaccary where he is paying £1: 2s: 2½d and, again for Roughlee, Henry Mitton paid £0: 2s: 4½d. The large difference in rental between these two people does not indicate that Henry Mitton had far less land under rental than Roger as Henry's main holding appears to have lain on the Barrowford side of the parish boundary. This meant that the same family were variously described as being of both Barrowford and Roughlee – the following records relate to the Mittons:[2]

1522: *Bernard Hargreaves surrendered a farm in Roughlee (which he had obtained from John*

---

[1] Thom. Potts, *The Wonderfull Discoverie of Witches in the Countie of Lancaster,* (Potts, 1613 - Chetham Soc 1845)
[2] W. Farrar, *Clitheroe Court Rolls*

Smith junior), to the use of John Robinson of Old Laund, Nicholas Robinson, Peter Smith and James Mitton, all of Roughlee.

1524: *John Robinson of Old Laund surrendered a farm in Roughlee (formerly in the occupation of William and Isabell Mitton), to the use of John Robinson junior, John Hartley of Roughlee, Nicholas Robinson of Roughlee and James Mitton of Barrowford.*

1525: *Lawrence Hargreaves and Henry Mitton sued James Mitchell for obstructing an ancient highway at Barrowford . . . 10s damages awarded to plaintiffs and a road for carrying hay, grain and dung.*

1528: *James Mitchell fined 20s for afray upon Henry Mitton and Lawrence Hargreaves within the Holmes (Water Meetings) at Barrowford.*

1532: *James Mitchell complains that Henry Mitton built a wall upon his land in The Holme . . a special jury of 24 men ordered the wall to be removed and the whikwood plantation to be removed and the watercourse to have its proper course as far as the little hole in the dyke.*

1532: *James Mitchell sued Lawrence Hargreaves and Henry Mitton for trespass of a way in Barrowford. . . Verdict for the defendants.*

1549: *Suite for ways between Lower Barrowford and Blacko (Higherford to Blacko Bar) . . . Bernard, Lawrence, James and Christopher Hartley, James Hartley of Fulshaw, James Hartley of Blacko, Lawrence and John Hargreaves, Lawrence Robinson, James Mitton and Lawrence Wilson versus Henry Bannester gent, Nicholas Smith and Christopher Robinson. Jury ordered a sufficient way to be kept between the Almys Kiln to a gap called Out Gait in Blacko on the land of Henry Bannester, Christopher Robinson and Nicholas Smith.*

1560: *James Mitton* owns land called Ridge End adjoining Laith Stiddes (or Latcherside) at the Old Laund, Town Pasture and Owte Blacko, all Barrowford.*

1571: *Higham Halmote . . John Mytton of Roughlee serves on a jury, along with Hugh Moore of Pendle; they find James Mytton of Lower Barrowford guilty of not making his boundary walls.*

Most of these court records relate to the lands within the area stretching from Blacko, over Pendle Water to the Water Meetings in Barrowford and along the Uthertone ridgeway to Ridgaling, Noggarth and the Launds. The Holme riverside (roughly stretching from Higherford Mill to Grimshaw's Wood) and Ridge lands were in the tenure of Henry Mitton whilst the Water Meetings Holmes were owned by Lawrence Hargreaves.

In 1527 a land dispute flared up and was to rumble on through the rest of the century; in that year a jury at the halmote declared that a farm and outbuildings, valued at £0: 22s: 2½d annual rent, had reverted to the king following the death of Henry Hartley and that his son, John Hartley, was his natural heir. As John was sixteen years of age he was officially a minor and therefore his uncle, Lawrence Hargreaves, was to be his guardian until he became of age. Margery Hartley (nee Hargreaves - Henry's widow) claimed her rights of dower from the estate and Henry Mitton objected to the granting of the tenancy until young John Hartley was of age and could *'fulfil the intention of the said will of his father.'*

Also in the year of 1527 Henry Mitton sued James Mitchell of Colne in a plea of land partition and trespass on Mitton's land at *Le Rigge* (Ridge Farm, above the Water Meetings at Barrowford). Mitton asked the court to provide him with security as *'he was in bodily fear of Mitchell;'* Christopher Nowell, bailiff of the King, gave Mitchell a summons to appear at Clitheroe Castle but he never turned up. He was therefore ordered to be imprisoned for contempt of court and four of his friends were to be found who would answer to the court - this was a common procedure whereby sworn statements by friends or family of the accused would render them to be liable to serve the sentence should the accused abscond.

At the 1540 halmote court an issue arose where Henry Mitton, of The Ridge, stated that his son John was the executor of the will of Henry Hartley; other records show John, the son of Henry Mitton receiving moneys due to the estate of Henry Hartley and this is because the Mittons were closely related to the Hartleys. By 1562 the property inherited by young John Hartley was occupied by Bernard Hartley and these lands and property became the subject of a dispute that was fit to grace the pages of a crime novel.

In 1598 Edward Whitaker, a member of the local Whitaker families and clerk/parson of Thorneyhill in Yorkshire, made an official complaint to the courts. The basis of this was that Whittaker was making representation on behalf of Henry Mitton against a number of the local landowners; to this end he stated that the properties and land occupied by Bernard Hartley of New Laund were actually the rightful property of Henry Mitton. Henry Mitton's father, yeoman James Mitton, appears to have died in 1562 as Whitaker states that this is the year in which Henry Mitton (a minor) inherited the properties of *Outeblakowe, Rydgende* and *Latcherside* from his father. These lands and farms stretched from the area of Blacko Foot, through High Ridge at Utherstone, along the Roughlee/Barrowford boundary through Ridgaling, along Noggarth and down to New Laund. Whitaker goes on to say that, as Henry was not of age, the properties were placed in the care of trustees; these were **Robert Bannester, Christopher Nutter, Lawrence Hartley** (son of Christopher of Lower Barrowford), and **Robert Bulcock** of Whitehough. At this time (1562) the properties were in the tenure of **Bernard Hartley** of New Laund. Things appear to take an unfortunate turn here as, according to Whitaker, one of the trustees married a daughter of Bernard Hartley and, when she became terminally ill, he conspired with the other trustees to have her sign the inheritance of Henry Mitton over to him, as her husband.[1]

Let us have a look at these trustees:

A **Robert Bannester** married Catherina Swier in 1599, she was possibly the half-sister of the Robinson brothers of Barley who were said to have been bewitched; Robert shared the same name as the Robert Bannister of Park Hill but it has been suggested that this latter Robert married a different woman.

Bernard Hartley had three daughters, Margaret by Joan his first wife, and Alice and Elizabeth by Margaret, his second wife. When Bernard died the property passed to his daughters and co-heirs. Of the three daughters of Bernard Hartley the Burnley burial index shows Alice Hartley of Laund being buried in 1599. It would appear that Elizabeth married a Robinson thus leaving the third daughter, Margaret, who can be shown to have married **Robert**

---

[1] W. Farrar, *Clitheroe Court Rolls,* (1912)

Bulcock at Newchurch in 1595 – this is the only record of any of the daughters of Bernard Hartley marrying a man named as a trustee within the land dispute. It can only be assumed that the above complaint related to the inheritance of one of the Hartley daughters, rather than the whole of their father's estate – **Christopher Nutter** married his cousin Ellen and inherited lands at Goldshaw and New Laund and therefore we appear to be left with the Robert Bulcock marriage; there are no local burial records for a Margaret Bulcock however.

Henry Mitton, then, appears to have had rights to the Hartley properties at Laund, through separate inheritances, in both 1527 and 1562. It is not clear as to the outcome of the court case but even if Mitton did regain at least some of his rightful inheritance he drew the short straw by being bewitched to death by his neighbours!

Smith

In 1602 the Hartley empire again became clouded when Lawrence Hartley was the subject of a complaint by Nicholas and Elizabeth Smith, of Barrowford, and Elizabeth Robinson of Laund. As part of his defence Lawrence stated that James Hartley had left New Laund to his brother, Alexander, who died without issue and therefore left the property and lands to his brother Bernard Hartley. However, Lawrence said that a dispute arose over the descent of the property through the re-marriage of Bernard's second wife, Margaret. On the 8th September 1572 a John Smith married a Margaret Hartley at Burnley and, if this is the remarriage of Bernard's second wife, we have the reason for the above dispute where Nicholas Smith (related to Margaret's second husband, John Smith) claimed his rights to the Laund properties.

The Smith family became firmly ensconced at Laund in the sixteenth century (following the Smith = Hartley marriage) but they had been farming within the locality for generations. The family were also prominent within other parts of the forest (notably at Dimpenley between Roughlee and Newchurch) and in the Briercliffe area of Burnley. In the 1507 period of deforestation John, Christopher and Peter Smith were mentioned as being tenants of the *Old Hold* of the forest at twenty marks per annum (around £1.40 in today's terms).

In 1522 Bernard Hargreaves transferred a farm in Roughlee to Peter Smith, the messuage had formerly been in the possession of John Smith. John Smith was of *Haynyate* (possibly Heys Lane at Dimpenley) in 1523 and the following year he was shown as being the co-tenant of a farm in *Whitely Haybothe* with Miles Nutter, father-in-law of Alice Nutter.

At the Higham halmote court of 1525 a farm of about fifty acres at Nether Roughlee (the Thorneyholme area) and *Watlyngforth* ('the ford by the [willow] wood' - probably a way over Dimpenley Clough) was shown as having been the property of Christopher Smith and his wife, Alice, throughout Christopher's life. The court then transferred the farm to William, son of John Smith, with an interest to widow Alice and James Smith. The tenancy was taken up by James Hartley and John Robinson of Laund. Two years later another farm of about thirty-four acres at Watlyngforth, in Nether Roughlee, was surrendered by John Smith to the use of John Robinson, son of John Robinson of Old Laund.

John Smith was sued by the Abbot of Whalley and his monk, Lawrence Forest, at the 1528 halmot for not paying tithes due to the Abbey at £0: 5s: 4d. Smith acknowledged and paid the debt before he was struck down by a thunderbolt!

In 1530 Margaret Hartley (widow of Henry) sued John Smith for failure to pay six year's rent on grazing for one cow. Smith stated that his rent was payable in arrears every three years and the case was settled. The next year saw John Smith being sued by Christopher Baldwin of

Wheathead for building a house on his land without permission (probably at Blacko Foot). Smith was ordered by the jury to pay Baldwin the same in compensation as it had cost to build the house. John Smith is in trouble again when, in 1532, he is sued by John Hargreaves (probably of the Higham family) for debt. The Smith family were also well established at Stone Edge in Over Barrowford and they appear in this capacity on a number of court rolls into the seventeenth century. A record shows the probable grandfather of Nicholas Smith who, in 1602, claimed his right to part of the Laund estates; in 1537 John Smith and his wife, Alice, surrender Stone Edge to the use of Nicholas, their son. Alice was the widow of James Bannister before marrying John Smith and her son and heir, James Bannister claimed his rights to the property. [1]

There is a strong possibility that John Smith gained the Stone Edge estate through his wife as the Bannisters of Park Hill owned the Over Barrowford master-tenancies. However, Nicholas Smith managed to produce written confirmation of his rights of acquittance and gained the tenancy of Laund upon an entry-fine of £0: 15s: 3½d. This particular record also shows that Christopher Lister esquire, of the Westby Hall family, had a claim on the Stone Edge property; Lister's attorney was Robert Derwen who was married to Margaret Bannister, the daughter of Alice Smith. Lister and Derwen attempted to forbid Nicholas Smith's entry to the property but appear to have failed. Here we have a direct link between the Listers and the Bannisters which can be further illustrated by a Colne court roll of 1570 showing that William Lister of Middop, esquire, surrendered by Christopher Hartley, of Barrowford, a parcel of land 'betweene le churche style and the hous in which Lawrence Blaykeye lived to Henry Bannester of le Parkehyll, gent.' The Listers had a firm foothold within Pendle Forest through their ownership of land and properties, especially around the Marsden area, and they were also close to the Bannisters of Park Hill– come 1612 the Malkin Tower and Westby holdings of these gentry families would touch base when Jennet Preston of Gisburn (hanged for witchcraft in 1612) and the Demdike family saw their paths so tragically cross. [2]

Still in the year of 1537 we see that John Smith has erred once again when he was fined 12d for the keeping of *Graihaunds,* for the purpose of chasing hares and other animals within the Forest of Pendle, without a licence. Again, in 1538, John Smith tries the patience of the courts when his old friend John Hargreaves sues him (and others) for pilfering land-rights on The Doles (the area around Dole House Farm) in the *intake* (newly cultivated land) of Roughlee. This time, however, Smith is exonerated.

In 1538 John Smith and Alice Nutter's father-in-law, Miles Nutter, sell off three acres of land owned jointly by them at Derleybanks Ende in Roughlee; the name of Derleybanks indicates an area used for the lord's deer hunting operation within the forest - the site of this was probably between Thorneyholme and Dimpenley. Also in that year Nicholas Smith is at it again, it appears that his father, John, had died and Nicholas was claiming his rights of ownership to Stone Edge. The jury decided that the case was too complicated for them and ordered a new jury of twenty-four men to decide the outcome. At the same court hearing James Smith, son of John, purchased a farm in the Roughlee area from John Bulcock, greave of Pendle; Lawrence Towneley (of Fulshaw and Stone Edge) stood surety for Smith.

The Smith *vs* Bannister feud raised its head again in 1545 when Henry Bannister of Park Hill sued Nicholas and Christopher Smith, of Stone Edge, for occupying lands in Over Barrowford that Bannister thought belonged to him. The lands in question were *'lying between the Almosse Kylne and Stone Edge in Outeblakoe.'* The dispute was solved by an official land-measurer

---

[1] *The Farrar Papers*, Manchester Central Library
[2] Jonathan Lumby, *The Lancashire Witch Craze,* (Carnegie, 1995)

(surveyor) who, at the direction of the court, laid out *mearstakes* from '*the Brygghyll upwards,*' both parties were then to occupy their share of the lands as then staked out. The *Brygghyll* is almost certainly the steep riverside bank area rising from the packhorse bridge at Higherford, up through the 'Dicky Nook' and Whittycroft to Stone Edge. The *Almosse Kylne* is difficult to locate but I take it to be the *'Alms Kiln'* and could well have been sited where the Old Corn Mill now stands above the Bridge Inn at Higherford.

Further to this, in 1530 Bernard and Lawrence Hartley sued Lawrence Hargreaves and other tenants of Lower Barrowford and the jury decided that both parties should occupy *'all those lands lying between the Kiln Yard and Barrowford Kiln as of ancient times'*. The Hargreaves family farmed around the Water Meetings area of Barrowford and the above description would apply to this district – there were, therefore, at least two kiln sites here, the *Kiln Yard* translates as the 'Kiln Enclosure' and either this, or the *Barrowford Kiln,* would probably have been *Almosse Kiln.*

Christopher Smith reappears in the records of 1547 when Bernard Hartley is shown to have owned a cottage and two gardens upon Blacko Hillside. The property was tenanted by Christopher Smith whilst the rights of ownership were reserved for Alexander Hartley, son and heir of Bernard. This property would be part of the Stone Edge estate and there is every possibility that it was in the area of Malkin Tower, if not the Malkin property itself.

John Smith of Roughlee is once more embroiled in a land dispute, this time he (and others) took Miles Nutter to court for unlawfully occupying land in Roughlee. The court of 1547 was held before a jury of twenty-four foresters who ordered that the land in question (*Meane Grounde* in Nether and Over Roughlee) should be divided between the tenants according to the size of their land holdings at the time.[1] Not to be included in this was a close called *Wattlyngforthe de le Heyheade Ende.*

Roughlee Old Hall and the Smiths

William, the son of John Smith junior, who was in in turn the son of John Smith, died in 1576 and his eldest son, John Smith, inherited his property of approximately thirty-three acres in Nether Roughlee and the smaller fifteen acre plot at *Watlingforthe.* John Smith went on to acquire much of the Smith family properties around Roughlee and, by the time of his death in 1598, he had become the most important person in Roughlee.[2] The Pendle Witch legend had always assumed that Alice Nutter lived at the Roughlee Old Hall and that her father-in-law, Miles Nutter, had built the property. This story had been propagated by a date-stone at the Hall which appears to show that the property was built by someone with the initials of MN in 1536. This stone, however, is almost certainly from another building; both the placing of the stone and the later date of the Hall verify this. Gladys Whittaker shows, however, that there is a weight of evidence for John Smith having occupied Roughlee Old Hall, she also suggests that he was the builder of the property – at his death he owned Old House and New House in Roughlee and it is likely that this latter property was the Old Hall.

---

[1] When an ordinary halmote court jury of 12 local foresters was unable to pronounce judgement upon a case a special jury of 24 men was called. These jurors were summoned from all of the Blackburnshire forests, rather than purely from the forest in which the dispute arose.
[2] Gladys Whittaker, *Roughlee Hall. Fact and Fiction,* (Marsden Antiquarians, 1980)

John Smith's wife, Alice, was the daughter of Henry Shaw who was a man of some substance, he originally hailed from Newsham over the Yorkshire border and built his wealth through trade as a clothier. The Shaws were an established family within the forest, they acquired lands and were friendly with the leading yeoman classes of Hartley, Nutter, Smith and Hargreaves. John Robinson, in his capacity as greave of Pendle Forest, surrendered a farm of around thirty-three acres called *Blackoe* in 1524 and among the six new co-tenants of this farm was Henry Shaw. The record also shows that chaplain William Hird proved his rights to this property; William Hird was a Chantry Priest at Whalley from 1508 to at least 1535 and could very possibly have been retained by the Bannisters at Colne as they owned the North Chapel at St. Bartholomew's.[1] In this chapel is a prayer, inscribed in illuminated Saxon figures on three boards of oak, a free translation from the Latin would be:

"O' Mary, Mother of Christ! I earnestly entreat Thee to succour and aid the World by the recital of such prayers in Heaven as gladden the heart and banish all spectral illusions in the hour of death, and that William Hyrd may find favour with Thee. And, O' Virgin Mother! I beseech Thee to have me in thy holy keeping, lest the powers of death prevail against me."

Henry Shaw's son, another Henry, married an Isabell Hartley; the family lived at Alkincoats Hall in Colne, (an estate encompassing a number of local farms). In 1625 Isabell Shaw, widow of the late Henry, left a will in which she made bequests to John Hartley, blacksmith, and the children of Richard Hartley of Coates-in-Craven (this family were descended from Bernard Hartley of Laund via his son John).

The Old Hall, Roughlee

The year 1560 was the year of John and Alice Smith's marriage and John's father, William Smith, surrendered a farm in Roughlee the objective being that John and Alice were to own the property. The surrender was subject to indentures made between William Smith and Henry Shaw in the form of a dower for Henry's daughter Alice. William Smith's wife, Isabell, was to retain a close called *Greystones* from the farm lands and this puts the site of the farm firmly within the Roughlee area of Dole House and Dimpenley. It is fairly certain that the present Roughlee Old Hall was erected sometime in the later sixteenth century and that John and Alice Smith occupied the property. John Smith of the Old Hall was buried at Newchurch in 1598 leaving three daughters; Alice (born 1578) who married James Oddie of Rimington in 1599, Margaret (born 1580 died 1631) married Hugh Hartley of Winewall in 1599 and Ellen (born 1583 died 1659) who married Henry Hartley of Roughlee and then Lawrence Roberts. The

---

[1] T.D.Whitaker, *History of Whalley*, (1st edition, 1881)

Marriage of Ellen to Henry Hartley, and Margaret to Hugh Hartley, saw the Old Hall property move into Hartley ownership and this family lived at the Old Hall well into the late seventeenth century. Margaret's grand-daughter, Ellen Hartley, was the daughter of James Hartley of the Old Hall and Dimpenley and she married John Hartley of Admergill in 1663. Following John's death in 1669 Ellen inherited the Old Hall.

Gladys Whittaker makes an interesting case for the youngest Smith daughter, Ellen, having had an illegitimate son called John who was raised as John Hartley. The local story goes that this son was called 'nephew' at the Hall but 'bastard' in the alehouse. Through evidence of wills and property Gladys shows that John Hartley could well have been the son of George, the third Earl of Cumberland, from Skipton Castle. A case is also made to explain the reason why Alice Nutter had so long been thought to have lived at the Old Hall. The fact that Alice Smith was the mistress of the Hall, and that she had a daughter also named Alice, led to early researchers, such as Harrison Ainsworth and Robert Neill, confusing the Alice Nutter legend with the Alice Hartley facts.[1]

More Smiths

In 1549 Nicholas Smith was again in dispute over Stone Edge when he complained that Christopher Robinson of Over Barrowford had taken lands that were his (Smith's) by right of inheritance from his parents, John and Alice Smith. Robinson defended his actions by saying that he had swapped the Stone Edge land for lands of the Smiths elsewhere in Barrowford.

Christopher Smith died in 1551 and his brother, John (they were probably the sons of John Smith) aged nineteen years, was admitted to Christopher's farm at a yearly rent of £0: 1s: 1d. John Halstead of High Halstead in Briercliffe was young John's guardian. This illustrates the strong link between certain families within the area of Briercliffe and Pendle Forest – in particular the Smiths of Roughlee were closely related to the Smith families of Pighole, Hill End, Hollin Grove and Hill Farm in Lane Bottom.[2] The Nutter families from Goldshaw and Waterside would go on to settle in Briercliffe and neighbouring Extwistle as the seventeenth century wore on.

Christopher Smith, the son of William and Isabell, made an official complaint in 1558 against the widow of Richard Baldwin and Henry Baldwin, both of Wheathead, stating that Richard Baldwin had owed Isabell Smith the sum of £8. Neither Richard Baldwin's widow, or Henry, were prepared to settle this debt as executors of his will. This Richard Baldwin (deceased) was probably the father of the miller, Richard Baldwin, who allegedly threw Old Demdike and her daughter off his land and lost his young daughter through bewitchment as a consequence.[3]

William Smith surrendered a close of land at the Greystones in Roughlee in 1559 to the use of William Mitton, of Roughlee, this close of around thirty acres was situated above the Dole House Farm on the Ridge Lane running from Noggarth Top down to Happy Valley.

Our old friend, Nicholas Smith of Stone Edge, had a son John who carried on the family tradition of suing the Robinson family of Stone Edge. In 1560 John went to court in order to

[1] Gladys Whittaker, *Roughlee Hall. Fact and Fiction,* (Marsden Antiquarians, 1980)
[2] Roger Frost, *A Lancashire Township,* (The Rieve Edge Press, 1982)
[3] Part Two of this book

prove his rights to twelve acres in Blacko as this land had once belonged to his grandmother, Alice. Smith complained that Christopher Robinson and his son, also Christopher, had seized the lands unlawfully but the jury found in favour of John Smith and he regained his land.

In 1564 William Smith was appointed as a *Fence Looker* for Roughlee and in the same year John Smith was fined 12d for keeping a *Gray Hawnd*.[1] In 1565 Margaret Blakey surrendered her part of a substantial farm in Roughlee to James Hartley (son of Bernard of the Laund) and William Smith (son of John junior) of Roughlee. This suggests that the Roughlee Smiths were closely related to both the Hartleys of Laund and the Blakey family of Roughlee and Blacko.

Early in the reign of James Ist (1603-1625) the Crown decided to contest the land tenure of the forest area and this caused a great deal of anguish and upheaval amongst the lesser landowners. The king's bare-faced cheek was rewarded by a compromised settlement whereby the tenants made a one-off payment to the Crown. Things quietened down for a while but by 1611 the king was up to his old tricks. He commissioned another enquiry as to the 'doubtful' land-holdings and new lands taken from wastes. The Crown commissioners appointed to oversee the new legalised robbery were none other than Sir Richard Molyneux and Sir Ralph Asshton, to whom John Nutter of Greenhead was servant.

The commissioners stated that they would only recognise copyholds if they were purchased from the king at £0: 9s: 4d per acre (twenty-eight years rent at four pence per acre). A carrot was offered here in as much as any tenant wishing to pay this sum was offered extra waste land, the ordinary people were understandably unhappy with this state of affairs. The gentry, however, were quick to spot an opportunity to acquire yet more land, this put them at variance with their smaller neighbours. Again, the Crown won the case and the copyholders of the manor of Ightenhill (Burnley) paid a settlement of £2,141: 10s: 10d – this ensured that the remaining waste lands were divided amongst them at a rental of six pence per acre. However, this incident would have caused much unrest and ill feeling on behalf of the poorer classes against the local gentry; furthermore one of the local yeomanry, in the shape of John Nutter, would have been firmly on the side of the Crown; this would surely have reflected badly on Nutter and his family whose standing within the local community would have been somewhat tainted.

The steward's deputies were despatched into the forest with their customary heavy-handed approach and demanded equal payment regardless of whether the inhabitants were struggling or prospering. It is perfectly reasonable, then, to assume that the poor would oppose the government authorities on the new tenancy order; to what extent, however, did the rich landowners see an opportunity to evict the smallholders adjoining their own lands and thus gain them for themselves?

Was the date of 1611, in which the Crown acted, of any significance to the round-up of the poor in the 1612 Pendle Witch Trials? Jennet Preston (of Gisburn), Anne Whittle (Old Chattox of West Close) and Elizabeth Southern (Old Demdike) all lived in dwellings upon large estates – in all of these cases their families may have previously held the tenancies of holdings upon these estates. Alice Nutter had, by reason of her dower, a veto on the sale of her deceased husband's Roughlee properties.

The ultimate objective (in 1612) of particular members of the forest gentry may have been to gain (or re-regain) certain tenements and closes of land inconveniently (for the gentry) occupied by the forest poor. If this is indeed the case then their accusations of witchcraft, and subsequent prosecutions of the nine executed Pendle foresters, worked a treat!

awful, awful, awful!

---

[1] *Fence-lookers* were local men responsible for checking the parish hedges and fences

Chapter Ten

People and Places Continued

Hargreaves

The Pendle Forest Hargreaves families of Goldshaw, Higham and Pendleside were somewhat unlucky in their dealings with the Pendle Witches. Alison Device, Demdike's grand-daughter, gave evidence at the 1612 trial that her brother, James Device, had;[1]

A Blacke-Dogge, which her said brother called Dandy, which Dandy did aske her said brother what he would haue him to doe, whereunto he answered, hee would haue him to kill **Iohn Hargreiues,** *of Gold-shey-booth: whereunto Dandy answered that he would doe it: since which time the said Iohn is dead.*

And at another time this Examinate confesseth and saith, That her said brother did call the said Dandy: who thereupon appeared in the said house, asking this Examinates brother what hee would haue him to doe: whereupon this Examinates said brother said, he would haue him to kill **Blaze Hargreiues** *of Higham: whereupon Dandy answered, hee should haue his best helpe, and so vanished away: and shee saith, that since that time the said Hargreiues is dead; but how long after, this Examinate doth not now remember.*

Alison went on to describe the Good Friday meeting at Malkin Tower:

And she further saith, she knoweth the names of six of them, viz. the wife of **Hugh Hargreiues** *vnder Pendle, Christopher Howgate of Pendle, Vncle to this Examinat and Elizabeth his wife; and Dick Myles wife of the Rough-Lee,* **Christopher Iacks** *of Thorniholme, and his wife; and the names of the residue, she this Examinate doth not know.*

Blaze Hargreaves was supposedly 'killed' by James Device, the wife of Blaze was called Jennet (she was buried at Padiham in 1600) and she was co-tenant, along with her son, of lands in Higham in which John Nutter, dean of Chester, was involved. We have met with this John Nutter previously in relation to his many land holdings. It is not clear if this **John Hargreaves** was the one with the alias of Jacks (possible the father of **Christopher Jackes)** but it is almost certain that these Hargreaves were related.

The alias of *Jacks* ran through the Thorneyholme and Dimpenley branches of the Hargreaves family, in 1635 a James (alias Jackes) Hargreaves of Dimpenley was buried at Newchurch. The 1539 Roughlee vaccary rentals show that **John Hargreaves** paid £0: 9s: 8½d for land and that a **Christopher Hargreaves** and **Edmond Crook** were farming at Whitehough and Thorneyholme, between the villages of Barley and Roughlee.

---

[1] Thomas Potts, *The Wonderfull Discoverie of Witches,* (Potts, 1613 - Chetham Society, 1845)

An *Acquittance,* within the Clitheroe court rolls, for £13: 6s: 8d is dated February 1593:[1]

- **Hugh** son of **Richarde Hargreaves** of Heigham Deyne, to John Nutter, rector of *Sepheton and Deane of Chester (by James Hartley, clerk, his attorney) -- for quitclaim of properties in Higham Deyne called the Over Felds, Bent and Backe Feelde, in the tenure of* **Hugh Hargreaves** and **Jennet** *his mother. Witnessed by Edmund Starkie, Ricardi Wodroff, John Nutter, Henric Nutter.*

- *Acquittance: for £70 8 May, 1593:* **Blaze Hargreves** *of Heigham, yeoman, and* **Hughe** *his son and heir, to John Nutter, Dean of Chester (by Edmond Starkie of Huntrode, gent.) . . . for quitclaim of properties in Higham Deyne called the Over Felds, Bent and Backe Feelde, in the tenure of* **Hugh Hargreaves** and **Jennet** *his mother. . . . Witnesses were Edmund Starkie, Henrye Nutter, Willmus Nutter and Richard Cople.*

   It would appear from this that the proper name of Blaze Hargreaves was actually Richard Hargreaves. Records relating to the Hargreaves families of Higham show that they farmed that area along with lands in Filly Close, Fence and West Close. The following records relate to this family:[2]

1539: *Roughlee Rentals: John Hargreaves pays 9s: 8.5d.*

1552: *Hugh Hargreaves of Higham was father to Blaize Hargreaves his heir and related to James and William Hargreaves.*

1554: *Hugh Hargreaves sought admittance to a messuage in Higham at £0:17s:6d which he occupied lately but was evicted for none-payment of rent. Katherine Shackleton forbade fine in right of inheritance of Blaze Hargreaves as son and heir of the said Hugh; John Hargreaves alias Jacke received land in Great Marsden from Robert Hargreaves and his son John*

1555: *John Hargreaves, alias Jack, of Nether Barrowford surrenders a messuage now in the tenure of Miles Nutter (Alice Nutter's father-in-law), John and Richard Nutter and to Elizabeth wife of Miles at £0:22s:2d.*

1566: *Blaize Hargreaves and others surrender premises in Higham to Jennet Pollard.*

1566: *Blaise Hargreaves rented land at Burnley Wood.*

   The appellation of Blaize (Blaze, Blaise) was applied to successive generations of this branch of the Hargreaves family. Why James Device wanted revenge upon John Hargreaves of Goldshaw and Blaise Hargreaves of Higham is unclear, the probability is that James was asked none-too politely to leave their land and as a consequence he had felt snubbed.

---

[1] A *quitclaim* was the release and disclaim of all rights, interest and potential legal action from the grantor of a property, or land, to the grantee
[2] W. Farrar, *Clitheroe Court Rolls,* (Vol 1, 1912)

Constable Hargreaves

Another player within the annals of Pendle Forest is the forest constable, Henry Hargreaves (yeoman) who appears to have rented lands in the Simonstone area to the west of the forest. The fact that there are two marriage records in existence for Henry Hargreaves complicates the search somewhat. The first marriage was at Colne where Henric Hargreaves married Elizabetha Lawe and the other was within the Whalley marriage entries where Henrye Hargreaves married Jenneta Feirnside in the December of 1598.[1] If this latter is our Henry then he would have been the brother-in-law of Anthony Nutter of Goldshaw who had married Elizabeth Feirnside at Whalley in 1598. Anthony Nutter it was who Old Chattox accused of favouring Demdike over herself and whose daughter Chattox bewitched. Being so close to the every-day machinations of the forest dwellers Henry Hargreaves would have brought an invaluable local knowledge to his official position as the eyes and ears of the his boss, the Justice of the Peace, Roger Nowell of Read Hall. In all probability Henry would have been around 35 years of age and in his sixth month as forest constable when he assisted Roger Nowell in his 1612 witch round-up.

Returning to the marriage record of Henric Hargreaves and Elizabeth Lawe on the 24th October 1602 at Colne; if this is indeed Constable Hargreaves then this raises the intriguing possibility that he was related to the chapman (traveller in small goods) John Lawe of Halifax who, in the March of 1612, was supposedly bewitched and crippled by Alison Device. This relationship would suggest that there was at least an opportunity for Hargreaves' boss, Roger Nowell, to use this Hargreaves/Lawe link in order to set-up the whole of the prosecution case that eventually led to the Pendle Witch Trials. [2]

The office of constable was somewhat of a poisoned chalice, having been chosen to serve a forester could not refuse to do so unless he could have afforded to pay for a stand-in to perform his duties for him; these duties would have included arresting local wrong-doers and escorting them to the Lancaster or Preston Assizes. This could have meant that the constable had to arrest his close neighbours or even his own family when the need arose, this could place him in a somewhat onerous position within the community and it has to be remembered that the office of constable was an unpaid one.

In his official capacity Henry Hargreaves visited Malkin Tower between Good Friday, 10th April, and Monday the 27th April, 1612, in order to search for evidence appertaining to the concealment of evidence. Chattox was said to have taken three 'scalps' from the graveyard at Newchurch St. Mary's and had consequently given a number of the teeth of one of them to Demdike to employ in her demonic activities.[3] Hargreaves was charged with the task of going to Malkin in order to find the teeth and found that Demdike had buried them; being guided by Demdike's ever-helpful grandson, James Device, Hargreaves soon found the teeth (along with a shaped clay image) buried some eighteen inches deep at the western end of Malkin Tower.[4]

The constable was also involved with James when he took him from Malkin, over the Edge of Weets on the old Gisburn Track (Coalpit Lane), to Westby Hall at Gisburn. This ancient route

---

[1] Blackburn and Leyland Hundreds - *Parish Records* - relevant local studies libraries and Preston Records Office

[2] It is also possible that the Lawe family received land at Barrowford - *The Lancashire Witch Conspiracy,* (Part two)

[3] Skulls were referred to as *scalps;* Chattox would have easily acquired a skull when a new grave would uncover a previous burial. The earlier bones were often left lying around until the Sexton had the time to place them within a charnel (bone) house

[4] These images, or *dolls* as they were known, were used to cause harm to the intended victim whereby pins were stuck into the image

followed a trackway from Malkin that can still be made out with some difficulty until it joins the ancient Black Dyke on Blacko Hillside, from here the track is clear as it skirts Weets Hill and drops sharply over the Edge of Weets towards Gisburn. The purpose of this journey to the Lister household was for James to formally identify Jennet Preston as having been at the Malkin Tower meeting on Good Friday.

The route over Weets Hill taken by James Device and Henry Hargreaves in 1612

Hargreaves of Water Meetings Farm

The Water Meetings of Barrowford is a picturesque place where the rivers of Pendle Water and Blacko Water meet. The area sits at the base of the western slope of Blacko Hill, at the junction of the parishes of Blacko, Barrowford and Roughlee. From the river valley an ancient route climbs westward through the Utherstone Woods and on to the ridge top. This ridgeway served our area for millennia as a major trade-route and the original track can still be followed through to Padiham Heights and onwards to Portfield and Whalley. On the riverside at the Water Meetings, where the ancient track climbs towards the ridgeway, is Water Meetings Farm and Cottage. There was a farm in existence here in the later sixteenth century as the Colne burial records show members of the Hargreaves family, of Water Meetings, being buried there. However, the property is not mentioned in the published court rolls of 1425-1567.

The present building is a linear three-cell house of two stories, formerly with a storied outshut to the rear. All details suggests a third quarter seventeenth century but the final layout results from alterations to the earlier build, probably of early seventeenth century date.[1] James Hargreaves' will of 1674 has an inventory which lists the parlour and lower parlour - both heated. In the middle of the seventeenth century the lower end of the building was turned into two rooms heated by corner fireplaces. One of these rooms has a plaster frieze around the wall, this is likely to be the lower parlour of the inventory. Also mentioned was a heated workshop, many yeoman's houses of this period had workshops attached for the purposes of wool-carding, combing, spinning and weaving the finishing cloth, also for the making of equipment.

The Hargreaves family name was synonymous with Water Meetings Farm but it is difficult to show a definite lineage beyond the seventeenth century. The Poll Tax records of 1660 show only one Henry Hargreaves, he lived with his son, James Hargreaves of Water Meetings.[2] In an

[1] Sarah Pearson, *Rural Houses of the Lancashire Pennines,* (HM Stationery Office, 1985)
[2] Doreen Crowther, *Unpublished Hargreaves family research,* (Nelson Library)

extract from the nineteenth century Manchester publication, *The Cotton Trade and Industrial Lancashire,* an interesting report shows a seventeenth century letter dated the 15th of July 1652. the letter is from John Bannister of Park Hill, gentleman, who had borrowed the sum of £200 from Henry Hargreaves (alias Hall) of Barrowford, clothier. Hargreaves is described by Bannister as *'a very rich and able man in estate who set out much money on hire,'* the loan to Bannister carried an interest rate of 8% and Bannister found Hargreaves *'a very hard, oppressing and vigorous man.'*

Henry Hargreaves, then, was a cloth dealer and money-lender; this combination was common at that period as the wealthier clothiers required a decent capital sum in-hand with which to pay their suppliers whilst they had to wait for payment from their customers. Given the lack of official banking facilities the forest moneyers would provide loans to many of their fellow yeomanry, many of the larger houses within Pendle were purchased through mortgages obtained from people such as Hargreaves.

On the 15th of December, 1656, Henry's grandson, Lawrence Hargreaves, also a clothier, married Ann Robinson of Marsden and on the 5th August, 1657, they baptised their son, John, at Colne. It appears that Lawrence and Ann moved to Marsden, possibly to Ann's family property, as James Hargreaves leaves in his will of 1673 *'one red pinter'* to John, son of Lawrence of Marsden Chapel. This James could have been the son of Lawrence Hargreaves who died in 1618. Henry the cloth dealer and moneyer died in the late 1650s as his will shows:

The Will of Henry Hargreaves (alias Hall) 1658: [1]

I Henry Hargreaves (alias Hall) of Barrowford in the County of Lancaster, yeoman, sick in body but of sound and perfect memory and understanding having made a will to settle that estate which God in his bounty has lent unto me: my worldly estate to be made into fourthings, it is my mind that the same be made into two equal parts: the first part thereof arranging for the sale of some of my goods and debts: the bounty to be paid to belong for all my children save James my son and heir: and the other part I quit and bequeath the estate of the house and lands wherein suit upon a mortgage from Lawrence Robinson redeemable by order from [. . . . . Thorpe ?] upon the payment of two hundred pounds and by the same now paid on three fourthings: the same is that my said son James shall have to his own use the said two hundred pounds: and whereas by my surrender that I herewith shall release all other of my lands within Barrowford aforesaid by the same of all my houses, barns, lands, messuages and stables with their appurtenances lying and being in Over Barrowford of the yearly rent to the Lord of the forest of [fourteen?] shillings; thereafter to the use of William Hartley of [Burnley?] and he is to be thereof feoffed; it is my last will that the forementioned shall stand and be therefore fined and seized for and to the last and behoof of my said son James and his heirs and assigns forever.

The foeffes to be paid first: I quit and bequeath unto my son Henry the sum of one hundred and forty pounds; I quit and bequeath unto my daughters Margaret and Ellen either of them the sum of thirty four and ten pounds; I also quit unto my daughter Elizabeth the sum of twenty pounds; and the remainder of all my goods chattels and debts after my funeral debts and expenses be paid and discharged quit and bequeath unto my said children Henry, Margaret and Ellen equally to be divided amongst them all interest attaining.

---

[1] Original held at Preston Records Office

Debts owing to me the testator:
Henry Blakey of Blacko - sixty eight shillings
William Nutter - forty shillings
Thomas Bannester - twenty shillings
[Ruth?] Shuttleworth [forty?] pounds
*Joseph Robinson - seven shillings (crossed out)

Joseph Robinson* of Little Marsden, yeoman, possibly the father of Ann Robinson (wife of Henry's son, Lawrence), is seen as one of the appraisers of the goods and chattels of James Hargreaves whose will of 25th March, 1673, shows that he devised Water Meetings, a field of eight acres called Whitelee and twelve acres in Blacko on copyhold rent of 13s: 4d to James, his eldest son and heir. James left his tenements in Barrowford and Salterforth to his youngest son, William. Other legacies were the sum of £21 to James Hilton and £20 to Elizabeth Hilton, the children of Margaret (James' daughter) wife of Edward Hilton.[1] His Worldly Goods went to his wife, Ann, five shillings to his grand-daughter Alice (the daughter of his daughter Elizabeth Dickinson), and five shillings to all his other grandchildren. His son, James Hargreaves, was the Executor.

James' belongings were valued by James Hartley of Wanless – John Hartley of Roughlee – John Blakey of Colne and Joseph Robinson of Little Marsden. The rooms in his property were: *The Parlour, The Chambers over the Lower Parlour, The House, The Lower Parlour, The Workshop and The Stairs, The Workshop, Parlour, The Milkhouse, The Kitchen, The Little Buttery, The House, Barn and other Outbuildings.*

James was the eldest son of James Hargreaves and inherited the Water Meetings estate but did not live there, instead he lived in Barrowford and rented the farm out to George Hartley.

Hargreaves Great House - now the White Bear

In 1687 James' son, John, died; either James or John had built Hargreaves Great House (the White Bear) in Barrowford. In 1667 John mentioned his *'new house,'* and other properties, in his will. However, if the date of the Great House is, in fact, 1667 then it must have been built by his father, James, as John was not born until 1664. This is probably the reason that James was not living at Water Meetings in 1674. John's elder brother, James, became the owner of The Great House and Heirs House,

---

[1] About this time the Hiltons rebuilt the house at Higher Park Hill in Barrowford

Colne, and went on to become the father of the later Hargreaves families.[1] James died in 1791 and his will of 1778 mentions his dwelling house as Hargreaves Great House and his inventory shows his effects are still at the Water meetings Farm.

On his death John Hargreaves left his infant son James, born 1684, in the care of his father James. John also had a son John, born 1685, and a daughter Jennet, born 1686. This son John was later given as living at Laund, this is the High Laund property to the north-west of Carr in Barrowford – it is possible that this property came into John's possession through marriage. The son James, had two surviving daughters; Catherine was born in 1709 and married her cousin, John, they later lived at Laund. The other daughter, Jennet, married James Lonsdale of Marsden and they inherited the lower part of Hargreaves Great House.

In November 1713 James Hargreaves of Barrowford, yeoman, was listed as the owner of the White Bear as was John Hargreaves of Barrowford. James Hargreaves was given as being of the Water Meetings.[1]

The 1803 Survey of Barrowford shows that Abraham Hargreaves owned the White Bear (here called Charles Farm) and Brew House. He also owned Greenhill Farm, above the White bear on Pasture Lane, the farm-track past this property was given as the occupation road to Higher Ridge and the Water Meetings.

In the later nineteenth century Water Meetings Farm, along with the Fleece Inn, Barrowford, was purchased by William Farrington Esquire of Leyland. The farm was occupied by Nicholas Dugdale; later occupants were the Sharp family.[2]

Fields attached to Water Meetings Farm were: *Meadow – Parrock – Coppice – Barley Croft – Wood South of the River – Holme of Bridge End – Bowling Green Holme – White Lees – White Lees Top – Rough Ing – Cock Hill – Wood Field – Lowest Dole Field – Middle Dole Field - Highest Dole Field* – the latter four contain an occupation road :

Buildings were: *The Farmhouse – The Barn – One Cottage – One Loomshop* (in occupation of Aaron Nelson) – *One Cottage* (in occupation of William Holme).

To this day the Water Meetings riverside Holme lands belong to the Hargreaves family.

---

[1] One of this family was Abraham Hargreaves of Heirs House who, in 1784, wrote a diary. This covered the time that he was setting-up his spinning operation in the old Park Mill, Barrowford. The diary is available at Colne Local Studies Library

[2] Albert J Morris, *In Those Days,* (Rieve Edge Press, 1998)

Chapter Eleven

Religion

Whalley Abbey

When William the Conqueror invaded England, on the 14th of October 1066, he was seeking a revenge that had long festered within him; he had the huff with King Harold for a number of reasons, not least of which was the fact that Harold had sworn over holy relics not to accept the English Crown. This peeved the Conqueror who saw the English throne as his by rights; he sought and received the blessing of the Pope for his invasion of England as he regarded it as a holy undertaking. Following his success William endowed the Battle Abbey at Hastings, the alter of which is said to cover the very spot where Harold fell, reputedly with an arrow in his eye, although certain medieval scribes had it that Harold survived to old age within a Cheshire abbey.

Following the example of their king, the Norman overlords erected the churches that we are familiar with, their squat architecture is instantly recognisable even though many of the structures were extensively altered at later dates. The Norman baronage, and the church, were the two influences that led to the later unified development of the forest area.

The Abbey of Whalley would eventually share the overseeing of society within the honour of Clitheroe with the Clitheroe overlords. Long before the founding of the Whalley Abbey a Saxon church had been dedicated to All Saints there, known as *The White Church under the Leigh* this would be a wooden structure, later to be replaced by a stone building. The rectors, or deans, were the lords of the town and, as they were allowed to marry, the succession of their position was hereditary. The office of dean was looked upon as that of a dignitary, rather than a purely ecclesiastical position, he was inferior only to the feudal overlords and, therefore, enjoyed a privileged existence.

Dean Liulphus was an incumbent at Whalley in the reign of Canute and had earned himself the name of Cutwulph when he cut off the tail of a wolf whilst hunting at Deansgreave in the Forest of Rossendale.[1] There is no doubt that the deans lived the high-life, tales of their hunting exploits were legendary, there can be no doubt either that their position was being eyed by the predatory overlords. This situation continued until the Lateran Council decreed in 1215 that the marriage of ecclesiastics was to be prohibited. Following this the deans had to resign their patronage to the chief lords who were not slow to take advantage of the situation. By taking the minimum qualifying religious orders the lords were able to 'absorb' for themselves the income of the church benefice, formerly due to the dean. Members of the Towneley family were Deans of Whalley but this male line died out around 1295.[2]

The story of the Cistercian Abbey of Whalley really begins at Stanlaw in the ancient parish of Eastham, Cheshire; Stanlaw Abbey appears to have been founded between 1172 and 1178 by John, constable of Chester. The de Lacy's were great benefactors of Stanlaw and through them

---

[1] T.D.Whitaker, *History of Whalley,* (1st Edition , 1881)
[2] *Towneley MSS*

the abbey held a fourth part of the advowson (income) of the rectory of Blackburn. It was Henry de Lacy, the third earl of Lincloln, who sanctioned the removal of the Stanlaw Abbey, between 1283 and 1285, to its site at Whalley. This was well received by the monks as they had long complained about their Stanlaw site being sea-swept and boggy. They were granted the rest of the rectory of Blackburn and allowed to construct their new abbey upon the glebe land that was the whole of the township of Whalley. On St. Ambrose day, in 1296, Gregory de Northbury, the eighth Abbot of Stanlaw, along with his convent, took possession of the old deanery – this would be their home whilst the abbey buildings were being constructed.[1] Following much wrangling between the ecclesiastical powers (including the Pope) the monks of Stanlaw finally made the new site at Whalley their official home and, according to Whitaker, the earl of Lincoln laid the foundation stone for the new abbey on the morning of St. Barnabas day (12th day of June) 1308. By 1330 the abbey buildings were advanced to the degree where the abbot and convent could move out of the deanery and into the new building. The abbey buildings were completed to the original design plans in 1444 under Abbot Eccles - the monks estimated that the project had cost around £3,000.

Not everyone was happy with this state of affairs, however. The Abbey of Sawley, near Gisburn, was established in 1147 when there is reference to a priest from Gisburn being present at the laying of the foundation stone. Sawley complained that the new abbey at Whalley contravened the rule that new abbeys were not to be sited too closely to existing ones. The Sawley monks maintained that the former rector of Whalley supplied them with corn from the parish of Whalley and that the foundation of the new abbey had caused an increase in demand for corn and goods to the extent that Sawley had to pay £30 per year in excess. In 1305 a compromise was reached whereby each house was to treat the other on equal terms, any monk found to be acting to the contrary benefit of the other house was to be punished.

Sawley Abbey was not adverse to standing up for itself as there are numerous incidents involving litigation between the abbey and other ecclesiastical houses through the ages. When Sawley Abbey was founded the Abbot wanted the right of Patronage over the nearby village of Gisburn but, in 1226, the Archbishop of York granted the Patronage to the nunnery at Gisburn under the Prioress of Stansfield (through the guidance of the powerful Percy family). Both Sawley Abbey and the Gisburn nunnery were very poor and a bitter feud existed between them, in 1285 the vicar of Gisburn was prosecuted by the Abbot of Sawley *'for entering the Abbot's warren and carrying off game.'*[2] Despite the presence of the abbey and nunnery this was not an area in which to linger; in 1401 the vicar of Skipton was returning from a visit to Sawley Abbey when he was murdered on his way to Gisburn. Twenty-four years later the rector of Gisburn, Thomas Banaster, asked his Bishop to *'reconcile the churchyard after the shedding of blood.'*

The abbey of Whalley prospered over the centuries, many grants of land, and in some cases whole townships, saw their power continually increase. The more land that they controlled and the more tithes they could extract from the parish; these were payments of a tenth part of the profits derived from the land, live-stock and labour of the inhabitants. In 1296 the tithe income to the abbey from Burnley parish alone was £47.[3]

The various parish churches were also responsible for the maintenance of the mother house at Whalley although, in 1396, abbey records show that: *'The parishes of Brunlay, Colne, Chirch and Huselynden to be free from the repairs of the mother church of Whalley,'* this did not

[1] Ven. Charles Henry Lambert, *Whalley Abbey - Yesterday and Today,* (Whalley Abbey Committee)

[2] T.D.Whitaker, *History of Craven,* (1st edition, 1805)

[3] W.Bennett, *History of Burnley,* (Volume 1, Burnley Corporation, 1946)

mean, however, that these parishes were exempt from other charges, such as the maintenance of the rector's house.

The abbey estate did not always run in a smooth and quietly religious manner as can be seen from the following *Exemplification of Pleas* in the Chancery. In the middle of the fourteenth century farms and associated lands in *Witton iuxta Blakburn* and *Whalleye* had been formally valued and were stated to have been: '..... *acquired without licence by Abbot John of Lindelay from Adam son of William of Raddeclif, outlawed for burning the house of John of Podeseye,* (in 1344 John Pudsey, of Bolton Hall in Bolton-by-Bowland, had his house deliberately burnt down)[1] *held by fee simple of Geoffrey of Chaterton, lord of Witton; the abbot also acquired without licence lands called Caldecotes in Great Penhulton from William Aygladde, chaplain, outlawed for rape against Alice, daughter of Adam of Heyleghg.'*

'*Also Abbot Robert of Toppecliff, predecessor of John of Lindelay, without licence acquired from John of Whalleye a messuage in Whalley valued 2s per annum which John held of the abbot in fee simple. All the above had been escheated together with 5s in money, 8 ells of woollen cloth, value 15d, and 10 ells of linen cloth value 6d, and 1 cow value 8s, and calf value 2s, and 1 horse value 10s, which belonged to the fugitive Thomas Horne who slew John of Newton in the monastery.'* [2]

Towards their nadir in Tudor times, the monks of Whalley were often accused of being too ready to live from the fat of the land, they were seen as being wealthy and indulgent. Many stories were told of the gallivanting of the monks, broadsheets with poems and songs about the errant prior were very popular as can be seen in this contemporary medieval ballad:

Quhere are ye boun', ye bolde prior,
With that ladye on yore knee?
I'm boun' to ye hills, I'm boun' to the dales,
I'm boun' to ye grey priorie

Abbot Paslew

Abbot John Paslew is possibly the best-known of all those who served within the auspices of the abbey at Whalley, he had the dubious honour of being the very last abbot there. Born to the Paslew family of Wiswell Hall (near Whalley) John Paslew entered the Abbey as a novice on the 21st September 1487. In the following year Paslew, aged about twenty-four years, went to Oxford where he eventually gained the degree of Bachelor of Divinity. Following a ten-year stint within the environs of Oxford University Paslew returned to Whalley where he was elected abbot on the 7th August 1507. By-and-large Abbot Paslew lived the life of a nobleman; he travelled widely and was generous in his hospitality whilst leading the Abbey in a statesman-like manner. [3]

A natural reaction of the Catholic gentry to Henry VIII's *Dissolution of the Monasteries* was to rebel, they organised an armed uprising in an attempt to persuade the king to reverse his

---

[1] J.W.Winder, *Pudseys and Parsons,* (St. Peter & St. Paul, Bolton-by-Bowland, 1972)
[2] T.D.Whitaker, *History of Whalley,* (First edition, 1881)
[3] Ven. Charles Henry Lambert, *Whalley Abbey - Yesterday and Today,* (Whalley Abbey Committee)

policies and restore the dissolved monasteries to their former owners. Robert Aske placed himself at the head of the rebellion, known as *The Pilgrimage of Grace,* and was soon joined by church dignitaries, the gentry and many of the labouring classes who all rallied to his standard of *The Five Wounds of Christ.* The whole of the county of Yorkshire were to be counted amongst Aske's number, this soon spread into Lancashire under the guidance of important local Catholics.

Amongst these were Nicholas Tempest, of nearby Bashall, and Sir Stephen Hamerton of Craven who had mustered some four-hundred men to follow them. On the 23rd October, 1536, this band of 'Pilgrims' descended upon Whalley Abbey in order to arouse the abbey and its parishioners to their cause. The monks of the abbey were understandably reluctant to become embroiled in the uprising, fearing for their future safety they would rather lie-low and take their chances. However, Tempest and his crew were not to be put off lightly and, after many hours of siege where they threatened to burn down the abbey barns, they were finally admitted. By force of arms Abbot Paslew was persuaded to swear allegiance to the Pilgrimage leader, Aske, whilst Hamerton rode to Burnley and Colne in order to coerce the parish priests there to gather their parishioners. Paslew would later be accused of supplying a horse and items of armour plate for the use of Tempest in the rebellion.

Whalley Abbey; engraved from Wm. Turner's 1794 work (History of Whalley 1881)

On the 25th of October the king's man, Lord Derby, let it be known that he was on his way to Whalley and intended to crush the rebels there before he moved into Yorkshire with the same purpose. Tempest and Hamerton, undaunted by the threat, called for a muster of all local males over the age of sixteen years to be assembled upon Clitheroe Moor in readiness for the battle to come. However, on the 27th of October, Aske met with the king's man in Yorkshire, the Duke of Norfolk, and effectively surrendered; letters were sent immediately to the Clitheroe contingent of Tempest and Hamerton informing them that the cause was lost, ordering them to lay down their arms and disperse their men. Unfortunately for the abbey, and especially Abbot Paslew, this communication did not arrive before a monk named Richard Eastgate, of Sawley Abbey, had been admitted into Whalley Abbey; the significance of this was that Eastgate was regarded by the Crown as a leading rebel in the Pilgrimage. The fact that Whalley had admitted him at such a sensitive time was seen as an act of rebellion and so Abbot Paslew had been compromised. The letter of surrender was finally received at Clitheroe on the 30th of October, 1536, Tempest and Hamerton then proceeded to Whalley where they disbanded following a sulk of many hours – this only served to rub salt into the royal wounds.

The *Pilgrimage of Grace* was, of course, seen by Henry VIII as a direct insurrection against his authority. It is thought that Paslew may have involved himself further (perhaps somewhat involuntarily) in the later stages of the Pilgrimage as letters have survived showing his efforts to distance himself from the affair (no doubt when he saw which way the wind was blowing!). In an apparent act of desperation he granted the king's secretary, Thomas Cromwell, a pension of ten marks per annum from the abbey funds in an attempt to placate the royal wrath; this was to no avail as will be seen from the following passage:[1]

'The monks were now reduced to humiliating and submissive circumstances. They were indeed fallen from that high estate, when kings were their tributaries, and empires too narrow for the wide grasp of their ambition. The following is a copy of Thomas Cromwell's indulgence, taken from the Towneley MSS:-'

'---To all estates due honour and reverence, and to all other, commendacioun in our Lord everlasting -- Know ye that we, John abbot of ye monasterie of our blessed Ladie of Whalley, in Com. Lanc. by ye assente and consente of ye convente have freely granted unto ye right honourable Mr Tho. Cromwell, secretarie, general, visitor and principal official to our most sovereign Lord Kynge Hen.VIII., an annual rent or fee of VI:XIII:IV. yerele, to be paide at ye nativitie of St. John Baptiste unto ye said Maister Tho. Cromwell. Wee, ye saide abbot and convent have put to ye same our handes and common seale .--Yeven at Whalley 1st Jan. 28 Hen.VIII.---'

'But every act of submission, every strategem and advice, had failed to ward off the blow. Within ten weeks from the date of this document there was neither abbot nor abbey of Whalley.'

'After the dispersion, imprisonment, and execution of the principal leaders of the rebellion, the day of reckoning and retribution was at hand. The Earl of Shrewsbury, by the king's orders, sent a herald with a troop of horse, who, taking Paslew, Eastgate, Haydock, and some others of the monks prisoners, they were arraigned at Lancaster castle, and convicted of high treason. On the 12th of March 1537, (Whitaker has it on the 10th) Paslew was conveyed back to Whalley for execution, where, in a field called Holehouses, immediately facing the house of his birth (at Wiswell, near Whalley) a gallows was erected, on which Paslew and Eastgate suffered punishment or martyrdom, for the story varies according to the bias by the party by whom it is told. Haydock was carried to Padiham, and died there the same ignominious death on the day following. The monks, driven from their asylum, escaped to France, with the

---

[1] John Roby, *Traditions of Lancashire,* (1st edition, Routledge, London, 1872)

exception of a few, who lingered near the scenes of their former enjoyments, hovering like departed hopes round the ruin to which they clung.'

Opinion is divided as to the site of Paslew's execution, folklore has it that he was executed either in the Abbey grounds, in Imps Field at Whalley, or at his former home in Wiswell.[1] However, the strongest argument seems to be that Paslew was hanged at Lancaster following his trial. A tombstone, said to be that of the Abbot is placed in the wall of the parish church but when it was moved from the church yard to its present position no actual burial was found.[2] Nicholas Tempest and Stephen Hamerton were executed at Tyburn.

The king ordered the forfeiture of the abbey's possessions, and the transfer of some of the monks who remained within the area, to other monasteries; at this point it is alleged that a shortfall in the amount of gold and silver plate belonging to the abbey came to light. This was said to be as a result of Abbot Paslew selling off the valuables to pay for his assumption to the height of a mitred abbot although this probably incorrect. The abbey remained as the property of the king until June 6th, 1553, when the abbey site, and the manor of Whalley, were sold to members of the local gentry, John Braddyl and Richard Assheton, for the sum of £2,132: 3s: 9d. Braddyl then built himself a new manor house at nearby Portfield whilst the Assheton family moved into the Abbot's House. Abbot Paslew's prior, Christopher Smith, was allowed to continue as a chantry priest at Whalley parish church because of his *'great age.'*

It is thought that the abbey buildings were rendered uninhabitable during the reign of Queen Mary as she was actively attempting to restore the displaced monks to their former abbeys; the structure at this time would still have rivalled the ruins at the Fountains and Furness Abbeys. Unfortunately, having survived the Civil War, Whalley Abbey was systematically dismantled during the reign of Charles II. The owner at that time paid groups of workmen to remove and carry off the stonework – they were paid to destroy the abbey fabric by the yard. A number of our parish churches claim to have parts of the abbey structure within their own, the gentry houses of the district also show architectural details relating to the abbey. It is said that much of the ornamental stonework from the windows and door-arches was dumped into the river on the abbey site.

From the time of the first Asshetons the abbey continued to be used as a private residence, in the late eighteenth century the site was accorded the status of a farm house. In 1866 the site was left in the will of John Taylor of Moreton Hall to Col. John Hargreaves of Broad Oak, Accrington who restored the property and made it his residence. In the 1920s most of the abbey site was purchased by the Manchester Diocese of the Church of England whilst a smaller part was purchased by the Catholic Church.

*   *   *   *   *   *   *

It is difficult to overestimate the role that the hegemony of Whalley Abbey played in the overall function of the thirty townships within its jurisdiction. Prior to the *Dissolution of the Monasteries* the 180 square miles that made up the parish of Whalley had no bishop, nor did it have a cathedral and therefore the abbey found itself central to the economic and spiritual lives of the tens of thousands of people within its extended environs. The abbey was a major

---

[1] J. Fell, *Window on Whalley,* (Countryside Publications, 1979)

[2] Ven. Charles Henry Lambert, *Whalley Abbey - Yesterday and Today,* (Whalley Abbey Committee)

landowner, employer and provider of alms to the poor of the district. The two *compotus* [1] lists for Whalley Abbey, compiled in 1478 and 1521, show that the income from the parish was drawn from the chapelries of Clitheroe, Downham, Burnley, Colne, Altham and Haslingden along with Blackburn, Eccles and Rochdale. Relating to the church income alone this rose from a total of £356: 17s: 5½d in 1478 to £592: 3s: 1½d in 1521 – these figures did not account for the farming incomes from the dependant farms. [2]

The abbey was not slow to capitalise on its equity and expanded its land holdings, it also spent copiously on entertaining the many people who had need to visit the abbey in either spiritual or commercial capacities. Building works, at the abbey and in the parishes, were an on-going source of employment, an example of which can be seen in the extension of Saint Peter's church in Burnley. Between 1521 and 1533 local masons were employed to enlarge the north aisle of the church, the head of this project being the Sellers family of Whalley who were attached permanently to the abbey building and maintenance team.

The extent to which the abbey succeeded in acquiring its wealth, lands, precious objects and power can be seen to have played a part in its eventual, and rapid downfall. The abbey estate as a whole presented itself as a valuable prize upon which Henry VIII had set his jaundiced eye; the embroilment of the last abbot of Whalley, John Paslew, in the ill-fated *Pilgrimage of Grace* was to provide the perfect excuse for the king to pounce on the abbey. Within a few months of Paslew's execution for high treason (March 1537) the whole abbey system had been virtually disbanded. The destruction of the estate was carried out with clinical precision, the king's authorities employed a great deal of propaganda by which they attempted to justify their actions – the abbey had become associated with the act of treason and this became attached by association to the monks. Furthermore the authorities were not slow to use the wealth of the abbey as a pointer towards the perceived avarice of its people, broadsides and ballads abounded whereby the monks were accused of living a high-life not expected of people of their particular calling; they were therefore unceremoniously ejected from their ecclesiastic home and sent on their way. As might be expected, Whitaker had something to say on the subject:

Had the Dissolution of the Monasteries been conducted on other principals than sacrilege and rapine, had the application of their revenues been directed by those high ideas of the inalienable nature of tithes and offerings which prevailed a century later, and in consequence, had their spiritualities been completely restored to officiating incumbents, while the temporalities, instead of being squandered with thoughtless prodigality, had been disposed of at an extended value, the necessities, even of Henry VIII, might have been abundantly supplied, and a wealthy, yet not overgrown establishment, have been formed as the basis of reformation. But as it was in fact conducted, nothing but the over-ruling Providence of God could have procured even a decent reception for the reforming clergy.

For on the sites of these great foundations, and among people among all other bound the old religion by interest, by imagination, by gratitude, and by regret, they were turned out, armed indeed with the word of God, but destitute of all external means to conciliate or to reward. On the very sites where whole districts had been feasted and pensioned, they had neither kitchens for hospitality, nor purses for alms. Dejected and dissatisfied, and many of them, it is

---

[1] The term *compotus* is often found in records and is simply the Latin for *account* or *audit*
[2] Whalley Church Records

probable, deeply tinctured with old prejudices, they performed their stated offices without spirit, and without effect, and they transmitted to their successors a people only Christian inasmuch as they had received the right of baptism, and only not Catholics, because the mass had been abolished among them.

It is an ill-wind that blows nobody good and the period following the destruction of Whalley Abbey can certainly be described as good for certain members of local society and these were the gentry. Locally important families such as Bradyll, Nowell, Assheton and Towneley were to benefit from the old abbey estates in no little way. The immediate benefactors of the fallen abbey were Richard Assheton of Whalley and John Bradyll of Brockhole; this partnership took stewardship of the abbey lands and within a few years were able to purchase the estates outright – Bradyll took the lands and Assheton moved his family into the former abbot's house.

The destruction of the central economic authority was to usher in a sea-change for certain people within the Pendle Forest communities, the former abbey lands changed hands and therefore many tenants found themselves with new masters to please. Whereby the authority of the abbey would have dealt with minor problems relating to its economic estates the local halmote courts at Colne, Higham and Ightenhill found themselves having to address an increasing number of small grievances. The loss of a cohesive spiritual authority was to have an even more profound effect upon the ordinary forest folk, as the care of the poor became a localised responsibility the local taxpayers began to resent the fact that they were required to pay for the upkeep of their neighbours. When the abbey oversaw the alms relief it was a case of 'out of site, out of mind' but the new relief brought home to people that *they* were actually paying for the poor within their community and resentment often ensued.

The pre-Reformation methods of worship had not disappeared under the new Protestant sovereigns, far from it in fact; many of the forest clergy continued with their 'traditional' Catholic-based services following the Reformation, paying only lip-service to the new ways. This can be partly explained by the fact that the Catholic form of worship was only slowly subjugated by the later Protestant forms - Henry VIII had set the ball rolling when he nationalised religion but the full-blown Protestant Reformation did not really take effect until the reigns of Henry's son, Edward VI (1547-53) and daughter, Elizabeth Ist (1558-1603). It also has to be remembered that the generation born before the Reformation had been raised within a strong Catholic culture, as had their priests. It would be impossible for strongly held beliefs to be subjugated within a single generation and it is no surprise, therefore, that pockets of Catholic 'resistance' existed at the time of the 1612 Pendle Witch Trials amongst certain gentry families and also amongst the ordinary people.[1] Other gentry families fully embraced the Protestant faith (sometimes for political reasons only) and prospered whilst their Catholic counterparts suffered confiscation of land, property and money – and sometimes their lives.

With some of the money appropriated from the wealthy monasteries during the *Dissolution*, Henry VIII created a bishopric and cathedral in the city of Chester, the distance of this new authority from its forest communities was, however, to prove telling. The loss of the spiritual authority of the abbey saw a marked downturn in the quality within certain factions of the clergy who were willing to serve the forest areas. The lack of ecclesiastical leadership led to a number of clerics with definite pre-Reformation leanings being attached to the livings within Whalley Parish; not least of these was one George Dobson who we met earlier. The parish church at Whalley attained the services of Dobson in 1558 and he was to serve there for the next

---

[1] Andrew W Snape, *English Martyrs - Whalley,* (Whalley, 2000)

thirty-three years. Dobson had an unfortunate trait in that he would only recognise the pro-Catholic worshippers amongst his congregation, a small clique formed and this, of course, upset the other parishioners. An extract from a letter sent to the bishop of Chester describes Dobson in the following terms:

He is......... a common drunkard, and such an ale-knight as the like is not in our parish, and in the night when most men be abed at rest then is he in the ale-house with a company like unto himself, but not one of them can match him in ale-house tricks, for he will, when he cannot discern black from blue, dance with a full cup on his heade, surpassing all the rest. [1]

This, at least, was the description of Dobson as his Protestant congregation saw him – a strong traditionalist (if not fully Catholic) cleric who was accused of promulgating the old doctrines and thus keeping the 'magic' suspicions of the simple forest-folk alive.

Other clerics were reported as being downright incompetent - an incumbent of Saint Mary's, Newchurch-in-Pendle, by the name of Sellers, was said to have refused to marry people and that he spent most of his time frolicking with the landlady of the Fence Gate alehouse! This was not an entirely local phenomena, nationally there are many recorded instances whereby Puritan clergy describe the whole of Lancashire as a spiritually barren area[2] - the inference here being that many pockets of Catholicism not only survived in the area but that they were positively thriving. As an illustration of this seventeen members of the Lancashire clergy, the incumbents of Whalley and Blackburn included, petitioned for action in 1590 as *'moste of the people refraine theire Parishe Churche, under pretence of theire Chapelles, and having no service at their Chapelles, com at [none] at all; but manye of them grow into utter Atheisme and Barbarisme, manie enjoye full securitie in Poperie and Popishe practices.'* [3]

The Gentry and the Church

We have seen that dichotomy between the rich and poor people of Pendle Forest hinged largely upon the acquisition of lands; although the area did not contain members of the true gentry class there were nevertheless a significant number of minor gentry. Apart from the ownership of estates (and the subsequent related political machinations) the main concern of these people was that of religion. As a direct consequence of the Tudor hegemony the local gentry fell decisively into two opposite camps - Catholic and Protestant.

In the extended medieval period leading up to the reign of Henry VIII it can be said that the vast majority of the English people were Catholic. The loss of the monasteries and other religious houses during the *Dissolution* of the 1530s brought an end to the continuity of Catholicism, the new Protestant order became firmly established under the passing of the *Acts of Supremacy and Uniformity* within a year of Elizabeth I ascending the throne. The pre-Reformation Catholic bishops were staunchly loyal to the Crown and therefore could be seen to fulfil the role of civil servants. This meant that the high-end Catholic opposition to king Henry's break with Rome was somewhat muted – with a few notable exceptions; both John Fisher,

---

[1] Whalley Church Records
[2] Lord Strange described the county of Lancashire, in 1583, as *'this so unbridled and bad an handful of England'*
[3] Rachel A C Hasted, *The Pendle Witch-Trial 1612,* (Lancashire County Books, 1993)

bishop of Rochester and Sir Thomas More, Lord High Chancellor of England, were executed for their refusal to accept Henry's 'supremacy.' This is not to say that there was no opposition at street-level; the ground-swell of unrest during the *Pilgrimage of Grace* (1536-7) and the *West Country Rising* (1549) saw many ordinary people joining forces with members of the gentry and the clergy alike in opposition to the new Protestant order.

Religious historians Michael Mullett and Leo Warren, in their book *Martyrs of the Diocese of Lancaster,* make the point that the older generation, born before the Dissolution and loyal to the old faith, had seen many changes in the official line regarding the religious practices of the population. Henry VIII had instigated *Catholicism Without the Pope,* this was enthusiastically taken up by Edward VI in his general *Protestantisation* (1547-53) followed by Mary Ist's rapid re-Catholicisation (1553-8). When Elizabeth I gained the throne in 1558 followers of the old tradition must taken the attitude of 'wait and see' – just how long would the new queen reign and to what extent would she enforce the anti-Catholic edicts of her father and half-brother? During this period some churches, and a Cambridge college, held on to their chalices and mass vestments in the hope that things would revolve full-circle and the Mass would once again return.

During the reign of Mary Tudor many new Catholic clergy were either ordained or converted to the faith and these people proved to be a problem when Elizabeth ascended the throne. Many refused to conform to the Act of 1559 and, of those who did, a great number continued to encourage Catholic practices within their own parish. Elizabeth's many Protestant Acts were to become collectively known as the *Penal Period* and during this time the penalties for refusal to adopt the new ways became increasingly severe. In 1571, 1581 and 1585 Acts were passed to make it an offence of high treason to call the queen a heretic, to be reconciled to the Catholic church or to be a Catholic priest (or harbour such) within the realm. This had the effect of sending the Catholic faith underground. Many secret places of worship existed locally, the gentry were able to hide their priests and chapels whilst ordinary people used isolated buildings such as barns for the hearing of Mass – Wilkinson's barn in the village of Barley was probably the said to have been used as a place of worship by Irish farm labourers until relatively recently.[1]

Elizabeth's reign saw the halls of academia purged of their former Catholic influence and this left a vacuum when the acquisition of Catholic learning was forced abroad. In 1568 a Lancastrian named Cardinal William Allen, who was the son of Jane Lister of Westby near Gisburn, founded a college at Douai in the Low Countries. This new academic centre produced an English New Testament in 1582 and an Old Testament in 1609-10. The Douai institution ran alongside the English College in Rome as the power-house of the Catholic mission to England. Many of the sons of Catholic gentry, usually the younger sons who would not inherit the family estates, were sent to Douai to train as priests in which role they would return to England and secretly provide for the spiritual needs of those who upheld the old faith.

---

[1] Burnley film-maker Sam Hannah - interview, 1963

Chapter Twelve

The Forest Churches

The folk of the early Pendle Forest, along with the other forests of Blackburnshire, were parishioners of the chapel of Saint Michael at Clitheroe Castle. In 1331 Abbot Topcliffe petitioned the king with his claim that Saint Michael's had always been a chapel with dependence upon the Abbey at Whalley - the earl of Lincoln had wrongfully abstracted the chapel from Whalley and, because it had no rights of burial or baptism, it could not be a free chapel. In 1334 the king accepted the superior rights of Whalley Abbey on the condition that the Abbey paid three-hundred marks for the recognition. Saint Michael's was part of the dower of Queen Isabella who, shortly before the king's verdict, had granted the chapel's chaplainry to Richard de Moseley; he had to be bought out of his new position at a cost of £40 for the rest of his life. Following these political manoeuvres by the Abbey the former forest parishes were transferred to Whalley.

The inhabitants of Pendle Forest were not required to attend the church at Clitheroe, or later at Whalley, as the ordinary services were held at their local chapels. Both Burnley and Colne had their own churches in 1121 and a chantry chapel was erected at Padiham in 1445. Marsden also came to have a chapel of its own although people from here often used Saint Bartholomew's at Colne. There was a certain snob-value attached to the attendance of a particular church, the great and the good would prefer to be seen at certain churches but not others. Many of the minor gentry, and yeoman classes, were happy to make use of the Colne church (the Bannisters and Towneleys had chantries there) but others preferred to travel from Pendle to Whalley parish church. Not only would people from Pendle attend Whalley to be seen in the 'right' company and hear the local business news, many of them had family within the Whalley area. A great number of Whalley people had migrated eastwards into the forest in search of farms to operate, especially following the deforestation of 1507.

It is possible that the more isolated areas of Pendle had the use of a place for the saying of mass long before the erection of the 'chapel of ease' at Newchurch-in-Pendle, perhaps as early as 1250. [1] In 1532 there is a record of '*a chaplain of the new chapel in Penhull*,' this would be the same chaplain of Goldshaw (Newchurch) who was appointed in 1529. The new church of Saint Mary's was consecrated by the Bishop of Chester, John Bird, in 1544 to serve the five forest booths of Goldshaw, Barley, Wheatley, Roughlee and Old Laund. The booths of Reedley Hallows, Filly Close, New Laund and Wheatley Carr were somewhat out on a limb as, being extra-parochial, they were not considered to be part of any chapelry, therefore the inhabitants were required to marry at Clitheroe.

Medieval society distinguished between wrong-doing as *sins against man* (these were dealt with by the halmote courts) and *sins against God*, these were to be heard before the church

---

[1] A *chapel-of-ease* was a place in which a travelling priest (from Whalley) would provide local religious service for the forest community; because of the distances involved in attending the existing churches at that time this would at least ensure that the forest dwellers had a modicum of spiritual guidance.

courts. A common method employed by the church was for the local priest to appoint overseers whose job it was to regulate moral wrong-doing. The overseers would report problems to the priest who, if he considered it necessary, would transfer the matter to the mother church of Whalley where the boothsmen formed juries under the auspices of the prior. Matters heard at Whalley concerned such improprieties as the none-attendance of Sunday worship, immoral behaviour, working for wages on the Sabbath, breach of promise, none-observance of wills, profanity, talking in church, the use of magic, celebrating the *black-fast* and thumping the vicar!

If marriage problems could not be rectified upon the advice of the churchmen then the matter could be referred to a higher authority. Some divorces did take place, those of Blackburnshire were often taken to Chester in order to prevent the details being aired locally; when divorce was granted the woman would often be placed under the charge of a male relative who was supposed to take care of her moral and monetary welfare. At Burnley a case was reported concerning one of the Ightenhill tenants – the Home Farm of Ightenhill Manor was originally 690 acres in extent but in 1534 the Towneleys divided it into fourteen farms, one of which was tenanted by Thomas Folds. This Thomas married an Isabell and was ordered by a Church court, in 1535, to separate from his wife on account of *'nearness of kin.'* Thomas ignored this order as he denied that the church court had any jurisdiction over him, in 1537 he failed to turn up for another hearing and subsequently both he, and his wife, were suspended from the church.[1]

It would be difficult to overstate the important role that the church fulfilled throughout society, especially during the whole of the medieval period and through to the nineteenth century. During an era when superstition did not carry the same stigma as it does in our modern scientific age the church provided a strong focal point for village inhabitants. The regular tolling of church bells signified many things such as the marking of Saint's days. The Sanctus and Angelus bells were constant reminders to the workers in the fields that they were to unify with their neighbours for worship whilst national celebrations, and warnings, were rung clear; weddings, baptisms and funerals were marked in this manner. Prayers, and thanksgiving for the crops, would comfort the poor whose lives depended upon them whilst the causes of disease and famine were quantified by the priest so as to enable his flock to retain hope in a mysterious world.

The priest, of course, had a much wider remit within his parish than simply marrying, baptising and burying people. Besides officiating at the normal church services the parish priest often took the role of the feudal greave; he was the peacemaker when trouble flared within his community. He organised alms for the needy, he would liase between the gentry and the commoners, he was often the first port-of-call when land disputes arose and he often found himself at the centre of parish musters in times of local and national conflict.

Along with the spiritual comfort offered by the village churches they also had a more practical role. When most people were living in timber-framed houses the stoutly built stone church would often be the safest refuge in times of trouble. Weapons were stored in the church buildings so that the inhabitants could run there from the surrounding fields when threats arose. The numerous Scots incursions into the area caused local people to be constantly on their guard and the church acted as a central muster point for them. St. Mary The Virgin, at Gisburn, had a dual dedication to St. Andrew, the patron Saint of Scotland – this may have been a diplomatic attempt to pacify the raiding Scots. [2]

---

[1] W. Bennett, *History of Burnley,* (Vol 1, Burnley Corporation, 1946)

[2] B. P. Tyrer, *St. Mary The Virgin,* (St. Mary P.C.C, 2001)

The measurement of each villein's strip of land needed to be accurately carried out, to this end the official *chain* (cut to a standard unit of length) would be kept in the church for the marking of plots and for the use of an arbitrator when disputes arose. Tools for the maintenance of the village, such as picks and shovels, along with certain pieces of agricultural machinery for the common use, were also housed in the church. The church was also the equivalent of the modern village hall as meetings concerning the area would be held there. The incumbent would stand outside the door after a service and announce any forthcoming events such as furniture auctions, punishments to be carried out in the stocks, recent Church Court verdicts and so on. Often a halmote court would order that the payment for the purchase of land, or repayment of debts, was to take place within the porch, or at the altar, of the local church, this added a degree of gravitas to the magistrate's ruling.

Marriage was seen in the medieval period as being largely a civil contract between a man and a woman, church marriages amongst poorer people were not very common up to the eighteenth century, especially in country areas. It was thought to be sufficient for a man and woman to hold hands with a female third party who would hear the contractors swear their oaths. The couple then considered themselves to be legally married and could sue for breach of contract if either person took up with another. In 1600 only eighteen weddings took place during the whole year at the parish church of St. Bartholomew's at Colne, by 1831 this number had increased to around one-hundred and sixty-seven – the growth in population was a factor to consider here.

Any widow, whose husband had died insolvent, re-married dressed only in a close-fitting sheet; this followed a tradition that this form of dress meant that neither the woman, or her new husband, would be liable for her former husband's debts.[1] James Carr lived at Langroyde Hall, Colne, in the nineteenth century and an acquaintance of his stated that, in the 1700s, his mother had regularly seen unchaste women being punished by having to wear nothing but a white sheet in Colne church. In the presence of the whole congregation the woman would be made to walk up and down the aisle; *'bare-foot and bare-legged, having a white sheet wrapped about her from the shoulders to the feet and a white wand in her hand. She was then to stand on a seat near the pulpit and recite the gospels after the vicar...'*

Chantries

Wealthy families played a vital part in the prosperity of the parish churches, to be a benefactor of either the building or the priest was accepted as a definite sign of high-status. In fact, the important families tended to compete with each other in the provision of gifts; these could take the form of monetary donations, enrichment of the church building, gifts of land, provision of church plate, stained glass windows, the alter and font, tapestries and furniture. As a consequence of this some of our parish churches were richly decorated indeed. The internal walls were usually rendered and, as most parishioners were illiterate, pictures of biblical scenes were painted on the plasterwork so as to provide a pictorial background to the scriptures. Lush embroidered fabrics would hang on the internal walls, the church plate would gleam in the prismatic rays of light streaming in through the coloured windows and a good priest could transpose the minds of his flock to the Garden of Eden for an hour or so (that is when he was not berating them for their sins!).

Of the benefits bestowed to the parish church by the wealthy it is probable that the most important, over the long term, was the establishment of a chantry. The patron of a chantry

---

[1] James Carr, *Annals and Stories of Colne,* (Colne, 1878)

required that prayers would be said for himself, his family and ancestors on a regular basis. To this end he would endow his chantry with either lands, money or property – land was by far the most common form of endowment. The rent and profits from chantry lands would pay for the support of a chantry priest, this was usually a person from the community employed by the patron. The provision of a chantry also meant that a part of the church was sectioned off, usually by means of a carved screen, this was then reserved for the sole use of the patron and his family. Within the private section was an alter at which the chantry priest would regularly say prayers in which he specifically mentioned the names of the founder, his family and ancestors. This, of course, meant that the wealthy were confident of an ongoing spiritual insurance. The chantry priest often ran a small school attached to the church and this would stretch his meagre income.

Saint Mary's and All Saints parish Church, Whalley

St. Mary's contains the St. Mary's and St. Nicholas (Mitton) chantries and the Kage pew, dating from 1534, was made for Roger Nowell of Read. Certain architectural pieces were removed to St. Mary's from the Whalley Abbey next door - these include superbly carved choir stalls installed in the abbey in 1430. T. D. Whitaker, the historian (History of Whalley etc;) was the vicar of St. Mary's from 1809 to 1822 - an impressive monument to him stands in the chancel.[1]

The chapel door of St. Mary's is one of the earliest parts of the building

[1] J. Fell, *Window on Whalley,* (Countryside Books, 1979)

Chapter Thirteen

Parishes

The present parish church of St. Mary's and All Saints at Whalley has its origins in the Norman period of 1206, the first incumbent there was Peter de Cestria (1235-1296). There are a number of traditions attached to this rector: he was reputedly the illegitimate son of the Constable of Chester, he held a number of other rectorships besides Whalley and he served as the moneyer in the king's court. Following the dissolution of Whalley Abbey the sovereign, Elizabeth I, appointed one George Dobson as the vicar of Whalley. He was not a popular choice as a letter of complaint written by his parishioners stated that: *'he too frequently visited the ale. . . . by dancing with a full jug upon his head at which sport he excelled all others.'*

With regard to the parish of Whalley, Whitaker shows that an inquisition was taken at Blackburn, in the year 1650, before Richard Shuttleworth, under the Commonwealth Seal. The object of this commission was to evaluate all the parochial vocations within the parishes of Blackburn, Whalley and Rochdale. The findings of the inquisition were that. . . .

Whalley: *consisted of 35 townships, Mr. William Walker was an able and orthodox divine minister and received from Mr. Thomas Assheton, farmer of the rectory, a stipend of £38.*

Padiham: *was parochial, consisting of the townships of Padiham, Hapton, Simonstone and Higham Booth, containing 232 families and 1106 souls. The minister was John Breares, A.M. who received a stipend of £6: 19s: 2d from the receiver of the county, and £33 from the county commissioners, and that the inhabitants desired to be made a parish.*

Colne: *the chapelry consisted of Colne township, Foulridge, Marsden and Trawden, containing, in the whole, 400 families. The minister, John Horrocks, A.M. was an able divine and received £11: 10s: 0d from the farmer of the rectory by order of the county commissioners, the inhabitants desired to be made a parish.*

Clitheroe: *the chapelry consists of that township, Chatburn, Worston, Merely and Heyhouses (Sabden), in all about 400 families. The minister, Mr. Robert Marsden, was an able divine and received £11: 10s: 0d out of the duchy rents, and £25 from the commissioners of the county. The inhabitants desired to be made a parish.*

Downham: *was parochial and contained within the township 300 families and Twiston contained 40 families. The minister, George Whitaker, A.M. received £10 from the farmer of the rectory and £30 from the county commissioners. The inhabitants desire to be a parish.*

Accrington: *was not parochial and consisted of the township of Accrington vetus et nova, &c. containing 200 families. The minister, Mr. Roger Kenyon, was an able and orthodox divine. The inhabitants desired to be a parish.*

Altham: *was parochial, consisting of Altham and part of Clayton, which contained 150 families. The minister was Mr. Thomas Jolly, an able divine, who received £10 from the rectory and £30 from the commissioners. The inhabitants desired to be made a parish.*

Briercliffe and Extwistle: *were distant from Whalley five miles, and from any other chapel almost six, and consisted of 100 families. The inhabitants desired to erect a chapel themselves. --- Whitaker makes a footnote:- 'These distances are not accurate, but the request was reasonable. Indeed a place of worship is exceedingly wanted in this remote and uncivilised tract.'*

New Laund, Reedley Hallows, Filly Close and Ightenhill Park: *distant one and a half miles from Burnley, desired to be united to that church (St. Peter's) and to be made a parish.*

Burnley: *chapelry consisted of that township, Habergham Eaves and Worsthorn and contained upwards of 300 families. The minister was Mr. Henry Morris, an able and orthodox divine, received from the duchy £11: 10s: 0d - from the inhabitants £4: 8s: 2d and from the commissioners £24: 1s: 10d.*

Holme: *had no minister or maintenance, but the inhabitants desired that it may be made a parish church, and that the parish consist of Cliviger, Worsthorn and Hurstwood, in all 100 families.*

Church: *consisted of Church, Oswaldtwistle, Huncote and part of Clayton, containing 200 families. The minister, James Rigby, A.M. received £10 from the rectory and £30 from the county commissioners. The inhabitants desired to be a parish.*

Henthorn, Coldcoats and Wiswall: *desired to be continued to the parish church.*

Haslingden: *consisted of that township and part of Rossendal viz. Newhalley, part of Rawtenstall Booth, Oakenhead Booth, Constable Leigh Booth and Crawshaw Booth, in all 300 families. The minister, Mr. Robert Gilbert, was suspended by the divines. The inhabitants desire to be a parish.*

Newchurch-in-Pendle: *was parochial, the chapelry consisted of most part of the Pendle Forest and contained 150 families. The minister was Mr. Edward Lapage, an able divine who received £39 from from the commissioners of the county. Wheatley and Roughlee desire to be annexed and made a parish.*

Goodshaw: *was not parochial and had a chapelry consisting of 70 families; but no minister or maintenance, saving a messuage and backside, value 10s: but the inhabitants desired to be made a parish.*

Whitewell: *was not parochial and had a chapelry of 116 families, but no minister or maintenance:- the inhabitants desired to be made a parish.*

Newchurch-in-Rossendale: *was parochial and consisted of Dedwen Clough, Tunsted, Wolfenden Booth, parts of Wolfenden and Bacup, in all 300 families. The minister was Mr. Robert Dewhurst, an able divine, who received no allowance but what the inhabitants give, who desire to be made a parish. Whitaker's footnote:- 'What was now become of the valuable estate belonging to this church, which escaped the commissioners of pious uses under Edward 6th. and still belongs to it?'*

The outcome of this inquisition, as stated by Whitaker, was '*out of one overgrown parish it was proposed to carve no less than 17, a change of little importance in itself and probably intended to answer no other purpose than that of placing the clergy on a footing of entire equality, better suited to the genius of a republic than subordination.*'

Burnley

Chantry land is not the same as glebe land, this was land owned by the mother church, often gifted to them, as was the case in 1342 when the daughters of Adam, son of the Clerk, granted twenty-one acres around St. Peter's in Burnley to the abbey at Whalley. By 1537 Whalley Abbey owned fifty-five acres of land in Burnley along with five houses and gardens commanding a yearly rent of £3: 7s: 8d, part of this was the property of St. Peter's but ultimately owned by the mother establishment. Whilst Whalley profited from the income of the parishes it also had a duty to provide a chaplain, maintain the fabric of the church and supply the communion goods, in 1298 the chaplain at Burnley parish saw his annual income increase from £2: 13s: 4d to £4.

The two main endowments at St. Peter's were the Towneley and Stansfield chantries. The Towneley chantry was founded in 1373 by Thomas de la Legh of Towneley and Hapton when he gave one third of his Towneley estate to his nephew Gilbert. A proviso of this grant was that a chantry should be established in Burnley church with a dedication to the Blessed Virgin Mary. In 1500 Sir John Towneley rebuilt this chantry and placed yet more land at its disposal.

Priests of this endowment were:

Nicholas Parker who died in 1481:

John Green (possibly) to 1500:

John Ingham 1500-1534:

Peter Adlington 1534-1546:

Saint Peter's, Burnley

Oliver de Stansfield of Heasandford probably endowed the Stansfield chantry before his death in 1340, the alter is dedicated to St. Anthony. The Haydock family inherited the Stansfield estates through marriage and they maintained the chantry. Lands at the disposal of this endowment were Perkinrood Farm, Coal Clough House (both in Burnley) and land near the village of Church. John Ingham, of Fulledge House (priest to the Towneley chantry), endowed the Rood Chantry early in the sixteenth century with six acres of land at Habergham Eaves. Parishioners had to make up the income of this chantry as the endowment in itself was not sufficient. The priest here was Richard Hitchon from 1534 to 1547.

The people of Burnley endowed the chantry of Saint Peter, the Patron Saint of the Burnley church, this was the main chantry and used the High Altar. William Booth of Oakeneaves Farm granted part of his farm in 1522 and in 1531 other lands were granted in Burnley and Higham along with a Towneley grant of sixty-eight acres at Shoreyhey and Hollingreave within the township of Briercliffe. From 1531 to 1550 the priest was Gilbert Fairbank who, in 1559, became the first headmaster of Burnley Grammar School. A fifth chantry was to be established but, by a convoluted series of sub-grants a Robert de Stokke, of Worsthorne, passed land valued at £5 to his son and appointed him as the chantry priest. This never took place, however, the situation was the subject of an enquiry which alleged that six books valued at ten shillings, the property of other churches, had been stolen by persons unknown. It was also alleged that the Abbot of Whalley, Nicholas del Yorcke, was in possession of the books but the outcome of this odd affair is unknown.

The *Dissolution of the Chantries* took effect locally between 1547-50 and this saw the Burnley chantries being robbed of their valuables, in this period all the chantry lands were confiscated by the Crown and sold off. The good people of Burnley were horrified to see their long-serving priests thrown into destitution and so they clubbed together and bought back these lands, they were then returned to the priests to enjoy for the rest of their lives.

Records of the early incumbents at Burnley are scant, the ones that do survive show: [1]

1220 *approx: Henry, Chaplain of Burnley. Owned land at Heasandford*

1275 *approx: John of Burnley. Granted land by de Lacy*

1275 *Walter, Chaplain of Towneley. Owned lands in Cliviger*

1348 *John, son of Adam, son of Walter, along with William Moton*

1368 *Richard of Burnley, Chaplain*

1369 *Elias of Habergham*

1397 *Robert of Bolton, Chaplain*

1440 *Walter the Chaplain.*

Colne

Colne parish church of St. Bartholomew's is reputed to have been founded by Robert de Lacy following the Norman Conquest. In 1122 the church at Colne was granted by the then lord of Clitheroe, Hugh de la Val, to the Priory of Pontefract but, when the de Lacys were reunited with their Clitheroe estates, the grant was revoked. In 1229 Henry III re-confirmed the grant but the transfer never actually took place.

Following the founding of the abbey at Whalley the area of Colne became part of that parish; although Colne does not actually lie within the bounds of Pendle Forest it was the major commercial centre for the people of the eastern forest. In 1296 the abbey had to find a chaplain to serve at Colne for an income of £2: 13s: 4d. By 1515 the fabric of the church building had

---

[1] W. Bennett, *History of Burnley,* (Vol 1, Burnley Corporation, 1946)

deteriorated to the extent that the Archdeacon of Chester authorised Edmund Bradyll and Henry Towneley to repair and restore it. In 1547 Archbishop Cranmer (of Canterbury) acquired the rectories of Whalley, Rochdale and Blackburn from Edward VI by way of an exchange of lands, this technically put Colne within the See of Canterbury. Villages falling within the chapelry of Colne were responsible for the maintenance of the fabric of the church of St. Bartholomew, as an early (undated) record of money owed by each township shows: [1]

'Ann acount what each towne are at a fifteenth towards repair of Colne Church, as under':-

Colne Towne parte of a fifteen is seven shillings and one penny halphpenny;

Townshipe parte at a fifteen is thirteen shillings and six-pence halphpenny;

Great Marsdene parte at a fifteen is fourteen shillings and two-pence;

Little Marsdene parte at a fifteen is seven shillings and six-pence;

Trawdene parte at a fifteen is eight shillings and four-pence halphpenny;

Fulridge parte at a fifteen is five shillings and eight-pence halphpenny;

Penle (Pendle Forest) *parte at a fifteen seven shillings and one penny*

St. Bartholomew's Parish Church, Colne

---

[1] James Carr, Annals and Stories of Colne, (Colne, 1878)

There were two separate chantries at St. Bartholomew's, one was endowed by the Bannister family and the other by the Towneleys of Barnside (Laneshawbridge to the east of Colne). The Bannisters rebuilt Park Hill in 1661 and mortgaged the largest part of the house, and the estate, to John Swinglehurst of Gill, near Gisburn. Another part of the house was sold to Mr. Yorker whose part passed to Gamaliel Sutcliffe of Stone Shey Gate, Heptonstall.[1]

Incumbents at Colne Parish Church

Sir John Hegyn	Living 1500
Sir William Fairbank	1520
Sir Robert Blakey	1535-1551
Sir John Fielden	1551
Roger Blakey	1592
Sir Lawrence Ambler	1596
Richard Brierley	Died 1635
Thomas Warriner A.M	Living 1645
Thomas Whalley	Died 1646/7
John Horrocks, A.M	1647-1669
James Hargreaves	1669-1693
Thomas Tatham	Resigned 1708/9
John Barlow	Died 1727
Thomas Barlow	1727-1731
Henry Smalley	1731-1741
William Norcrosse	1741-1751
George White, M.A	1751-1789
Roger Wilson, L.L.B	1789-1811
John Hartley, B.A	1811-1817
Thomas Thoresby Whitaker, M.A	1817
Philip Abbott	Resigned 1819
John Henderson	1819-1876
William Clifford, M.A	1876-1908
Stephen Peachey Duval, D.D O.B.E	1908-1924
Alan Prangley Thorne, M.A	1924-1936
George Edward Brigstock, M.A	1936-1938
John Ross Macvicar, M.A	1938-1955

[1] Jesse Blakey, *Annals and Stories of Barrowford,* (SP, Nelson, 1929)

The Bannisters fell on hard times as can be seen from a record dated 1713:

'Barrowford – relief of John Bannister of Parke Hill, a debtor prisoner at Lancaster Gaol.' [1]

The act of splitting the estate eventually (and predictably) created problems with the ownership of the Bannister chantry (or choir as it was commonly called) and in 1743 the Bannisters and the Swinglehursts appeared before the Consistory Court of Chester to settle their disagreement. The Court ruled that the Swinglehursts were to have the northern part of the choir, along with four pews, and the liberty to stand, sit, kneel and hear divine service therein. Henry Bannister and his successors were reserved the right to bury their dead under the northern part of the choir – providing that they replaced the seats afterwards!

In 1541 Lawrence Towneley, of Barnside, prosecuted Thomas Towneley (and others) in the Duchy Court for *'tortious possession of an isle, or quere, in the parrish church of Colne.'* Lawrence Towneley's Bill of Complaint was addressed to The Right Hon. Sir William Fitzwilliam, Knight, Earl of Southampton and Chancellor of the Duchy of Lancaster. In this long, rambling letter, Towneley addresses himself as *'your daily Orator'* and states that his grandfather, Lawrence Towneley, had bequeathed the chantry to him. He goes on to state that George Houghton, gent, of Greenfield, Colne, had no rights to the use of the Towneley chantry and that: [2]

'One son-in-law of ye said Geo. Houghton, Thomas Bannester, James Ridioaughe, with diverse other Ryotous & evyll disposed p'sons, by the commandment of said George Houghton.......'

To cut a long story short the basis of the complaint was that the above mentioned gang broke down the door of the Towneley chantry during a service and frightened the worshippers. They then went on to break up the choir seating before nailing the chantry door closed! In answer to these accusations Thomas Towneley refuted all the charges and the outcome was that the Court virtually told both parties to clear off and stop wasting their time! The owners of Greenfield Hall continued to occupy their rightful pew adjoining the Towneley choir and nothing more was heard of this strange dispute. The Towneley choir eventually became the property of Captain Edward Every-Clayton, of Carr Hall, through his grandmother who was of the Barnside Towneley family.

The list of Colne Incumbents contains a number of people with the appellation of *Sir* – this is not because Colne had an irresistible appeal to those holding a knighthood; they took the title upon themselves as this was common practice when a clergyman had not taken a degree. James Carr has it of John Horrocks (1647-1669) that he was;

'A Puritan from Horrocks Hall and, according to Walker, a person so notoriously vicious in his life that he was forced plainly to tell his people they ought to do as he said and not as he did.'

The Clitheroe court rolls show entries relating to the grant of lands to the Colne chantry priests:

---

[1] *The Farrar Papers,* (Manchester Central Library)
[2] *Towneley MSS*

1508-09: To this halmote came Christopher Diconson and surrendered one garden called Malkenyerd with the appurtenances in Colne to the use of John Hegyn, chantry priest...... granted.

These entries are particularly interesting as it is probable that they refer to the site upon which the legendary Malkin Tower stood. The reason for this is that a Richard de Marsden held Blacko in 1323 at a rent of twenty shillings. The rent was raised to twenty-two shillings and raised again when Blacko was granted to de Marsden in fee for a sum of twenty-eight shillings and eight pence. This rent was eventually forgone as de Marsden donated twenty marks towards the king's overseas ventures. In 1344 parts of Blacko were granted to Richard de Marsden with the other parts going to his son John. A provision of this grant was that upon the death of John the lands should be given as chantry land to a chapel at Colne, or elsewhere, for the provision of the saying of mass for the souls of Richard de Marsden, Avice (his wife) and their family.

In 1524 John Robinson, greave of Pendle;

'surrenders one messuage and appurtenances called Blacko at ten shillings and eleven pence per annum rent which William Emmott, Thomas Driver, Richard Mitchell and James Hargreaves delivered to him, to the use of John Kippax, Roger Hartley, Henry Walton, John Hargreaves, Henry Shaw and Nicholas Marsden jnr. William Hird, Chaplain (by his attorney John Wallis) forbids fine for certain covenants between them. '

William Hird was a Chantry Priest at Whalley from 1508 to at least 1535, he could possibly have been retained by the Bannisters at their Colne chantry as they owned the North Chapel at St. Bartholomew's. In this chapel is a prayer, inscribed in illuminated Saxon figures on three boards of oak: a free translation from the Latin would be:

'O' Mary, Mother of Christ! I earnestly entreat Thee to succour and aid the World by the recital of such prayers in Heaven as gladden the heart and banish all spectral illusions in the hour of death, and that William Hyrd may find favour with Thee. And, O Virgin Mother! I beseech Thee to have me in thy holy keeping, lest the powers of death prevail against me.'

Richard Greenacres, gent and deputy steward of Blackburn, lived at Worston and his daughter, Frances, married Nicholas Assheton of Downham (1590-1625); in 1551 Richard took;

'a messuage & other buildings, land, meadow, pasture and feeding ground lying on Blacko Hillside within the Pendle Forest in the occupation of Christopher and Lawrence Blakey at ten shillings yearly, which late belonged to the finding and maintenance of a priest within the church of Colne, to the use of Robert Blakey, late incumbent of the said service ('Sir' Robert Blakey incumbent at Colne 1535 - 1551) for the term of his life, and after his death to the use of him and the said Richard Greenacres.'
– it is unclear as to which particular farm in Blacko this refers to.

1564: 'John Foulds surrenders part of a garden called Mawkynyarde lying in the north end of Colne to Christopher Dyconson for a yearly rent.' The description of this property as being *'in the north end of Colne'* almost certainly relates to the property that stood within the area of the present Malkin Tower Farm at Blacko and is the same property referred to in 1508/9.

The following is a valuable record of the Great and the Good of the extended Pendle Forest area within the earlier seventeenth century. The rights to seats within Colne parish church were allotted in accordance with the individual's land and property holdings.[1]

Allotment of seats in Colne Parish Church 1635:

A Certificate of a Commission granted by the Bishop of Chester to Nicholas Mitchell, Lawrence Hargreaves, Robert Smith, John Biggin, James Robbard, James Hartley of Wycoller, and Henry Parker, Churchwardens for alottment and Division of the Stalls, forms and seats in the Church,... now by them divided and alotted amongst the Parishioners as followeth; April ye 11th 1635 :-

Impremis. For the stalls and forms adjoining to ye Chancell on Sun-side of ye Mid Alley they allot as followeth: The first double form at Chancel back and the second next adjoining to the length of one form, they do allot and appoint to Nicholas Townley, esq., for his house at Greenfield and the tenements of Henry Baldwin, Henry Haughton, Lawrence Hartley of Bridge End, Roland Waley and the tenement lately belonging to Henry Mancknowle of Marsden. Impremis. The third form next adjoining, one length they do allot to John Bannister of Park Hill, gent., for his tenants at Great Hey (Foulridge).

Item. For the other forms at chancel back adjoining to the South Alley (that is to say:- the first double form and the second next adjoining they do appoint to Mr Lawrence Habergham for his house and lands at Foulridge Hall and Robert Emmott for his house and lands at Standroyd.

Item. The third form to the two last allotted to Mr Habergham and Robert Emmott they do allot for the ancient men of the parish to sit in.The rank between mid alley and south alley allotted as followeth:- Impremis. The first double-seated form through between the Alleys they do appoint to Mr Henry Doughty, gent., and William Emmott for their chief mansion houses.

Item. They do allot a stall on the south side of the great pillar to the tenants of Mr Doughty at Waterside.

Item. The second form to the pillar they do allot to William Hartley of Bradley and Alexander Parker for their mansion houses.

Item. The third form adjoining the pulpit and great pillar they allot and appoint to Richard Kippax of Marsden.

Item. The double form on the west side of the great pillar, and adjoining to the pulpit they allot to Mr Lawrence Townley of Stone Edge, for Fulshaw and pasture lands, and Edward Spencer for Lomeshaw lands.

Item. The fifth through next beneath the pulpit, they allot to Ambrose Walton for Clough-head, and William Sagar, younger, for Barkerhouse and the lands late belonging to Lawrence

---

[1] *The Barcroft Family Papers* (Preston Records Office)

Willson of Bradley (viz. Lawrence Whittam, Edward Marsden and Henry Higgin.)

Item. The sixth form they allot to William Emmott for his lands in Wycollar, Robert Folds of Trawden, John Cunliffe for his wife's lands in Winewall, Henry Shaw for his lands at Blackow, and James Hartley of Wanlas and Alexander Hartley of Blackow for his house and lands at Blackow.

Item. The seventh form they allot to John Hargreaves of Barrowford, Henry Blakey of Blackow, and Christopher Hartley of Barrowford for a house and lands bought of James Shackleton.

Item. The eight they appoint for Ambrose Barcroft for his house and tenement belonging to John Smith, tenant, Thomas Acrondly of Acrondly, Richard Holgate of Foulridge and William Hartley of Ackrondly.

Item. The ninth they appoint to James Emmott for Delves land, and for his wife's land, and John Bannister for his wife's land at Southfield and Richard Hargreaves of Edge-end.

Item. The tenth they appoint to Nicholas Townley, esq., for James Ridehalgh's tenement called Holehouses, Lawrence Ormerod of Schofield and the heirs of one Dawson, also Henden lands late belonging to Robert Rushton (that is to say) Joseph Rushton, John Lee, Edward and James Whitaker and Richard Kippax for Birdielands. [1]

Item. They appoint to James Wilson of Southfield, Gyles Hammond for Catlow lands, Robert Hargreaves for land at Southfield and Henry Lee of Catlow.

Item. The twelfth they appoint to the heirs of Christopher Folds, for lands in Barrowford, William Hanson or his wife for church lands in Colne, Nicholas Parker for part of Mitton's land and Nicholas Townley esq., for Rycroft tenement at Standroyd, Henry Hartley at Barrowford for part of Mitton's land and Lawrence Ormeroyd for Michael Greenwood's house and Thos. Sutcliffe for Christopher Fold's house in Barrowford.

Item. The thirteenth they appoint to Geoffrey Shackleton of Trawden for a house in Trawden, James Shackleton for the same, for land of James Hartley alias Lores in occupation of John Bancroft and John Hartley, son of Roger, and the lands lately belonging to Henry Hartley of Trawden viz. James Hartley for Lores lands, Roger Folds Christopher Hartley, Robert Hartley of Gilford Clough for several parts of the said land and Robert Folds for James Hartley's land.

Padiham

Dedicated to Saint Leonard, Whitaker states that the present church building at Padiham is too good for its supposed founding around 1440, he dates the structure to the time of Henry

---

[1] *Birdie* was the nickname of certain members of the Hartley family of great Marsden. *Birdielands* appears to appertain to a fowl-rearing operation within the Hendon district of Great Marsden owned by the Hartleys

VIII, the body of the church having been rebuilt in 1776. He quotes a memorandum from the Towneley records:

'Whereas Kynge Henry ye VI did graunt unto one Mr. Joh. Maresheale a lycense, dated VII Feb. an. regni XXX. to purchase certayne landes for ye use of a chauntrie priest at ye churche or chapel of Padyham, which sayde lycense of late tyme was in custodye of Syr Jhon Townley, knt. ye sayde Syr Jhon hath putte ye saide lycense into ye sure custodye of ye abbott and convent of Whalley forever.'

The following is a list of the incumbents at St. Leonard's, up to the time of Whitaker writing his *'History of Whalley - 1881'*:

Oliver Hall	chantry 1460	John Breres A.M	1644
William Boothe	chantry 1470	Roger Barton	1665
Hugh Hargreaves	1538	Elisha Clarkson	1676
John Hey	1551	Robert Sheffield	1685
John Baxter	1573	John Grundy	1694
Walter Borset	possibly	John Holmes	Kildwick
Robert Hill	1627	John Fishwick	1793
John Burtomwood	1633	John Adamson	1793 -

Padiham parish church served the large estates of both Gawthorpe and Huntroyd. The manor of Padiham was never granted out following the Norman Conquest; the de Lacy Inquisition of 1311 shows there to have been two free tenants, John Whitacre had been granted a total of 44 acres and Richard, son of Mawe, had twenty-five acres. By the year 1800 the patron of the church was L.P Starkie, esquire, of the nearby Huntroyd Hall.

Clitheroe

We have seen that Clitheroe Castle held the chapel of St. Michael; outside the castle walls there is also the church of St. Mary Magdalen. There has been a church on this site since at least 1122 when the building was granted to the Priory of St. John in Pontefract. The castle chapel never had a graveyard and consequently the burials took place at St. Mary Magdalen; before the founding of outlying churches, such as Newchurch-in-Pendle and Newchurch-in-Rossendale, some of the inhabitants of the forests had to carry their dead for a distance of almost twenty miles to Clitheroe.

The tower of St. Mary's dates from 1400 and the church has an interesting sundial which is thought to date from 1757 (although the base is much earlier). Besides three crosses dating to the tenth century the churchyard also holds a number of stone coffins, these are thought to date to the thirteenth century. Near to the coffins is a large block of stone, said locally to be part of a Roman pillar, and the stones from the early Norman church here are contained in the south entrance.

Incumbents at Clitheroe

Hugo Calellanus de Clyderhow	Henry 11
Petrus Caps. de Clyderhow	Henry 11
Henricus Clericus de Clyderhow	---------
Johannes son of Henry Cap, de Clyderhow	13 Edward 111
Henry de Mitton	1379
William Slater	1551
Edward Lawson	1569
Martyn Dyckson	15?8
William Richardson	uncertain
Robert Marsden	1657
William Banckes	1672
Stephen More	1696
Thomas Taylor	1701 buried 1737
James Cowgill	1743
James King D.D	1743
Thomas Wilson B.D	1775

St. Mary Magdalen
Clitheroe

Buried at St. Mary Magdalen, in 1682, was the famous metallurgist, Dr. John Webster, who wrote *'The History of Metallurgy'* and *'A Display of Supposed Witchcraft.'* Webster was also a historian and occultist, following his death a commemorative brass plaque was placed on the nave of St. Mary's, it shows the following mysterious diagram and inscription (translated from the Latin):[1]

Those who understand this figure will know me to have understood it too. Here lies a man unknown and sunken in a sea if contumeley, yet bore it well and cherished much of times gone by, that he might learn the secrets of wise men and come to know what fire and water do. John Hyphanyes or Webster, in Spinosa, his country house amongst the hills in a woodland Yorkshire parish where cuckoo sings.

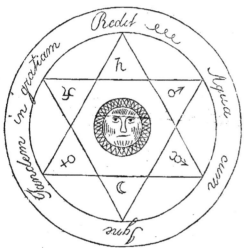

Born Feb 3 1610 and parted from this life at 72, June 18 1682. And thus on his death-bed bade farewell to this world. Golden peace to the living and eternal rest to the dead.

With fire and water he will at last be restored to grace.

Newchurch-in-Pendle

There is evidence for a *chapel of ease* having existed at Newchurch in the year 1250, the later chapel was dedicated by the Bishop of Chester on the 1st October 1544. The church of St. Mary's at Newchurch served the Forest of Pendle when the nearest churches would be at Colne and Burnley.

Each of the forest booths that St. Mary's served, Goldshaw, Barley, Wheatley, Roughlee and Old Laund elected a church warden, eventually the booths of Barley and Wheatley were combined leaving the church with four wardens.

The tower of St. Mary's was restored in 1653 and again in 1712, this part survives yet another rebuild in 1740. The church was restored both in 1884 and 1902. The parsons at Newchurch were reliant upon rents from the glebe-lands until the 1920s when these lands were sold in

---

[1] E. Peel & P. Southern, *The Trials of The Lancashire Witches*, (David & Charles, 1969/1972)

order to increase the parson's 'living.' Generally the parishioners from Roughlee westwards through Pendle would attend St. Mary's whilst the villagers of Blacko and Barrowford would attend the church at Colne (or, more rarely, Whalley). Below the clock on the tower of St. Mary's can be seen an oval feature, this is widely believed to be symbolic of the all-seeing 'Eye of God.' Although this is a nice story, the feature was designed to be an aperture. This would allow for the sexton, the curate or the churchwardens within the building to monitor the main church approach; this was necessary in order to begin bell-ringing at the approach of a wedding (funeral bells were tolled long before the cortege approached the church). This would also provide for light within the staircase to the upper tower. The tower of Whalley parish church also has a very similar rectangular window in exactly the same position as the Newchurch 'eye.' It is probable that the placing of this type of small orifice stems from the earlier times when churches incorporated battlements etc., as forms of defence.

Curates and incumbent curates at St. Mary's, Newchurch-in-Pendle

Johnnes Specke	1529	John Anderton	1721-1731
William Salter	1532	Henry Ward	1731-1735
Thomas Hird	1537	William Habbs	1735-1767
Giles Parker	1562	Wilfred Burton	1767-1791
Nicholas Rishton	1567	Thomas Higginson	1791-1804
James Ellis	1568	William Barton	1804-1814
Thomas Varley	1569	John Whittaker	1814-1825
Christr Nuttall	1607-1608	John Rushton	1825-1843
Johan. Town	1610-1611	T.M.Gosling	1843-1865
John	1620-1621	Commonwealth: Edward Lapage	1650
John Nowell	1621-1623	**Vicars:--------------**	--------------
Rcd Armistead	1625-1626	Nicholas Germon	1865-1870
Thomas Palem	1627-1635	James H Horrox	1870-1905
Robert Hole	1635-1636	Stephen P Duval	1905-1908
John Horrocks	1637-1638	Geoffrey C Fletcher	1909-1912
Robert Hartley	1669-1673	Charles C Weston	1913-1937
Paul Byrsteme	1673-1675	Edgar Smithies	1937-1944
Wm Wilkinson	1675-1683	John Barnes Wallis	1944-1951
Thomas Ingham	1683-1685	William Frankland	1952-1960
Thomas Ellis	1690-96	John N Rome	1961-1980
Jon Glasbrook	1717-1721	John P Richardson	1981-

Around 1950 Jean Walton wrote a booklet entitled *Pendle Forest Folk* covering the history of Newchurch from around the time of her birth in the late nineteenth century. She records that from its inception in the sixteenth century the church of St. Mary's was known as *New Cross* and in later times as *The Cathedral of the Forest*. Jean's grandfather, Henry Bailey of Wheatley, was a stone-mason and worked on the church during the 1852 rebuild and restoration.

St. Mary's, Newchurch-in-Pendle

The School House served as the accommodation for the school master in the early twentieth century, the bottom room, which opens on to the churchyard, was known as *'The Bone House'* due to the fact that it was once used as the charnel house, bones from pre-existing burials found during the digging of graves were stored here. Funerals usually employed a couple of jet-black Belgian horses to pull the hearse; as soon as the cortege was sighted, at the top of Nanny Maud Hill, the church bells began to toll 'the passing bell.' The custom of giving out the Arval Cake was still practiced in the early twentieth century, this was a form of sponge cake given to the mourners, along with a glass of wine; this practice appears to have been peculiar to the Lancashire area.

Jean tells a couple of stories of 'Kirk' people during the later 1800s: The first is an illustration of the reserved attitude, and tendency to understatement, adopted by most country folk: An old farmer who lived at Dimpenly (the small valley below the village of Newchurch) had been drinking with his cronies in the village's Lamb Inn. On his way home down Sparble Lane, as it passes St. Mary's graveyard, he happened to meet with what he described as a "*boggart.*" This took the form of a white headless figure carrying something under its arm. As the figure approached it dropped its burden which rolled to a halt at the farmer's feet. The old man glanced down and saw a bony head staring up at him; being neither astonished or frightened the farmer pointed down at the skull and addressed the apparition "*Hey up lad, tha's dropped summat!*"

In the later nineteenth century a vicar of Newchurch had been visiting friends at Whitehough and had a most convivial evening, too convivial in fact because as he tottered on his way back to the vicarage he fell in the river near Narrowgates Mill. Fortunately he managed to crawl out of the water and fell asleep on the river bank. The following morning two farm-hands were passing Narrowgates when they heard a loud snoring noise. Climbing down the river banking to investigate they took one look, found it was the parson, and went on their way with these parting words "*It's nobbut t' parson! He won't be needed 'til Sunday!*"

The reverend G. C. Fletcher (1909-1912) is remembered by Jean as being a high-church man and a good person to his flock. He had been moved to the fresh air of Newchurch from a very large and poor parish in London - no doubt this move was for the benefit of his health. Rev. Fletcher was a vegetarian, this was beyond the comprehension of the local farming community; when he first arrived one of the village elders was heard to remark that *"t' Parson looks as if he needs a good slice o' summat that's been driven through a gate!"*

Newchurch Village; 1910

The 'Castle' and 'Bastille' are behind the trees on the left. Behind the group is the Old Friendly Inn and facing down the hill is the Lamb Inn

Downham and Twiston

The unspoilt village of Downham shows its lineage in the *ham* suffix indicating a Saxon settlement. The manor of Downham was owned by a Saxon named Aufray (a corruption of Alfred) who granted it to Ilbert de Lacy, the manor was re-granted to the Dyneley family in 1353 by the Duke of Lancaster. The Starkie family of Huntroyd are descended from the Dyneley family; in 1558 the manor passed to Roger Assheton and it has remained in the ownership of this family to the present day.

The parish church at Downham is dedicated to St. Leonard, the existence of a church here is mentioned in the eleventh century. A major restoration of St. Leonard's was undertaken in 1910 during which Saxon, or early Norman, foundations were uncovered. The parish of Downham covers an area of over 3,000 acres within the townships of Downham and Twiston, it was originally part of the parochial chapelry of the parish of Whalley. When the abbey at Whalley was established it is recorded that the Chaplain of Downham received a stipend of four marks and the tithes of the area were worth ten marks.

The present tower of St. Leonard's appears to have been built in the fifteenth century but the rest of the church from that period was pulled down in 1800. The body of the church was rebuilt but not to a high standard, this was demolished prior to the 1914-1918 War and replaced by the present building to the design of the architect Sir Mervyn McCartney.[1]

We have seen that Richard Assheton co-purchased the Whalley Abbey estate, including

---

[1] *Downham Parish Church,* (DPCC booklet, 1950)

Downham, at the *Dissolution of the Monasteries;* upon his death, in 1578, Richard left no children and so the manor of Downham passed to his great-nephew, Richard Assheton, who died in 1625. The de Lacy Inquisition of 1311 shows the state of land holdings in Downham whereby 127 acres was let to *tenants at will:* 10 oxgangs in bondage *to certain natives:* 9 tofts to *certain cotarii* and a toft and 2 acres to *Henry de Downham.* Freemen of Downham were Walter de Waddyngton, Henry de Dounom, Henry son of Henry, Alan son of Robert, Thomas de Chatburne, Hugh de Donom and the heirs of Richard the Clerk.

The halmotes of *Penelton, Worston and Downom* were worth £1 per year, the total rental payable to the lord was £7 14s 3d. The neighbouring township of Twiston was held under John de Twisleton around 1300, and in 1327 John de Dyneley granted his capital messuage (manor house) and water mill in Twistleton to Richard de Greenacres. The village had its own chapel, as is shown in the Whalley Abbey records; this was dedicated to St. Lawrence but has been lost, the site is marked on earlier maps as being on the road from Lowergate to Ings End.

An interesting early custom, long abandoned, was the Downham village wakes – here a man and woman dressed as the king and queen and a Crown was carried before them in procession. This was traditionally said to be a 'right' bestowed upon the village in ancient times. When this practice died out it was replaced by the custom of around ten women chasing the village men-folk on Easter Tuesdays. When caught the men were grabbed and lifted, or 'heaved,' from their feet in a practice said to allude to the resurrection of Christ. The last 'true' Downham Queen is said to have died in Burnley in the early nineteenth century.

The old Downham stocks

Such, then, was the early development of the Forest of Pendle

Part Two

The Lancashire Witch Conspiracy

Roger Nowell's Lament

We gather close in our justice halls
To damn the poor of the Greenwood tall,
Pious minds in manors grand,
Yet dark we wring our bloodied hands

Full fine are we with titles close
As we turn their words to gain our cause,
And Aye! We tell of sharp danger posed
When Demdike steps on the Devil's toes

Through Pendle's ground in man's time to come
How will they judge of our deeds now done,
And what will they say of these days gone by
When we took their poor and hanged them high?

And of the damned in death's dungeon sour
Where spirit ebbs in night's dark hour,
Their dread will sound o'er Gallows Hill,
Who fought for them then,
Who weeps for them still?

J A Clayton

Contents: Part Two

The Lancashire Witch Conspiracy

Chapter One

The Lancashire Witch Trials of 1612 are commonly held to have been the most important event of their type within British history. Carried out by religious zealots, and those in search of fame and fortune, the witch-hunts of our medieval and early modern past were protracted and often brutal. Little wonder, then, that the Pendle Witches still hold a strong influence over the forest psyche; the local historian can carry out very little research without bumping up against the legend of the Witches.

In 1911 a historian by the name of Frank Hird published a collection of stories relating to the county of Lancashire. This publication, entitled *'Lancashire Stories,'* can still be found in local studies libraries and included an essay covering the legend of the Lancashire Witches. Because of the clear and concise nature of Hird's text it is fitting to include it here as a 'potted' introduction to the subject. Furthermore, it is interesting to see the approach of a writer from almost one-hundred years ago; it is apparent from this that the subject of the Pendle Witches has progressed little in the interim. Until now little has been known of the lives of the main cast within the story that was not known in the nineteenth century. To redress this there are new observations, facts and clues within the following text of *'The Lancashire Witch Conspiracy;'* these will hopefully extend our present knowledge of the subject and allow for a sound basis on which further research can be carried out. Here, then, is Frank Hird's essay:

The Lancashire Witches

▷In the early part of the seventeenth century the inhabitants of the Forest of Pendle, with few exceptions, must have been miserably poor and ignorant, since they had little communication with the outside world. Superstition exists in the district to this day. When James I was on the throne it held absolute domination over the simple minds of the inhabitants. And no belief was stronger than that in witchcraft. Upon this belief two old women, called Elizabeth Southerns and Anne Whittle, but better known in the chronicles of witchcraft as Old Demdike and Old Chattox, had played for many years with great success. Both these women were old, and both pretended to possess supernatural powers, and were therefore bitterly opposed to one another. Each woman had her following amongst the credulous peasantry, and in their anxiety to outvie one another each represented herself as more death-dealing, destructive and powerful than her neighbour, and the one who could show the most damage done to man or beast (whether real or not was quite immaterial) was more likely to get a larger custom for her charms and philtres, and horrible incantations.

It is a curious fact that, despite the bitter rivalry existing between these two women, the son-in-law of one of them, whose own wife was afterwards executed as a witch, paid the other an annual dole of meal to be exempt from her charms and witchcraft. As one of the many writers on the subject says, *"Where the possession of a commission from the powers of darkness was thus eagerly and ostentatiously paraded, every death, the cause of which was not perfecly obvious, whether it ended in a sudden termination or a slow and gradual decline, would be placed to the general account of one of the two agents of the devil, in those parts, as the party responsible for these unclaimed dividends of mortality. Did a cow go mad, or was a horse unaccountably affected with the staggers, the same solution was always at hand to clear negligence and save the trouble of inquiry; and so far from modestly disclaiming these atrocities, the only struggle on the parts of Mothers Demdike and Chattox would be which should first appropriate them. And in all this it must not be forgotten that their own credulity was at least as great as the credulity of their neighbours, and that each had the power in question was so much an admitted point that she had long ceased, in all probability, to entertain any doubt on the subject."*

Little wonder therefore that the doings, real or imaginary, of these two old women should become a scandal throughout the Forest of Pendle, and when James I launched forth his famous treatise on witchcraft and demonology, *"one of His Majesty's Justices in those parts, a very religious honest gentleman painful in the service of his country,"* Roger Nowell, took up the case of these self-accused witches. They were brought before him and both having made confession, they were committed to take their trial at the next Lancaster Assizes on charges of various murders and witchcrafts. At that time the Clerk of the Assize Courts was one Master Thomas Potts, who left a full record of the proceedings. Besides Mother Demdike and Mother Chattox, their two daughters, Alison Device and Anne Redfearne, were also committed. Master Potts tells us that the four women had not been in Lancaster Castle a week *"when their children and friends being abroad at libertie, laboured a speciall meeting at Malking Tower in the Forrest of Pendle, upon goocl-fryday, within a weeke after they were committed, of all the most dangerous, wicked, and damnable witches in the country, farre and neare. Upon good-fryday they met, according to solemne appoyntment, solemnized this greate festivall day according to their former order, with great cheare, merry company, and much conference. In the end, in this great assemblie it was decreed that M. Covell. (he was the gaoler of Lancaster Castle) by reason of his Office, shall be slaine before the 'next Assises, the Castle of Lancaster to be blown up."*

The evidence that this great meeting of witches ever took place was based solely upon the testimony of a child of nine, Jennet Device, the granddaughter of Mother Demdike. The child was intelligent and cunning and there is an ugly suspicion that she glibly repeated a lesson she had been taught. Who taught her the lesson can never be known, but the activity which Roger Nowell displayed in arresting all those who were said to have attended the witches' convention on Good Friday, casts considerable doubts upon his motives. Amongst those arrested was Alice Nutter, a lady of good family and a fair estate at Rough Lea. There is every reason to believe that she was in no way implicated in the doings of the so-called witches, and that the child Jennet Device was bribed by some of her relatives, who in the event of her death would inherit her property,to introduce her name. In addition to this Roger Nowell was one of her bitterest enemies: Alice Nutter won a lawsuit against him with regard to the boundary of their respective properties, he having claimed a portion of her land. The only charges made against her were that she had been present at the meeting at Malkin Tower on Good Friday, and had joined with Mother Demdike and Elizabeth Device in bewitching to death an old man called Mitton. The only witnesses against her were Elizabeth Device and her two children James and Jennet.

As a result of Jennet Device's evidence Mr. Justice Nowell sent as prisoners to Lancaster, Elizabeth Device, daughter of Old Demdike, and her son James, Katherine Hewitt, John and Jane Bulrock, Isabel Robey, and Margaret Pearson, as well as Alice Nutter, making in all twelve persons accused of *"the most barbarous and damnable Practises, Murthers wicked and devilish conspiracies."* The confession made by Mother Demdike to Roger Nowell on the second of April could only have sprung from hallucination or have been deliberate lying. Master Potts says, *"She was a very old woman, about the age of Fourscore yeares, and had been a Witch for fiftie yeares. She dwelt in the Forrest of Pendle, in waste places, fitte for her profession. What she's commited in her time no man knows."* Mother Demdike in her confession fixed the period of her practice in witchcraft at twenty years. She said that one day as she was returning home from a begging expedition she met, near a stone pit in Gouldshey, a spirit or a devil in the shape of a boy, one half of his coat black and the other brown. He bade her stay, saying to her that if she would give him her soul, she should have anything she wanted. Old Demdike inquired the spirit's name and was told it was Tib, and *"in hope of such gaine as was promised by the sayd Devill or Tib, was contented to give her Soule to the said Spirit."* During the next five or six years Tib appeared to Mother Demdike at various times and *"always about Daylight Gate,"* that is towards the evening, asking her what she would have or do. She always answered nothing. But about the end of the sixth year, one Sunday morning as she sat asleep with a child upon her knee, the spirit appeared to her in the shape of a brown dog, and as she was only wearing a smock it succeeded in drawing blood from under her left arm. Awaking suddenly she cried, *"Jesus, save my child,"* but she had no power to say *"Jesus save me,"* whereupon the brown dog vanished and for a space of eight weeks, she was *"almost stark mad."*

The only name mentioned in Mother Demdike's confession is that of a man called Baldwyn, who, when he and her granddaughter Alison Device, went to ask for money, called them witches and drove them away. Mother Demdike was blind, but as her granddaughter was leading her away, Tib appeared and said to her *"Revenge thee of him,"* to which Old Demdike replied *"Revenge thee either of him or his."* The spirit vanished out of her sight and she never saw him again.The most curious fact about this case is the diabolical readiness with which the Device family not only confessed they were witches, but testified against other people and against their own flesh and blood. Old Demdike in her confession said nothing as to any evil befalling Richard Baldwyn, but her granddaughter, Alison Device, said that the day after Baldwyn ordered them off his land, she heard that one of his children had fallen ill, and that after languishing for about a year, had died, and upon oath this woman stated she verily thought *"that her said grandmother did bewitch the said child to death."*

Old Demdike at the end of her confession said, *"That the speediest way to take a man's life away by Witchcraft, is to make a Picture of Clay, like unto the shape of the person whom they mean to kill, and dry it thoroughly; and when they would have them to be ill in any one place more than another, then take a Thorne or Pinne, and prick it in that part of the Picture you would so have to be ill: and when you would have any part of the Body to consume away, then take that part of the Picture and burne it. And when they would haye the whole Body to consume away, then take the remnant of the said Picture and burne it: and so thereupon by that means, the Body shall die."*

Mother Chattox whom Master Potts describes as *"a very old, withered, spent, and decrepit creature, her sight almost gone,"* made her confession after a few weeks' imprisonment in Lancaster Castle. She declared that she was *"seduced to condescend and agree to become subject unto that devilish abominable profession of Witchcraft"* through the wicked persuasion and counsel of Mother Demdike. She also had her familiar spirit, who was called Fancie. She declared that at the time of the initiation she heard Tib say to Mother Demdike that she should have *"gold, Silver, worldly Wealth at her will. And at the same time she saith, there was victuals viz. Flesh, Butter, Cheese, Bread, and Drink and bid them eat enough. And after their eating, the devil called Fancie, and the other spirit calling himself Tib, carried the remnant away. And she saith that although they did eat, they were never the fuller, nor better for the same; and that at their said Banquet, the said spirits gave them light to see what they did, although they neither had fire nor candle light; and that there were both the spirits and devils."*

The old woman admitted having bewitched to death one man. Nor were women alone concerned in this chapter of horrors. James Device, Old Demdike's grandson, not only confessed to his own participation in the craft, but testified against his mother, his grand-mother and his sister Alison. His evidence was given in the matter-of-fact way which distinguishes that of all those who made confessions, they all speak as if witchcraft were an ordinary every-day reality, and as if evil spirits went about the countryside in various disguises. James Device declared that on a certain Shrove Tuesday, his grandmother bade him go to church to receive the sacrament. He was not to eat the bread but to bring it away with him, and hand it to *"such a Thing"* as he should meet on his way homeward. But he disobeyed and ate the wafer. On his way home, when about fifty-yards from the church, he was met by a *"Thing in the shape of a hare"* which asked him if he bad brought the bread according to his grandmother's directions. He answered that he had not, whereupon the Thing threatened to tear him to pieces, but when he called upon the name of God, it disappeared.

A few days later a thing in the shape of a brown dog met him near the new church in Pendle. It asked him for his soul, promising him in return that he should be avenged on his enemies. To this Device made answer that his soul was not his to give but was his Saviour Jesus Christ's, yet as much as was his to give he was contented to yield to the spirit. Within two or three days of this meeting, James Device went to Carre Hall, where Mrs. Townley, after charging him and his mother with having stolen some of her turf, bade him begone. As he went *"forth of the door the said Mistress Townley gave him a knock between the shoulders."* A day or two later a black dog met him, and reminding him of the insult put upon him by Mrs. Townley, directed him to make a clay image like Mrs. Townley and he would help him to destroy her. Bidding Device to call him Dandy, the spirit disappeared. The next morning he made an image of clay of Mrs. Townley, and dried it the same night by the fire. Every day he crumbled away a piece of this image. At the end of a week it was all gone and two days later Mrs. Townley died. In the following Lent, one John Duckworth of the *Lawnde* promised James Device an old shirt, but when he went to get the gift, Duckworth refused to give it to him, and he was driven away. As he was going out of the house, the spirit Dandy appeared to him, and said *"Thou didst touch the said Duckworth."* This James Device denied but the spirit answered, *"Thou didst touch him and therefore I haye power of him...."* whereupon Device expressed his wish to the spirit that Duckworth might be killed. Within a week Duckworth was dead.

"Who but Witches can be proofes, and so witnesses of the doings of Witches?" asks Master Potts, *"since all their Meetings, Conspiracies, Practices, and Murthers are the works of darkness? But to discover this wicked fury God hath not only raised meanes beyond expectation by the voluntarie Confession and Accusation of all that are gone before to accuse this Witch (being Witches, and thereby witnesses of her doings), but after they were committed by meanes of a child to discover her to be one and a Principall in that wicked assembly at Malking Tower, and so devise such a damnable course for the deliverance of their friends from Lancaster, as to kill the Gaoler and blow up the Castle, wherein the Devill did but labour to assemble them together, and so being known, to send them all one way...."* Such was the arraignment of Katherine Hewitt.

She was accused of being present at the famous convention of Witches on the previous Good Friday at Malkin Tower. The only evidence against her was that of the Devices – mother, son and daughter. James Device swore that not only was Katherine Hewitt present at the meeting at Malkin Tower, but had there confessed that she had killed the child of a man named Foulds at CoIne. Elizabeth Device gave the same evidence. That imp of unspeakable wickedness, Jennet Device, whom Master Potts conceived to have been divinely inspired for the rooting out of witches, completed the chain of evidence against the unhappy woman. Called into court, she was directed by the judge to identify Katherine Hewitt. Without the least hesitation, the child went up to her and, taking her by the hand, accused her of being a witch. She described the place in which she had sat at the witches' feast on Good Friday at Malkin Tower, and then proceeded to relate their conversation, *"without any manner of contrarieties."* Upon this evidence Katherine Hewitt was condemned to death, and because she protested her innocence to the end, was branded as an impenitent.

Old Mother Dcmdike died in prison before the trials took place, a victim of ill-treatment. The 'confessions' made by this old woman, her daughter, and two grandchildren, as well as that of Old Chattox, were, in all probability, given under the promise that if they told the truth their lives would be spared. There is no record of any of the Lancashire witches being put to the torture, although this horrible means of extorting confessions was resorted to in other parts of the country. Yet remembering the superstitious belief in witchcraft which characterised the age, a belief that in the opinion of some of the most enlightened men warranted any means being used to extract the truth, Master Potts' description of James Device's appearance when he was brought to trial, gives rise to the assumption that in his case, at any rate, torture had been employed. We must remember that Master Potts was an official of the court, and that great stress was laid, both in his account and in the judge's summing up, of the fact that the confessions were "voluntarie." Of James Device he says, *"This wicked and miserable Wretch, whether by practise, or meanes, to bring himself to some untimely death and thereby to avoid his Tryall by his Countrey, and just judgement of the law; or ashamed to bee openly charged with so many devilish practises, and so much innocent blood as hee had spilt; or by reason of his imprisonment so long time before his Trial (which was with more favour, comisaration and reliefe than hee deserved) I know not: But being brought forward to the Barre, to receive his Tryal before this worthie judge, and so Honourable and Worshipfulle an assembly of justices for this service, was so insensihle, weake and unable in all thinges as he could neither speake, heare, or stand, but was holden up when hee was brought to the place of his arraignement to receive his trial!."*

James Device certainly deserved his fate, for, in addition to testifying against his mother, Elizabeth Device and his sister Alison, he was instrumental in sending three absolutely innocent women to their death - Katherine Hewitt, whose case has been already mentioned, Anne Redfern, and Alice Nutter. There seems every reason to believe that these two last women were accused of witchcraft by the Nutter family. Anne Redfern was the daughter of Old Chattox, but there was nothing to show that she had taken any part in her mother's supposed magic arts of witchcraft. Some eighteen years previously a young man, named Robert Nutter, had made improper advances to Anne Redfern and had been repulsed. Six months later he died of a languishing sickness, and this was the evidence on which Anne Redfern was hanged! Old Demdike declared to Justice Nowell that she had seen Anne Redfern and Old Chattox making three clay figures of Robert Nutter, his wife, and his father. James Device said that he saw three figures of clay, half-a-yard in length, at the end of the Redferns' house; one of these figures Anne Redfern was crumbling in her hands. He could not say who the figures represented. Robert Nutter's sister declared that there had been a quarrel between her brother and Anne Redfern about Whitsuntide, some eighteen or nineteen years before. Her brother had told her of the quarrel, and within a week or a fortnight he had fallen ill, *"and so languished until about Candlemas then next after, and then died."* During the time of his sickness Robert Nutter *"did a hundred times at least say that the said Anne Redfern and her associates had bewitched him to death."* She also said that her father, Christopher Nutter, shortly after her brother's death, also fell sick, and after languishing for some months he, too, died. The elder Nutter likewise *"did sundry times say that he was bewitched, but named nobodie that should have done the same."*

The evidence of John Nutter, Robert's brother, completed the case against the unhappy Anne Redfern. He said that about Christmas time some eighteen or nineteen years previously, whilst riding from Burnley with his brother Robert and his father, he heard the former say *"Father, I am sure I am bewitched by the Chattoxes, Anne Chattox and Anne Redfern her daughter; I pray you cause them to be layd in Lanc.aster Castle."* To this the elder Nutter replied *"Thou art a foolish lad, it is not so, it is thy miscarriage."*

Then Robert Nutter, weeping, said, *"Nay, I am sure that I am bewitched by them, and if ever I come again (he was then ready to go to Sir Richard Shuttleworth in whose service he was), I will procure them to be layd where they shall be glad to bite lice in two with their teeth....."* At this point occurred one of the most moving scenes in this horrible trial. Old Chattox was brought forward to be examined. She admitted making the clay figures, and falling upon her knees she confessed, and, with tears streaming down her withered cheeks, implored the mercy of the court for her daughter, whose innocence she protested. This appeal had no influence upon the besotted prejudices of the judge and jury who condemned this woman to death for the 'murder' of Robert Nutter upon evidence that was only hearsay, and was clearly inspired by the spite of enemies.

A shadow even more sinister rests upon the case of Alice Nutter. In those days to be accused of witchcraft was practically to be condemned. The ordinary rules of evidence were of little or no avail to the accused. She might bring the most convincing proof that she was fifty miles away from the spot on which she was declared to have taken part in the witches' orgy. The firm belief in the power of witches to ride through the air, to transport themselves where they would in a few moments, discounted all such evidence. Amongst this band of wretched women Alice Nutter was the only person of any condition or degree. The Demdikes and Chattoxes were practically mendicants. Alice Nutter was a lady of considerable fortune, of good family, and as Heywood says in his *Lancashire Witches, "I knew her a good woman and well bred, of an unquestion'd carriage, well reputed amongst her neighbours, reckoned with the best....."*

Master Potts, in his description of the trial of Alice Nutter, declared there were two types of persons who practised witchcraft: one which was in great misery and poverty, *"for such the Devill allures to follow him by promising great riches and worldly commodity; others though rich yet burn in a desperate desire of revenge,"* This he advances as the reason for Alice Nutter, *"a rich woman who had a great estate, and children of good hope: in the common opinion of the world a good temper, free from envy or malice...."* finding herself accused of witchcraft. The charges against her were both childish and absurd. She was accused of having killed Henry Mitton by witchcraft, because he had refused to give Old Mother Demdike a penny! The judge and jury accepted the evidence of Elizabeth and James Device that they had heard Old Demdike say she and Alice Nutter had bewitched Henry Mitton to death. The second charge was that she had taken part in the meeting at Malkin Tower on Good Friday, and here again the evidence of Elizabeth and James Device and that of the horrible child Jennet, satisfied the jury. As in the ease of Katherine Hewitt, Jennet Device identified Alice Nutter in the court, and taking her by the hand accused her of being a witch, describing the place she had oecupied at the feast, and the whole of the conferences which took place, It was in vain that Alice Nutter protested her innocence, but to quote Master Potts, *"Nothing would serve, for Old Demdike, Old Chattox and others had charged her with innocent blood which cries out for*

Revenge and will be satisfied. And therefore Almightie God, in his justice hath cut her down."

There can be little doubt but that Alice Nutter was the victim of a foul conspiracy. Her children showed the greatest anxiety that she should confess; neither they nor any member of her family made any effort to save her, or to clear her from the unsubstantiated charges brought against her. They accepted the finding of the court that their mother and kinswoman was a witch simply because the Devices, who were confessed witches, had said that she was one. Who knows what bitter family quarrels lay behind this appalling passiveness? We have no record of the character of Alice Nutter. She may have been a hard woman, or, on the other hand, she may have had bad children; but whatever lies hidden, it is impossible to dismiss the conviction that, in order to secure her money, her own family were passive, if not active, agents in her destruction.

Some one must have coached that child of darkness, Jennet Device, and rewards or promises of pardon doubtless bought the ridiculous evidence of Elizabeth and James Device. Alice Nutter died maintaining her innocence. Potts says, *"She died very impenitent; inasmuch as her owne children were never able to move her to confess any particular offence, or declare anything, even in articulo mortis, which was a very fearfull thing to all that were present."*

The trial of Elizabeth Device followed that of Old Chattox, she is described as having been branded with a preposterous mark in Nature, even from her birth, which was her left eye standing lower than the other, the one looking down, the other looking up, so strangely deformed, as the best who were present in that honourable assembly and great audience did affirm, they had not often seen the like. When Jennet Device was put up to give evidence against her mother, the latter broke out into such a storm of curses and reproaches that the child *"with weeping tears cried out to my Lord the judge, and told him she was not able to speak in the presenee of her mother."* Nothing would silence Elizabeth Device, and the learned judge, seeing in her curses and threats nothing but an attempt to terrify the child into withdrawing the statements she had already made to Mr. Nowel, ordered her removal from the court, Jennet was then placed upon a table in the presence of the whole court, and there gave evidence that her mother was a witch, and that she had frequently seen her familiar spirit, which was called Ball, in the shape of a brown dog, James Device told practically the same story.

On August 13th, the day after their trial, Old Chattox, Anne Redfern, Elizabeth, James and Alison Device, Alice Nutter, Katherine Hewitt, John Bulcock ancl his mothor, were taken to Gallows Hill, amidst the insults and execrations of an infuriated populace, and there they were hanged. Old Chattox and the Devices were convicted on their own confession, but the others were legally murdered on the unsupported testimony of these miserable wretches. Nothing marks more strongly the credulity of the age than the acceptance of the evidence of Jennet Device. Although she confessed to having taken part in her mother's practice of witchcraft, she was pardoned as King's evidence. What became of her after the extinction of her family, which she herself so largely helped to bring about, is not known; but in all probability she dragged out a miserable existence, an outcast, everyone in Pendle Forest pointing the finger of scorn at the murderess of her mother, her brother, and her sister.

There is a tradition, which, if based on fact would show that a retributive punishment awaited her. She is supposed to have heen the Jennet Davies who was condemned to death for witchcraft in 1633, together with Mother Dickinson, but was not executed. ◁

Chapter Two

The Listers of Westby and Jennet Preston

In the March of 1612 the Pendle Witch round-up was gathering pace. There was, however, a precedent for these events and this is where a gentry family, some three-miles to the east of the Pendle Forest (over the Yorkshire border) was causing a stir. The Listers of Westby Hall, an estate just outside the village of Gisburn, had been through trying times. Although the family were certainly not alone in experiencing the pressures caused by the past fifty-years of religious strife the Listers took their inter-family tensions to a new height. The resultant misjustice here saw an innocent woman dragged to the gallows; as it will be seen, as a direct consequence of this nineteen people from Lancashire were to be arraigned on witchcraft charges at the Lancaster Assizes in the following August. This is the story of Jennet Preston of Gisburn.

A name that is synonymous with the Gisburn area of West Craven is that of Lister – the family was first mentioned at Gisburne in 1312 and eventually the title of Lord Ribblesdale applied to this branch of the family, a name that has long been connected with the village through the extensive Ribblesdale estates and Gisburn Park. A potted history of the family is that, in the early fourteenth century, a John Lister of West Derby married Isabel de Bolton who was the widow of Roger de Clitheroe. Isabel was the daughter and co-heiress of John de Bolton, of Bolton-by-Bowland and Middop, bowbearer of the Forest of Bowland and was descended from Leofric, king of Mercia and his wife, Lady Godiva of Coventry, who also had two sons, the youngest of whom was Hereward the Wake. The eldest son was Algar who succeeded Leofric to the throne. Clitheroe was part of Mercia at that time. Hereward became general of the English forces after 1066 and held out on the Isle of Ely.

The Listers of Gisburn therefore hold a direct kinship with the Mercian royal family and the coronet on top of their coat of arms is the heraldic emblem of this connection - this can be seen in the Ribblesdale chapel in Gisburn parish church. The marriage of Isabel de Bolton and John Lister brought the areas of Middop, Rimington, Gisburn and Clitheroe into the Lister family. Adelaide Lister, sister of the fourth Baron Ribblesdale, was the last of the Gisburn Listers and died in 1943. The seat of the Listers was originally at the fortified manor house of Arnoldsbiggin on the edge of the villages of Gisburn and Rimington but in 1520 Thomas Lister married Effamia de Westbye, of neighbouring Westby Hall, and this brought Westby into Lister hands. Arnoldsbiggin was demolished in the 1730s to provide stone for the refurbishment of the Lower Hall (Gisburn Park), this being the property to which the Lister family were to move. [1]

On the site of the present Gisburn Vicarage, to the east of the parish church, once stood a fine Jacobean house belonging to Henry Marsden, one-time Member of Parliament for Clitheroe. In the seventeenth century the Listers had become sufficiently wealthy to be able to buy the lordship of the Manor of Gisburn from the Marsdens. They went on to buy the Rectory of the Church and the house that, unfortunately, they demolished.

---

[1] Baines, *The Listers of West Craven*

Westby Hall; the seat of the Lister family in Gisburn

This sketch shows the Hall during the period of the 1730s when the neighbouring property of Arnoldsbiggin (seen to the left) was being demolished. The materials from this earlier group of building were used to refurbish the Lister property at the Lower Hall in Gisburn

In 1597 a lease records a nice example of the boon work (work carried out in lieu of rent) owing to the lord of the manor by a tenant when Thomas Lister, son and heir of Thomas Lister esquire, of Westby-in-Craven, leases to William Monkes, husbandman, a messuage and land within the rectory of Gisburn at an annual rent of nineteen shillings and six pence plus boon rents of: *'One day ploughing, one day mowing, one day shearing of corn in harvest, two hens at Christmas and four horse loads of coal to be supplied to Westby Hall.'* Also included in the lease are the provisions that George Harrison was to be allowed space within his garden so that he could thatch his new house in Gisburn as required, no ash or elm trees were to be felled and all grain was to be ground at the Lister's mill in the lordship of Newsholme.

A sixteenth century lease shows the hamlet of Admergill, between the Lister lands of Middop and the Nutter lands of Roughlee, being granted to John Lister who never actually took up ownership of the area: *'Lease to John Lister of a tenement in Barnoldswick called Hadmargill now in the tenure of Alexander Hartley, Nicholas Blakey, and Christopher Hanson, and another tenement now or late in the tenure of Christopher Mitchell with the woods and underwoods at a rent of £4: 0s: 8d (for the former 64s. and for the latter 16s: 8d).'*

The Lister family was also prominent at Colne and Thornton-in-Craven following the purchase of the manor there by one William Lister, son of Christopher, in 1556. The extent of the manor at that time was thought to include the manor house, some sixty cottages, a watermill and lands at Hague-in-Craven, Kelbrook and Earby along with the Thornton church advowson. The Listers of Thornton supported Parliament during the Civil War, Sir William Lister fought for this cause at the Battle of Marston Moor in 1644 and the next year saw him commanding the Yorkshire troops. Sir William's eldest son, Captain William Lister, was killed at the Battle of Tadcaster whilst fighting for General Fairfax in 1642. To gain an idea as to the extent of the influence of the Lister family their accounts for the years 1761-1773 included rents due for the estates of the late Thomas Lister at:

Grange Meer, Sawley, Gisburn, Bracewell and Barnoldswick, Hellifield, Swinden, Nappa, Newsholme, Horton, Malham, Grindleton, Bolton and Paythorne; with moduses in lieu of tithe; Rimington, Twiston, Clitheroe, Pendleton, Oldham, Denton, Middleton, Brinnington and Romeley, etc. A list of the estates belonging to Thomas Lister dated 1785 shows that he owned property at Gisburn, Grangemeare, Rimington, Horton, Newsholme, Swinden, Paythorne, Twiston, Bracewell, Barnoldswick, Bolton, Grindleton; Also properties at Malham Water House i.e, East Malham, West Malham, Kirkby Malham; At Clitheroe, Pendleton, Chatburne and also at Whalley rectory, Oldham and Werneth along with a house in George Street in Hanover Square, London. Nineteenth century records showed the local estate tenants in Gisburn, Newsholme, Horton, Paythorne, Gisburn Forest, Rimington, Middop, Mitton, Clitheroe, Sawley, Whalley, Colne, Bolton, Slaidburn, Burnsall, Bracewell, Barnoldswick, Long Preston, Thornton and Burnley.

Jennet Preston

Although the Listers lived in Yorkshire the southern boundaries of their lands ran hard against those of Pendle Forest. Lister lands on White Moor shared a boundary with the forest on Blacko Hillside, the probable site of Malkin Tower here being some four miles from Westby Hall. Events within the Lister household in the year 1607 were to have a resounding effect upon the forest-folk over the border because, in that year Mr. Thomas Lister of Westby Hall died. The following is an abridgement of the evidence used by the prosecution at the Assize Court in York during the 1612 trial of Jennet Preston for the supposed killing of Thomas Lister by means of witchcraft:

The Arraignment
and Triall of Ienet Preston of Gisborne in Crauen, in the Countie of Yorke, at the Assises and generall Gaole-deliuerie, holden at the Castle of Yorke, in the Countie of Yorke, the seuen and twentieth day of Iuly last past. Anno Regni Regis Iacobi Angliæ &c. Decimo & Scotiæ

Thereupon were diuerse Examinations taken and read openly against her, to induce and satisfie the Gentlemen of the Iurie of Life and Death, to finde she was a Witch; and many other circumstances for the death of M. Lister. In the end Anne Robinson and others were both examined, who vpon their Oathes declared against her, That M. Lister lying in great extremitie, vpon his death bedde, cried out vnto them that stood about him; that Ienet Preston was in the house, looke where shee is, take hold of her: for Gods sake shut the doores, and take her, shee cannot escape away. Looke about for her, and lay hold on her, for shee is in the house: and so cryed very often in his great paines, to them that came to visit him during his sicknesse.

Being examined further, they both gaue this in euidence against her, That when Master Lister lay vpon his death-bedde, hee cryed out in great extremitie; Ienet Preston lyes heauie

147

upon me, Prestons wife lies heauie vpon me; helpe me, helpe me: and so departed, crying out against her. These, with many other witnesses, were further examined, and deposed, That Ienet Preston, the Prisoner at the Barre, being brought to M. Lister after hee was dead, & layd out to be wound vp in his winding-sheet, the said Ienet Preston comming to touch the dead corpes, they bled fresh bloud presently, in the presence of all that were there present: Which hath euer beene held a great argument to induce a Iurie to hold him guiltie that shall be accused of Murther, and hath seldome, or neuer, fayled in the Tryall.

Jennet Preston was said to have been *'of Gisborne in Craven in the Countie of Yorke'* and it is likely that she was born Jennet Balderston as, in 1587, a woman of this name married William Preston at Gisburn Parish Church.[1] William was possibly of the Preston family of Giggleswick where, in 1572, Roger Preston and Agnes Lund had a child Alice baptised. Having seen that the Lister estate of Westby ran up to the Pendle Forest boundary, and that Jennet Preston was almost certainly a Balderston before marriage, the following Letter of Attorney sets the old grey-matter in motion:

1496: *William Balderston, clerk, and Edmund Whitehead, chaplain, elected Miles Kippax and James Marsden their attorneys with respect to 'Lande lyeing next Blakhowe within the forrest of Penhill.'*

This might just have a bearing on the Jennet Preston story; Balderston and Whitehead appear to have been granted lands to the east of Blacko (towards White Moor) as either the benefit of a chantry, income for a parish incumbent or both. Who the benefactors, or grantors, of this land were escapes me but we have two clues in that Kippax and Marsden were landowners in the neighbouring parishes of Marsden and Colne whilst members of the Lister family held lands and property throughout these parishes. Coupling the fact that a Colne Lister might have granted lands to his parish and chantry priest, and the fact that the Listers would have owned the lands mentioned in the above Letter of Attorney, we have an interesting possibility. Did Jennet Preston's family actually have the tenure of a slice of the Lister estate? If so, perhaps there was not the massive social gulf between herself and her friend Thomas Lister senior as we have previously taken for granted. We would also have to have to ask if Jennet's position led Thomas Lister junior's persecution of her?

According to the church records Jennet Preston would have been aged thirty-eight years when Thomas Lister died in 1607. Jonathan Lumby makes a strong case for Thomas Lister and Jennet Preston having grown up together in the Gisburn area and they had possibly been life-long friends. Far from being an accusation against Jennet, Lister's deathbed statements could well have been an expression of his wish to have his friend (mistress?) Jennet at his bedside – the term *"she lays heavy on me"* having the meaning of *"she is on my mind."* Lumby shows that Thomas Lister probably collapsed and died at the marriage of his sixteen year-old son, Thomas Lister junior, at Bracewell Church. Thomas senior lay dying and cried out for Jennet in front of the assembled wedding guests and this would be highly embarrassing for his wife, Jane (formerly Jane Greenacres of Worston), and son, Thomas. The latter married Jane Heber, daughter of Thomas Heber of Marton. Having earlier tried and failed to have Jennet Preston

---

[1] Jonathan Lumby, *The Lancashire Witch Craze,* (Carnegie, 1995)

prosecuted for the killing of a child of the Dodgeson family (probably from the Gisburn locality) Lister junior eventually found an unlikely ally in James Device, grandson of Elizabeth Southern of Malkin Tower.

Jennet Preston was said to have taken against the young Lister following his failed attempt to prosecute her for practising witchcraft and James Device stated that she had attended a meeting of witches at Malkin Tower on Good Friday, 10th April 1612 – this was four days after Jennet's acquittal at York. One of the purposes of this *'diabolical'* meeting was, according to James Device, for Jennet Preston to enlist the aid of her neighbours in Pendle to bring about *'the utter ruin and overthrow of the name and the blood of this gentleman.'* In other words, according to the evidence of the young Device, Jennet planned to murder Thomas Lister junior and, just for good measure, his uncle Leonard Lister (1575-1618) of Cowgill on the outskirts of Gisburn. In the year 1600 this Leonard had married Anne Loftus of Coverham Abbey.

.... *'the said Iennet Preston comming to touch the dead corpes, they bled fresh bloud presently.'* Contemporary writers on the subject of witchcraft were dedicated to the empowerment of the dead by finding ways in which a body could communicate with the living. As far as the courts of the day were concerned the bleeding of a corpse when touched by the supposed murderer was damning evidence of guilt. In reality there are circumstances under which a corpse, shortly following demise, can be seen, or caused, to bleed but the evidence quoted in witchcraft and murder trials rarely said exactly from which part of the body this blood issued. Surgeons of the day were fond of *'bleeding'* ill people so as to relieve the body of *'stagnant humours'* – a corpse could therefore carry any number of fresh wounds on the skin surface, a suspect being forced to touch one of these lesions shortly following death could cause blood to well up, even if only a droplet or two.

The other obvious explanation for a corpse bleeding is that the witnesses lied about the appearance of blood. In the case of Jennet Preston the witnesses to the event were described as *'many others present,'* Lister's servant, Anne Robinson, being by inference one of these. It has to be remembered that a servant within a large, important household at this time would have 'followed the party-line' of their master. In reality the supposedly extinct medieval feudal system still applied (albeit in a watered-down fashion) to the larger estates such as Westby. It has to be a consideration, therefore, that the witnesses to the damning of Jennet Preston were 'guided' by Lister's determination to eradicate Jennet from his life – to what extent did the will of their master cause a conflict within the minds of the witnesses within the legal and moral ethics of lying under oath?

Having his witnesses in place and his case prepared young Lister enlisted the aid of his father-in-law, magistrate Thomas Heber of the neighbouring village of Marton, and had Jennet indicted at the July 1612 York Assizes where she was summarily convicted and executed on the Knavesmire (the present site of York racecourse). Many friends, family and neighbours of Jennet vociferously protested her innocence, probably because they knew the real story of her good relationship with Thomas Lister and the jealous acts of his young son following his father's death. This alleged incidence of witchcraft took place in Craven and was actually a precursor to the larger Pendle Witch Trials and executions that would soon take place over the county border. Jennet was first accused of witchcraft in 1607 and this would create a mind-set of suspicion amongst the local, inter-related gentry that would simmer until coming to a head in Pendle some five years later. Further to this, the judges Altham and Bromley, who were to try the Pendle cases at Lancaster later in the year of 1612, were the judges at the trial of Jennet

Preston and this created a legal framework within which Roger Nowell could operate – he would have plenty of time to assess the Westby case and set out his methods of interrogation accordingly. By the time of the August Assizes of 1612 Nowell's case for the prosecution was finely honed so as to press all the right buttons with Altham and Bromley.

It is clear, then, that the trial of Jennet Preston at York cannot be taken in isolation to the consequent Pendle cases. Indeed, it can be said that the Lister family were as heavily involved in the ownership of property within the extended area of Pendle Forest as they were within any of their other estates. Throughout the later sixteenth century, and certainly through the first half of the seventeenth century, the Listers held many acres of land and numerous farm properties. The main branch at Westby Hall worked alongside other family members in Colne and at Stirk House (Gisburn) in their constant land acquisitions – large areas of Marsden (Nelson) and Colne fell within their hegemony as did many of the properties relating to the Pendle accused. As an example, the Listers were close to the Bannisters of Park Hill and the Towneleys of Barnside, Stone Edge and Carr Hall; as a consequence of inter-marriage between these three gentry families the Listers had control (at least in part) over the properties attached to the Stone Edge estate in Blacko – Malkin being one of these. The Towneleys owned most of the farms around Wheatley Booth, including Black Moss and probably the farm where Demdike's son, Christopher Holgate, lived and we shall see more on this later.

Can it be any wonder, then, that when Master Lister shouted the Forest of Pendle jumped? There can be no doubt that the Westby manor would have been aware of the existence of so-called witches at Malkin and West Close; having been tolerated for many years perhaps it was felt that the time was right to play the trump-card. The cousinhood of local gentry would have heard their staff and tenants speaking in hushed voices, telling stories of witchcraft that were both wondrous and terrible in equal measure, how the women at Malkin Tower could heal or kill at will and how the people of West Close went in fear of their lives. Having manipulated Jennet Preston into a position where she could be said to have openly attended the 'diabolical' Good Friday meeting at Malkin Tower master Lister could now show his hand. His friend Nowell already had his troops in place and the military-like operation swung into action – not only did Nowell's plan progress like clock-work, he was dealt the best of all possible hands when young Jennet Device innocently tripped into his office at Read Hall to give her 'evidence'.

This stone object, found at Calf Hall in Barnoldswick, is thought to be a 'witch-ball.'

Half of the base is missing, the ball would originally have blocked the hole in the base and therefore stopped any stray spirits from entering.

These objects were usually placed within the farm dairy to protect the milk from being soured.

Photo: Nic Ashworth

Chapter Three

Thomas Potts and Roger Nowell

Potts

In the year 1613, a few months following the Witch Trials of the previous August at Lancaster Assizes, Thomas Potts published his first-hand account of the proceedings under the title of *The Wonderfull Discoverie of Witches in the Countie of Lancaster*. Potts was the Associate Clerk on the Northern Circuit during the autumn sessions; he was also possibly the Clerk of Arraigns on the summer circuit of 1612. In this capacity he was responsible for drafting indictments and producing examinations and witness statements to the court as required. The following is an illustration of the responsibilities assigned to Potts: [1]

'Because the two judges divided to hear Crown (criminal) and civil cases separately, the clerks were also empowered to act as one of the 'judges', as two were theoretically required in each type of trial. Another pamphlet describing a witchcraft trial, The Most Strange and Admirable Discoverie of the Three Witches of Warboys (London 1593), describes Edward Fenner as 'for that time ... Judge alone,' a representation of common practice as if it were exceptional, because it was not legally defensible. This careful presentation of reality, framed within an ideal which did not exist in practice, warns us against that in reading Potts' work, we may be reading an account that is economical with the truth: justice is always represented as infallible in pamphlets.'

King James I

Potts was the client of Sir Thomas Knyvet, Baron of Eskrick and privy Councillor who was an effective channel for Potts to gain the ear of the king when presenting his glorification of the authorities involved in the Pendle trials. Knyvett would have known that the *Wonderfull Discoverie* would have been well received by James I; this would reflect not only upon himself as patron of the book but also upon Potts and the trial judges. Knyvet was the man who made the discovery of explosives in the cellars of the House Of Commons and effectively foiled the Gunpowder Plot[2]. As a keeper of the Jewell House under Elizabeth I Knyvet held a certain amount of respect but this was never a high-flying position. Following the Gunpowder Plot he became a favourite of king James and was appointed Warden of the Mint, he was also made a knight and privy councillor, was guardian to James' daughter Mary and, in 1607, was made Baron of Escrick. Unfortunately for

---

[1] Marion Gibson, *Thomas Potts' Dusty Memory*, (The Lancashire Witches – Poole, ed, Manchester University Press, 2002)
[2] See chapter below on this

Knyvet his skills in handling money were somewhat limited and thousands of pounds of royal funds were lost. He held on to his position by exaggerating the threat to James' person from the Catholics and promoting himself as Keeper of the King's Person.

The publishing of the *Wonderfull Discoverie* in 1613 was fortunately timed so as to revive the fortunes of Knyvet within the royal court. In the *Dedicatorie* of his pamphlet Thomas Potts sets out his intention of ensuring that there would be no mistake as to where his loyalties lay:

To The Right Honorable, Thomas, Lord Knyvet, Baron of Escrick
in the Countie of Yorke, my very Honorable good Lord and Master
And To The Right Honorable and Virtuous Ladie,
The Ladie Elizabeth Knyvet
his wife, my honorable good Ladie and Mistris.

To the modern eye the above dedication is a touch oily but it manages to go downhill from here onwards:

Let it stande (I beseech thee) with your favors whome profession of the same true Religion towardes God, and so greate love hath united in one, Jointly to accept the protection and Patronage of these my laboures, which not their owne worth hath encouraged, but your Worthinesse hath enforced me to consecrate unto your Honours. To you (Right Honorable my very good lord) of Right doe they belonge: for to whom shall i rather present the first fruits of my learning then to your Lordship: who nourished then both mee and them, when there was scarce any being to mee or them? And whose just and upright carriage of causes, whore zeale to Justice andd Honorable curtesie to all men, have purchased you a Reverend and worthie Respect of all men in all partes of this Kingdome, where you are knowne .... and so on and so forth!

Potts did not fare badly from his publication; under royal patronage in 1615 he was granted the keepership of Skalme Park where the favourite hounds of the king were trained. In 1618 he was granted the *'office of collecting forfeitures on the laws concerning sewers, for twenty-one years.'* Having the remit to appoint collectors under his keepership Potts could now consider himself as a minor patron, not too bad a position for a lowly clerk who had no university training.

Potts' account of the trials, then, can be viewed to a certain extent as propaganda with the intent of exalting the wisdom of all those in authority concerned with the removal of so many diabolical witches from the country – not to mention the fact that they had probably foiled another instance of the Gunpowder Plot!

Potts is at pains to explain that he provided us with a true and honest account of the trial proceedings, an account taken straight from the records at Lancaster Castle and therefore irrefutable. Unfortunately this cannot be substantiated and we have to look at Potts' motives for his publication. He wishes for the reader to stand in awe of the successful legal machinations so expertly carried out by His Majesty's northern authorities and Westminster judges. We are lucky on the one hand that Thomas Potts reported his version of events in that frenzied year of 1612, without the *Discoverie* we might well have never heard of the Pendle Witches – on the other hand the evidence provided to us almost four-hundred years ago must be examined not only with sympathy for the mindset of the day but also with the evidence furnished to us by both common sense and the hard facts of surviving written record.

If we were to remove the statements of the accused from the context of a witchcraft trial, and strip them of their fanciful Faustian embroidery, the many instances of diabolical happenings quoted within the Pendle Witch Trials would be rendered both normal and totally insignificant. Having said that, this does not detract from the fact that we have a written (if inaccurate) record of Pendle Forest folk within the early modern period. It is of great value to our local history, and the memory of a number of local people to whom gross injustice was done, to seek the true facts wherever possible.

Nowell

James Ist was convinced that he was continually being targeted by the ill-meant attentions of the proponents of witchcraft both at home and abroad. When he acceded to the English throne in 1603 James had been king of Scotland for some thirty-six years (since the age of one in fact) and had grown up within the strict Scottish Reformation. He was a scholar of Protestant theology and his studies included the subject of witchcraft. Not being the most stable of characters James appears to have become somewhat obsessed by the *'science of demons'* and to this end he published a treatise on witchcraft in 1597 entitled *'Daemonologie, in Forme of a Dialogue, Divided into Three Books,'* this was reprinted in London as *'Daemonologie'* when he gained the English Crown. This unfortunate work was to become the reference text for all those in authority who were charged to uphold the law in James' kingdom. Not least of these proponents of the king's views on the subject of witchcraft were the circuit judges, Justices of the Peace and the Puritan gentry – the very people who were central to the prosecution of the Pendle Witch Trials. When, in his official capacity as magistrate, Roger Nowell of Read Hall began to receive official complaints of witchcraft on his patch there was a weight of bias upon

his shoulders, whether he realised it or not he was just as much a victim of the paranoid atmosphere of the times as was the lowliest forest dweller; unfortunately it was to be the latter who would 'carry the can' for this state of affairs.

Read Hall; an engraving of about 1750

So; who exactly was this Roger Nowell who would play such a leading role in our local folklore? He married Katherine Murton in 1551 and was the son of Roger Nowell and Florence Starkie (nee Atkinson) who had married on the 25th January 1551 at Padiham – witnesses had been *Alexander Ryshton, Georgius Shuttleworth, Henrye Thomson,* and *Robte Bell.* At the time of this marriage Florence was the widow of Laurence Starkie of Huntroyd Hall. One of the Starkie offspring of this marriage, Nicholas, inherited Cleworth Hall in Lancashire and it was here that a celebrated case of supposed witchcraft occurred when Starkie's two children began to have fits in 1595. Not long afterwards Starkie's three other children began to suffer the same symptoms followed by a maid and an elderly relation. To illustrate the mindset of the day the symptoms of these people were immediately assigned to possession by the devil whereas today the case would be viewed as nothing more than adoptive hysteria. To cut a long story short, Starkie hired a professional 'wise man' in the shape of one Edmund Hartley, his remit being to effect a cure upon the affected people within his household. It is probable that Hartley was a close relative of John Hartley of Liverpool, clerk and servant to John Nutter (the dean of Chester), the Starkies owned estates in Huyton (Liverpool) where John Hartley was based – no doubt John Hartley, or dean Nutter, were able to recommend Edmund Hartley to the Starkies as being 'the man for the job' – with consequences!

Through the use of herbs, potions and psychology Hartley regained some degree of control over the mass hysteria within Starkie's domain. Things quietened down for about one year but Hartley began to demand increased payment for his services. The children began to grow wilder and related that Hartley had kissed them and laid on their beds – Freudian tales of furry devils and little holes began to emerge and this proved to be too much for Starkie who accused Hartley of employing the use of witchcraft. He was therefore arraigned at the Lancaster Assizes of 1597 and sentenced to death. The first attempt at hanging failed when the rope snapped and Hartley hit the ground standing; stupefied and amazed at his survival he decided that he must have been guilty after all and didn't think twice about saying so - gibbering and obviously in shock Hartley proclaimed his guilt loudly and clearly! At this point he was strung up again, this time with more success.

The salient point of this story is that Nowell, who was closely related to the Starkies, would have followed these events closely; by 1612 the Starkies had removed to the family seat of Huntroyd. The fact that this estate was almost adjacent to Nowell's home at Read, and that Nowell was related to Starkie, would have ensured that he could draw upon Starkie's experience as prosecutor during Hartley's witchcraft trial. In fact this whole peculiar episode within the everyday life of the gentry could be said to have been the trial-run (no pun intended) for the major events that were to unfold in 1612.

Roger Nowell was also related to Alexander Nowell (1507-1602) who was dean of Saint Paul's throughout the reign of Elizabeth I, despite the fact that she detested him! Alexander Nowell has been credited with the invention of bottled ale; when on a fishing trip he decanted a jug of beer into a bottle and placed it in a net in the river to keep cool. At the end of the day he noticed that the beer had fermented slightly within the bottle and this gave it a pleasant aerated quality. He worked out that the fermentation process could be carried on once beer had been sealed in a container and passed the knowledge on to a friend in the brewing trade. Alexander's brother Lawrence became the dean of Lichfield and another brother, Robert, became a prominent lawyer and held the post of Queen's Attorney of the Court of Wards and moved in the highest of circles; Queen Elizabeth's minister, Lord Burghley, was an executor of Robert's will.

Roger Nowell could also boast as second cousins John Wolton, Bishop of Exeter and Dr William Whittaker, Regius Professor of Divinity at Cambridge and a relative of T. D. Whitaker the historian. The Nowells were also closely related to the local gentry families of Towneley, Sherburne of Stoneyhurst and Bradyll of Portfield and Whalley. Roger's son, Christopher, married Eleanor Shuttleworth of Gawthorpe Hall whose family employed Robert Nutter of Greenhead who was supposedly bewitched to death by Chattox. Another relative, Margery Whitaker born 1595, is said to have been the clerk to Roger Nowell. It is often claimed that

Roger Nowell had cause to prosecute Alice Nutter of Roughlee in the 1612 trials because of a contentious land dispute between the two families of Nowell and Nutter. There does not appear to be any direct evidence for this but confusion may have arisen from the fact that another family by the name of Nowell lived in the forest. John Nowell of Wheatley, Laund and Fence was, for a period, steward of the forest and as such he dealt with many land transactions in the Roughlee area.[1] John Nowell was possibly the same *Johnes Nowels gent,* who married Letissia Bradyll in 1575. The Nowell family of Laund owned lands in different areas of the forest, a descendant farmed at Bank Stile Farm on the present Church Street in Barrowford in the nineteenth century and another shot his wife with a Colt .45 pistol at his Barrowford home in March 1897. Roger Nowell was constantly in either conflict or discussion over land deals of his own, we see later that he was often at odds with his neighbours, and even his own family, over rights to lands around his home of Read.

In the March of 1558 a Poll was taken amongst the following worthies as to whether John Bradyll of Whalley should be allowed to erect a private area of twelve-feet by four-feet within Whalley Parish Church on account of him having erected a mansion house at Whalley and having nowhere to worship in which to serve God:

Sir Richard Shirburne, John Towneley, Richard Asshetone, Thomas Catterall and Thomas Nowell, esquires, Gilbert Moreton, Edmund Starkie, Henry Riley, John Crumbooke, George Shotillworth, Anthony Watesone, John Whiticarr, Hugh Shotillworth, John Paslewe, Thomas Willicell, Christopher Smyth, Randle Holcar and John Lawe, gents., and Bernard Shotilworth, John Cundeclif, Richard Dogesone, John Lee, Henry Holcar, Francis Webster and William Seller, *to John Braddill of Whalley, esquire;........*
.......with the assent of George Clarke, vicar, and Christopher Seller of Penhultone, John Tasker of Wiswall, John Colthurste of Letell Mitton, George Grenefelde of Whalley, John Norram of Reade, Thomas Whiticar, Edmund Cockeshote of Symondeston, ⸱Lawrence Whiticar of Padiham and James Robert of Hapton, churchwardens. Sanctioned by William, Bishop of Chester.

Many of the names of the great and the good are assembled here, some bear a direct relationship to the 1612 trials amongst which are: **Richard Assheton** who married Isabel Hancock of Pendleton and died in 1597 reputedly at the hands of Elizabeth Southern. **Thomas Catterall** was probably related to one Isold de Heton who, in local folklore, was the grandmother of Elizabeth Southern and whom we shall meet with presently. We have seen that **Thomas Nowell** was uncle to Roger Nowell. **John Lawe** was a yeoman within the Whalley area as were members of his extended family. Between 1581 and 1596 a branch of the family had settled in Wiswell, near Whalley and were regularly mentioned on the Catholic recusancy rolls as having had their goods seized. We have met briefly with John Lawe the chapman who was reputedly bewitched in Colne Field by Alison Device - more of this later.

Richard Dogesone, the Dodgesons of Pendle Forest and Gisburn had an unfortunate habit of allowing their children and animals to become bewitched, at least according to the trial records. **William Seller** carries the name of the family who were regular masons on the

---

[1] W. Farrar, *Clitheroe Court Rolls* (Vol 2, 1912)

Whalley Abbey site and who built a large part of the parish church of St. Peter's in Burnley. Further to this, the daughter of Elizabeth Southern (Elizabeth Device) was accused of having her daughter, Jennet, illegitimately by a man called Sellers. **John Crombock** was of the Clerk Hill family in Whalley and his son would marry into the family of Nutter of Greenhead. **Randle Holker** was a large landowner and a neighbour of Roger Nowell, Randle's son, John, had a son Randle and he will figure later in our story.

September 1580: Feoffment and Release for £20: William Farrington of Worden to Ralph Assheton, esquire, Nicholas Starkie, William Crumbocke and Richard Risheton, esquires, ... messuages in Reade, late of Thomas Deyne called Deynes Place, in the tenure of John Seller* .... for the use of Roger Nowell of Reade, esquire. Witnessed by Richard Shuttleworth, Edmund Starky, William Shotleworth, John Wodroffe, Henry Feilden. *John Seller of Read farmed Deynes Place, a property formerly tenanted by Thomas Dean. It is possible that Thomas was the brother of John Dean of Newfield Edge in Middop whose wife, Jennet, was supposedly bewitched by John and Jane Bulcock.

August 1598: Myles Whittaker of Symoundstone, yeoman - surrender to Roger Nowell of Reade, esquire, farming concerns in Symondstone........

October 1598: Josias Proctor of Warsell, Co. York, gentleman, surrender of concerns to Roger Nowell of Reade, esquire, Reade, Harwood and Dinckley* in Co. Lancashire and Stanlowe, Lofthouses, Wakefield, Sandall and Wentbridge in Co. York..... * This will prove to be of interest to our story at a later stage when we see that Nowell could here have been taking over the family lands of Elizabeth Southern

December 1598: Roger Nowell of Reade serves quitclaim upon Thomas Whitacres* of Symonstone, yeoman, for properties in Symonstone.... *The Whittaker families of Simonstone and Holme-in-Cliviger were related - this will have a bearing on our story later.

May 1612: A Royal Commission of James I is sent to the Quorum of esquires Roger Nowell of Read and Nicholas Bannester of Altham, Justices of the Peace, to act in the case of a disputed deed of bargain and sale: Thomas Rothwell and Roger Kenyon plaintiffs versus Edmund Starky* and others............ *Edmund Starky married Ann Hancock of Lower Higham in 1560 and they were the parents of the Nicholas Starkie of Cleworth and Huntroyd on whose case Roger Nowell was expected to pass fair judgement. Was this a case of keeping nepotism within the family?

June 1600: Ellize Robinson of Gouldshaiebooth, yeoman, to Mr. John Nutter, Dean of Chester (by John Nutter his servant)...... to the use of Anne, the second daughter of Ellize Robinson, for her preferrment in marriage. Witnessed by: Roger Nowell, Edmund Starkie, Roger Nowell, Henry Nutter and Rychard Bawdine......

We shall meet again with dean Nutter presently, Henry Nutter of Sabden was a relative of his. It is probable that the Richard Baldwin mentioned here was not Demdike's enemy, the miller of Wheathead, this was more likely to have been Richard Baldwin from the Simonstone area. The two Roger Nowells were the father and son of Read Hall.

August 1633: *Roger Nowell of Reade esquire serves quitclaim to Thomas Whitacres of Symonstone, gentleman for all his part of the manor of Symonstone....... *This Roger was the son of magistrate Roger Nowell (Nowell senior died in 1623). The above sample of records relating to the Nowell estates show that Roger Nowell, in common with most gentry of the time, was not averse to claiming or re-claiming lands and property wherever possible. In the years after the 1612 trials he was constantly at odds with his son, Roger, over his Read and Simonstone holdings. In fact Roger junior took his father to court in a bid to prove that he did not owe *suite* to him in respect of Nowell senior's manorial rights.[1] We have, then, at least a flavour of the man who instigated the Pendle Witch trials.

Having built up their fortunes under Elizabeth I the Nowell family were keen to be seen to serve the new king, to this end Roger signed the *Loyal Address of the Lancashire Gentry,* a document welcoming James I to the throne. Nowell's standing within the extended area of Lancashire was considerable and it did him no harm to be seen to actively pursue the king's enemies within his own area of control. The imposition of religious uniformity throughout the Forest of Pendle, and the wider parish of Whalley, served as an example to people that the laws of the Protestant church were to be obeyed. Prosecution of the poor also avoided any embarrassing, or potentially troublesome reaction from the Catholic gentry. The Whalley Parish Registers of 1538 to 1601 show Roger Nowell having six of his ten children baptised:

August 8th 1582: **Rogerus Nowell** *filius et heres (son and heir) Rogeri Nowell de Readehale*
May 21st 1586: **Maria Nowell** *filius Rogeri - Armiger (arms bearer)*
March 7th 1587: **Florentia Nowell** *filius Rogeri - Armiger*
July 1591: **Alexander Nowell** *filius Rogeri - Armiger*
February 18th 1592: **Issabella Nowell** *filius Rogeri – Armiger*
June 24th 1596: **Robtus Nowell** *filius Rogeri - Armiger*
July 15th 1600: **Katherina Nowell** *filius Rogeri - Armiger*

Papers held at the Preston Records Office show an interesting and potentially damning snippet of information regarding the Nowells: [2]

February 1612: *A Bill of Complaint is presented to the Lord Chancellor by Roger Rigbye of Ditton, gentleman, against Roger Nowell of Reade, gentleman and son of Roger Nowell, and others, for alleged fraud and unlawful retention of documents relating to the office of Clerk of the Peace....*

This record suggests a matter of possible impropriety on Nowell junior's part just one month before his father began to prosecute the case of the Pendle Witches. Is it unreasonable to suggest that this might just be the fulcrum upon which the Pendle Witch case hinged? Certainly, by prosecuting such a high profile case within his district, Roger Nowell senior would have thrown a smoke-screen over the accusations being levelled against his son.

---

[1] W. Farrar, *Clitheroe Court Rolls* (1912)
[2] Unpublished Papers / *The Nowells of Read*

Chapter Four

Hubble-Bubble, Religion and Trouble

> *'Stinking boots, mucky combs, rotten girdles, filthy rags and*
> *gobbets of wood under the names of parcels of the Holy Cross'*

Such was the description of the contents of abbey cauldrons given by those charged with propagating the anti-monastic Tudor propaganda of the *Dissolution*. Shakespeare would take this up and run with it in 1606 when he wrote *Macbeth*, his *'witch's brew'* would fire the imagination of witchcraft commentators up to the present day. Often these steaming, bubbling cauldrons, constantly stirred by a cackling old hag with a huge wart on the end of her nose, were said to contain certain human body parts. The basis of this can be seen within the Tudor persecution of Catholics whose martyrs were a constant source of ghoulish souvenirs. When cut down from the gallows the bodies of those Catholics condemned for treason were often divided into quarters; following this the gathering of onlookers would surge forward and cut off any part of the body within reach. Handkerchiefs were soaked in the blood of the executed person and these, along with fingers and toes, would become sought-after relics of the deceased.

This fate was to befall one Edmund Campion whose thumb was removed following his execution and never recovered. Campion it was who led a Catholic mission into Lancashire in 1580 in the hope of raising backing for his cause amongst the county gentry. Campion set out from Stratford and arrived at Houghton Tower, the seat of the Houghton family near Preston; it is thought that at that time the young William Shakespeare might have been a servant at Houghton Tower. From this base Campion travelled the local estates of the area on his recruitment drive; amongst the families he stayed with over the following six months were the Heskeths at Rufford, Listers of Westby, Allens at Rossall, Southworths at Samlesbury, Sherburns at Stoneyhurst, Tempests at Bracewell, Towneleys at Towneley Hall and the Worthingtons at Standish. [1]

By the year 1612 it is clear that the art of detecting witchcraft had become somewhat standardised. It was only necessary for a person to be accused of being a witch for them to be thrown into the dungeons of the Well Tower at Lancaster Gaol. When the unfortunate accused person was tried it was simply a matter of proving that he or she had some kind of mark upon their body, where a witches familiar had sucked, to condemn them. Along with, or instead of this 'evidence,' a witch could be proven guilt on the slender evidence of hear-say or a rambling, nonsensical 'confession' taken under duress. The ducking-stool and pricking-tool were also favourite methods employed to prosecute the unfortunate people accused of witchcraft. The former was a wooden seat whose pivotal arrangement allowed for the accused to be placed in the chair and ducked beneath the water. If the person drowned then they were a witch and if they lived they were also a witch! The River Calder at the bottom of Cuckstool Lane, in Burnley,

---

[1] Richard Wilson, *The Pilot's Thumb*, (The Lancashire Witches, R.Poole, Ed. – Manchester University Press, 2002)

was one of the main places within Pendle where the barbaric practice of 'ducking' took place. The 'pricking-tool' was a form of bradawl and was employed by the witch-finder to jab into some part of the anatomy of the accused. If this action drew blood (as it would) then the accused was guilty. Where the accused was a younger woman (as was often the case) her interrogators very often stripped them naked before carrying out their 'inspections' – this, of course, was intended to be a show of power by the (male) interrogator and to further the ignominy suffered by the victim. On top of this, what could be better for the case of the prosecution than if the accused were to be old, haggard, ugly, deformed, a nuisance to their neighbours, parish and landlord and also suffering from some kind of dementia - or better still, *all* of these?

Taking the accounts of *'diabolical witchery'* published by scholars of the time one single thread is apparent above all others and that is the presence of the devil. William Perkins was the leading Puritan writer of his age and a friend of William Whittaker, who was in turn a relative of Roger Nowell. In 1608 Perkins published his *'Discourse of the Damned Art of Witches'* in which he wrote: *'The ground of all witchcraft is a league or covenant made between the witch and the devil, wherein they do mutually bind themselves together the one unto the other. For his part (the devil) promises to be ready to his vassals command, to appear at any time in the likewise of any creature, to consult with him, to aid and help him.'*

The feature of actual consort directly with the devil is notably absent in most cases of English witchcraft trials and the Pendle trials were no exception.[1] This did not deter the redoubtable prosecution, however, enough evidence of the old Catholic practices was apparent in the spells and incantations that the accused admitted to using. Further to this, Nowell would be well aware of the writings of Perkins and was at pains to ensure that the accused of the Pendle Trials were given every opportunity to brag about their own personal demons or *Familiars*. No self-respecting witch would be without one of these as they were an essential part of the toolkit when they were out to impress others of their perceived powers. To the forest-folk, many of the small animals around them served the purpose of Familiars, hares, cats and dogs were their favourites; this is no surprise as these animals constantly surrounded them. The endowment of animals with spiritual powers is as old as the hills and in the case of the Pendle Forest would have filtered down the generations here from the Iron Age, if not before.

Many of the Pendle accused appear to have owned up, or even boasted about having the companionship of a Familiar and this was grist to Nowell's mill – the presence of a malevolent Familiar firmly linked the accused to the devil. At least this would be the case by the time that the jury heard the evidence. On the subject of witch Familiars, Chetham Society notes from the nineteenth century state that:[2]

'Bernard, who is learned in the nomenclature of familiar spirits, gives, in his Guide to Grand Jurymen, *1630, the following list of the names of the more celebrated familiars of English witches. 'Such as I have read of are these: Mephistophiles, Lucifer, Little Lord, Fimodes, David, Jude, Little Robin, Smacke, Litefoote, Nonsuch, Lunch, Makeshift, Swash, Pluck, Blue, Catch, White, Callico, Hardname, Tibb, Hiff, Ball, Puss, Rutterkin, Dicke, Prettie, Grissil, and Jacke.'*

---

[1] E. Peel & P. Southern, *The Trials of the Lancashire Witches*, (David & Charles, 1969/1972)
[2] Notes in Potts' *The Wonderful Discoverie of Witches*, (Chetham Society)

'In the confession of Isabel Gowdie, a famous Scotch witch, (in Pitcairne's Trials, vol. iii. page 614,) we have the following catalogue of attendant spirits, rather, it must be confessed, a formidable band. 'The names of our Divellis, that waited upon us, ar thes: first, Robert the Jakis; Sanderis, the Read Roaver; Thomas the Fearie; Swain, the Roaring Lion; Thieffe of Hell; Wait upon Hirself; Mak Hectour; Robert the Rule; Hendrie Laing; and Rorie. We would ken them all, on by on, from utheris. Some of theim apeirit in sadd dunn, som in grasse-grein, som in sea-grein, and some in yallow. 'Archbishop Harsnet, in his admirable Declaration of Popish Impostures, under the pretence of casting out Devils, 1605, a work unsurpassed for rich humour and caustic wit, clothed in good old idiomatic English, has a chapter 'on the strange names of these devils,' in which he observes, 'It is not amiss that you be acquainted with these extravagant names of devils, least meeting them otherwise by chance you mistake them for the names of tapsters, or juglers.' Certainly, some of the names he marshalls in array smell strongly of the tavern. These are some of them: Pippin, Philpot, Modu, Soforce, Hilco, Smolkin, Hillio, Hiaclito, Lustie Huffe-cap, Killico, Hob, Frateretto, Fliberdigibbet, Hoberdidance, Tocobatto, and Lustie Jollie Jenkin.'

The apparent readiness of the Pendle accused to admit to having Familiars suggests that they were actually a necessary accessory, a powerful Familiar would lend weight to the wise person's claim to be able to heal and protect themselves and their fellow foresters or, when conditions dictated, to bring harm to others. Interestingly, whenever a Familiar appears in the confessions (in relation to the charge of murder by witchcraft) the accused admit that their Familiars were responsible for actually carrying out the foul deed and it was, therefore, out of their own hands. The Familiars had taken it upon themselves to harm or kill the victim whilst the accused stood by – *"Good heavens, now look what you have done you naughty little Familiar* (or words to that effect!).

Chattox had her *Fancy*, Elizabeth Southern had her *Tibb*, James Device had his *Dandy* and Elizabeth Device had her *Ball*. It is difficult at a distance of some four-hundred years to read the mindset of these individuals in this respect. To what extent did they actually believe in their animal Familiars and just how much of this phenomenon was silly superstition? Certainly, these people were born-and-bred into an age of superstition and belief in the power of nature. A constant exposure to such tales and beliefs from birth could well have implanted a strong notion within a person's psyche, to such an extent perhaps that they believed that hares conversed with them. Further to this we know that the wise-people were expert herbalists and had no shortage of materials to work with in God's great garden. Within reach of everyone were common plants whose effect upon the human body were both powerful, dangerous and well known. The soporific effects of flora such as valerian, St. John's wort, hen-bane, 'magic mushrooms' and birch leaves meant that they would have been seen as basic stock within the armoury of the healer. The experience of the healer would be necessary when medicines, salves and potions containing the more dangerous plants such as Bella Donna were administered, in the wrong hands these would have been deadly. Given the fact that mind-altering drugs were freely available at the time exactly what part would these have played in the many instances of apparent fantasy reported by the accused?

There is also another consideration here and that is the power of hypnotism. In 1873 the Burnley historian, T. T. Wilkinson, and John Harland of the Chetham Society, published a book entitled 'Lancashire Legends and Traditions.' The book includes a tract on witchcraft in the Pendle area – this was supposedly an early piece unearthed by Harland and translated into modern English. The authors were of the opinion that the treatise was written early in the reign of James I as there is no mention of the execution at Lancaster of the Pendle Witches. Although this early date is unconvincing the tract raises the interesting possibility that a part of the wise person's armoury was hypnosis;

The Humoures of Roger and Doll with the Maner how they were served by a Lancashire Witch

Roger and Doll being got in a merrie humour, one day meeting with Margery, began to swear at her, and called her "Leaden Heels," but she passed by as if she minded it not. They had not gone far before there was a style to go over;- but when they was on the top, they could not get down on either side, fancying there was ponds of water about them, till some travellers came by, who, finding them thus mounted on the wooden horse in a strange posture, made them dismount. However, not satisfied, she watched their motions, and found them in a barn that stood by the road, where the cows used to be driven in to be milked. There, being seated upon the strawe , toying together, and wondering at what had happened, ... Margery, who stood there invisible, sprinkled Roger with a certain dust, which changed his very countenance, making it appear to his mistress like an ass's head; which so frightened her, that she gave a lustie spring, and throwing him quite down, she got up, running, and crying out, "The devil! The devil!" This so terrified Roger, that he followed, crying out, "What ails you? --- What ails you?" In this manner, to the laughter of a great number of people, they ran until they were so tired, they were forced to lie down, being no longer able to hold out. Thus, at this time, her revenge was satisfied.

To what extent this might be based upon the experience of the author is pure speculation but anyone who has witnessed a stage hypnotism show will surely recognise the close similarities here between the above story and the antics of those placed under the influence of hypnosis. There is also the consideration that the *"certain dust"* sprinkled over Roger was some kind of hallucinogenic drug.

The reported instances of witchcraft show that most of the 'bewitched' people in the 1612 trials were landowners, or related to landowners – this is commonly thought to be as a consequence of them having been regularly targeted by the accused and having need to throw the begging poor off their lands. As we have seen, the Hartleys were heavily involved in land tenancy around Malkin, was it pure coincidence that Katherine Hewitt was accused of having in hand the bewitching of a child of Michael Hartley of Colne?
Roger Nowell himself had interests in land and business within the area and he was closely allied in land holdings at Simonstone with the relations of Alice Nutter. The Listers of Westby were friends and business colleagues of the Bannisters and owned the neighbouring Yorkshire lands to Malkin. The Moore family of nearby Ball House was related to Hugh Moore, gent of Higham Dean who had his ale turned sour and his son John 'killed' by Chattox. Henry Mitton, who was said to have fallen victim to Demdike and her daughter for refusing Demdike a penny, lived a short distance from Malkin at Ridge, this farm is on the heights of Utherstone Wood overlooking the Barrowford Water Meetings and half-way between Malkin and Alice Nutter's home. Robert Nutter, of the major landowning family of Nutter at Greenhead, was supposedly killed by Chattox and her daughter, Ann Redfearn, for making lewd advances towards Ann.

Robert's father was also suspected to have been the victim of witchcraft, Chattox and her family lived on land at West Close where he was a sub-tenant under lord Shuttleworth. The Robinsons of Foothouse Gate, in Barley, were akin to the Nutters in their land acquisitions and went the same unfortunate way as Robert Nutter and his father, this time as victims of Demdike.

Richard Assheton of Downham Hall was (allegedly) an extremely high-profile victim of Demdike, (the reason for this has never been explained) and the death of Ann Towneley of Carr Hall, another member of a local gentry family, was offered to the Assizes as a juicy plumb in the prosecution of James Device. Assheton was one of two exceptional victims, in relation to distance from the Pendle Forest core around which the accused were said to have operated, Jennet Dean of Newfield Edge (situated in Middop on the Blacko to Gisburn road) being the other. The latter could well have been connected (if not related) to the Bulcocks of Pendle who allegedly bewitched her and sent her mad.

In later chapters we see that there is a correlation between the accused and their supposed victims – in particular, the avaricious land requirements of the forest yeomen and husbandmen created a great deal of both inter-family and trans-family friction. Few of the neighbouring farmers were immune to the economic pressures of growing land ownership, it is probably fair to say that rich and poor alike were aware of this tension and would easily become embroiled in arguments over having shown favour to one or other of the protagonists. This is illustrated in the statements of the accused whereby Demdike would not directly approach certain houses yet she was 'favoured' by Anthony Nutter over other healers to treat his cattle. Again, Chattox would not approach Bull Hole Farm, she preferred to stay a field's distance and send her daughter to the door, the wife of Hugh Moor, however, actually employed Chattox to card wool. When the complex inter-communal politics were coupled with the regular begging operations of the Demdike family amongst their neighbours it is becomes apparent that there would have been a pressurised store of ill feeling just waiting to be vented.

When Chattox, or Demdike, walked the trackways of the forest it is quite easy to picture them meeting with many other members of the community on a daily basis. What is not as easy to imagine is the reception that they would receive along the way – what percentage of their fellow wayfarers would have given a friendly nod, stopped for a few words of gossip; what percentage would sneer and chide them or indeed threaten them; and what percentage would have dived into the nearest hedge in order to avoid them altogether? In the work of Thomas Potts we are told that the neighbours of the accused were queuing to tell their own particular story of devilment and murder, these grisly tales often stretched back over decades but had not been forgotten. To what extent, then, were these tales, rumours and legends provided in the form of relief by the foresters, only too pleased to get things off their chests and see an end to the witch families? Perhaps there was another incentive for people to run to the authorities with their accusations, were they 'invited' by the prosecution to come forward with even the smallest snippet of gossip that could be woven into full-blown proof of guilt? Did the forest people who were willing to furnish accusations actually realise the seriousness of their actions, were they indeed aware that many of their own neighbours were facing the gallows or were they told that this was just a routine, niggling problem that would quickly be dealt with, perhaps with a small fine here and there? In the end, when the forest had lost a number of its families to the Lancaster rope, did their former neighbours sleep easily in their beds – were the villages, fields, byways, alehouses, farmsteads and hills now free from nuisance? Was the community now spiritually cleansed leaving only good, God-fearing neighbours; did people now skip along the pathways with a song in their hearts whilst the brooks happily babbled along their silvery tinkling way?

Well actually, no! The surviving court records paint a picture of the post-1612 trial forest as being much the same as it had been previously. Before the soil upon the graves of the accused had settled there were the usual violent outbursts where the landowners around the Water Meetings were beating each other up, forming gangs and threatening their neighbours with guns, diverting the river so that it would wash away the fences of other farmers and accusing each other of manifold sins - and the men were just as bad! The names cropping up in relation to this behaviour in the early seventeenth century were exactly the same names as had been troubling the courts one-hundred years earlier; one has to ask why these anti-social types had never been the subject of the wrath of the authorities to the extent that the poor of 1612 were. The obvious answer here is that those who were so obviously prone to violence were capable of organising and defending themselves in a manner not available to the elderly women and children who, according to Master Potts, were so dangerous that they had to be wiped from the face of the earth!

Gunpowder Treason and Plot

As the son of the Catholic Mary, Queen of Scots, James I was expected to be much less severe against the Catholics than Elizabeth had been, in fact the Catholic hierarchy had petitioned in order to gain his favour for some time before he ascended to the throne upon the death of Elizabeth I in 1603. Some Catholics even believed that he might lift the persecution, and allow them to worship freely; the new king, however, was under pressure from many members of the House of Commons who were strongly anti-Catholic. He also became less sympathetic towards Catholics following the discovery of a series of minor Catholic plots. The *'Bye Plot'* of 1603 was a conspiracy to kidnap the king and force him to repeal anti-Catholic legislation whilst the *'Main Plot'* was an alleged plan by Catholic clergy and nobles to remove the king and replace him with his cousin, the Catholic Arabella Stuart.

Although a Protestant, James' wife, Anne of Denmark, converted to Catholicism; one of a number of factors that led many Catholics to hope for toleration under his rule. These final hopes were dashed when it became clear that James was not going to honour his pre-reign promises to the Catholics, in fact he denied ever making them and the persecution under him was going to be worse than under Elizabeth. James now made clear his utter detestation of papists, he stated that *'the bishops must see to the severe and exact punishment of every Catholic,'* he made a new proclamation on February 22nd, 1604, ordering all priests out of the realm and also reversed his repeal of recusancy fines, these became payable immediately with arrears. At James' request a Bill was introduced into the House of Commons on April 24th to classify all Catholics as excommunicates, an idea which had been presented to and rejected by Elizabeth as being too severe. Tesimond describes the effect of this bill: *'In consequence, they were no longer able to make their wills or dispose of their goods. The effect of this law was to make them outlaws and exiles; and like such they were treated. There was no longer any obligation to pay them their debts or rents for land held from them. They could not now go to law or have the laws protection. They could seek no remedy for ills and injuries received. In a word, they were considered and treated as professed enemies of the state.'*

The Catholics saw this as a disaster as it was thought that it would lead to their utter ruin. It was also the final straw for a group of dissident Catholic gentry who had been gathering together across the country for some time, thoroughly disillusioned with the treatment that they and their fellows had received for many years the matter came swiftly to a head. The leader of this group, Catesby, almost immediately after the passing of the Act, sent for his cousin Thomas Wintour and revealed the Gunpowder Plot to him at a meeting with Jack Wright at his house in Lambeth. Catesby felt that *'the nature of the disease required so sharp a remedy'* and that the Plot was a morally justifiable act of self-defence against the oppressive rule of a tyrant. But he saw the Plot as an act of last resort and was determined to leave no stone unturned in his quest to remedy the situation by peaceful means and without bloodshed. To this end, he sent Thomas Wintour to Flanders to meet with the Constable of Spain, who was on his way to England to conclude the peace negotiations between Spain and England. He was to *'inform the Constable of the condition of the Catholics here in England, entreating him to solicit his Majesty at his coming hither that the penal laws may be recalled, and we admitted into the ranks of his other subjects.'*

This, of course, was to no avail and so Catesby and his co-conspirators went ahead with their plans to blow up the Houses of Parliament and the king along with them. Guy Fawkes had been recruited into the plot on the strength of his experiences in the Low Countries where, as a munitions expert, he had worked with gunpowder; he was therefore entrusted with the task of obtaining the powder and placing it within the House of Commons cellars.

During October of 1605 Fawkes rented a storage room beneath the intended target and placed there some thirty-six kegs of powder. These were covered by bundles of faggots and on Wednesday 30th October Fawkes inspected the cellar again to satisfy himself that the gunpowder was still in place and had not been disturbed. In the meantime a letter, known as the Monteagle Letter, warning of the intended danger had found its way into the hands of the authorities and a search of the cellars was carried out on Sunday 3rd November, it is possible, even likely, that the powder was found by the authorities at this stage but, wishing to catch the plotters red-handed, this was kept quiet.

A few of the leading conspirators met in London and agreed that the authorities were still unaware of their actions. However, all except Fawkes made plans for a speedy exit from London. Fawkes had agreed to watch the cellar alone; having already been given the task of firing the powder his orders were to embark for Flanders as soon as the charge was fired and spread the news of the explosion on the continent.

On the following Monday afternoon, the Lord Chamberlain, Thomas Howard, Earl of Suffolk, searched the Parliament buildings accompanied by Monteagle and John Whynniard. In the cellar they came upon an unusually large pile of billets and faggots, and saw Guy Fawkes whom they described as *'a very bad and desperate fellow.'* They asked who owned the pile, and Fawkes replied that it was Thomas Percy's in whose employment he worked. They reported these details to the king describing Fawkes as a man *'who seemed to be shrewd enough, but up to no good.'* They again searched the cellar, a little before midnight the following night, this time led by Sir Thomas Knyvett. Fawkes had gone forth to warn Percy that same day, but returned to his post before nightfall. Once again the pile of billets and faggots was searched; the powder was discovered, and this time Fawkes was arrested. On his person they discovered a watch, slow-matches and touchwood. Fawkes later declared that if he had been in the cellar when Knyvett entered it he would have *'blown him up, house, himself, and all.'* When the House of Commons briefly assembled on the morning following the arrest of Guy Fawkes the Clerk, Ralph Ewens, added a note to the official records:

'This last night the Upper House of Parliament was searched by Sir Tho. Knevett; and one Johnson (Johnson was the assumed name of Guy Fawkes), *servant to Mr. Thomas Percy, was there apprehended; who had placed Thirty-six Barrels of Gunpowder in the vault under the House, with a purpose to blow King, and the whole Company, when they should there assemble. Afterwards divers other Gentlemen were discovered to be of the Plot.'*

Thirteen of the main conspirators were eventually apprehended, most of them being tortured and executed – many other known Catholic sympathisers were also arrested and questioned in the aftermath of the plot. Effectively the Gunpowder Plot increased the hostility of the nation to the Catholics and the penal laws were again enforced. Catholics who had begun to attend Church were now required to take the sacrament, churchwardens and constables were fined if they did not prosecute recusants and were rewarded for their success when they did so.[1] New fines were inflicted on those who kept Catholic servants and recusants were forbidden to come within ten miles of London. They were forbidden to practice as attorneys or physicians; they could not be executors of a will, nor guardians of children, they might not be married except in the Church of England and their books could be destroyed, and their houses visited by the magistrates in search of arms. It is said that courtiers bought from the king the shameful privilege of seizing land and property belonging to the wealthier Catholics. In our own area Nicholas Bannister of Altham was a trusted agent of the Crown whose remit was to strip local Catholics of a large percentage of their property.[2]

Life under James, then, was no more a bed of roses for the Catholics than it had been for the past sixty-five years. In the few years leading up to the Witch Trials the social environment was uneasy, the government, and therefore their underling gentry, could well be described as being skittish. The Catholic gentry went about their business with more than the occasional glance over their shoulder whilst the Protestant gentry, within the limits of their own particular power-base, took pains to court the king. A Puritan attitude was beneficial here, anyone who thought themselves to be anyone was constantly seen in church and heard to preach the Protestant doctrine loud and clear, behind the scenes, however, there was much disagreement between high Puritan clergy as to what exactly constituted the official spiritual line.

One thing was for certain, if gentry families such as the Listers of Westby and the Nowells of Read were to enjoy the continuing favour of the king they had to respond in kind; furthermore, any deed or service they provided to benefit the Crown had to gain the ear of Westminster – publicity was the name of the game. It was of little use to industriously serve the king from a Lancashire backwater if he was unaware that you were doing so – the thing that was required here was a sound network of fellow civil servants stretching from the depths of the forest down to London. The local gentry were not shy in this department and what better way to catch the king's eye than to be seen to foil a dastardly attempt on His Majesty's authority by a socially disingenuous group of demon-worshipping terrorists ensconced within the diabolical Malkin Tower? Armed to the teeth with barrels of gunpowder this treacherous band were all but ready to blow the Castle at Lancaster sky high until our brave local Justices, employing all their available wit, intelligence and supreme loyalty to the Crown, stepped in and foiled the new Gunpowder Plot at the last minute.

---

[1] Andrew W Snape, *English Martyrs – Whalley*, (SP, Whalley, 2000)
[2] *Farrar Papers,* Manchester Central Library

On Good Friday 1612 Roger Nowell was able to provide written evidence that a diabolical meeting of witches took place at Malkin Tower and that the main purpose of this meeting of some twenty witches was to blow up the prison at Lancaster Castle, in so doing they would kill the governor and release their colleagues incarcerated there. No matter that this group were actually families of poor elderly people and children who, in the cases of Ann Whittle and Elizabeth Southern, had survived in a harsh and unforgiving environment for over seventy winters. In later life at least, these matriarchs were without the aid of men-folk and had reared their children and grandchildren to the best of their ability; in reality these people had probably harmed not a single person. No matter either that Nowell's 'evidence' was based upon the disjointed testimony of a child and the twisted words of a naive young man. These facts were of no consequence to certain social-climbing landowners ensconced within their halls and mansions. As we shall see, when the opportunity of settling old scores (in the case of Thomas Lister) and being seen to foil another Gunpowder Plot (Roger Nowell) presented itself the truth would not be allowed to stand in the way of excellent propaganda. The Northern Circuit of Westminster Judges in the coming August was to be attended by James Altham and his colleague, Justice Edward Bromley. Roger Nowell knew these judges well, he knew their methods and was able to gather his 'evidence' for the Witch Trials in such a manner that would impress them when he would present his case before them in the coming August. The first cog within a larger wheel of injustice was set in place.

An ancient wall at Spen, above Roughlee Village.

The ghost of Old Demdike is said to walk the night-time forest

Chapter Five

The Road to Gallows Hill

The following is a synopsis of the series of events of 1612 with the prosecution's flowery references to spirits, Familiars and voodoo-type dolls stripped away.

18th March 1612: The Scene - Malkin Tower: The bejewelled meadow stretching out to the hills from the aged face of Malkin Tower suddenly releases an overnight guest as, his lungs bursting with morning-song, a skylark rises into the bright morning air. All is quiet for a few moments until the soft rasping breath of a brown hare layers upon the remnants of a dawn mist, mingling with the smoky primeval perfume of newly-fuelled oakwood. The hare carelessly crests the hill brow, stops and listens; the age-rusted creak of neglected hinges rents the air and, within the leap of a split-second, he is gone from Old Malkin's sight. If he had cared to dally for a few seconds longer the hare would have realised the cause of this vulgar invasion of his morning; he would have seen the door of the humble dwelling fly open to reveal the dishevelled form of a young woman. This is Alison Device and, as she wipes the troubled night from her eyes, she stretches, yawns, spits on the floor and shouts *"Eyup mother, wot a gradely day for't witchin'."* Another, older and more careworn voice drifts into the crisp morning air from deep within the house *"Nay lass, tha's bin witchin' most o't week, it's brass as we needs now."* Alizon curses quietly to herself as she pulls on her hob-nailed boots, *"Aye, reight, I'll be off into t'badlands o' Trawden fer a bit o' beggin' then."*

. . . . Demdike's grand-daughter, Alison Device, sets off from Malkin Tower on a begging spree to Trawden Forest and in so doing it can be said that she set in motion a train of events that would reverberate through the forest for centuries to come. Alison meets a trader by the name of John Lawe at Colne Field and asks him for a few pins. Lawe would later say that he refused to open his pack whilst his son, Abraham, would give evidence that his father gave Alison the pins. Whatever the case may be the official line is that John Lawe took the huff at being pestered and cursed by Alison and, suffering what appears to have been a stroke, collapsed in Colne Field. He was taken into what was probably the Greyhound Inn in Market Street (demolished around 1790) where Alison, obviously shaken at the events, looked in at him before continuing on her way.

21st March: Halifax; Abraham Lawe receives a letter informing him of his father's condition.

29th March: Abraham Lawe goes to Colne and is informed by the local people that his father had been the victim of Alison Device who, being the granddaughter of the infamous Demdike, must have used witchcraft to strike him down. Lawe, finding Alison, takes her to Colne and confronts her with his sick father – Alison is contrite and confesses.

30th March: Roger Nowell examines both Alison Device and Abraham Lawe at Read Hall.

After she admits to having a Familiar, in the shape of a black dog, Nowell decides that there is sufficient evidence to hold Alison.

2nd April: Demdike and Chattox are examined at Ashlar House in Fence by Nowell. Also present are John Nutter, Margaret Crooke and James Robinson. Accusations of witchcraft fly thick and fast and more local people are brought into the fray.

4th April: Chattox, Demdike, Anne Redfern and Alison Device are packed off to the Well Tower at Lancaster Castle to await trial in the coming August.

6th April: Jennet Preston is tried at York Assizes after being accused by Thomas Lister of killing a child of the Dodgeson family in the Gisburn area. She is acquitted.

10th April: This being Good Friday some twenty witches hold a *'diabolical'* meeting at Malkin Tower. The local constable, Henry Hargreaves, is well aware of this gathering and informs Nowell that it has taken place.

27th April: Roger Nowell and his fellow Justice, Nicholas Bannister of Altham, are again at Fence, this time to examine the Device family of Elizabeth, James and Jennet. Another bout of apparent confession, recrimination and accusation breaks out – James and Jennet are only too happy to chat with the nice magistrates about their party at Malkin. The fate of those they insist were in attendance at the Good Friday gathering is now sealed.

27th July: Jennet Preston is again tried at York, this time on a charge of having bewitched to death Thomas Lister of Westby. Roger Nowell has sent the relevant witness statements relating to the Good Friday Malkin meeting to York Assizes. Jennet is said to have enlisted the help of others to kill Lister and his brother, she is found guilty and sentenced to death by the same judges who would later try the Pendle accused.

17th August: The Lancaster Assizes are officially opened for business.

18th August: Elizabeth and James Device, along with Chattox, are found guilty. Chattox's daughter, Anne Redfern, is found not guilty of murdering Robert Nutter of Greenhead.

19th August: Anne Redfern is tried for the murder of Christopher Nutter of Greenhead and this time is found guilty. Alison Device, Margaret Pearson, John and Jane Bulcock, Isabell Roby, Alice Nutter and Katherine Hewit are all found guilty. The Samlesbury accused are found not guilty.

The following are sentenced to death (Elizabeth Southern had died in Lancaster Gaol, probably in May, before the trial): *Elizabeth Device: James Device: Alison Device: Anne Redfern: Alice Nutter: Anne Whittle (alias Chattox): John Bulcock: Jane Bulcock: Isabell Roby: Katherine Hewit.*

20th August: The condemned are executed at a public hanging on Gallows Hill in Lancaster.

When the Assize judges, Bromley and Altham, arrived at Lancaster in the August of 1612 they were presented with a calendar of proceedings; this took the form of a list of the accused to be tried within their sessions, the cases against them and the order in which they were to be tried. The following is the list presented by Covell, the governor of Lancaster Gaol and coroner for the Lancaster district: [1]

Vpon Sunday in the after noone, my honorable Lords the Iudges of Assise, came from Kendall to Lancaster. Wherevpon M. Couell, presented vnto their Lordships a Calender, conteyning the Names of the Prisoners committed to his charge, which were to receiue their Tryall at the Assises: Out of which, we are onely to deale with the proceedings against Witches, which were as followeth.

Viz

❑ *Elizabeth Sowtherns alias Old Demdike of Malkyn Tower Who dyed before shee came to her tryall*

❑ *Anne Whittle, alias Chattox of West Close*

❑ *Elizabeth Deuice: Daughter of old Demdike of Malkyn*

❑ *Iames Deuice: Sonne of Elizabeth Deuice of Malkyn*

❑ *Anne Readfearne: Daughter of Anne Chattox of West Close*

❑ *Alice Nutter of the Roughlea*

❑ *Katherine Hewytte of Colne*

❑ *Alice Grey of Colne: Found not guiltye*

❑ *Iohn Bulcocke of Mossende*

❑ *Jane Bulcocke of Mossende*

❑ *Alizon Deuice: Daughter of Elizabeth Deuice of Malkyn*

❑ *Isabell Robey of Windle*

❑ *Margaret Pearson of Padiham*

---

[1] Thomas Potts, *Wonderfull Discoverie,* (Potts, 1613 – Chetham Society, 1845)

Also indicted on the charge of witchcraft at the August Assizes were a group of people from the Samlesbury area, four miles to the east of Preston: the case against this group of accused collapsed when it was found that the charges had been maliciously falsified by the family of Jane Southworth.[1]

Although **Isabell Roby** was not from the Pendle area she is of interest to the local case; she was accused of being a dangerous witch within her home area of Saint Helens (Liverpool) and her case was brought by Sir Thomas Gerard of Bryn whose family seat was The Brynne near Ashton-in-Makerfield. Sir Thomas's father was a notorious Catholic recusant who had been involved in subterfuge against the Crown; he eventually conformed (at least in public) and held on to the majority of his estate which, in turn, he passed on to his son Sir Thomas. Thomas's younger brother was one John Gerard who, as a leading Catholic missionary, played a major role in the Gunpowder Plot for which he was imprisoned – Gerard did not take kindly to this and so he escaped to France.

Furthermore, we will see that there was a strong network between the owners of many Liverpool estates and our local forest gentry. Not least of the links between the two areas was John Nutter of Newchurch-in-Pendle, dean of Chester and parson of Sephton (Sefton), whose sponsor was the earl of Sephton. Nutter's right-hand-man was clerk John Hartley, also of Liverpool and close relative of the Pendle Forest Hartley families. Along with properties within Liverpool dean Nutter had rights to lands adjoining the estates of Gerard in Wigan and Ashton.

The prosecution of Isabell Roby, at the same time as the Pendle Witches were being arraigned, would almost certainly have been as a consequence of her nemesis, Sir Thomas Gerard, being close to the major players of 1612 i.e.; Roger Nowell, the Towneleys, Thomas Lister, Nicholas Bannister, Sir Richard Shuttleworth, the earls Molyneux of Sephton, Thomas Heber, the Asshetons and, beneath this strata of society, the local minor gentry such as the Nutters of Greenhead, the Bannisters of Barrowford and the Hartleys of Old Laund. Gerard would very quickly have heard through the old (underground) Catholic grapevine of the feeding-frenzy that was happening within Pendle Forest; reputations were to be enhanced by arresting a few poor wretches and offering them up to the seat of idiocy occupied by the Sovereign. If his mates in Pendle were finding witches then Gerard was not going to be left out – unfortunately for one Isabell Roby.

There is no greater, or more intense, a proponent of a subject than a recent convert and so it was with the newly-Protestant Sir Thomas Gerard who went out of his way to court the king; he was almost the first to purchase one of the new baronetcies, at a cost of £1,000, in May 1611. Out to prove himself as worthy of his role as a Justice of the Peace, Gerard would need to have a high-profile case under his belt – what could be better then than a nice juicy anti-Catholic witchcraft case? In mid-March of 1612 Gerard had played a part in securing the evidence of Abraham Lawe whose father had supposedly been bewitched on Colne Field. Having seen that there were going to be royal brownie-points aplenty in the coming months Gerard jumped onto the band-wagon and indicted a witch for himself.

Another pertinent example of the intensity found within times of religious strife is where a representative of the queen, in 1595, wrote a letter regarding the common practice of Catholic sympathisers openly moving letters and information around the country. The letter writer would have had all the recusant carriers of letters arrested. He was obviously wary of tackling

---

[1] For a more detailed view on the Samlesbury trial see Jonathan Lumby: *The Lancashire Witch-Craze*

this problem head-on as he did not know whom he could trust: [1] *'I dare not geve my voyce to any commissioners concerning taking of preestes and seminaryes . . . . excepte Nicholas Bannister* (and others) *and I am in conscyence perswaded that everie peculier of theise would spende all the buttons att theyr doublettes to purge Lancashyre from idolatrie, papistrie, seditios seminaryes and theyr favorytes.'* This gives us a definite insight into the pervasive air of treason and subterfuge of the period and also we see Roger Nowell's co-magistrate, Nicholas Bannister, in a true light.

The evidence against Isabell Roby was that anyone who happened to disagree with her fell ill and died. Despite the testimony of a prosecution witness, who firmly stated that Roby was not a witch, she was found guilt and sentenced to death. When Abraham Lawe's father took the stand in another case the judge took pity on him and called upon Gerard and Sir Richard Houghton (of another long-standing Catholic family) to provide for him.

Margaret Pearson lived just outside the Forest of Pendle in Padiham but, as this bounds onto the Higham and West Close areas of the western forest, she would be familiar to the Pendle accused. This was the third time that Pearson had been arraigned on a case of witchcraft, on this latest occasion she was accused by Chattox of *'riding a mare of Dodgeson's to death.'* Another witness, Jennet Booth, also from Padiham, said that she had visited Pearson's husband whilst Pearson was in prison and a toad had hopped out of a pile of firewood. On the strength of this puerile 'evidence' Margaret Pearson received a sentence of pillory in the stocks of the main county towns, followed by imprisonment for twelve months.

Katherine Hewit of Colne was the wife of clothier John Hewit. She appears to have been a friend of **Alice Grey** who, having been found not guilty (although arraigned on much the same evidence as Hewit), figures little in the trial reports. Hewit was accused of bewitching to death one Anne Foulds; on the 4th July 1608 *Anna Ffouldes, daughter of Nicholai,* was buried at Colne. Hewit was also accused of *'having in hanck a child of Michael Hartley's of Colne.'* The meaning of this term is clear whereby *hanck* means 'in hand' but the origin is rather dubious; it may come from the Scots word *'to hanck,'* i.e. *'to have,' 'to holdfast'* or *'secure.'* Jamieson's Scotch Dictionary also shows *hanck* as possibly being from *'handkill'* meaning *'to murder,'* or lastly, the meaning may be metaphorically taken from the *'hanck'* signifying a skein of yarn or worsted which is tied or trussed up.

Katherine Hewit was also known as **Old Mouldheels**, this could be related to the fact that she was married to a clothier (a dealer in cloth). Handloom warps had a *size* of animal-fat applied to them to stiffen and strengthen the thread, this was sometimes over-applied in order to bulk out the cloth and as a consequence the warp became shiny and susceptible to the growth of mould on the surface of the textile. The warp was then known as a *'mouldy warp.'* The word *'Heels'* was a suffix commonly applied to a nickname relating to the nature of an individual, for example *'Leaden Heels'* described someone who moved slowly or dawdled. The shiny, slippery nature of a mouldy warp, coupled with the heels suffix might, therefore, have been the reason why the name *Mouldheels* was applied to Katherine Hewit; did she have a tendency to move quickly or bustle around? Alternatively, were the Hewits well known for their slippery nature within the cloth trade? Victorian novelists often used the term *'as shiny as a mouldy warp.'*

Another cause of mouldy warps was in the dying process; if dark colours were required, and there was not enough black or dark brown sheep's wool available, lighter brown wool was dyed

---

[1] *Bannister of Altham Papers,* Lancashire Records Office

by boiling it together with steel filings. This was done over and over again according to an exactly scheduled process of eight days; such treatment, however, damages the wool as it becomes brittle and mouldy.[1] Textile terms would have come easily to Hewit as she would no doubt work in some capacity in her husband's trade. In certain counties of England the farmer's enemy, the mole, is known within folklore as a *'mouldy-warp'* although it is uncertain that the name applied within this part of Lancashire.

It is likely that the Hewits lived in the Waterside area of Colne as there is a record of a John Kenyon having illegally erected a number of cottages there in the later part of the sixteenth century and one of the tenants there was one *John Hewytte*, clothier, and family.[2] A land transfer of May 1561 shows that Thomas Robinson of Goldshay and his brother, John Robinson, surrendered to Agnes Hewit, formerly the wife of Nicholas Blakey and now the wife of John Hewit, the tenancy of a farm, garden and fifteen acres of land in Colne by the oath of John Kenyon etc. In 1563 and 1568 John Hewit is mentioned as being co-tenant of this small farm in Colne at seven and-a-half acres. Nicholas Michell, who farmed at Old Earth Farm in Colne, surrendered the property and this may have been the area where John and Agnes Hewit were tenants. It is not clear as to the relationship between this John Hewit and the John Hewit who was the husband of Katherine Hewit. The probability is, however, that they were related as the name was relatively uncommon. On the 18th February, 1615, a *John Huett de Townhouse* (Great Marsden) was buried at Colne, the Townhouse area is close to Colne Waterside but it is not known if this was Katherine's husband. In 1620 a Colne rental list shows that a John Hewet *'rented a cottage upon the wastes of the manor of Colne at £0: 3s: 4d per year.'* [3] Being from Colne meant that Katherine Hewit was not strictly of the Pendle Forest. The others, then, were the Pendle Witches proper and at their head was **Elizabeth Southern,** alias **Old Demdike,** of Malkin Tower. The historic line on this family is that Elizabeth Southern had a daughter, **Elizabeth,** and a son **Christopher Holgate.** The daughter, Elizabeth, married **John Device** and they had daughters **Alizon** and **Jennet** and a son **James.** We will see presently that Alizon was actually baptised with the name of Alicea and I have therefore used the spelling of *Alison* within the text

John and Jane Bulcock were mother and son of Moss End at Newchurch, Jane was the wife of Christopher Bulcock.

Alice Nutter was the widow of landowner Richard Nutter of Crow Trees, Roughlee.

Old Chattox was described as being around eighty and lived at West Close below the village of Higham. Chattox's real name was **Anne Whittle** and her daughter, **Anne Redfern,** was the wife of Thomas Redfern (Redfeirne) by whom she had at least one child, a daughter named Marie. Chattox's other daughter, Elizabeth, was commonly known as Bessie Whittle. It is not clear if the name of Whittle originated through the family having lived at Whittley (modern White Lee, an area near to West Close), or from the Whittle-le-Woods area of Chorley – this latter suggestion is possible as there was a major concentration of the name in that area in the

[1] *Woollen Dying*, Unpublished text, Unknown author
[2] W. Farrar, *Clitheroe Court Rolls* (Vol 1, 1912)
[3] *Rentals for the Manor of Colne,* (Colne Local Studies Library)

sixteenth and seventeenth centuries. The Newchurch-in-Pendle, Burnley and Padiham parish records show a distinct paucity of the Whittle surname, in fact there is but a single relevant entry and that is where a *Jenneta Whyttle* was buried at Newchurch in 1576. Given the extreme rarity of the name locally the assignment of this person to the family of Anne Whittle would not be a serious offence.

In 1563 there is evidence that the Whittle family were small tenant farmers as Edmund Stevenson surrendered a parcel of land (around two acres) to *Christopher Whittles*. Along with this parcel Stevenson also granted Whittles a . . . *'Turbary in Red Mosse, Goldshaw, sufficient for a fire to be spent and burnt on said parcel to the use of Christopher Whittles and his assigns for 29 years at £0: 7s: 4d per year.'* This suggests that Whittles had a house on the parcel of land.[1] Edmund Stevenson had farmed land at East Delph, adjacent to Bull Hole Farm in Newchurch, for a number of years and another land record shows him letting a close of the Bull Hole Farm estate to Christopher Whittles. The turf-fields (*turbary*) were part of the moss below Newchurch village on which Higher Moss, Moss Nook and the Bulcock property of Moss End were situated. Bull Hole was the farm belonging to John Nutter whose cow Old Demdike was accused of killing. Christopher Whittle found himself in front of the magistrates in 1567 when he and James Moor, of Higham, were each fined 20d for making an affray together.

Other Whittle family members were Humphrey, baptised May 1562 at Whalley; Isabella Whittle, daughter of William, baptised February 1568 at Whalley; Nicholas Whittle, son of William, baptised December 1570 at Whalley; Oliver Whittle *molendarius* (miller) of Altham buried September 1570 at Whalley; Nicholas Whittle married Ana Blackburn, April 1581 at Whalley; Isabella Whittle, daughter of Nicholas, baptised June 1590 at Whalley. In 1587 the records of Great Harwood parish church show that William Whittle *'oweth 12d for burial of Old Whyttle wyffe.'*

Anne Whittle was gleefully described by Potts as having been a shambling old crone of about eighty years, she muttered and mumbled to herself, her lips continually moving but *'saying no man knows what.'* His description is aimed at consolidating the opinion of his readership into the general belief that a dangerous hag had been removed from society. There was no empathy with this poor, possibly senile woman who found herself before the Lancaster court – just a certainty that she deserved to die. Taken from Potts' account the following is the statement accorded to Old Chattox:

The Confession and Examination of Anne Whittle alias Chattox, being Prisoner at Lancaster, taken the 19 day of May,

First, the sayd Anne Whittle, alias Chattox, sayth, that about fourteene yeares past she entered, through the wicked perswasions and counsell of Elizabeth Southerns, alias Demdike, and was seduced to condescend & agree to become subiect vnto that diuelish abhominable profession of Witchcraft: Soone after which, the Deuill appeared vnto her in the liknes of a

---

[1] The common rights of *turbary* (peat-cutting) within the forest were for sufficient fuel to be available to supply a single fire per property.

Man, about midnight, at the house of the sayd Demdike: and therevpon the sayd Demdike and shee, went foorth of the said house vnto him; wherevpon the said wicked Spirit mooued this Examinate, that she would become his Subiect, and giue her Soule vnto him: the which at first, she refused to assent vnto; but after, by the great perswasions made by the sayd Demdike, shee yeelded to be at his commaundement and appoyntment: wherevpon the sayd wicked Spirit then sayd vnto her, that hee must haue one part of her body for him to sucke vpon; the which shee denyed then to graunt vnto him; and withall asked him, what part of her body hee would haue for that vse; who said, hee would haue a place of her right side neere to her ribbes, for him to sucke vpon: whereunto shee assented.

*A*nd *she further sayth, that at the same time, there was a thing in the likenes of a spotted Bitch, that came with the sayd Spirit vnto the sayd Demdike, which then did speake vnto her in this Examinates hearing, and sayd, that she should haue Gould, Siluer, and worldly Wealth, at her will. And at the same time she saith, there was victuals, viz. Flesh, Butter, Cheese, Bread, and Drinke, and bidde them eate enough. And after their eating, the Deuill called Fancie, and the other Spirit calling himselfe Tibbe, carried the remnant away: And she sayeth, that although they did eate, they were neuer the fuller, nor better for the same; and that at their said Banquet, the said Spirits gaue them light to see what they did, although they neyther had fire nor Candle light; and that they were both shee Spirites, and Diuels.*

*A*nd *being further examined how many sundry Person haue been bewitched to death, and by whom they were so bewitched: She sayth, that one Robert Nuter, late of the Greene-head in Pendle, was bewitched by this Examinate, the said Demdike, and Widdow Lomshawe, (late of Burneley) now deceased.*

*A*nd *she further sayth, that the said Demdike shewed her, that she had bewitched to death, Richard Ashton, Sonne of Richard Ashton of Downeham Esquire.*

A scene more awash with pathos than that of Anne Whittle's courtroom appearance can hardly be imagined; when her daughter, Anne Redfern, was being sentenced in court Old Chattox fell upon her knees and wept loud and long. She said that she fully admitted her guilt but that her daughter was entirely innocent; the protective mother pleaded with the judges to spare the life of her daughter but her entreaties fell upon deaf-ears – she might as well have asked for the moon.

The main reasons for the demise of Anne Whittle and her daughter was the enmity between this West Close family and their near neighbours, the Nutters of Greenhead. We shall meet with this family in detail but for now suffice it to say that Anne Redfern appears to have been the victim of a spoilt younger son of the yeomanry who, not able to have his own way when asking for sexual favours from an older married woman, threw his toys out of the pram. The person in question, young Robert Nutter, died in Chester (probably of consumption) a number of weeks after a fall-out with Anne Redfern; Robert's father, Christopher Nutter, died later the same year, again probably of the same disease and this was seen as having been a consequence of Anne Redfern and her mother bewitching them. The daughter was actually found not guilty of the first charge of murder but Demdike had made a tit-for-tat confession stating that she had seen Chattox and Anne Redfern making 'pictures' (clay models) of the Nutters to facilitate their deaths. This proved to be more than enough to convict Chattox and her daughter; both were duly hanged. (*For the Chattox/Redfern genealogy see page 295*).

Anne Redfern and her husband Thomas lived at West Close along with Anne's mother, Old Chattox; it is not clear if they all actually occupied the same property but this is probably the case. We are reasonably sure that Anne and Thomas had a daughter as the testimony of James Device stated that he saw the three Redferns together i.e, Anne, Thomas and daughter Marie. The Marriage of *Thomas Redfeirne* and *Ann Brown* in 1583 is interesting as this could well provide us with the marriage of Chattox's daughter. The fact that Ann possibly carried the name of Brown indicates that her mother could have had this name before marrying a Whittle. Alternatively, it was common practice for unmarried women to give the father's surname to a child; Whittle could have been Chattox's birth-name and she had her children by a man named Brown. According to witness statements Chattox had at least one other daughter, Elizabeth (Bessie) and this could possibly have been the Elizabeth Brown who married a Thomas Ellott in 1596. This latter family were based at Carry Bridge on the eastern edge of Colne Field. The following parish record entries relate to Newchurch unless otherwise stated:

1576: Ellis Brown (burial)

1581: Ellena Brown (baptism)

1581: Elena Brown (burial)

1581: Jenneta Brown married John Hartley

1583: Agnes (Ann) Brown married Thomas Redfeirne

1593: Ellis Redfeirne son of Robert (baptised Burnley)

1596: John Redfeirne (burial)

1596: Elizabeth Brown married Thomas Ellotte

1609: Marie Redfeirne married Richard Clayton

It is apparent from the parish records that the family of Thomas Redfern lived in Burnley, to the south of the Pendle Forest boundary. The lack of a surname within the registers cannot be taken as firm evidence that a particular family by that name did not exist – having said that, the incidence of recorded names does at least provide a demographic clue. Relating this to the Redfern family within the sixteenth century, it is apparent that this surname occurred within the records only very rarely. In fact, the four instances recorded in the above (proposed) genealogy comprise the whole of the local register entries.[1] Given this apparent scarcity of the Redfern name the marriage of Thomas Redfern and Agnes Brown can be taken as *'best available evidence'* for their having been the characters within the Pendle Witch story.

---

[1] Burnley *St. Peter's Parish Records*: Padiham *St. Leonard's Parish Records*: Colne *St. Bartholomew's Parish Records*: Newchurch *St. Mary's Parish Records*: Whalley *St. Mary's Parish Records*

Chapter Six

Give a Witch a Bad Name

There can be little doubt that the accounts left to us by Potts of the 1612 witch trials are blatantly biased; this is evident when he embroiders his account of Elizabeth Southern having lived at Malkin for a good number of years – the impression conveyed by Potts is one of a festering, evil, malodorous entity ensconced within that carbuncle of the forest, Malkin Tower. For many years this seat of the devil had been smouldering with the witch's curse but, at last, the cavalry had arrived in the form of Roger Nowell and Co; the forest would now be rid of the inhuman brood at the hands of which they had suffered for so long!

We shall see presently that there was probably a good reason why Elizabeth Southern lived at Malkin. It is highly probable that Southern and her family would have carried out work relating to the woollen weaving process, perhaps carding new wool, spinning or even weaving pieces – the produce from this could have been exchanged for rent with the owner of Malkin or, as the property was surrounded by woollen merchants at that time, the family's goods may have raised hard cash with which to pay their rent. This income would also have been supplemented by regular forays into the forest to beg for food and a few coppers. Along with many other people in their situation Demdike and her family would feel no need to hide the fact that they resorted to begging around the district. We do not know if this was a daily necessity or if they begged only in times of particular need; in fact there is every possibility that the term *begging* is a misnomer when applied to the Demdike family. It could have been the case that certain farming neighbours were only too happy to supply their spare blue-milk and oatmeal from the bottom of the sack to the Malkin family. Rather than begging expeditions one or other of the family might have done the farm-rounds as a matter of regular course in order to obtain their everyday consumables. The others would stay at home to carry out any weaving-related work they might have had; this would not preclude James and Alison from wandering the forest in search of any easy opportunity, however!

It is clear that local farmers would not tolerate an number of beggars, or strangers, on their lands and this is illustrated by T D Whitaker in his *History of Whalley* whereby he positively condones the shooting of the riff-raff who trespassed upon the holdings of the landowners – especially where the gentry were concerned the 'common sort' were obviously dispensable within the social scheme of things!

The local overseers would not interfere with the practice of begging to any degree as begging would have kept the family from having to claim on the limited local poor funds. In fact it was not uncommon for a poor woman to run an alehouse to gain a small income, although alehouses were usually frowned upon they were openly accepted when providing a living for the poor; a survey of Pendle Forest in 1655 showed that there were twelve alehouses, three of which were run by women.[1] Even more unwilling to accept the methods of the begging poor were the

---

[1] Mary Brigg, *The Forest of Pendle in the Seventeenth Century*, (Paper, Lancs / Cheshire History Soc. 1963)

Puritan element within society; to these people begging was anathema in the eyes of God, able people should toil for their bread and ask nothing of their fellow man. Given that many of the gentry (and other figures of authority) were of a Puritan bent the nails were ready to be driven firmly into the coffins of the disaffected poor – or at least a certain section of the poor in Pendle society who were ripe for the plucking.

Roger Nowell and his fellow Justice of the Peace, Nicholas Bannister of Altham, were members of the local Justice Quorum.[1] At times Nowell would interview the accused alone, apart from his assistant, this was the case on the 2nd of April when he examined Elizabeth Southern at Ashlar House in Fence (the house of James Wilsey):

The voluntarie Confession and Examination of *Elizabeth Sowtherns*

He (Roger Nowell) said Elizabeth Sowtherns confesseth, and sayth; That about twentie yeares past, as she was comming homeward from begging, there met her this Examinate neere vnto a Stonepit in Gouldshey, in the sayd Forrest of Pendle, a Spirit or Deuill in the shape of a Boy, the one halfe of his Coate blacke, and the other browne, who bade this Examinate stay, saying to her, that if she would giue him her Soule, she should haue any thing that she would request. Wherevpon this Examinat demaunded his name? and the Spirit answered, his name was Tibb: and so this Examinate in hope of such gaine as was promised by the sayd Deuill or Tibb, was contented to giue her Soule to the said Spirit: And for the space of fiue or sixe yeares next after, the sayd Spirit or Deuill appeared at sundry times vnto her this Examinate about Day-light Gate, alwayes bidding her stay, and asking her this Examinate what she would haue or doe? To whom this Examinate replyed, Nay nothing: for she this Examinate said, she wanted nothing yet.

And so about the end of the said sixe yeares, vpon a Sabboth day in the morning, this Examinate (Elizabeth Southern) hauing a little Childe vpon her knee, and she being in a slumber, the sayd Spirit appeared vnto her in the likenes of a browne Dogg, forcing himselfe to her knee, to get blood vnder her left Arme: and she being without any apparrell sauing her Smocke, the said Deuill did get blood vnder her left arme. And this Examinate awaking, sayd, Iesus saue my Child; but had no power, nor could not say, Iesus saue her selfe: wherevpon the Browne Dogge vanished out of this Examinats sight: after which, this Examinate was almost starke madd for the space of eight weekes.

Just how much of this 'voluntary' confession can be taken as the verbatim statement of Demdike is open to question. If the statement is genuine then, at best, we have the ramblings of a deluded mind; she is said to have been awoken by a brown dog after which she was *'starke madd'* for two months. From the statement this incident can be extrapolated to an approximate date of 1598/99 by discounting twenty years from 1612 and then adding six years. At the time of this incident Elizabeth Southern was obviously not a well woman and it is interesting to note that, as we shall see later, Elizabeth had a grandson named Henry who died at the age of four in 1599.

---

[1] A *Quorum* was made up of judges whose experience placed them in a senior position within the local legal system

Close inspection of the whole of Potts' accounts within his *Wonderfull Discovery of Witches* shows a common thread in that a fanciful story, embellished with devils, spells, voodoo-type dolls, familiars and flying horses. Intertwined within this rubbish can be found what appears to the unbiased observer as a sound core of truth. In the case of Demdike's 'confession' this becomes apparent if the fantasy is stripped away; it may also serve us well to consider that many of the 'confessions' of the various accused appear to be extremely arbitrary in relation to the passage of time, some statements when taken at face value are muddled at best.

Demdike was woken with a start when she was bitten (or dreamt that she had been bitten) by the brown dog, if this dog had been her own then it might simply have jumped up in order to gain her attention as dogs are wont to do. To embellish this small, ordinary recollection, Nowell could easily have slipped his own terms into the statement; Demdike uttered the words *"Jesus save my child"* followed by the statement that *"she had no power to ask for help for herself"* were perhaps Nowell's interpolated words and turned a trivial and mundane event into 'proof' that the examinate must indeed be a witch.

Great play is made of the fact that Demdike's familiar, Tibb, was a boy dressed in a coat half brown and half black although this was a common style of workman's coat at the time. Having met the boy near a quarry in the Newchurch area (probably Higher Delph or Faugh's Delph) he becomes the Devil incarnate. The bones of the fact could well be that Demdike did meet a young lad and he made some kind of an impression upon her; certainly the description (probably an embellishment on behalf of Nowell) of the coat is designed to embroider the character of the boy by giving him a devilish air. Was this designed to provide subtle overtones of the biblical boy Joseph and his multi-coloured coat? The lad appeared at various times, always at *daylight-gate* (dusk) and always bidding her to stay. The fact that Demdike first met the lad on her way home suggests that this too might have been around dusk. Was the lad at a regular place at a regular time, perhaps a farmer's lad on his way home from the fields and merely wanting some company to walk with for a while? If this were the real story related by Demdike to Nowell it would be a simple matter for him to add a few frills by assigning the boy as an agent of the Devil, ready and willing to carry out evil deeds at Demdike's bidding. As an illustration of the fact that many of the statements made by the accused were at best confused, Demdike stated on the same day that the boy was named Tibb and also that her familiar was a black cat named Tibb.

We have seen that the witch's Familiar was central to the prosecution, the accused appear to have readily admitted to having access to their own private little demons in the shape of cats, dogs, boys and, in the case of Chattox, a ,*thing like a Christian man.'* It is possible that the likes of Demdike and Chattox would vie with each other in order to have perceived access to a supernatural aid. The person with the most powerful reputation would gain the most employment from the people in need of their services. To this end it is probable that the accused would mention this to Nowell – given the likelihood that nobody had previously thought to demonise the 'standard practice' of the accused they would see no danger in admitting to having access to what amounted to a tool of their trade. In all probability the animals referred to as Familiars would have been the pets kept by the accused. It was common practice to keep dogs for protection and to catch any game that might have been available. There are a number of instances of local people owning dogs in the Clitheroe Court Rolls, examples being:

1537: *James Hartley of Blacko fined 4d for keeping an objectionable dog (canem irracionabilem) to his neighbour's injury.*

1555: Henry Bannester of Parkhill and James Hartley of Blacko fined 12d each for keeping an unruly tenant in John Robinson alias Bewse who with his dogs drove away his neighbour's beasts.

1560: John Blakey keeps a dog called 'a shepe werier.'

These records, of course, show only the dog owners who had broken the byelaws. Given the propensity for country people to imbue their animals (hares, cats, dogs, owls etc,) with a zoomorphic spirituality, and taking into account that these animals existed in far greater numbers than they do today, it is no surprise that the accused related closely with them. Cats in particular were closely associated with witchcraft, from at least the Norman Conquest to the nineteenth century most villages had their own particular stories attached to these animals. A favourite was where a cat belonging to an elderly woman would be injured in some way, usually by breaking a leg, the following day the unfortunate cat's elderly owner was found to have exactly the same injury. The accused, such as Demdike, would have been seeped in this lore throughout the whole of their lives and would see nothing wrong in relating to their interrogators the fact that they owned animals and knew the folklore associated with them. From the time when animals were regarded as the messengers of local deities this part of the countryman's culture had survived almost intact.

A matter of relevance here is the manner in which the statements of the accused were manipulated by the magistrates to ensure that the person in control of the Familiar was seen to have actually channelled its demonic powers towards their own evil ends. It is interesting that many of the statements within Potts' account of the trials show that the Familiars of the accused appeared 'out of the blue' – at a salient point within the related story a Familiar, or spirit, would be at the service of the witch and would be only too willing to kill on their behalf. When this occurred the witch would be taken aback, somehow they appeared unable to relate the actions of the Familiar to their own intentions. This raises the question of the depth of belief that the accused held in their own abilities or powers; if they did indeed think that they might have been responsible for the death of another person then the transference of guilt to a third party might assuage their own perceived guilt. The guilt transference might also have been an attempt on behalf of the accused to deflect their own prosecution. There is also the possibility that the magistrates used autosuggestion in their methods of interrogation to plant the idea within the minds of the so-called witches i.e, that they were indeed responsible for the deaths of their neighbours – this might elicit the response that it was the spirit who killed and not the accused directly.

In the circumstances whereby the accused were interviewed by a magistrate acting alone, where was the failsafe to assure fairness? When Nowell acted within his Quorum, along with his fellow Justice, Nicholas Bannister, would the latter question Nowell's methods? When the written 'confessions' were submitted as pure fact to the August Assizes, at Lancaster Castle, who acted for the defence, who cross-examined the prosecution in order to gain even a hint at the truth?. . . . Not one solitary person is the answer.

The Baldwin Connection

Elizabeth Southern died in Lancaster Gaol before the start of the August trials and was therefore never convicted of any crime; this, of course, did not prevent Thomas Potts including her alleged confession in his *Discoverie*. He obviously considered that it would be a waste of valuable propaganda to omit such a juicy piece of diabolism; the brilliant detective work, carried out by Roger Nowell, in arraigning the damnable brood of highly dangerous witches had to be reported. Another extract of Demdike's 'confession,' taken by Nowell at Ashlar House, shows the enmity that existed between the Malkin group and their neighbours:

And vpon her examination, she (Elizabeth Sowthens) further confesseth, and saith. That a little before Christmas last, this Examinates Daughter (Elizabeth Device) hauing been to helpe Richard Baldwyns Folkes at the Mill: This Examinates Daughter did bid her this Examinate goe to the sayd Baldwyns house, and aske him some thing for her helping of his Folkes at the Mill, (as aforesaid:) and in this Examinates going to the said Baldwyns house, and neere to the sayd house, she mette with the said Richard Baldwyn; Which Baldwyn sayd to this Examinate, and the said Alizon Deuice (who at that time ledde this Examinate, being blinde) get out of my ground Whores and Witches, I will burne the one of you, and hang the other. To whom this Examinate answered: I care not for thee, hang thy selfe: Presently wherevpon, at this Examinates going ouer the next hedge, the said Spirit or Diuell called Tibb, appeared vnto this Examinat, and sayd, Reuenge thee of him. To whom, this Examinate sayd againe to the said Spirit. Revenge thee eyther of him, or his. And so the said Spirit vanished out of her sight, and she neuer saw him since.

This alleged confession points us in an interesting direction; as is the case with other 'confessions' of the accused, it is necessary to read between the lines to gain some semblance of truth. The altercation with the miller, Richard Baldwin, was also referred to in a statement taken by Nowell from Demdike's granddaughter, Alison Device. Alison allegedly reported that her grandmother said that she would '*pray for Baldwin both still and loude,*' this was then taken by the prosecution as evidence that Demdike had put a spell upon Baldwin following which his daughter died. The term '*pray*' is open to conjecture in this context but the die is firmly cast when Demdike apparently admits that she bade her Familiar to take revenge upon Baldwin. This event appears to have occurred late in the year of 1611; the spirit was said to have appeared unto Demdike and then vanished out of her sight – given that Demdike was blind at this time it is difficult to credit these given 'facts.' The only other explanation here would be that Demdike 'saw' the spirit in her imagination which would suggest a degree of mental instability; given that Alison did not mention the appearance of Demdike's spirit in her own statement there would have been ample opportunity here for a defence lawyer to shoot the prosecution down in flames.

Alison Device told Nowell that she thought Demdike had killed Baldwin's daughter – in fact Ellena, the daughter of *Richardi Baldwyn de Whithead*, was buried at Colne on September 8th 1610. Ellena was but one of many of the Baldwin family of Wheathead to have died in this period, from the late sixteenth century a family member, usually a child, died almost every other year for a period of some twenty years.[1]

Elsewhere in the *Discoverie* we are told that Baldwin's daughter had fallen ill shortly after her father's argument with Demdike and lingered about a year before her death. Demdike states that the altercation took place '*a little before Christmas last.*' As her statement was taken in the

---

[1] Colne St. Bartholomew's Parish records

spring of 1612 this should refer to the Christmas of 1611 but this cannot be correct. There would only have been a space of four months between the incident and Demdike's statement – if the burial record of Ellena Baldwin definitely refers to the miller's daughter then the incident must have taken place before Christmas 1609. This appears to be another example of the sporadic, and often arbitrary, nature of the facts within the statements of the accused.

Alison Device stated that she had many times heard her grandmother curse Richard Baldwin and there is no reason to doubt this given the account where Baldwin reacted angrily to Demdike and her daughter, Elizabeth Device, when they approached his house. This is commonly said to have been the reaction of a man who was at the end of his tether with the Demdike family – if Elizabeth had indeed carried out work at Baldwin's mill, however, she would have been entitled to expect payment in some form; why then did Baldwin hit the roof?

The following (abridged) last will and testament of James Baldwin was transcribed by Peter Wightman (of Colne) and provides interesting reading:

*O*n *the ninth day of January in the three and thirtieth year of our most gracious and sovereign lady Queen Elizabeth (1591) I James Bawden of Colne in the county of Lancaster glover sick in body but whole in mind do ordain and make this my last will: my worldly goods to be divided into three equal parts - the first thereof to my wife in her own right - the second to my sons John Bawden and James Bawden - the third divided as twenty shillings to my youngest son James Bawden, I give to Lawrence Botheman four yard of new grey cloth, one pair of new shoes, a pair of stockings, a pair of breeches and a jerkin being all of sheep grey and twenty stone of hay. I give unto John Bawden my part of one hundredth of Calve skins and all my part of sheep skins the wool thereof being pulled, and also all my instruments wherewith I do dress any leather, and the residue of my part of goods I will shall be equally divided to the said John Bawden, James Bawden, Annyse now wife of the said Lawrence Botheman,* **Elizabeth Davye** *alias Bawden and* **Jennet Davye** *alias Bawden supposed to be the bastard daughters of me the said James Bawden. I make executors Elizabeth my wife and John Walker of Colne desiring* **Christopher Bawden** *of the Weethead to see this my last will and testament be fulfilled as my trust is in him. . . . the estate is valued by Christopher Dicconson and Henry Bawden, yeoman of Greenfield.*

So. . . . somewhere along the line James Baldwin, of Colne, had two daughters by a woman called Davye and they were still living at the time of Baldwin's will in 1591. The names of Baldwin's daughters, Elizabeth and Jennet Davye, correspond to the names of Elizabeth and Jennet Device of Malkin but this, of course, proves nothing as Elizabeth and Jennet were common given names at the time. We will see the argument later for the name of Davye, Davis, Device and Devise being of the same phonetic root and the following might be of interest to our subject of the Baldwin will. Anthony Baldwin, of Trawden Forest, died on the 8th October 1724 and left all of his goods and chattels to his sister, Margaret Baldwin; Margaret died the following year and her will states:[1]

I Margaret Baldwin of Oakenbank within the Forrest & Chase of Trawden give devise & bequeath unto Thomas Wilson of Beaver in the Forrest of Trawden yeoman & **David Davis**

---

[1] Doreen Crowther – *Transcribed Colne Wills*

of Wycholde (Wycoller) in the Forrest and County aforesaid yeoman & Richard Sutcliffe of Todmerden in Hundersfield yeoman the sum of twenty pounds of Current Brittish money. I give unto Mary Cowgill my servant the sum of ten pounds of current money; Item I give unto John Baldwin my nephew the sum of fifteen pounds; Item I give unto William Baldwin my nephew the sum of fifteen pounds; Item I give unto James Baldwin my nephew the sum of fifteen pounds; Item I give unto Elizabeth Wife of John Blaikey of Marsden the sum of fifteen pounds; Item I give unto Margaret Wife of Richard Boyes of Colne the sum of fifteen pounds; Thomas Wilson & David Davis aforesaid joynt & lawful Executors of this my Will.

The will of James Baldwin in 1591, and the above will of Margaret Baldwin some 134 years later, proves little in relation to the Device name other than a link between the Baldwins and the Device family. Here then, we can return to the question posed earlier 'why did Richard Baldwin hit the roof when Elizabeth Southern and her daughter appeared on his land?' The plain answer is that we do not know for certain but we must consider the fact that Elizabeth Device could well have been related to the Baldwin family through her husband, John Device. If so, the fact that the Demdike family were related to his own family through the illegitimate offspring of his (probable) brother James would have been enough to grossly offend the high Protestant morals of Richard Baldwin. The un-Godly family of *'witches and whores,'* as he unkindly named Demdike and Elizabeth Device, would have been a constant thorn in his side. The fact that his neighbours, and moreover, his fellow church congregation, would have known of the relationship would have been enough to cause him a serious bout of apoplexy. It has to be born in mind here that Richard Baldwin was not only a local church worthy but he also rubbed shoulders with the Great and the Good of Pendle Forest. Records show that he often witnessed marriage contracts and other official papers and, in this capacity, would have had occasion to work alongside Roger Nowell in certain matters of officialdom. Given this state of affairs is it any wonder that Richard Baldwin's Malkin 'neighbours from hell' (as he would see them) were arraigned and tried for witchcraft when the opportunity arose?

Furthermore, Richard Baldwin's sister, Ellena, was related by marriage to Henry Hargreaves, the constable who, under Roger Nowell's instructions, carried out most of the arrests of the Pendle accused in 1612. Richard Baldwin's brother named a daughter after his sister as records show that on the 10th of January 1613 Ellena Baldwin, daughter of Christopher of Wheathead, was buried at Colne. In 1597 a Richard Baldwin married Jenneta Hartley at Newchurch-in-Pendle and on the 16th of April 1612 a Jenneta Baldwin of Wheathead was buried at Colne – the records do not give the status of Jenneta but she was possibly Richard's daughter as, on the 5th of June 1617, the wife of Richard Baldwin of Wheathead was buried at Colne.

In a paper to the *Historic Society of Lancashire and Cheshire* (1963) Mary Briggs reported that Richard Baldwin left a will in 1617 in which he stated that he was: *'Trusting . . . to be one of the Electe number that shalle inherite his heavenly and everlasting kingdom . . .'* Mary showed that this differs from the standard requirement within wills to ensure a Christian burial and that Baldwin was exercising a particular sectarian doctrine. The will also shows that Baldwin had three daughters, Elizabeth, Margaret and Mary all of whom *'Shall have, occupy and quietly possess the easte end of my now dwelling house and barne there adjoyninge for and during the terme of twelve yeares next after the decease of me. . .'*

Three years later, in 1620, Richard's brother, John Baldwin of Wheathead, left a will in which the inventory totalled £180 thus showing that he was a substantial yeoman at the time of his death. Having no children John left what amounted to the major part of his property and goods to his wife: *'Jennet, my wyffe shall have halfe part of all my goodes as the laudable custome giveth her. . .'* The other half was to go to nephews and nieces. Half of the estate does not appear to have been a majority but the usual custom was to divide property and goods by thirds; a third to the youngest children, a third for the wife's dower and the other third was known as *'the dead's part'* and paid for funeral expenses plus any outstanding debts of the deceased, legacies and legal fees. Jennet died in the following January and she left the same inventory as her husband:

The halfe parte of 4 oxen and 3 stiers	*£16: 0: 0*
Halfe of 8 kyne and 4 calves	*£12: 3: 4*
Halfe of 9 yonge beastes	*£ 7: 0: 0*
Halfe of 1 meare, sadles and other furniture	*£ 2: 0: 0*
Halfe of seaventeen sheepe	*£ 2: 0: 0*
Halfe of 1 swyne	*£ 0: 15: 0*
Halfe of waynes, wheles, yockes and teames and other husbandrie geare	*£ 3: 16: 8*
Halfe of 1 Ireon Chimney, reckontrie, brandret fyre poate, tonges and spittes	*£ 0: 13: 4*

Jennet would probably have received an income from her half of the farming operation, the nephews and nieces would only receive their share upon her death. The Wheathead farming estate supported at least three families of Baldwins during the same period although it appears that Richard operated separately as a miller. Richard Baldwin's father, Henry, and brother Christopher, were churchwardens at Colne in 1601. Richard Baldwin also figured in the arraignment of Anne Whittle when the prosecution furnished a statement supposedly given by her where she says that her spirit wished to kill the wife of Richard Baldwin but she stopped this from happening. Richard Baldwin would not appear to have been very popular amongst certain (apostate?) members of the Pendle Forest community!

At the time of James Baldwin's will there were two neighbouring Christopher Baldwins, one lived in the hamlet of Admergill below Blacko Hill and the other was living at Wheathead. There are two Wheathead properties, one is the Higher Wheathead on the Burnt Moor high above Admergill and the other is known as Lower Wheathead and is situated at Lanefield off Wheathead Lane (SD 847 418). However, just to confuse matters, on some pre-nineteenth century estate maps the property of the present Lower Wheathead is actually shown as Higher Wheathead. We know that the present Lower Wheathead Farm was the Wheathead of Richard Baldwin, the miller who turned both of the Elizabeths off his land, as it just within the boundary of Pendle Forest whereas Higher Wheathead is situated on Burnt Moor in the parish of Brogden (detached) – Richard Baldwin was *'of Roughlee.'* The Baldwins had been involved in land acquisition within Roughlee Booth for many years as the Clitheroe Court Rolls illustrate:

1507: *There is another pasture and vaccary called Overoughlee and Netheroughlee otherwise Roughlee Boothe whereof the old rent was £9 by year the same now taken by Christopher Baldwin, Christopher Smith, Peter Smith, John Smith, John Byby, Henry Mitton, William*

Mitton, Richard Nutter, Lawrence Nutter, Piers Robinson, John Robinson, Bertram Robinson and Nicholas Robinson for 20 marcs per year. Improved yearly £4: 6s: 8d.

1515/16: John Bawdeyn fined for cutting wood and greenwood in Castyclough (Wheathead) and William Bawden likewise.

1525: Presented at the Great Inquest taken from the Forest of Pendle that 1 messuage and appurtenances in Roughlee called Wheat Head in said Forest at £0: 33s: 4d per annum rent has reverted to the King upon the death of John Baldwin and that Henry Baldwin, his son and heir, is 8 years old. John Baldwin forbids fine for 40s of money: and also came to the court Ellen and Joan Baldwin and forbid fine for their dowers for the term of their lives. Said Henry Baldwin finds surety, Peter Robinson and William Baldwin. Admitted.

1525: William Baldwen, Henry Baldwin and the wife of Christopher Baldwen were amerced at 6d each for breach of the Birelag (bye-laws) and not making the Rengyorde (ring-fence) at Wolfenbanck (above Wheathead).

1525: William Baldwen fined 12d, the wife of John Baldwen 2d and the wife of Christopher Baldwen 2d for trespass with their beasts on Roughlee Common.

1531: John Hirst sues William Baldwin, the relict of Christopher Baldwin and the relict of John Baldwin for debt.

1531: Christopher Baldwin sues John Smith of Barrowford for building a house on his land. The jury ordered Smith to give Baldwin the same value in land.

1532: John Hanson alias Jenkin and Henry Baldwin both fined 4d for cutting down and removing greenwood from Wulfaw Bank.

1537: Henry Baldwin sues William Baldwin for 40s damages for oppressing his pasture at Wheathead.

1546: William Baldwin of Wheathead 'kept so unreasonable a way that the king's subjects were not able to pass' - this refers to Baldwin neglecting Wheathead Lane adjoining his property.

1539 Rentals: Roughlee

John Hargreaves	9s: 8½d	Miles Nutter	11s: 1¼d
William Mitton	11s: 1¼d	Miles Robinson	5s: 6¼d
Nicholas Robinson	9s: 8½d	Jo Smith snr	5s: 6¼d
Rich Bibbye	4s: 2d	Wm Baldwin	11s: 1¼d
Wife of Chr Baldwin	11s: 1¼d		

1551: *William Baldwin of Wheathead surrendered a messuage and other buildings in Roughlee at £0: 16s: 8d to the use of Nicholas Baldwin son of said William. Henry Baldwin claimed half of the messuage by inheritance. Henry later surrendered all his title at Wheathead at £0: 33s:4d in the present holding of William Baldwin to Nicholas and Christopher Baldwin.*

1552: *Land dispute - In 1551 Lawrence Hartley surrendered land in Barrowford at 4s to Christopher Hartley his son. James Hartley of Blacko disputed fine because of his inheritance. Dower reserved to Johanne late wife of Lawrence Hartley for life. In 1552 James Baldwin of Blacko seized the land at 10s, jury ordered land to return to Christopher Hartley.*

1555: *Christopher Baldwin versus Henry Baldwin for obstruction of road and watercourse and the door of the complainant's barn and broke his hedges. Henry Baldwin complains that Christopher Baldwin obstructed the right course of water between his land and unjustly fixed a gate on his land.*

1556: *Christopher Baldwin complains that Henry Baldwin dammed and diverted the water course. Jury direct course to be put back as it was.*

1558: *Christopher Smith, executor of Isobell Smith, complained against the relict (widow) of Richard Baldwin, and Henry Baldwin executor of the testament of Richard Baldwin, in a plea of debt to £8.*

1564: *Henry Baldwin of Wheathead by James Hartley tenant of Blacko, surrenders a messuage and other buildings at £0:33s:4d to the use of Lawrence Blakey, John Swayne of Southfield and John Swayne of Foulridge. Intent: Christopher Baldwin (son of Henry) now occupies the above buildings at 40s paid to his father, residue of premises to the father – Henry Baldwin of Wheathead, by James Hartley tenant of Blacko, surrenders a messuage and other buildings at £0: 33s: 4d to the use of Lawrence Blakey, John Swayne of Southfield and John Swayne of Foulridge. Intent: Christopher Baldwin (son of Henry) now occupies the above buildings at 40s paid to his father, residue of premises to the father.*

1570: *Henry Baldwin of Wheathead, Christopher Baldwin senior of Wheathead and Nicholas Baldwin were each fined 2d because they kept their sheep upon the common pasture of Shelfield (Marsden) of which area they were not tenants.*

1575: *Henricus Baldwine married Eliza Shackleden at Newchurch*

Colne Wills relating to Wheathead residents:

Nicholas Baldwin 1587:
Christopher Baldwin 1594:
Richard Baldwin 1617:
Jennet Baldwin Widow 1620:
John Baldwin 1620:
John Baldwin 1661:

1608/9 Rentals: Roughlee Vaccary

Chris Nuttall clerk	3s: 3¼d	Henry Robinson	7s: 7d
John Bulcock	3s: 0d	**Chris Baldwin**	£1: 13: 4d
Richard Baldwin	16s: 8d	**John Baldwin**	16s: 8d
Robert Smith	16s: 1½d	James Slater & wife	3s: 8½d
Chris & Simon Blakey	13s: 10d	James Ridehough	5s :6½d
Roger Mitton	£1: 2s: 2½d	Miles Nutter	11s: 7d
William Robinson	5s: 4d	John Crook	12s: 0d
John Varley	11s: 4d	Henry Mitton	2s: 4½d
Hugh Hartley	16s: 0d	Ellen Hartley	15s: 7d
John Robinson	10s: 10d	John Cunliffe	£1:18s:1d
Wm Hartley alias Trock	6s:0: 25d	heirs of Henry Hartley	0s:6d

A number of the Colne and Roughlee Baldwins were involved in the corn milling trade; in 1536 miller, Richard Bawden, paid tithes from corn sheaves to the Abbot of Whalley at either ten pence or ten shillings (the record is unclear). In 1546 James Bawden, a miller, was fined four pence for overcharging for multure at the King's Mill in Colne. James, who made the above will in 1591, was a glove-maker at the time of his death but could have been the miller of 1546 – his executor, Christopher Baldwin (son of Henry Baldwin and brother to Richard Baldwin, miller of Wheathead) was involved in the Foulridge mill operation as the following Foulridge Manor record shows:

13th July 1594: *Award of Barnarde Towneley of Hurstewoode, gent., Robart Jackson of Worsthorne, and Christofer Bawdwen of Weethead in Pendle, yeomen, concerning disputes between lords and owners of Foulerygge over allotments and rebuilding of mill.*

It is generally thought that Baldwin's Mill, where Elizabeth Device helped out, was the corn mill that was situated in Roughlee near to the residence of Alice Nutter at Damhead. However, this mill was owned by Lawrence Towneley who, in 1609, paid £0: 2s: 0d rental, this compared with his rental at Carr Mill of £1: 0s: 0d and illustrates the difference in the size of the two operations. In the October of 1569 Henry Towneley, of Carr Hall (Barrowford), surrendered Carr Mill to Thomas Lister of Westby, Richard Smith, Lawrence Towneley and John Hartley of Admergill, yeoman. At the time of the 1609 rental returns for Roughlee Booth the tenant of the Roughlee Mill was John Nutter, the son of John Nutter who was the son of Ellis Nutter of Reedley Waterside and this family tenanted both the Roughlee mill (built 1598) and the Carr mill at Lower Barrowford. This is of interest because the Damhead area in which the Roughlee Mill was situated was owned by the family of Alice Nutter's husband; this property eventually descended to the Nutters of Waterside. This would appear to negate the argument for Richard Baldwin having owned/worked the Roughlee Mill.

An estate plan of Lower Wheathead shows that there was a parcel of land on the edge of Henry Baldwin's land known as *Oastgate Clough*. The word 'oast' is now taken as meaning 'hop drying oven' but during the medieval period oast had the generic meaning of *kiln. Oast-gate,* then, would have been the trackway to the kiln suggesting that there was a grain-related operation upon Wheathead land; this could have been a kiln site for the malting of barley for the brewing process, a kiln for the treatment of wheat and oats, or both. In the neighbouring hamlet of Admergill there was a corn-drying operation of some kind as a number of grooved rack-stones can be found in the field walls around the immediate area of the buildings.

Field names from an Admergill estate plan show that a riverside close was known as the Mill Field and this, along with the evidence of the rack-stones, points to there having been a corn mill on the site.[1] This mill was in fact much closer to Lower Wheathead than was Damhead, higher up the Roughlee valley, and this could well have been Baldwin's Mill. Christopher Baldwin who was either the brother or nephew of Richard, was at Admergill at this time and Richard could well have shared in any milling operation there. John Hartley of Admergill, as we have seen, had an interest in the Carr corn mill and there is the strong possibility here that he was involved in milling at Admergill along with Christopher Baldwin. John's will of 1623 shows that, on the 21st of August in that year, the Admergill operation had corn growing in the fields to the value of £14. Corn, then, was being grown on a commercial scale within the Wheathead and Admergill areas; other crops besides wheat were grown locally, rye, oats and barley were staple corn crops, the latter being indicated by the field name of Barley Holme in Admergill. The Admergill Baldwins, then, were very possibly the *'folks of Richard Baldwin'* whom Elizabeth Device helped out.

In 1589 a Richard Baldwin, of *'Wanless in Blakey in Coln'* was shown as a yeoman farmer. He was the tenant of the Blakeys of Blakey Hall; Lower Wanless is the farm now standing upon the Leeds and Liverpool canal where it once served as an inn known as The Grinning Rat. There is every possibility that a small milling operation was located here as the farm sits astride the juncture of the two streams draining Blacko Hillside. It is not clear whether the Richard Baldwin here named is the same as the Richard of Wheathead – it is a possibility as he could have been named as the tenant of Wanless even though his main property was at Wheathead.

In 1609 Richard Baldwin tenanted some sixty acres of land within Roughlee whilst his brother, Christopher, paid for one-hundred acres. The difference in landholding between them was possibly on account of Richard running his mill operation whereby Christopher would be primarily a farmer.

An early photograph of cottages within the old Roughlee Mill area

Photograph: S. Regan

---

[1] An estate plan relating to the 19th century sale of Admergill Hall Farm is available at Nelson Local Studies Library *(Doreen Crowther Files)*

Chapter Seven

Elizabeth - A Device By Any Other Name!

In his will James Baldwin bequeathed a portion of his goods to '**Elizabeth Davye** alias *Bawden* and **Jennet Davye** alias *Bawden supposed to be the bastard daughters of me the said James Bawden.'* There is no doubt that a family by the name of Davye lived within the Colne area in the later sixteenth century; the records also show two entries for Deves;

1509: *William Mitchell, Nicholas Dugdell and* **Alan Deves** *were fined for making an afray upon John Hegyn and for drawing blood. As they had no means of support they were punished bodily (in the stocks).*

1531: **Alan Deves** *made an afray upon Nicholas Mitchel*

1534: *The jury present George Blakey, clerk, and* **Alan Deves** *for making an afray together and the said George for drawing blood from the said Alan.*

21st April 1607: *Alicia, the illegitimate daughter of* **Jacobi Davye** *was baptised;*
20th April 1608: **Jacobi Davye** *buries his son, Johannes;*
28th May 1611: *Anna the daughter of* **Jacobi Davie** *is buried;*
21st March 1612: **Laurentius Davie** *de Colne is buried;*
17th July 1614: *Jacob, the son of* **Jacobi Davie** *is baptised;*
4th August 1617: *Jacob Lee de Catlaw married the wife of* **Jacobi Davie;**
2nd August 1616: *Margareta, daughter of* **Jacobi Davie** *is baptised;*
18th August 1618: **Jacob Davie** *married Agnes Abilsburye;*
11th October 1619: **Jacob Davie** *de Barrowford was buried;*
29th March 1621: *Thomas, son of* **Jacobi Davie** *is baptised;*
13th May 1630: **Jacob Davie** *was buried.*
25th July 1633: *Johes Cotton married Agnes* **Davie;**

There are no records for the name of Device or Devise but three for Alan Deves, the rest relate to the name of Davye and Davie. There is a strong probability that the Alan Deves, who was prone to getting into scrapes with his neighbours in 1509, 1531 and 1534, would have been related to John Device, the husband of Elizabeth. Because the Davye family surname only appears within the Colne parish records when Alicea is baptised in 1607 it is unsafe to assume that the family were not in the area previously; it might just be the case that Jacob Davye had been the first in his family to have his children baptised. It has to be remembered that most of the common people did not use the church to baptise their children or to marry; also, church records do not begin until (commonly) the mid-sixteenth century. This is the main reason that we have a struggle to allocate a particular family to others of a similar name. As an aside, in Colne there was a hill called Davie Hill from where Roger Foulds was buried in 1644 (Anne Foulds of Colne was bewitched to death by Katherine Hewit) and this provides at least a consideration that the Davye/Davie family was actually living locally for a good number of years prior to 1607.

An interesting point arises where Alan Deves was put in the Colne stocks; this was the form of punishment commonly meted out for minor misdemeanours where the guilty person was unable to afford to pay a fine. The man that Deves assaulted, John Hegyn (Higgin), was the incumbent at Colne parish church at the time of Deves's first court appearance. In this capacity Higgin was granted the income from land and buildings at Malkin; this was the result of this land, along with another area of Blacko Hillside, having been granted to the Colne parish church before the 1507 deforestation. In a complex web of over-tenancy, sub-tenancy and inter-marriage not only were the Towneleys and Bannisters the landlords of the Stone Edge estate, of which the property of Malkin formed a small part, but also the Listers of Westby Hall were heavily involved in land ownership around and upon Blacko Hillside. By the middle of the nineteenth century the Malkin Tower farm property was part of the Bannister estate of Park Hill and this would suggest that this family had exercised control over this particular site, as over-tenants, for a number of years.

Why, then, did William Mitchell, Nicholas Dugdell and Alan Deves attack John Higgin? Two of the three protagonists were local men; a branch of the Mitchells lived at Colne Church Style whilst another part of the family farmed around Lower Ridge in the Water Meetings area of Barrowford. The Dugdales were also a Barrowford farming family. In 1531 Alan Deves also assaulted Nicholas Mitchell whose brother, Richard Mitchell, had a quarter share in the tenancy of a Blacko Hillside property (possibly Malkin) in 1524, the beneficiary here being one William Hird, a chantry priest. Deves appears to have taken a break from assaulting his neighbours as he does not appear again until 1534 when he was at it again with another Colne chantry priest in the form of George Blakey. I take this chap to be the brother of 'Sir' Robert Blakey who was incumbent at Colne between 1520 and 1551 and was very likely to have been the beneficiary of the Malkin property. This is because Robert Blakey, in 1540, was accused by Bernard Hartley of trespass through not keeping his fences *between the Juddefield and the Long Rodes upon Le Blacke Dyke.*' This was the area of Blacko Hill immediately above the Malkin property. This same property was mentioned again in the court rolls of 1551:

'The messuage and other buildings, land, meadow, pasture and feeding ground in the occupation of Christopher and Lawrence Blakey at 10s per annum, which late belonged to the finding and maintenance of a priest within the church of Colne, to the use of Robert Blakey, late incumbent of the said service for the term of his life and his heirs.'

This was the end of the property as long-term glebe/chantry land and the property surrender was no doubt a direct consequence of the 1547 Act for the *Dissolution of the Chantries*. This Act saw the breaking up of the private chantry chapels and altars within parish churches on the grounds that they were based upon superstition. At the time the blow was softened by Elizabeth Ist's chancellors promising that the money diverted from the former chantries would be redirected into other church affairs; this never happened and the Act proved to be nothing other than a windfall for the exchequer to spend on its foreign policies.

Where Alan Deves lived is not known but the question arises as to whether the attacks upon Higgin and Blakey were related to their roles as beneficiaries of the income generated by the Malkin property? We have seen that there is reason to believe that Alan Deves was local to the Blacko area but can we accept that he would have reason to rough up his parish priest? To illustrate the possibilities here it is worth quoting the story of one Gilbert Fairbank whose brother 'Sir' William Fairbank was incumbent at Colne, following John Higgin, from 1520 to 1535. Gilbert was the incumbent at St. Peter's in Burnley and was therefore the beneficiary of church lands in the form of a farm and eleven acres of land in the Habergham area of Burnley. In 1550 Fairbank wrote a petition to Sir William Paget explaining that the local farmers would not accept the fact that he had the rights over the Habergham lands and had taken the law into their own hands: [1]

Concereninge 1 mease and 11 acres with appurtenances there (Habergahme) . . . I have always takin proffittes thereof until ye 2nd day of Maye laste when Edmunde Whitacres, Richarde Bothe, Margretta Batersbye, Johes Hargraves, Henricus Emote and Thos Emote, with force of armmes, that is to saye with bowes, swordes, bucklers and other weapones defensive, in a most riotouse manner entered into said mease and land and expulsed this plaintiffe from everye part thereof and will no wise suffer him to enjoye ye same to this plaintiff's utter inpoverishmente.

This record conjures the image of a wild-eyed Margaret Batersbye, sporting an apron and huge hob-nailed boots, running amok on the Habergham farm, screaming like a banshee whist she twirled the leg-bone of an ox frantically above her head - whilst this was happening the poor old priest would have been cowering behind the nearest pig stye!

This incident shows the depth of feeling that surrounded ecclesiastic land grants. This was by no means an isolated incidence of unrest but most of the church land holdings appear to have been peaceable. When a parish incumbent held true glebe lands there was little for the neighbouring farmers to complain about because Whalley Abbey had in all probability held these lands for many years. It has to be remembered, however, that the chantry priest was usually a poor, unqualified parishioner who was simply paid (usually by the gentry) to pray for the patron's family on a regular basis. The grant of lands to the use of a chantry priest often saw an *'offcumden'* (none-local person) take over the property rents that a farmer had previously paid to the same family of over-tenants for generations. Furthermore there were cases where a chantry priest was granted a tithe of the farm turnover and it would be natural for the beneficiary to wish to maximise the income from his holding – he might well have been constantly pushing the farmer of the property to increase the farm yield. In these cases there would have been a degree of resentment on behalf of the farmer who saw the profits from his hard labour disappear into the priest's pocket.

It might also be the case that former common lands were taken into providing a priest's living; this could well have been the case with the Habergham lands of Gilbert Fairbank. It would upset the locals no-end to lose their former grazing and turf rights, little wonder then that in Fairbank's case the Habergham farmers wound up Margaret Batersbye and let her loose! To the common parishioner the chantry priest, as a privately employed individual, served little purpose – in fact he would often have been viewed as a parasite. In stark contrast to this the *Dissolution of the Monasteries* saw the removal of many of the livelihoods accorded to parish priests – at this time it was common for parishioners to actually buy lands and donate them to their priests, presumably the popularity of the individual priest within his parish would play a part in the amount of acreage donated in this way.

---

[1] W. Bennett, *History of Burnley,* (Vol 1, Burnley Corporation, 1946)

Returning to the attack by Alan Deves upon John Higgen and George Blakey, can it be purely coincidental that Higgin and Blakey might well have enjoyed the income from the Malkin lands, or neighbouring lands? If Deves farmed in some capacity within the area then we could well have a definite link between the Deves family and Malkin Tower. Jacob Davie of Barrowford (buried 1619 at Colne) could have been a relatively close neighbour of the Device family at Malkin Tower as the property then stood in Barrowford.

Device – Found At Last!

Having looked at the number of incidences relating to the surname of Device we have seen that the name only occurs within Colne, Burnley and the Pendle Forest in the form of Deves, Davye and Davie. These latter two instances belong to a family where the Christian name of Jacob occurs in most of the male children and, because they appear late on the scene, they are of little obvious consequence for our purposes. All hope of locating the husband of Elizabeth is not lost, however, as it now appears that we do actually have this family within the records of Saint Mary's at Newchurch-in-Pendle.[1] There are a total of five entries within the Newchurch registers for the surname of **Denis** and a single one for **Dennis**. This surname was extremely uncommon within our area, occurring nowhere else within the whole of the extended forest area, other than at Newchurch, over the 180 year period covered by the early registers:

❖ 1590: *John Dennis* married Elizabeth Ingham*

❖ 1590: *Jacobus (James) Denis (baptism)*

❖ 1593: *Alicea (Alison) Denis (baptism)*

❖ 1595: *Henry Denis (baptism)†*

❖ 1599: *Henry Denis (burial)†*

❖ 1600: *Jenneta Denis (baptism)*

❖ 1600: *John Denis* (burial)*

We know that the church officials wrote names phonetically and it is highly probable that the name of **Denis** was actually the name of **Devis**. Even if the name *Devis* was entered correctly into the original records there is a good chance that the original record transcribers would have misinterpreted these. This is perfectly understandable when copying early records as the letter *n* often resembled the letter *v*. The names and dates within the records strengthen the probability of the **Denis** records having actually been the **Device** family. The very first one to appear is the baptism, in the year of 1590, of Jacobus Denis; care must be taken as the obvious

---

[1] *The Registers of Newchurch-in-Pendle*, 1574-1754, (Lancashire Parish Register Society – 2002)

meaning of this Christian name would be Jacob. However, the appellation of *Jacobus* was from the Latin *Iakōbos,* this was a cognate of *James* and *Jacob* but the common practice was to write *Jacob* as *Jacobi* and *James* as *Jacobus.* This varied somewhat between church officials as some used the English word *James* at the same time as others were using the Latin. The consistency of a particular clerical hand can often be followed in the spelling of surnames over a period within parish registers, each successive cleric having their own ideas on the subject. (For more on this see *Appendix III*). In the case of Newchurch Saint Mary's the same incumbent, one Thomas Varley, served from 1569 to 1607 and therefore he would cover the whole of the Denis family records – this run of records can be seen to relate directly to the family of Elizabeth Device.

- ❖ In the year 1590 **Elizabeth Ingham** married **John Dennis;** this date fits perfectly with our present knowledge of the family, other than the Ingham surname; this will be covered in due course.

- ❖ Again, in the same year of 1590, **James Denis** is baptised, this is the same year that John and Elizabeth married and indicates a 'shotgun wedding.'

- ❖ Three years later (1593) we see the baptism of **Alicea (Alison) Denis.**

- ❖ **Henry Denis** is baptised in 1595 but died as an infant in 1599.

- ❖ In 1600 **Jenneta (Jennet) Denis** is baptised. According to Jennet Device (in 1612) her father, John Device, died '*about eleven years agone*' and this corresponds with the burial of John Denis in 1600.

Following the baptism of Jenneta Denis there were only two further relevant entries at Newchurch, one in 1635 for a Devis burial and another in 1682 for a Davis burial; the Burnley St. Peter's records show that in June, 1583, a Thomas Wynter married Anne Devies.

Do we finally have in the Newchurch *Denis* records firm evidence for the family of Elizabeth Device? On the basis of *'best available evidence'* it is indeed reasonable to accept these records as relating to Elizabeth Device and her family. This is progress indeed within the Pendle Witch legend and will allow us to make further inroads into the story as we proceed. With this new evidence we can now put a definite age to the Device children; in 1612 **James Device** would have been around twenty-one and not the callow youth as we supposed from the writings of Potts. **Alison Device** would have been a young woman of around eighteen years of age and young **Jennet Device** would have been eleven, rather than the nine years ascribed to her by Potts. In due course these slightly revised ages of the Device children might have a bearing upon their alleged statements. It is clear that Elizabeth had another child named Henry who died at the age of four, no doubt this is the reason for him never having been mentioned within story.

Elizabeth Device was Elizabeth Southern's only daughter as far as we are aware. Elizabeth was said to be somewhere in the region of forty years of age at the time of the trials and, because of an unfortunate deformity in one of her eyes, she is often unkindly referred to as *'Squinting Lizzie.'* Potts tells us that she had one eye higher than the other, the one eye looked up and the other down; the hidden inference being that this deformity, within the context of this isolated corner of the forest, was the product of inbreeding. This is probably not the case, however, as this deformity is far more common than might be thought, it is often caused by an accident, especially in young childhood. If a child falls heavily onto the side of the skull, or cheekbone, this causes displacement of the various bone structures within the face and, as the bones set into adulthood, so does the deformity set exactly as that ascribed to our unfortunate subject.

Elizabeth Device, then, appears to have been rather unfortunate in both her physical appearance and in her unwitting relationship to a local Puritan worthy by the name of Richard Baldwin. The fact that Elizabeth enlisted the aid of her aged and blind mother to approach Richard Baldwin on her behalf raises a couple of points. Elizabeth Device was unwilling to ask Baldwin for her dues – was this because of the old enmity between the families? Was Elizabeth of a shy disposition because of her disfigurement or was she emotionally challenged to such an extent that she was incapable of communication upon this level? With regard to this latter possibility Potts stated that Roger Nowell could not extract any kind of submission from Elizabeth during their initial interview. Her stubborn refusal to either incriminate herself, or make any kind of statement, showed that either she was aware of the dangerous situation in which her family found themselves or she was incapable of communicating with Nowell. If she inclined to shrink from social contact, as the Baldwin episode might suggest, Elizabeth would probably have become sullen and uncooperative when confronted with Nowell's authority.

According to Potts, it was only when Elizabeth realised that her own son and daughter (James and Jennet) had accused her of causing death by witchcraft did she finally confess to being a witch. However, the story does not add up here; when Elizabeth stood before the Lancaster Assizes she maintained her innocence by pleading not guilty. Nowell then pulled his master-stroke by calling Jennet Device to testify against not only her own mother but the whole shebang of the gathered accused. Potts fains surprise at the appearance of Jennet, calling her *'This unexpected witness;'* here he gives the impression that God Himself had sent the child trotting along to the court in order to carry out His work in routing out the ubiquitous devil from amongst the poor foresters.

Quite naturally, when confronted by her own child making accusations that would lead to her death, Elizabeth went berserk. Potts says that she screamed and cursed and so frightened the child that Elizabeth had to be physically removed from the courtroom. This has been used by many writers upon the subject as proof that Elizabeth was mentally unstable but the circumstances were such that even a well-balanced character might snap when confronted with such a gross miscarriage of justice as this so patently was. Potts also made the telling statement that Elizabeth denied having made any confession as she was dragged from the court – there is here a strong suggestion of there having been an interpolation of facts by either the prosecution or, later, the writing up of the case by Potts.

Above all others, this particular period within the two-day trial leaves the modern mind stunned by its sheer lack of respect by the authorities for the lives of subordinate humanity. It is always dangerous to try to judge the opinions and actions of a period where the mindset was decidedly different to modern ideas; especially where justice and the rights of the individual (as opposed to the rights of the state) were concerned. However, this does not preclude an expectation of basic humanity between the ages of history; as a medieval philosopher said *"The same heart beats in the breast of all mankind."*

There has always been an argument (rightly or wrongly) for the taking of life in extreme circumstances but the single prerequisite must be that the full force of justice is openly seen to be applied. Where does this leave the Great and the Good who were appointed to oversee the justice system in 1612? When the poor wretches were dragged from the dungeons (Demdike having died there) of Lancaster Gaol, and summarily tried for their lives on charges of gobbledegook and fairytale, a child of eleven was their principal witness. The prosecution was therefore damned in the eyes of posterity and the judges joined in for equally good measure by both allowing and condoning the unacceptable.

Christopher Holgate

Further to the Denis entries at Newchurch, the *very next entry* in the church records to that of the marriage for John Dennis and Elizabeth Ingham shows the marriage of **Christopher Holgate** and Isab. Robinson. Christopher Holgate was described in the prosecution evidence as being the uncle to the Device children and, if we take it that Elizabeth Device was the true child of Elizabeth Southern, (rather than the adopted daughter or step-daughter), he would in all likelihood have been the son of Elizabeth Southern. Whether he was the full or half-brother to Elizabeth Device is not clear at this stage. The Newchurch marriage record of 1590 shows Elizabeth Southern's daughter getting married and she could well have married in a double wedding with her brother, Christopher; the two couples were certainly married within a short period of each other. As with Elizabeth and John Dennis the marriage of Christopher Holgate coincides with the baptism of their first child – Alicea Holgate was baptised at Newchurch in 1590. Moreover, the other Holgate children were given exactly the same names as the offspring of Elizabeth and John Dennis i.e; Alicea, Henry, Jennet and (next generation) James. The following are all Newchurch-in-Pendle entries unless otherwise stated:

The Family of Christopher Holgate:
1590: *Alicea (Alison) Holgate (baptised)~*
1592: *Anna Holgate (baptised)*
1594: *Jenneta Holgate (baptised)†*
1595: *Jenneta Holgate (buried)†*
1596: *Henry Holgate (baptised)††*
1596: *Henry Holgate (buried)††*
1600: *Maria Holgate (dtr Chris of Pendle, baptised Padiham)*
1604: *George Holgate (baptised)*
1607: *Henry Holgate (baptised) † † †*
1609: *Christopher Holgate (baptised) ***
1610: *Christopher Holgate (buried) ***
1611: *Jennet Holgate (baptised)*

The Next Generation
1626: *Henry Holgate (baptised, son of Henry)*
1632: *James Holgate (baptised, son of Henry or George)*
1632: *Anna Holgate (baptised, daughter of Henry or George)^*
1636: *Isabel Holgate (baptised, daughter of Henry or George)*
1636: *Isabel Holgate (buried, possible wife of Christopher)*
1637: *Alice Holgate married Thurstan Garstang~*
1640: *John Holgate (baptised)**
1645: *Ellena Holgate (baptised)*
1647: *Isabella Holgate (baptised)*

1655: *James Holgate (baptised)*
1664: *Henry Holgate (burial)* † † †
1664: *John Holgate (burial)**
1673: *Anna Holgate (burial)^*

So... who were the Holgates by whom Demdike apparently had a son? In 1443 a Richard Holgate was one of the free tenants of Pendleton, by the time of the *New Hold* within Pendle Forest the family appear as two definite branches, one in the Colne/Foulridge area and the other in the forest itself. In 1507 William Holgate was fined at the Ightenhill halmote for digging turfs on a pasture called *The Flange*, in the Goldshaw area, this land was tenanted by James Hargreaves and Robert Bulcock. By 1513 it becomes clear that the Holgates were tenants in their own right as Henry Hartley of Pendle surrendered a farm and other premises in Barley (around twenty-two acres) that Richard Holgate had delivered to him. Two years later a farm at Wheatley Hay Booth (£0: 8s: 11d rental) reverted to king on the death of William Holgate, his son and heir was Richard Holgate and Richard's younger brother, Thomas Holgate, sought admittance to the property. This was obviously the cause of some ill-feeling within the family as another record of 1515 shows that Margaret Holgate, the widow of William, and her son Thomas complained against Richard Holgate for illegally entering their farm at Hay Booth.

In 1523 it is apparent that Richard Holgate had the lifetime tenancy of another farm at Hay Booth, this was no doubt an inheritance from his father and possibly the reason why his mother wished the other property to be tenanted by her younger son. In this instance John Hargreaves complained that Roger Hartley, Thomas Varley and Robert Varley were occupying the farm illegally as Richard Holgate had granted him the tenancy on contract. The three defendants were the feoffes of Richard Holgate and were, therefore, holding the property on his behalf. Richard Holgate found surety for his tenancy by John Smith and Miles Nutter.

The township of Barley included the four original farming operations that were carved out from the forest areas, these were Barley Booth, Wheatley Booth, Hay Booth and Whitehough. This region is formed within a strip of high land running from Stang Top in the east, through the Black Moss area and onwards to the slopes of Pendle Hill above the village of Barley. We see a further land transaction involving the Holgates when, in 1524, John, Richard and Robert Bulcock, along with Thomas Varley, surrendered a farm and other buildings in Hay Booth (£0: 8s: 11d rental) to the use of Richard Holgate. Richard again found surety for his tenancy by John Smith and Miles Nutter - he was obviously friendly with these, the two wealthiest men in Roughlee.[1] Given that this latest record for Holgate property was of exactly the same rental as that of the previous recorded property (in Hay Booth) it is fair to say that this was the Holgate family farm and Richard Holgate had finally become the official tenant there. It also seems fair to suggest that this particular farm would have been the property on which Demdike's son, Christopher Holgate, and his family were living in 1612.

In this case they would most probably have been under-tenants of either the Listers of Westby or the Towneleys; Charles Towneley owned most of the farms around Barley and in 1532 he decreed that the income from Black Moss Farm should go to the use of Richard Dancer (chaplain) and Stephen Ellis (clerk and schoolmaster). John Robinson senior farmed at Black Moss and he stated that by rights he had the tenancy for the term of his lifetime. This appeared

---

[1] John Smith probably built Roughlee Old Hall and Miles Nutter was the father-in-law of Alice Nutter

to cut no ice with the court and Dancer and Ellis were admitted as tenants. Following a certain period the ownership of the property was to transfer to Lawrence Lister, son of William of Middop esquire, and to his heirs forever. This came to fruition as a later record of 1562 showed that Anthony Lister of Stirk House (Gisburn) owned Black Moss at a rent of £0: 5s: 8d; William Bulcock had the tenancy of part of the property for life at a rent to Lister of £0: 40s: 0d. William Ridehalgh owned the other part of the tenancy, on the same terms. This nicely illustrates the juicy profits to be had from being the over-tenant of a property at the old fixed rent to the Clitheroe overlords; multiply Lister's profits by the large number of farms that he held and it becomes clear why the gentry were prospering at this time.

Christopher Holgate was described by Jennet Device as being her uncle *'of Pendle'* in order to distinguish him from a Christopher Holgate who lived in Colne at that time. This latter branch, also closely related to the Holgates of Fouridge, were the largest group of the Holgate family within the area. Christopher of Pendle married Isob. Robinson of the Barley family (with whom we have already met). This family farmed at Black Moss, Foothouse Gate and Whitehough, all of which fell within the district of Hay Booth, as did the Holgate property. It is also worth considering here that if the Holgate farmstead of 1612 was not the actual property owned by Richard Holgate then Christopher may well have gained the tenancy via his marriage to Isob. Robinson. Whilst on the subject of Christopher's wife, she is mentioned in one single instance within the statements of the accused when Jennet Device describes those who attended the Good Friday meeting at Malkin Tower: *'Christopher Howgate of Pendle, vnckle to this Examinate, and Elizabeth his wife.'* It is apparent, however, that this is the product of an ancient 'typo' somewhere along the line. The parish record relating to *Isob. Robinson* may have been mistakenly written by a church official but the likelihood is that the name was mixed up somewhere in the translation between the witness, the magistrate, the court statements and Potts' account. Many other discrepancies of this nature occur and it is unsafe to assume that all names, dates and ages etc, within the *Wonderfull Discoverie* are in fact true verbatim accounts. After all, we have seen that one man's Dennis is another man's Device!

Christopher Holgate and his wife were amongst the few named persons at the Good Friday gathering to escape with their lives; for some reason they were never prosecuted but lack of evidence against them is not the first reason for this that springs to mind. Most of those who were executed at Lancaster lost their lives on the basis of an almost farcical prosecution case. One possibility for the Holgate's escape is that they had a number of dependant children – in the twenty years following their marriage (1590) the Holgates had produced nine children, three of whom had died in infancy. Christopher was now also to lose his mother, sister, nephew and niece at a single stroke.

Demdike's son, then, appears to have married into the Robinson family of Barley and this begs the question as to why her daughter, Elizabeth Device, allegedly brought about the deaths of both John and James Robinson of Barley? According to the statement of James Device his mother, Elizabeth, had killed John Robinson for having accused her of having a child by a man named Sellers; this is yet another example of inter-family tension within the forest. We are left with the vexed question as to who Richard Holgate's father was, is there a clue in his naming his sons Henry and James? This is a possibility but his sister Elizabeth also named her sons Henry and James, unless Richard and Elizabeth shared the same father (we shall see that this is unlikely) the clue does no hold much water. Taking the family of Holgate within the Hay Booth area of the forest it might not be entirely unreasonable to suggest that Christopher may have been a grandson of Richard and Thomas Holgate's generation.

We have seen that a long established family of Holgates lived within Foulridge – the dominant male name throughout the generations of this family was Henry. As landowners around the village of Foulridge the family is reasonably well documented in the court rolls and they would have known Elizabeth Southern very well. In 1592 Commissioners for the Crown came to Colne with the remit of surveying the manor and separating it from the waste lands; to this end they enlisted the help of local elders within the community to describe the ancient boundaries. One of these witnesses was one Henry Holgate who was described as a venerable incumbent of Colne and *'of the age of three score years and five'* thus putting his year of birth at 1527. This puts him

roughly in the same generation as Elizabeth Southern and adds to the other circumstantial evidence of his Christian name being Henry, along with his having been a neighbour of the Malkin family. Admittedly we do not have sufficient evidence to name Christopher Holgate's father but we have at least furnished the story with a half-viable theory – more on this later.

Black Moss Farm; home of the Bulcock family

Elizabeth Ingham

The name of Elizabeth Device is firmly fixed within the psyche of anyone with an interest in the Pendle Witch legend, a legend that we have, in fact, been exposed to for generations. It can be difficult to assimilate new evidence into the firmly established folklore because there is often a counter-balance somewhere along the line. And so it is with the Southern/Device confederacy long held to have been the lynchpin within the story of 1612.

Having seen that Elizabeth Device carried the surname of Ingham prior to her marriage to John Dennis (Device) it becomes apparent, as in all genealogy research, that the extended family is becoming ever more complicated. For instance, what was the marital status of Elizabeth Ingham at the time of her marriage? Was she born an Ingham or had she married an Ingham and been widowed in the interim? If she was indeed born with the Ingham surname why was her mother apparently called Southern? As we proceed with the life of Elizabeth Southern we have now a vital piece of evidence to work with in the Ingham name of her daughter; this evidence has previously been unforthcoming but is potentially invaluable in the search for the real person behind the unfortunate appellation of Old Demdike . . . . .

Chapter Eight

Elizabeth Southern

It is with good reason that Old Demdike is the most widely recognised character within the Pendle Witch legend – throughout the *Wonderfull Discoverie* many references are made to her having introduced a number of others into the black arts; this suggests that she was a major player within the local circle of wise-women during the later sixteenth and early seventeenth centuries. The following is the statement said by Roger Nowell to be the confession of Elizabeth Southern:

The voluntarie Confession and Examination of
Elizabeth Southerns alias Demdike, taken at the Fence in the
Forrest of Pendle in the Countie of Lancaster.
The second day of Aprill, Before Roger Nowell of Reade Esquire, one of his
Maiesties Iustices of the peace within the sayd Countie, Viz

The said Elizabeth Sowtherns confesseth, and sayth; That about twentie yeares past, as she was comming homeward from begging, there met her this Examinate neere vnto a Stonepit in Gouldshey, in the sayd Forrest of Pendle, a Spirit or Deuill in the shape of a Boy, the one halfe of his Coate blacke, and the other browne, who bade this Examinate stay, saying to her, that if she would giue him her Soule, she should haue any thing that she would request. Wherevpon this Examinat demaunded his name? and the Spirit answered, his name was Tibb: and so this Examinate in hope of such gaine as was promised by the sayd Deuill or Tibb, was contented to giue her Soule to the said Spirit: And for the space of fiue or six yeares next after, the sayd Spirit or Deuill appeared at sundry times vnto her this Examinate about Day-light Gate, always bidding her stay, and asking her this Examinate what she would haue or doe? To whom this Examinate replyed, Nay nothing: for she this Examinate said, she wanted nothing yet. And so about the end of the said six yeares, vpon a Sabboth day in the morning, this Examinate hauing a litle Child vpon her knee, and she being in a slumber, the sayd Spirit appeared vnto her in the likenes of a browne Dogg, forcing himselfe to her knee, to get blood vnder her left Arme: and she being without any apparrell sauing her Smocke, the said Deuill did get blood vnder her left arme. And this Examinate awaking, sayd, Iesus saue my Child; but had no power, nor could not say, Iesus saue her selfe: wherevpon the Browne Dogge vanished out of this Examinats sight: after which, this Examinate was almost starke madd for the space of eight weekes.

And vpon her examination, she further confesseth, and saith. That a little before Christmas last, this Examinates Daughter hauing been to helpe Richard Baldwyns Folkes at the Mill: This Examinates Daughter did bid her this Examinate goe to the sayd Baldwyns house, and aske him some thing for her helping of his Folkes at the Mill, (as aforesaid:) and in this Examinates going to the said Baldwyns house, and neere to the sayd house, she mette with the said Richard Baldwyn; Which Baldwyn sayd to this Examinate, and the said Alizon Deuice (who at that time ledde this Examinate, being blinde) get out of my ground Whores and Witches, I will burne the one of you, and hang the other. To whom this Examinate answered: I care not for thee, hang thy selfe: Presently whereupon, at this Examinates going ouer the next hedge, the said Spirit or Diuell called Tibb, appeared vnto this Examinat, and sayd, Reuenge thee of him. To whom, this Examinate sayd againe to the said Spirit. Revenge thee eyther of him, or his. And so the said Spirit vanished out of her sight, and she neuer saw him since.

A̶nd further this Examinate confesseth, and sayth, that the speediest way to take a mans life away by Witchcraft, is to make a Picture of Clay, like vnto the shape of the person whom they meane to kill, & dry it thorowly: and when they would haue them to be ill in any one place more then an other; then take a Thorne or Pinne, and pricke it in that part of the Picture you would so haue to be ill: and when you would haue any part of the Body to consume away, then take that part of the Picture, and burne it. And when they would haue the whole body to consume away, then take the remnant of the sayd Picture, and burne it: and so therevpon by that meanes, the body shall die.

There is a weight of evidence in favour of Malkin Tower, the residence of the Southern clan, having been situated on Blacko hillside (see later chapters on this). Until the late nineteenth century the area of Blacko, or Blakey as it was commonly named, was a part of Over Barrowford and, as a fellow Barrowfordian, I have long held an interest in Elizabeth Southern and her family. Admittedly, if the contemporary accounts of the family are even partly true, you would not want to meet them on a dark night but this is the impression we are meant to glean from the writings of Potts – the more repulsive he could make the accused the more sympathy he would engender for the argument that his court had rid the country of a diabolical nuisance. In his preamble to the *Wonderfull Discoverie* Potts had this to say about Elizabeth Southern:

T̶herefore I pray you giue me leaue, (with your patience and fauour,) before I proceed to the Indictment, Arraignment, and Tryall of such as were Prisoners in the Castle, to lay open the life and death of this damnable and malicious Witch, of so long continuance (old Demdike) of whom our whole business hath such dependence, that without the particular Declaration and Record of her Euidence, with the circumstaunces, wee shall neuer bring any thing to good perfection: for from this Sincke of villanie and mischiefe, haue all the rest proceeded; as you shall haue them in order.

S̶hee was a very old woman, about the age of Foure-score yeares, and had been a Witch for fiftie yeares. Shee dwelt in the Forrest of Pendle, a vast place, fitte for her profession: What shee committed in her time, no man knowes. Thus lives shee securely for many yeares, brought vp her owne Children, instructed her Graund-children, and tooke great care and pains to bring them to be Witches. Shee was a generall agent for the Deuill in all these partes: no man escaped her, or her Furies, that euer gaue them any occassion of offence, or denyed them any thing they stood need of: And certaine it is, no man neere them, was secure or free from danger ......the common opinion of the Kinges subjects for the losses of their Children, Friendes, Goodes, and Cattle, (as there could not be so greate Fire without some Smoake) ......
In the end, Roger Nowell esquire, one of his Maiesties Iustices in these partes, a very religious honest Gentleman, Painefull in the service of his Countrey: whose fame for this great service to his Countrey, shall liue after him, tooke vpon him to enter into the particular examinations of these suspected persons: And to the honour of God, and the great comforte of all his Countrey, made such a discouery of them in order, as the like hath not been heard of ......

It is interesting that Potts makes no mention of any physical deformity or mental defect relating to Elizabeth Southern as, whenever the opportunity arose, he took great delight in pointing out the afflictions carried by others of the accused. He puts her age at around eighty years, in other words she appeared elderly but in those days of low life expectancy it is probable that people would have appeared to be much older than their true years. A clue to her real age might be seen in the fact that it was common practice to name children after the reigning royal family of the time; was Elizabeth Southern therefore named after Henry VIII's new daughter, Elizabeth, born in 1533? . . . . We shall see.

Demdike and Folklore

As might be expected a great deal of folklore has grown around the legend of the Pendle Witches. Memories within the forest run deep and local country people have long passed stories down the generations concerning ghouls, boggarts, goblins and witches. My wife's aunt was brought up at Extwistle Hall, a lonely sixteenth century mansion on the outskirts of Burnley and Worsthorne. She recalled that as a child the long winter evenings were passed by her father recounting stories of local ghostly happenings and goblin funerals at the end of the lane to the Hall. This oral tradition was quick to encapsulate the stories of Old Demdike who, along with other local ghostly celebrities, would figure prominently in our local entertainments – the dull, flickering shadows cast by candlelight, creaking old floors, the wind howling in the pitch-black night would all add to the atmosphere of magic engendered by the story-teller. Unfortunately, in the case of my wife's aunt, the stories were told so well that she was left traumatised by them and refused to leave the house for days afterwards!

A relevant story recounted by a farmer from the village of Barley shows the other side of the coin to the standard witch-tales. Born in the later nineteenth century the farmer, by the name of Hargreaves, recalled his parents telling him that a shepherd was employed by local farmers to tend their sheep on the moors of Pendle Hill. This had been common practice for centuries but in this particular case there had been a long drought and the moorland becks and springs had dried up. The sheep were mangy and were worth very little due to their poor wool through the lack of decent grazing – the shepherd would be paid according to the amount of wool the sheep produced and he knew that he might starve that year. Sitting on a stone on Pendle's brow the shepherd presented a sorry site, he was startled by someone approaching from behind and turned to see a local wise-woman who had the reputation of being a witch. *"What's up lad, art tha not well?"* The shepherd recounted his tale to the woman and she suddenly struck her staff into the ground; a gush of water ensued from deep within the earth and this spring has been known as Deep Clough Spring ever since and has never dried up. The farmer used this tale as an illustration of the locally held feeling that witches could '*carry out good deeds as well as bad.*' This story also illustrates another powerful, and tangible, string to the bow of the wise-person and that is the art of water divination.

With the month of October comes the ancient festival of Hallowe'en. The shops are laden with the associated paraphernalia of the festival and that means, by and large, witch outfits, pointed hats, grotesque masks, plastic broomsticks, false warty noses etc., etc. The original purpose of the All Hallows festival having been largely forgotten as Hallowe'en now descends into an orgy of self-imposed 'horror' and, even worse, the American practice of '*trick or treat.*' The standard image now of the witch is of an old crone, flying on her broomstick, her massive nose silhouetted against a huge full-moon; accompanied by her black cat and wearing a pointed hat the witch flies to goodness-knows-where in search of consort with some demon or other.

We do not have to search far for the origins of these images, they grew out of fertile imaginations during the Victorian period and one man in particular can be seen to have a propinquity to the matter – William Harrison Ainsworth. Ainsworth it was who provided us with the romantic novel *The Lancashire Witches;* first published in 1849, this book, above all others, propagated the legend of the Pendle Witches. Ainsworth was born in Manchester in 1805 and qualified as a solicitor in London in 1826, whilst still in his teens he became a successful writer of essays and reviews. In 1833 Ainsworth published his book, *Rookwood,* and this almost immediately propelled him into the realms of literary fame.

In 1845 James Crossley, a partner in Ainsworth's father's legal practice, had edited the reprint of Potts' *Wonderfull Discoverie of Witches* for the Chetham Society and Crossley suggested to Ainsworth that he might care to write up the story. Ainsworth eagerly took to the task and in the years 1846 and 1847 he and Crossly made frequent visits to the Pendle area in search of local colour relating to the witch legend. On most of their visits the pair stayed at Bridge Cottage in Whalley, at the time this property functioned as a Young Ladies Seminary conducted by one of Ainsworth's relatives. They also stayed at the vicarage in Newchurch-in-Pendle from where the curate introduced them to local characters, of which there was certainly no shortage!

Ainsworth spent much of the following year of 1848 in writing his novel and it was immediately serialised in the Sunday Times, printed privately in book-form in 1849 and officially published in three volumes under the sub-title of 'A Romance of Pendle Forest.' Through various reprints, in differing formats, the novel became affordable to the masses and best-seller status quickly followed. The novel describes the local Pendle landscape accurately but a large dollop of artistic licence is applied to the actual story of the Pendle Witches. Whilst the principal characters are all given roles their locations and social class are purposely mixed up, an example being where Alison Device speaks with a 'posh' accent; the reason for this is eventually seen to be that she is the daughter of Alice Nutter! From the perspective of a local person I find the dialogue, when spoken by the common people, to be somewhat confusing – to all intents and purposes the locals are given to speaking with a pronounced Scottish accent! Having said that, the book is a good read and a nice example of the style of its day, furthermore it contains accounts of folklore related to Ainsworth on his local visits and these are well be worth perusing in our search for the true character of Elizabeth Southern. In fact, within Ainsworth's often garbled history, we will see that there is a stronger element of fact than we might have previously given him credit for.

Isold de Heton and Demdike

A short extract from *The Lancashire Witches* describes the situation of Old Demdike's home of Malkin Tower and Ainsworth then carries the story on to her birth: '. . . . *then once again, in the reign of Henry VI Malkin Tower became a robber's stronghold, and gave protection to a freebooter named Blackburn, who, with a band of daring and desperate marauders, took advantage of the troubled state of the country, ravaged it far and wide, and committed unheard of atrocities, even levying contributions upon the Abbeys of Whalley and Salley, and the heads of these religious establishments were glad to make terms with him to save their herds and stores, all attempts to dislodge him from his mountain fastness, and destroy his band, had failed.'*

'*Upon one occasion it chanced that he made a visit in disguise to Whalley Abbey, and, passing the little hermitage near the church, beheld the votaress who tenanted it. This was Isold de Heton. Ravished by her wondrous beauty, Blackburn soon found an opportunity of making his passion known to her, and his handsome though fierce lineaments pleasing her, he did not long sigh in vain. He frequently visited her in the garb of a Cistertian monk, and, being taken for one of the brethren, his conduct brought great scandal upon the Abbey. The abandoned votaress bore him a daughter, and the infant was conveyed away by the lover, and placed under the care of a peasant's wife at Barrowford. From that child sprung Bess Blackburn, the mother of old Demdike; so that the witch is a direct descendant of Isold de Heton.*'

When we take the above text, and substitute Edward II for Henry VI, we have the period of unrest when Thomas, the earl of Lancaster, revolted against the king. Thomas was defeated in battle at Boroughbridge and executed at his castle in Pontefract on 22nd March 1322. As we have seen in Part One, this left the honour of Clitheroe, and Pendle Forest, completely rudderless – a breakdown in law-and-order quickly followed. The forests were robbed of their game and Scots and locals alike plundered the local farms. The clergy were far from immune as can be seen when, later in the year of 1322, a gang from Marsden (now Nelson) raided the Abbey at Whalley and upset the Abbot somewhat when they pinched £5,000 worth of goods. The Abbot's demeanour would not have been improved when he was robbed again in 1347; this time we see that Queen Isabella's treasury at Whalley was robbed of £2,000 in cash and £3,000 in goods along with many charters and papal bulls, furthermore many of the Queen's houses in the Forest of Bowland were burnt down.[1]

Records of the following year show that there was still civil unrest, reports of people disturbing the peace were common, a few of those who were actually prosecuted for this were Robert the son of Henry Catlow of Marsden, Thomas his brother and Adam the Turner of Marsden. John of Higham was prosecuted for '*Impersonating the representative of The Duchy of Lancaster and obtaining 'puture'* (taxes) *from the inhabitants of Marsden and Colne.'* Things did not begin to return to any semblance of normality until late in the year of 1324. Perhaps, because Ainsworth was aware that, historically, there had been a high degree of unrest within the forest, he based his Blackburn character upon one of the many real-life outlaws who abounded in earlier times.

The tale relates that Blackburn and Isold de Heton lived together at Malkin Tower before coming to a sticky end; Demdike, the great-granddaughter of Isold de Heton, then takes up residence there. The question is, of course, how much truth can we assign to the story? Having seen that there is at least a historical basis let us have a look at the enigmatic Isold de Heton:

During the fifteenth century the landowning families within the Whalley area included the Catteralls, Brockholes, Hetons and Talbots. On the 3rd February, 1329, John de Brockholes gave to Thomas Talbot, son of Edmund Talbot, all his lands and tenements in Bashall near Whalley and the Catteralls owned much land and property at Little Mitton.

At some time in the early part of the fifteenth century the Catteralls were possessed of the Manor of Heton, a small village on the west bank of the river Lune, south of Lancaster and east of Heysham. John de Catterall, who probably died in 1441, gave the manor of Heton to Roger de Brockholes, whose father John de Brockholes was living in Heton in 1402. It is very possible

---

[1] W. Bennett, *The History of Marsden and Nelson*, (Nelson Corporation, 1957)

that Isold de Heton had married a younger son, John, of the Catteralls of Catterall and Little Mitton (near Whalley) thus endowing him with the manor of Heton for life. This John de Catterall arranged for the transfer of the Heton manor to his distant relation, Roger de Brockholes, on his death. On the death of John, or before if he was suffering from a terminal illness, Isold used her influence with her close relatives at Mitton (one of whom was a monk at Whalley) to obtain the position of recluse at the abbey. The appointment of the position of anchorite was in the gift of the king, and Isold would not get it without some influence in the region.

Henry VI, under privy Seal, appointed Isold de Heton, a widow, as recluse at Whalley on July 6th in the fifteenth year of his reign (1437-8.) Her appointment at Whalley coincided very closely with the transfer of the manor of Heton from John de Catterall to Roger de Brockholes. The position of recluse was not as austere as might be imagined, Isold would had the security of a home, her weekly food allowance would include twenty-four loaves of bread and eight gallons of beer, she would also have had a weekly cash allowance and the benefit of two servants to look after her.

So far, so good – the Isold de Heton in Ainsworth's story was in fact a real person. Further to this, he has the freebooter, Blackburn, disguising himself as a monk and visiting Isold (with definite none-monkish intentions) in her hermitage. Isold is then found to be with child and abandoned in great shame by the abbey. Again, this is based on fact as in 1440-41 the abbot, John Eccles, petitioned Henry VI to close the Hermitage at Whalley because of misbehaviour by the anchorites, specifically naming Isold de Heton as having broken her vows and living outside the hermitage *'this two yere and more'*.

'Her vow was probably taken in the first fervours of sorrow, which soon wore off, so that the widow grew weary of her confinement, and broke loose from her vows and her cell together. Vowesses like these . . . . seem to have been in general a disgrace to their profession.' [1]

Such was the shame brought onto the abbey by the behaviour of Isold and her servants that a written representation to the king was formulated:

To The Kyng
oWre Sovereign Lord &c.

Be hit remembryd that the plase and habitacion of the seid recluse is within place halowed, and nere to the gate of the seyd monastre, and that weemen that have attendyng and acquayntyd to the seyd recluse have recorse daily into the seyd monastre, for the livere of brede, ale, kychin, and other thyngs for the sustetacyon of the seyd recluse accordyng to the composityon endentyd above rehyrsed: the whyche is not accordyng to be had withyn such religyous plases. And howe that dyvers that been anchores and recluses in the seyd plase aforetyme, contrary to theyre own oth and proffesyon, have brokyn owte of the seyd plase, wherin they were reclusyd, and dpartyd therfrom wythout eny reconsilyatyon. And in especyal how that now Isold of

---

[1] T. D. Whitaker, *History of Whalley,* (First edition, 1881) –Whitaker relates his own opinion here

heton that was reclusyd in the seyd plase, at denomynatyon, and preferment of owre
Sovereign Lord Kyng that nowe is, is broken owte of the seyd plase, hath departyd
therfrom contrary to her own oth and professyon, not willyng not entendyng to be
restoryd agayn, and so livyng at her owne liberte by this two yere and more, lyke as
she had never bin profyssed. And that dyvers of wymen that have been servants ther
and attendyng to the recluses afortym have byn misgovernyd, and gotten with chyld
withyn the seyd plase hallowyd, to the grete displeassaunce of hurt and disclander of
the abbeys aforeseyd, &c. . . . [1]

The petition had the desired effect as Henry VI dissolved the Whalley hermitage endowed by his ancestor, Henry duke of Lancaster, and replaced it with a chantry for the benefit of the soul of the duke. Isold was summarily ejected from the abbey; Whitaker records a local Whalley legend that Isold broke a leg on the steep hillside of Whalley Nab whilst trying to escape the attentions of the monks from the abbey. To illustrate the inter-relationship, or cousinhood, of the local gentry relating to the story of Isold de Heton it is necessary to provide a somewhat convoluted account of their lands and marriage practices – therefore this text is contained in *Appendix I* of this book.

Old Demdike

The appellation of 'Old Demdike' translates as *'Demon Woman,'* the obvious connotation of the name suggests that the recipient of the title was feared and loathed within the community. Certainly there had to be a reason for acquisition of the name and in earlier times it was applied (as an adjectival suffix) to strong women within a more matriarchal society – an excellent case-in-point here is the name of the famous early British queen, Boudicca. Here we have the proto-Celtic word *boudīko* meaning *'victorious'* and the addition of the *'dicca'* or *'dike'* suffix thus giving us *'victorious woman.'*

The Pendle Witch case has attracted scholars of every discipline and we have been furnished with many professional opinions regarding the underlying social and psychological undercurrents appertaining to the 1612 witch trials. Amongst these are Robin Briggs of Oxford University and Dr Euan Cameron of the University of Newcastle-upon-Tyne, the following observations are based upon their general writings on the subject;

'Demdike, at around eighty, was extremely advanced in years and this would play a part in
the way in which others would see and judge her. The older women tended to be wise women
and healers, titles which by definition involved age. A further explanation lies in the fact that
older people, especially those who were senile, exhibited eccentric or anti-social behaviour
that made people uncomfortable and tended to invite accusations. Older people were also less
physically powerful and therefore they were perceived to have been more likely to resort to
magic to defend themselves or to take revenge. Furthermore, underlying the depiction of the
strong-willed older matriarch was a deep male fear of sexually experienced, independent
women. This is partly the reason that old widows were particularly susceptible to charges of

---

[1] Whitaker's *History of Whalley* reproduces this transcript of a letter from *Whalley Church Records*

witchcraft. There is no definite trend related to the marital status of witches when accused of witchcraft. However, the percentage of unmarried (widowed or never married) was higher than the percentage of those married. Among the unmarried the widow was most likely to be accused. In a patriarchal society, a women who was not under the control of a husband or father was a source of concern. The other cause for fear was that the number of unmarried women was increasing, these women were often considered a burden on society.'

For married couples there were two main sources of danger, one being conflict and inter-familial tensions. This allowed for the expression of otherwise socially unacceptable feelings, for example where a child made accusations against a parent. The second cause was when friction occurred over property, this often belonged to the man of the household and, although married women had no independent wealth or property, they often worked alongside their husbands. They were, therefore, fully involved in the working and improvement of family lands and property and often found themselves involved in disputes over rents, labour or even possession of these lands.

The reasons for the Demdike appellation, then, are manifold; we can see that an elderly woman, with a strongly independent character, would have made the men within the neighbourhood somewhat uncomfortable; especially those in authority and with a more Puritan leaning. The strong matriarch would, therefore, have been the target of derision from certain members of the community, not least the lay and church authorities. Perhaps Demdike grew increasingly cantankerous with age, after all she would have lived an extremely hard life despite which she successfully (and possibly single-handedly) raised at least two children – just to add insult to injury she lost her sight at some stage in later life. On the other side of the coin, Demdike may have earned her title through the somewhat grudging respect of the community, it is apparent that she was called upon by neighbouring farmers to cure their ailing livestock. She may well have been an outstanding herbalist and healer, she could possibly have acted as the local midwife in her younger days. She certainly appears to have been the longest serving person within her craft of all the Pendle accused and might, therefore, have worn the Demdike tag as a badge of honour.

However. . . . there is also a strong possibility that nobody in the Forest of Pendle actually called Elizabeth Southern *Old Demdike,* nor Anne Whittle *Old Chattox.* In their so-called confessions the accused bandy the names around like confetti, Demdike this and Chattox that; closer inspection, however, shows a definite interpolation of the name within the prosecution statements and this must have been a deliberate policy on behalf of either Potts or the examining magistrate, or both. The wording within these statements relates an odd mixture of first person and third person thus giving the *impression* that the words were directly attributable to the examinate. Reading the *Wonderfull Discoverie* in this light it becomes apparent that the only person who could be proved to have actually employed the Demdike title was Thomas Potts, this he did as voraciously and as often as he possibly could. There is not a single instance within the Assize Court prosecution documents where there is proof that anyone other than the magistrates, and Potts, addressed the elders of the accused as Demdike and Chattox. Words were constantly put into the mouths of the accused, ideas were floated before them and these were quickly adapted to their culture and, in turn, translated by the prosecution into evil malpractice. This was shamelessly designed to horrify the Assize judges (not that they needed much persuasion to hang a few wretches here and there), the jury and the Crown authorities.

It is highly possible that neither of the descriptive nick-names of Demdike and Chattox has been used within any context locally other than when referring to the trials; were they to have been standard colloquial nick-names it is fairly certain that the elders of the local area would still have used them within living memory and this is not the case. These names are not used by the people of Pendle, in town, in the country or on the farm other than in relation to the Pendle Witches.

We have, then, a strong slant within the *Wonderfull Discoverie* towards the language that Potts saw fit to employ for maximum impact on the justices and jury. Had Potts' pamphlet been written by a working person from within the community of the Pendle Forest then we would have had a Pendle Witch tradition at variance to the one that we now know – it is highly possible, in fact, that under these circumstances we would have had no Pendle Witch tradition at all!

Demdike - Southern

As we have seen, it is very possible that Isold de Heton had married John Catterall of Mitton and we are informed by Potts that, at the time of the 1612 trials, Demdike's surname was Southern (Sowthernes). In 1316 Robert de Southerne re-granted Great Mitton Hall to Thomas de Southerne for life, after which his son Thomas then his brother Adam who granted lands here to Thomas Talbot in 1343. Later in the reign of Edward II (1307-27), Isobell Southerne, heiress to Sir John Southerne, married Walter de Hawksworth of Hawksworth near Otley thus bringing the Mitton property to that family. It is fact, then, that a family in the Whalley area, carrying the locally rare name of Southern, had a solid pedigree linked with the Talbots and Catteralls *et al*. Further to the Southern association; in 1616 *'John Braddill of Portefeild in Whalley esquire, and Richard Sowthen of Whalley, gentleman'* surrender lands, they do this again in 1622. Richard Southen was actually the servant, or right-hand-man, of John Bradyll and in this capacity he knew Bradyll's many tenants around the Whalley area. Richard Towneley esquire granted to Sowthen, along with Sir John Talbot of Salebury, George Shuttleworth of Asterlee, and Thomas Greenefield of Whalley, lands at Barneside and Monkroyd (Laneshawbridge), Foulridge, Carry Heyes (Colne) and Low Mashey in Little Marsden (probably Massey House in Brierfield), Colne, Wrightington and Goosenargh.

Apart from Elizabeth Southern there are few other examples of the name in local records, a rare exact phonetic match can be seen when a Jenneta Southan was buried on the 3rd January 1619 at Whalley. In 1637 the Colne baptism records show; *'Johannes fili Johanis Sowthard de Trawden illegi 17th December.'* Two possibilities of a misspelling of the name are shown when on the 19th March 1610 an Isabell Suttherd is buried at Newchurch-in-Pendle; this latter is phonetically close to Southern and cannot be ruled out of the search. A perusal of the incidence of Southern families in the sixteenth century shows that, nationally, there are a few scattered examples but a significant cluster of people carrying the name appears in the area of Holme in Lincolnshire. In 1584 a *Richard Sothorne,* of Penwortham, had his will proven in the Consistory Court of Lincoln. There is the possibility of a link here (admittedly tenuous but nevertheless worthy of consideration) between the Southern family of Whalley and the Lincolnshire families. The Clitheroe overlords of the de Lacy family were, at one time and another, earls of Lincoln and their strong connections with that area brought a number of people into the parish of Whalley.

Many families whose origins were in Lincolnshire, Nottinghamshire and South Yorkshire moved into our area because of their links with the de Lacy hegemony of the Clitheroe overlords. Often these people were attached to the Clitheroe Authority as stewards, overseers, foresters and estate managers whilst others worked within the lord's vaccary system. Furthermore, the Nowells of Read held substantial lands around the Wakefield area – in 1480 Roger Nowell founded a chantry at the altar of St. Peter in the church of All Saints in Wakefield. The Nowells gradually appropriated the whole township excepting one estate and this continued in the Holker family of Read; the Holkers were substantial yeomanry and owned lands within Pendle Forest.

A number of instances occur within Pendle Forest land transactions whereby the Holkers crop up in close proximity to the main players within the witch trial story. On the 14th May 1599 Roger Nowell esquire, John Holker gentleman (son of Randle) and John's son and heir Randle, all of Read, went to court with a land dispute concerning Read Moor. The outcome of the Duchy Court proceedings was that Roger Nowell was to own the moor as freehold and John Holker was to have two farms in Read with lands on the edge of the moor. The Holkers were also to have rights of pasture on the moor, other than a parcel called *Conyer Clappers upon Hassilhurst* which Nowell was to enclose. Nowell was also granted the right to enclose 140 acres of the moorland other than ten acres adjoining *'a certaine littel sike or sprynge called ye Warme Wall.'*

In 1610 John Holker, son and heir of Randle Holker and his wife Jennett of Read, was married to Elizabeth, daughter of James Hartley, yeoman of Barley. John Holker and his brother, Nicholas, were to have the income from Holker properties in Read and Simonstone used by John Robinson (son of Edmund) of Old Laund and Robert Bulcock of Whitehough. This is interesting as we have a link between Roger Nowell of Read, a close neighbour of the Holkers, and the Robinsons of Barley with whom the Demdike clan were at odds. Also, Robert Bulcock of Whitehough would have been related to Christopher Bulcock of Moss End in Newchurch whose wife, Jane, and son, John, were implicated in the Good Friday gathering at Malkin Tower and lost their lives in consequence.

The Gatehouse, Lancaster Castle

Chapter Nine

Would the Real Elizabeth Southern Please Step Forward?

On the subject of Elizabeth Southern's origins how much credence can we give to the Blackburn connection? Ainsworth has it that Southern was the granddaughter of a *'freebooter called Blackburn'* who eventually settled at Malkin Tower. There are almost no references to the Southern name, and very few to that of Blackburn, within the Pendle Forest but a relatively large number of these within the Whalley area (within whose parish the forest area fell). This is interesting when we look at Ainsworth's account of Demdike's grandparents, Isold de Heton and the marauder, Blackburn, who supposedly came from the Whalley area into the forest.

In a land and property surrender of 1579 we have a William Blackburn involved as a tenant (on the Bradyll estate) of farms at Billington on the outskirts of Whalley – as shall become apparent shortly, this William Blackburn appears to be of importance within our search. William's brother, George Blackburn, is shown to be farming the Bradyll estate at Dinckley (possibly the Grange or Hall farms there) some four kilometres to the west of Whalley along with a neighbour who was part of the Holker family. As a coincidental aside we see in this document that a parcel of land in Dinckley was called *Maulkin Ees* and in the tenure of a John Talbot; the *Ees* appellation relates to an island or neck of land formed by the Ribble.

Bess Blackburn

The following marriage entry, in the Whalley parish records, relates to the outlined text box (top-right) in the Blackburn family tree (opposite page):

Whallias Nupt (Whalley Marriage)
Thomase Hingaham et Elizabethe Blackburne; 15 Jun 1563

This marriage record has, until now, been of no significance to the Pendle Witch story. However, we are now privy to the information that the daughter of Elizabeth Southern was almost certainly named Ingham. This would appear to provide the breakthrough that we have been seeking. The **Thomas Ingham = Elizabeth Blackburn** marriage could very well be actual confirmation of the story that Demdike was a daughter of the Blackburn family from Whalley – or Billington to be more specific. The Whalley parish records provide us with an interesting record where an Elizabeth Blackburn was baptised on the 18th April 1541. Although baptisms are not a strictly accurate indicator of the actual birth date of an individual there is no harm in assuming a date of birth within a year or so – if the 1541 entry were to be the baptism of Elizabeth Southern then she would have been aged around twenty-three when she married Thomas Ingham and around seventy-one when she died (as Elizabeth Southern) in 1612.

We have seen the folklore related by Ainsworth following his visit to the forest in the mid-1800s; with the available recorded evidence to reinforce the argument it now seems highly probable that at this time Ainsworth picked up the local knowledge that Demdike had been named Blackburn and that she had moved into the Pendle Forest from the Whalley area. We even have a tantalising Isolde de Hetton suggestion in the early Robert Blackburn = Isolde marriage; however, Isolde Blackburn's pre-married surname is uncertain and cannot be pursued. It is clear that the Blackburns farmed for many generations within the same extended area centred upon Whalley, in fact the Billington lands adjoined with Whalley lands. We see that William Blackburn was running farms on the core Bradyll estates at Billington in 1579; it is not clear if this holding was gained through earlier Blackburn holdings or through marriage of the Blackburns into the Bradyll family. *(See also the early Blackburn genealogy on page 295).*

The Blackburn Family (proposed)

All Whalley records

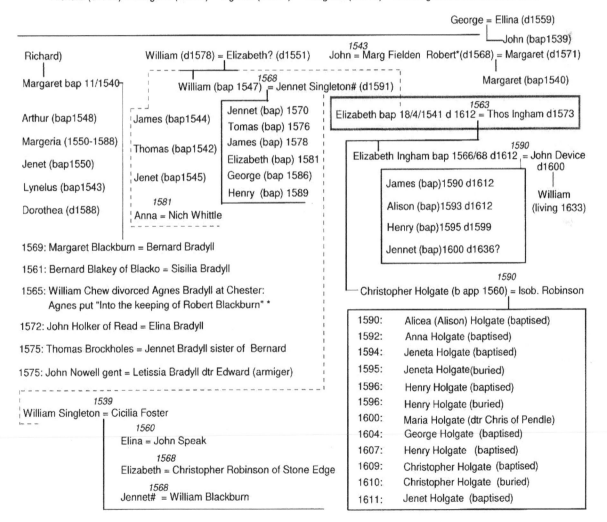

That there was an erstwhile link between the two families is not in doubt, Agnes Bradyll was entrusted into the guardianship of Robert Blackburn following her divorce in 1565 – this raises the probability that Agnes was either Robert's daughter or his sister. Furthermore, in 1569 Margaret Blackburn married Bernard Bradyll who was brother to John and the son of Edward, the recipient of Whalley Abbey lands.

To gain an idea of the extent of the lands occupied by William Blackburn (and others) in Billington, and the lands farmed by William's brother, George, in neighbouring Dynckley, we have a land dispute document of 28th March 1547 where Robert Morley is the deforciant in a case brought by John Crombock and Edward Bradyll: [1]

'Itemes of a capital messuage, with the appurtenances, 2 messuages, 3 gardens, 3 orchards, a water-mill, 100 acres of land, 100 acres of meadow, 100 acres of pasture, 50 acres of wood and underwood, and 60 acres of moor, moss and turbary, and 16 shillings of rent.'

There is no doubt that the Blackburn family were important landowners throughout the extended area around Whalley; the earliest recorded member of the dynasty appears to be one John Blakeburne who had a son Adam de Blakeburne who was, in the thirteenth century, a steward of Blackburnshire. In the mid-thirteenth century Adam held lands at Ribchester and Clayton-le-Dale and a record of the mid-thirteenth century shows that the Blackburns were acquiring lands. In their relationship with the Bradyll family the boot of hierarchy had been on the other foot as, in 1280, Avice Billington left to Beatrice, daughter of Adam de Blakeburne, an income of 20d and the homage from Roger Bradyll associated with Billington lands. Another surrender of the period saw Mathew de Worthsthorn convey to Adam Blakeburne the homage and service of Adam de Legh (the ancestors of the Towneleys) held in Worsthorne. Also in this area Adam was to receive the homage and rents of Gilbert de Hurstwood, Adam son of Elias, Robert son of Nicholas, Robert de Newcastle and Henry de Windle; from the latter he was also to receive an annual rent of one pair of white gloves.

Adam de Blakeburn appears to have a son, Henry, who married Elicia and is recorded in 1290 as holding lands, probably from his father, at Walton-le-Dale. Another of Adam's sons, John, is recorded in 1309; in 1339 a John Blakeburne is shown to have been owed suit by the Radcliffe family for lands at Wiswall near Whalley. By 1330 a William Blakeburne had appeared on the scene, he was shown to hold lands at Leyland (Preston) in 1331. In 1342 Gilbert Blakeburn has a son, Robert, who holds land at Hoghton (Blackburn) and in 1344 Robert's wife is shown to have been Isolde Blackburn. In 1349 Robert and Isolde are tenanting lands at Preston and by 1369 owned land alongside the Molyneux family. In that same year Robert Blackburn, son of Robert, was said to have been of Erley. John Blackburn, son of Robert, farmed at Halewood (Preston) in 1350 and in 1382 he farmed at Smerley in Hale. A Richard Blackburn appears in 1366 as does John again in 1376. Robert, son of John, surrenders his properties in Kenyon and Much-Wolverton to his father in 1388 and Richard is farming at Standen and Clitheroe in 1392. By 1410 a Robert Blackburn was shown as owning lands in Knutsford (Cheshire) and we then have a large gap in the records until we see Ralph Blackburn farming the old family holdings at Walton le dale in 1492. Ralph had a daughter, Constance, who married one Edmund More.

---

[1] *The Bradyll Papers*, Preston Records Office

In 1508 John, the Abbot of Whalley, granted to Robert Blackburn, land called *Bensonfield* in Billington at a rent of ten shillings. In 1583 Thomas Blackburn owned buildings on Freergate in Preston town and is shown again in 1595 as owning property at Walton le Dale. Some 260 years after we first saw John Blackburn owning lands at Wiswall we have another mention (1600) of the family where another John Blackburn still farmed the same area. A Guild record of 1632 shows that Richard Blackburn, of Dinckley, was a woollen webster.[1] Six years later Robert Blackburn of Billington took the lease of a farm in Great Harwood, near Whalley, from Henry Blackburn. The lease also included closes of land called *Pie Dowle, Great and Little Broom Bank* and *The Wood;* the lease, at £30, was for the benefit of Robert Blackburn's son, William.

Singleton

William Blackburn married Jennet Singleton in 1568 and it is probable that this William was the brother of Elizabeth Southern; the two were baptised within six years of each other. A perusal of the names given by William Blackburn and his wife, Jennet (Singleton) to their children shows exactly the same Christian names as those given by Demdike's daughter to her children and by Demdike's son to his offspring. William also names a child Elizabeth, after his proposed sister, or mother (after whom Demdike was possibly named). Demdike's children, Christopher Holgate and Elizabeth Ingham, appear then to have named their children after their Blackburn cousins.

The Singleton family were comparable in status to the Blackburns and, in similar fashion to that family, their landholdings stretched along the Ribble from Preston towards Whalley. The earliest records for the family (1200) show an Alan de Syngleton owning lands at Whittington and Freckleton and by 1244 he also had a holding at Singleton. In the 1300s the family, in the shape of Gilbert, Thomas, Adam, Robert and Nicholas, were ensconced firmly within the manor of Broughton (on the outskirts of Preston) at Broughton Tower. In the following century a James Singleton, of Broughton, had a son, Robert whose descendant Edward Singleton was prosecuted for his Catholic beliefs; this was also the case in the early 1600s when another Edward of the Broughton estates was punished for recusancy. In the fifteenth century a Nicholas Singleton had part of the manor of Brockholes and his son, Richard, lived at Bank Hall in Broughton. Other estates held by the family included Goosenargh, Woodplumpton and Staining. Richard's grandson, Henry, married the daughter of John Singleton of Singleton Hall and this takes us full-circle back to Adam de Syngleton who is said to have built the original property in 1260. The building, situated at Goosenargh, is now known as Chingle Hall and is reported to be haunted by no less than sixteen individual spirits!

In the year 1410 we catch a glimpse of the family when *Richard de Tounley* grants lands *'All the manors and messuages etc. which I have by rights of inheritance of John my father in the county of Lancaster'* to Nicholas de Syngleton, his son Thomas and Richard de Syngleton chaplain.[2] We see them again in 1492 when they are involved in a property transfer between Constance Blackburn (daughter of Ralph and widow of Edmund More) and Ralph Whalley. The property, called Hanscha, was the inheritance of Constance and Robert Syngleton witnessed the deed.

---

[1] *Township Guilds* – Preston Records Office
[2] *Towneley MSS*

A farm and fifteen acres of land was, in 1592, in the possession of Thomas Singleton esquire, of Broughton Tower (Preston) and his son, Edward Singleton. The land was said to have been at Durton, this was probably Dutton some two kilometres north of Ribchester (there is a property called Singleton House at Ribchester to this day). In 1597 the Countess Dowager of Derby and Sir Richard Molyneux divided the manor of Ulnes Walton and a recipient of part of the estate was Robert Singleton, gent. John Bradyll of Portfield (Whalley) son and heir of Edward Bradyll, of Brockhall, granted (1598) former Whalley Abbey lands to Thomas Singleton, Doctor of Divinity and principal of Brassenose College in the University of Oxford. Thomas, as we have seen, had earlier been the beneficiary in the will of John Bradyll's father, Edward.

Taking it that Demdike's brother, William Blackburn, married Jennet Singleton on the 4th October 1568 another relevant parish record entry (Whalley) heaves into view. Four days following the marriage of William and Jennet we see Christopher Robinson of Stone Edge (Blacko) marrying Elizabeth Singleton who appears to have been the sister of Jennet.[1] Things become interesting here when the following land surrender is taken into account;

1570: *Bernard Blakey surrenders 1 messuage and 40 acres of land at Blacko to James Hartley (son of Bernard of Laund) and Simon Blakey (son of Bernard) as feoffes (to hold the property in trust)* . . .

The intent of the surrender was that the farm, then in the possession of Christopher Robinson senior, was to go to Christopher Robinson junior for the extent of his natural life. Following his death the property was to pass to any lawful issue of Christopher and his wife Elizabeth (Singleton). If there were to be no issue then the property was to pass to any rightful heirs of Christopher on condition that one-third of the property went to Elizabeth Singleton for her dower - she was also to receive all profits from the farm for the extent of her natural life.

Our interest in this lies in the fact that Bernard Blakey's wife was one Sissilia Bradyll (they married at Whalley in 1561), thus making him a relative by marriage of Elizabeth Southern; likewise, Elizabeth Singleton, wife of Christopher Robinson who held large amounts of land around Blacko, was probably sister-in-law to Demdike's brother. So . . . we have long wondered why Demdike appeared to be untouchable within her perceived fortress of Malkin Tower and now we might just have a major clue. The reason for her having lived on the Blacko Hillside could very well have been that her family, in the shape of either the Robinsons or the Blakeys, had provided a small property for her on the edge of the Stone Edge estate. This probably came about following the demise of her husband, Thomas Ingham. Whether Elizabeth Device moved into Malkin with her mother at the time of her father's death is not known – she possibly moved her family across the ridgeway between the West Close area and Blacko following the death of her husband, John Device, in 1600.

Ingham

Demdike's daughter carried the surname of Ingham at the time of her marriage to John Device in 1590 and Elizabeth Blackburn married Thomas Ingham in 1563. In the sixteenth century, branches of the Ingham family were located from Whalley through to Colne; there were definite

---

[1] *Whalley Parish Records* and unpublished genealogies held by Clitheroe Local Studies Library

concentrations of them on the periphery of the forest area at Read and Padiham but the main families were to be found in a small area of Burnley. The site of highest status regarding the Ingham properties was the farming operation at Fulledge (Burnley), this incorporated Turf Moor, now the site of the Burnley Football Club stadium. A branch of the Ingham family of Fulledge farmed at Lower Timber Hill Farm (Burnley), this family farmed the eighteen-acre holding here for most of the sixteenth and seventeenth centuries. In 1544, on the occasion of his marriage, John Ingham's father granted him six acres lying in two fields named Marled Earth and Over Hartshead together with the west part of the house comprising a cellar, a room over the cellar and a stable built next to the cellar and room. In 1588 Robert Ingham junior was taxed eight shillings on his goods at Timberhill. In the early seventeenth century it is clear that the Ingham families were heavily involved in the woollen trade as listed as suppliers of cloth on the same document were Richard Ingham of Ightenhill, Edward Ingham of Ightenhill, Thomas Ingham, and George Ingham.[1]

In 1522 John Ingham, a priest at Burnley from 1500 to 1534, was related to both Sir John Towneley and the Inghams of Fulledge House. John held land at Smallshaw (Burnley) and in other parts of the area. He officially informed his sister (Alice Barcroft) and his nephew (Richard Tattersall of the Ridge) that if they did not stop bickering between themselves as to who was to inherit his properties then he would leave the lot to found a chantry in Burnley church. Further to this, in 1529, we see that John Ingham bequeathed his properties to the Burnley church!

Within the forest proper were the Inghams of West Close, Higham and Inghams Farm in Reedley Hallows. The Inghams were also established in farming at Colne Edge, between Blacko and Colne. From here, in 1600, Lawrence Ingham had a daughter Grace baptised at Colne followed by Henry (1600-died 1607), James (1602) William (1606 died 1608) Richard (1608) and Robert (1610). In the neighbouring manor of Foulridge, during the sixteenth century, there was a close known as Inghams Tenement; this was freehold land held by the Stephenson family of Ball House and indicates the presence of an Ingham family here at a reasonably early date. Topographically closer to our story is the Stone Edge estate where, in 1637, Sarah Ingham had an illegitimate son, Joseph, by Christopher Hall of Barrowford Water Meetings. Although late in date for our purposes this latter record shows that the Ingham family were living at Stone Edge and had probably done so for a number of years. On the 18th May, 1607, Isabella Ingham of Blacko was buried at Colne and, again, we see that the Inghams were living within the area of Elizabeth Southern's home at Malkin Tower. The family were still farming in this area some thirty years later as the Preston Assize Recognizance Rolls show that Abraham Ingham, and Sarah his wife, of Barrowford, were ordered to keep the peace to Mary Parker of Stone Edge. There had obviously been a disagreement between the Inghams and Mary Parker and this had led to some kind of physical assault – in the same year of 1637 an official arbitrator provided a testimonial in the dispute between these parties.

As far as the birth of Demdike's daughter goes we have two records in Whalley parish, in the years 1566 and 1568, showing the baptism of two children named Elizabeth Ingham. One of these could well have been Demdike's daughter who would become Elizabeth Device; certainly the 1566 date of baptism fits well with the 1563 marriage of Elizabeth Blackburn = Thomas

---

[1] W. Bennett, *History of Burnley*, (Vol 1, Burnley Corporation, 1946)

Ingham. If we do indeed have here the records appertaining to Demdike and her daughter then the question arises as to whether the family were living in the Whalley area following their marriage or had they moved into the forest? The fact that a baptism was carried out at Whalley is irrelevant in terms of location; it does not strictly follow that a child baptised in one *local* parish church was actually born in that parish – as we have seen, the extended forest area (including Colne and Burnley) fell within the parish of Whalley. It is highly possible that the Thomas Ingham and his new wife were either based at, or had moved to the Fulledge, West Close and Higham areas to farm. They might have lived on a farm belonging to another family member and had their daughter Elizabeth there following which they had her baptised at Whalley. If this was the case then the evidence tends to lean towards the Inghams having lived around the Pendle Forest area of West Close as Elizabeth married John Dennis/Device at Newchurch. Further to this we have the marriage at Burnley, in 1597, of John Nutter (1567-1636) of Chamberhead (Reedley Waterside) to Ann Ingham (1568-1630) the daughter of John Ingham. As we shall see later this John Nutter was a close relative of the Nutter family of Greenhead; two members of this branch (Robert and Christopher) were said to have been killed by Old Chattox. An interesting question arises here – was Ann Ingham closely related to Demdike's husband, Thomas Ingham? If so we may well have a reason why Demdike and Chattox appeared to be mortal enemies; Demdike would have sided with the Nutters who were not best pleased with their Chattox family neighbours at West Close. In this same vein it might also be worth mentioning that, in 1581, Anna Blackburn married Nicholas Whittle at Whalley; again, do we have a family relationship between Chattox's name of Whittle and Elizabeth Blackburn (Demdike)?

A picture now begins to emerge whereby we have a credible insight into Demdike's earlier life, a period that has remained a complete mystery to us from the time that Ainsworth gleaned snippets of information relating to the matter. Before proceeding I must return at this point to the subject of Demdike's son, Christopher Holgate. Having speculated that his father was from the local forest area it is now possible to extend the search into the area of Demdike's possible early stamping grounds of Whalley. No Holgate entries are recorded at Whalley parish church and this suggests that there were few families of this name using the place. The neighbouring Forest of Rossendale, however, did have a family of that name and they show up regularly in the Clitheroe Court Rolls; one such record dates from 1570 and we see Christopher Holgate (son of John) and Hugh Hey (with his wife Jennet) surrendering a farm at Wheathead in Wolfenden. This was located in the area of the Forest of Rossendale shown by the following record, found in the *Act Book of the Ecclesiastical Court of Whalley:*

1519: *John Ormerod juror for Rossendale, comprising 'Constable Le Bacok booth, Tunstede, Wulfendene, Dedwyne Cloghe, Rowtenstalghe, Crawshabothe, Goodshaghe, Love cloghe, Wulfenden cloghe.*

Was the Christopher Holgate of Rossendale actually the father of Demdike's son? There is no definitive reason to take Demdike's son as a close relative of the Colne/Pendle Holgate families, especially as we are now casting our genealogical net further afield; neither is it unreasonable to suggest that Demdike might have had an illegitimate child before her marriage to Thomas Ingham. If this were to be the case then she would have been no more than twenty years of age at the time. Following this through, Demdike married Thomas Ingham in 1563 when she already had a small son, Christopher; there is every likelihood that her family married off the young

Elizabeth to Thomas, this was common practice in such cases. Following the marriage the small family of three moved to Thomas Ingham's locality in the Burnley/Pendle Forest district. They shortly became the proud parents of a baby daughter who they named Elizabeth, a name carried by the child's mother, grandmother and cousin. There is a possibility here that baby Elizabeth was born with a congenital deformity whereby she was either simply cross-eyed or one of her eye-sockets was misaligned within the skull frame; alternatively the child could have fallen onto a hard object within her formative years and dislocated an eye socket. Whatever the unfortunate circumstances it is likely from later reports that young Elizabeth grew up as a shy child, she would probably have had a tendency not to look people directly in the eye and this would have given her the appearance of being strange and shifty.

At the approximate age of twenty-six Elizabeth married John Device at St. Mary's, Newchurch; it is likely that Device was quite a bit older than Elizabeth as, in 1633, it becomes apparent that he already had a son, William, when he married Elizabeth.[1] Device, then, could well have been a relatively elderly widower in 1590; perhaps his young bride thought that this was the highest number on the dice that she was likely to throw in the matrimony stakes as her disfigurement would deter younger, more eligible men. Whatever the case may be John Device died ten years after his marriage and was buried in the churchyard at St. Mary's.

A number of clues point towards the young Demdike family having lived within the western forest before migrating eastwards to Malkin. Demdike and daughter Elizabeth knew the West Close, Higham, Newchurch areas of the forest well and appear to have been on close terms with a number of the inhabitants there. Chattox stated that Anthony Nutter, who farmed near Newchurch, 'favoured' Demdike over herself and Demdike's granddaughter, Alison Device, was a friend of Anthony Nutter's daughter, Ann. This is shown when Chattox entered Nutter's house one day and found Alison and Ann laughing together, taking it that the girls were disrespecting her Chattox was said to have bewitched Ann who died shortly afterwards. Demdike is often seen within the 1612 trial statements as scurrying around the West Close area with piggins (single-handed buckets) full of milk. She was abroad on this task when she happened to come across Chattox and her daughter making clay 'pictures' of the Greenhead Nutters in order to cause their untimely deaths. A viable explanation here is that the Demdike family lived and worked in that area; if this was indeed the case then why did they end their days at the probable Blacko site of Malkin Tower?

The possible explanation for this is that Demdike's husband, Thomas Ingham, died; the Whalley records tell us that three people by the name of Thomas Ingham were buried there on the 8th February 1573, the 17th December 1573 and the 22nd February 1587. Any one of these could relate to Demdike's husband; if he had died in 1573 then she would have been left with a son of approximately thirteen and a daughter of around nine. No records to show any transfer of land in relation to Thomas Ingham, or claim of dower by Elizabeth Ingham, have been forthcoming and it is therefore likely that his widow and young family were left without means of support other than working on the land of Thomas's relatives. These are possibly the same family who show up in the Padiham parish records as follows:

Maria Ingham father Johnis Ingham de Westclose baptised 12 May 1609

---

[1] Evidence given by Edmund Robinson in the 1633 Pendle Witch case – see Chapter Fourteen below

Elizabetha Ingham father Thomae Ingham de Westclose buried 24 Feb 1603

Elizabetha Ingham father Johnis Ingham de Pendle baptised 02 Jun 1611

Jenneta Ingham father Johnis Ingham de Pendle baptised 27 Apr 1617

Jana Ingham father Johannis Ingham de Pendle baptised 24 Oct 1619

Thomas Whitaker father Thomae Whittaker de Simonstone et Margarita Ingham father Johannis Ingham de West Close bapties 05 May 1622

It is probable that the above Thomas and John Ingham were related to Demdike's husband, this could have been a reason for Demdike frequenting the area of West Close. The Clitheroe Court Rolls for Ightenhill show a number of Ingham entries amongst which are:

1443: *Free tenants:John Ingham of Burnley:- Robert Ingham of Little Marsden:- John Ingham of Padiham:- William Ingham of Pendle*

1507: *John and Katherine Ingham, Robert and Isabella Ingham and William Holgate were fined for digging turf on a pasture called le Flange in the occupation of James Hargreaves and Robert Bulcock (Goldshaw?)*

1513: *George Ingham complained against James Hargreaves, chantry priest, in a plea of debt for 10 marks:- John Ingham (son of Humphrey) of Fulledge had sons John (then a minor) and William*

1532: *William Ingham, his wife Elizabeth and son John had a capital messuage (large property) at Burnley Wood:- a John Ingham was the son of Henry:- a John Ingham surrendered the farm of Tinkler House in Padiham*

1540: *William Ingham and his wife Elizabeth hold the Burnley Wood property at £0: 8s: 0d*

1541: *Humphrey Ingham is dead (his wife is Margery) and leaves Padiham properties of Tinkler Field, Knightley, Burn End, Sabden Bank and a house there*

1545: *John Ingham and Hugh Halstead, yeomen, pay John Crook the sum of £15: 9s: 0d for the close and farm (with appurtenances) of West Close for 20 years*

1546: *John Ingham of Padiham made afray upon Isabell and Alice Crook and drew blood:- John Ingham farmed lands at Haggot gate and Moor Gate in Goldshaw*

1547: *John Ingham of Fulledge was dead and his son and heir was Robert Ingham:- Richard Ingham was the son of Richard of Burnley Wood*

1556: *William Lister surrendered 4 farms, 4 crofts and 4 gardens in the occupation of William Ingham and John Holden on the south side of Colne to Henry Mitton*

On the 1st February 1559 Lawrence Habergham granted a parcel of land at Colne, known as The Yng, to the foundation of a grammar school. In 1577 Robert Ingham, rector of Stockham Pelham in Hertfordshire, owned a house and land in Alfrethen, Essex. The property was rented to his nephew, John Ingham of Whalley, at £3 per annum; Robert declared that following his death the £3 rent should be paid towards the maintenance of a Free Grammar School in either Burnley or Colne.

By the year 1619 it is clear that the Fulledge estate farmed by the Inghams was in the ownership of Laurence Ormerod of Burnley who had placed it in the care of John Nutter and Ellis Nutter, of New Laund, as trustees. Ormerod had died before 1619 and John Nutter had also died in that year. The lands within the trusteeship of the Nutters were given as:

A capital messuage called Fulledge (Fulledge House): 7 other messuages in Burnley with all their appurtenances: 71 parcels of common waste in Burnley, Burnley Wood, Habergham Eves and Little Ightenhill.

The surviving trustee, Ellis Nutter of Waterside, granted admittance to the lands and property to Robert Ingham junior of Fulledge. As a final word on the Ingham family we see them, in 1562, fraternising with the local gentry. Laurence Habergham had married Margaret Ingham of Burnley, Margaret was the daughter of Jennet Ingham and Sir John Towneley. The story goes that Sir John had married Jennet Ingham but the marriage was not officially recognised because of Jennet's lowly birth. Laurence Habergham had previously been married to Grace, the natural daughter of Sir John Towneley and therefore the marriage of Laurence and Margaret was declared to be incestuous. However, Whitaker *(History of Whalley)* states that he found evidence to show that the case was referred to the Archbishop of York who, pouring oil upon troubled waters, found that Sir John's child, Margaret, was born during the lifetime of his wife. The marriage of Laurence and Margaret, therefore, was legal because the law of incest did not extend to relations between putative children. Just how close this marriage brought Demdike's husband, Thomas Ingham, to the high-status Towneley and Habergham families is anyone's guess!

Sketch of a stoneware 'Witch-bottle' found behind a fireplace in Trawden during the 19th century. These bottles could be used as either protection against witchcraft or to cause injury to a witch. If injury was intended to be the outcome then the bottle would be filled with human hair, nail parings, bent nails and copper pins.

A 'heart' made from fabric would be stuck with pins and also placed in the bottle which was then corked and buried. The Trawden example was found to contain bent nails and hair and was probably designed to afford protection.

Chapter Ten

Jennet Device

Having seen that the child of eleven, Jennet Device, was instrumental in the conviction of many of the accused, what exactly was her 'evidence' proffered so triumphantly to the court by Roger Nowell? The following takes up Potts as he describes the events immediately following Elizabeth Device's courtroom outburst against her daughter:

The Examination and Euidence of Iennet Device, Daughter of the said Elizabeth Device, late Wife of Iohn Device, of the Forrest of Pendle, in the Countie of Lancaster. Against Elizabeth Device her Mother, Prisoner at the Barre vpon her Arraignement and Triall. viz

In the end, when no meanes would serue, his Lordship commanded the Prisoner (Elizabeth Device) *to be taken away, and the Maide* (Jennet Device) *to bee set vpon the Table in the presence of the whole Court, who deliuered her euidence in that Honorable assembly, to the Gentlemen of the Iurie of life and death, as followeth. viz.*

Iennet Deuice, Daughter of Elizabeth Deuice, late Wife of Iohn Deuice, of the Forrest of Pendle aforesaid Widdow, confesseth and saith, that her said Mother is a Witch, and that this shee knoweth to be true; for, that shee had seene her Spirit sundrie times come vnto her said Mother in her owne house, called Malking-Tower, in the likenesse of a browne Dogge, which shee called Ball; and at one time amongst others, the said Ball did aske this Examinates Mother what she would haue him to doe: and this Examinates Mother answered, that she would haue the said Ball to helpe her to kill Iohn Robinson of Barley, alias Swyer: by helpe of which said Ball, the said Swyer was killed by witch-craft accordingly; and that this Examinates Mother hath continued a Witch for these three or foure yeares last past. And further, this Examinate confesseth, that about a yeare after, this Examinates Mother called for the said Ball, who appeared as aforesaid, asking this Examinates Mother what shee would haue done, who said, that shee would haue him to kill Iames Robinson, alias Swyer, of Barlow (Barley) aforesaid, Brother to the said Iohn: whereunto Ball answered, hee would doe it; and about three weekes after, the said Iames dyed.

And this Examinate also saith, that one other time shee was present, when her said Mother did call for the Ball, Her Spirit. who appeared in manner as aforesaid, and asked this Examinates Mother what she would haue him to doe, whereunto this Examinates Mother then said shee would haue him to kill one Mitton of the Rough Lee, whereupon the said Ball said, he would doe it, and so vanished away, and about three weekes after, the said Mitton likewise dyed.

The flow of content here is obviously contrived; the pronounced hand of biased-intent shines through when we recall that the statement is that of an eleven year old child. The description accorded to the word of Jennet in relation to the spirit, Ball, follows through the story and is standardised throughout – far too standardised in fact! That the accused were prone to imbue their animals with extraordinary powers is highly possible, probable in fact; this would allow the almost totally powerless within society to attain at least a modicum of (perceived) control over their own social standing. Elizabeth Device may well have returned home from her day in the forest with a piggin of blue-milk and a scant copper or two; she might have been the subject of derision by her neighbours during the day. In this case it would be little wonder that she would return home in a mood of despondency, with little good-will to extend to her fellow man. Sitting by the fire she might have stroked her brown pet dog, Ball, for solace and muttered of the constant ills done to her and how sweet any revenge would be if this were possible; *"Eeh lad, 'ow grand it'd bifo't setthi abaht worrittin' yon mon!"* [1]

It is not clear whether the multitude of dogs cropping up within the statements of the accused actually belonged to them (as pets) or if the dogs were semi-strays wandering the neighbourhood and visiting people on a regular basis in search of scraps. This is entirely possible as it would be unlikely that dogs were kept solely as pets by the poor, they would have to earn their living by catching rabbits, hares and game from the surrounding moors. The suggestion in Jennet's 'evidence' points to the dog, Ball, having appeared at various intervals throughout the story, this lends weight to the animal having had some kind of close-tie with the Device family.

Whatever the case might have been, Jennet was repeating the conversations overheard within her family over a period of many years; a small percentage of the people who had been perceived to insult her family would become ill or die and this was then automatically assigned to the mutterings of her mother or grandmother. Elizabeth Device would not deny the rumour that she had 'killed' someone by using her powers; this was useful ammunition with which to arm herself against the outside world. Jennet was stating as fact that she knew her mother had been a witch for some three or four years but this did not seem to strike anyone as having been questionable at the time. Certainly the judges did not take the view that Jennet, being only around six or seven when Elizabeth apparently became a witch, was not capable of presenting justifiable evidence in what amounted to a murder trial.

Jennet Seller

Elizabeth Device was said to have given her reason for killing John Robinson of Barley as revenge for him having accused her *'of having an illegitimate child by one Sellers.'* Elizabeth's youngest child, Jennet, is commonly taken to be the child she was accused of having by Seller and this is the most acceptable explanation because Elizabeth's husband, John Device, had died in the same year that Jennet was born. The argument has been made for John having been senior in years to Elizabeth and it has been suggested that this is one reason why she might have 'played away.' There is also the story, related to me by Andrew Turner, of Malkin Tower Farm, that the folklore around the Blacko Hillside has it that Elizabeth Device was raped and the

---

[1] Roughly translated from the vernacular as *"I say Old Chap, how lovely it would be if I could possibly allow you to assault my protagonist in your inimitable canine fashion!"*

perpetrator, in an attempt to make amends, gave the family a plot of land. It is worth remembering here that Richard Baldwin called Demdike and Elizabeth Device *"Witches and whores,"* can we take it, therefore, that Elizabeth Device was the 'whore' and Demdike the 'witch'? This would point towards Elizabeth having had a tryst with a man named Seller, possibly whilst her husband was still living. It is just possible in the natural scheme of things that, if John died early in the year 1600, Elizabeth could have taken up with Mr Seller following John's death and still produced a child within the same year – she would have had to be quick though!

This is as far as we can take this Seller connection, well almost . . . The Seller surname was well established within the Whalley area where they were neighbours of the Blackburns. In 1546 a William Seller, churchwarden, rented land called *Screyestall Land* in Whalley from John Bradyll and, in 1580, John Seller farmed at Deans Place in Read. William Farrington transferred the property of Deans Place Farm to Roger Nowell, this was witnessed by Henry Fielding of Goldshaw, a relative of the Demdike/Blackburn family. One of the first curates at Newchurch was William Seller, he was reported as being unsatisfactory in 1535, it was said that he did not hear confessions and refused to marry people; he was suspended in 1536. William Seller of Pendleton was a churchwarden at Whalley parish church in 1590. As was the case with most of the families who originated in Whalley, the Seller name grew thinner on the ground as it approached the forest. That is not to say that there were no Sellers hereabouts as, by the early seventeenth century, they were farming at Wanless (below Blacko), Wheathead and Burned Moor (Admergill). It is also believed that, during the period leading up to the 1612 trial, a Seller farmed at White Moor Farm just a few hundred metres to the east of Malkin Tower Farm.[1]

As a final note on the Seller/Jennet Device mystery there is a very interesting entry in the Newchurch burial records where we find:

Jennet Seller alias Devis: sepult (interpolated entry): 22nd December 1635 [2]

In all probability this is the burial of Jennet Device. In Part One we saw that the Baldwin will mentioned a Jennet Davye but the above burial record names Jennet as both Seller and Devis; this precludes the Baldwin/Davye connection. It would appear that Jennet (quite understandably) changed her name to that of her father following the execution of the rest of her family. There is also a strong hint here that Jennet would have gone to live with her father although there is also the possibility that she changed her name and went to live with her uncle, Christopher Holgate; whatever the case may have been it is clear that Jennet lived out the rest of her post-trial days in the forest. In the 1633 Pendle Witch case, as we shall see later, Jennet was implicated when a Robinson lad accused her, along with her half-brother, William Device, of being a witch.

Jennet Device, then, died in the winter of 1635, aged 35 years, and was buried at Saint Mary's. The curate was Robert Hill and amongst the small group of mourners on that December day would have been Jennet's Holgate relatives along with her Seller family. The following churchwardens at the time were John Robinson, Laurence Robinson, James Ridehalgh and

---

[1] E. Peel & P. Southern, *The Trials of the Lancashire Witches*, (David & Charles, 1969 / 1972)
[2] *Sepult* (burial); *interpolated entry* means the burial was entered into the parish register at a later date

Thomas Varley; this latter was a friend of the Holgates and the curate who officiated at the marriage of Jennet's mother and John Device. What did the curate say as Jennet was buried? What was said amongst that sad, graveside gathering of the events some twenty-three years earlier when Jennet played a major part in the deaths of her family? At least Jennet was afforded a Christian burial, this was more than those who were executed in August 1612 were afforded. The actual fate of Jennet's grandmother, Elizabeth Southern, following her demise in the dungeon of the Well Tower at Lancaster, is unknown. There was no reason that she could not have received a Christian burial as she was never actually tried and convicted of any crime – she died an innocent woman.

John Device

John Device was said to have paid an annual contribution of one *aghendole* of oatmeal to Chattox – an *aghendole* was originally the term used for a 'hand out' ('dole' is still used in this context) where *aghen* and *hanck* share the same root for 'hand' or 'in hand.' The aghendole equivalent in weight today would be around eight and-a-half pounds. Alison Device said that the reason for John Device providing this contribution to Chattox was to gain protection for Device's family, property and goods against the powers of Chattox. Again this hints at John having been elderly, perhaps too frail to resist the Whittle/Redfern family. The first year that John Device missed paying the contribution he fell ill and died, during his final illness he constantly blamed Chattox for having bewitched him.

To accept this story at face value we must also accept that Demdike, as John's mother-in-law, stood idly back and allowed her rival (and former student in witchcraft) to blackmail her family without retaliation. Demdike had apparently been practising her craft for many more years than Chattox and must have seen herself as being at least the equal of her great rival. We have no explanation for this, nor do her family's statements shed any light on this curious incident; why would the family of the supposedly most omnipotent witch in the whole area pay for protection from another witch who was subordinate in power? There is surely more to this than meets the eye; a somewhat tenuous link exists between Chattox and the Demdike family through a Whittle/Blackburn marriage and a Brown/Hey/Holgate connection. Further to this, Demdike and Alice Nutter allegedly bewitched Henry Mitton and, as we saw in Part One, Henry Mitton was related to the Hartley family of Laund. We have also seen that it is probable that one of Chattox's daughters married into the Hartley family. This could provide a reason why Demdike appears to have taken against poor old Henry Mitton; this would illustrate that the extended families of Chattox and Demdike were fair targets within their witching games!

Another explanation for the mystery springs to mind and that centres upon Chattox's daughter, Bessie Whittle, sister to Anne Redferne. Bessie was said by Alison Device to have broken into the *'fire house'* at Malkin Tower and stolen a quantity of clothing and food following which she had the audacity to turn up at church wearing Alison's best bonnet![1] This could just furnish us with the character of Bessie Whittle, a burglar and bare-faced (but not bare-headed) with it! Having broken into the firehouse at Malkin Tower, and stolen the goods from the Device family, did John Device pay protection to Chattox in order for her daughter to leave them alone?

---

[1] *Firehouse* was the description used in order to differentiate a domestic dwelling from commercial buildings or to describe the heated part of a large house

If Bessie was some kind of latter-day Calamity Jane perhaps John wished to keep the peace rather than risking an all-out war between the different factions within the forest. Certainly, the method of settling these types of dispute within the forest was often the use of open conflict; many records of physical assault survive from this period when the law was seen as a last resort. It was not uncommon for families, armed with muskets and staves, to confront each other over some perceived wrong doing by their rivals – many instances of this type stemmed from, or involved, a petty land dispute.

Alison Device

Alison (or *Alicea,* according to her baptism record), was the eldest daughter of Elizabeth Device and she was to play a pivotal part within the case of the Pendle Witch Trials. In our story the episode of Alison Device and the chapman (traveller in small goods), John Lawe, ranks alongside the persecution of Jennet Preston and the Good Friday gathering of the clans as a judicial watershed. On the 18th March, 1612, Alison unwittingly triggered the roundup of 'witches' throughout the Forest of Pendle. Having decided to take herself off to the farms of the Trawden area, probably on a produce-gathering mission, Alison left Malkin and headed south down the ancient trackway of Slipper Hill. This old route took her over the Wanless Water beck and on up the hillside, past the huge stone marker on the wayside and to the top of the ridge known as Colne Edge; she may have stopped here for a chat with her Ingham relatives before resuming her journey. Her way then took her down into the North Valley before reaching the steep ascent to the top of the market town of Colne. Alison headed for the crossroads above the old church from where she intended to take the road east through Colne Field and make for Carry Bridge, the gateway into Trawden Forest.

Events undertook a disastrous turn as the young woman began to leave the town behind; not far along the road she happened upon a foot-weary traveller heading in the opposite direction. The man's name was John Lawe and what happened next was to go down in the annals of history. His mind being set only upon washing down the dust of the road in one of the Colne ale-houses, Lawe passed Alison without so much as a sideways glance. Unfortunately Alison was not so set upon her journey and took the opportunity to ask the traveller for a small packet of pins; these copper pins were used to peg woollen cloth 'pieces' onto wooden frames. As a 'petty chapman' John Lawe would have been carrying these pins, along with a number of other small commodities that farmer's wives in the outlying areas would require. Having been diverted from his vision of foaming ale, Lawe reacted to Alison's request with a dismissive grunt, he could not be bothered to remove his back-pack, undo the straps and find the requested goods. Taking this cursory dismissal as a personal affront Alison gave him a piece of her mind before they parted, each setting off again in opposite directions.

They had not been parted for a period of two minutes when Alison heard a commotion behind her; turning she saw Lawe slumped in a ragged heap in the middle of the road. It is apparent that the chapman had suffered a stroke from the stress of having been in an argument with Alison. He was picked up by passers by and taken the short distance into the Greyhound Inn at Colne where he was laid on a wooden bench.[1] Having followed these events from a distance

---

[1] Commonly known as the *Dog,* this inn stood at the top of Colne Market Street and was demolished long ago

Alison peered around the door of the inn to see what the situation was; having taken a look at Lawe she then appears to have resumed her foray into Trawden Forest.

That, at least, is the official version of events according to Potts. . . . as usual, however, statements relating to the unfortunate episode do not stack up. In fact the more the situation is studied the more contrived it appears to become; to further this argument let us have a closer look at the Colne Field incident, beginning with the *Wonderful Discoverie*:

The CONFESSIONE
of Alizon Device, Prisoner at the Barre: published and declared at time of her Arraignement and Triall in open Court

*S*He saith, That about two yeares agone, her Grand-mother, called Elizabeth Sothernes, alias Dembdike, did (sundry times in going or walking together, as they went begging) perswade and aduise this Examinate to let a Diuell or a Familiar appeare to her, and that shee, this Examinate would let him suck at some part of her; and she might haue and doe what shee would. And so not long after these perswasions, this Examinate being walking towards the Rough-Lee, in a Close of one Iohn Robinsons, there appeared vnto her a thing like vnto a Blacke Dogge: speaking vnto her, this Examinate, and desiring her to giue him her Soule, and he would giue her power to doe any thing shee would: whereupon this Examinate being therewithall inticed, and setting her downe; the said Blacke-Dogge did with his mouth (as this Examinate then thought) sucke at her breast, a little below her Paps, which place did remain blew halfe a yeare next after: which said Blacke-Dogge did not appeare to this Examinate, vntill the eighteenth day of March last: at which time this Examinate met with a Pedler on the high-way, called Colne-field, neere vnto Colne: and this Examinate demanded of the said Pedler to buy some pinnes of him; but the said Pedler sturdily answered this Examinate that he would not loose his Packe; and so this Examinate parting with him: presently there appeared to this Examinate the Blacke-Dogge, which appeared vnto her as before: which Black Dogge spake vnto this Examinate in English, saying; What wouldst thou haue me to do vnto yonder man? to whom this Examinate said, What canst thou do at him? and the Dogge answered againe, I can lame him: whereupon this Examinat answered, and said to the said Black Dogge, Lame him: and before the Pedler was gone fortie Roddes further, he fell downe Lame: and this Examinate then went after the said Pedler; and in a house about the distance aforesaid, he was lying Lame: and so this Examinate went begging in Trawden Forrest that day, and came home at night: and about fiue daies next after, the said Black-Dogge did appeare to this Examinate, as she was going a begging, in a Cloase neere the New-Church in Pendle, and spake againe to her, saying; Stay and speake with me; but this Examinate would not: Sithence which time this Examinat neuer saw him.

What, then, are we to make of this incident? We have in John Lawe a stout traveller who one would have expected to have been reasonably fit given the long distances he would have journeyed in the course of plying his trade. Having met with the eighteen-year old Alison, who asked if he would sell her a few pins, Lawe is driven into such a state of apoplexy that he suffers a major stroke. To our modern ears this story, in its officially reported form, is somewhat difficult to believe; having said that, it is possible that the prevalent fear of witchcraft was present in Lawe's mind when he met Alison; perhaps her perceived powers caused him to be overcome by his fear. This would be a possible explanation on the condition that Lawe knew

Alison and was aware that she had a reputation as being a powerful and dangerous witch – this seems unlikely when it is considered that nowhere was Lawe reported to have known Alison previously. Furthermore Lawe would have been a man of the world, his trade would bring him into contact with all manner of humanity and Alison would probably not have been an obvious threat to him.

In an attempt to get to the nub of the matter we have to consider the statements of both Alison and Lawe; both of them mention the presence of a black dog. Alison stated that her Familiar was a *'Blacke Dogge'* who conveniently appeared following Lawe's refusal to empty his pack; even more conveniently the black dog spoke to Alison *'in English,'* following which she commanded it to lame the chapman. Lawe's statement ran on similar lines whereby he said that *"he saw a great Black-Dogge stand by him, with very fearefull firie eyes, great teeth, and a terrible countenance, looking him in the face, whereat he was very sore afraid."* It is not unreasonable to assume, then, that Alison did indeed have a canine companion, this was understandable for a young girl who was given to roaming the forest areas alone at all times of day and night – a fierce dog would offer good protection. The fact that both Alison and a large black dog appeared simultaneously at the Inn, following Lawe's collapse, reinforces this argument.

Alison was angry following her dismissal by Lawe and she could well have reacted by setting her dog on him. However, this does not appear to be the whole story; it is made quite clear that Alison was contrite immediately following Lawe's collapse and at her trial, this does not suggest the character of an aggressive girl. The most likely explanation to my mind is that when Lawe met with Alison he had her marked down as a scruffy beggar-girl with no means of paying for the goods that she had requested, he reacted by shouting in order to deter her from pestering him further and the dog, perceiving a threat to his mistress, attacked him. Lawe ran towards Colne market place with the snarling, snapping dog in angry pursuit; fear, anger and the effects of the sudden two-hundred yard sprint (approximately forty-roods) caused Lawe to have a stroke and collapse on Colne Field. Having helplessly watched these events unfold Alison at least showed some concern by looking in on Lawe. When Alison's statement was being prepared the presence of the dog proved to be grist to Nowell's mill and it very quickly became transformed into an ethereal spirit whose sole intent was to satisfy Alison's evil disposition.

The official line was that a letter was sent to John's son, Abraham Lawe, who was described as a cloth-dyer. It is thought that Abraham lived in the Halifax area and this is very possible, as we shall see a little later. The letter from Colne arrived with Abraham around the 21st March and he set off to see his father who he described as *'being paralysed on one side all save his eye.'* By the time his son had arrived John seems to have regained his speech as he is able to relate that Alison Device had caused his lameness by bewitchment.

Now, it is possible to detect a faint whiff of subterfuge here. There is every possibility that the traveller, John Lawe, was actually visiting Colne on business, rather than having been a native of the area. This is illustrated by the fact that his son lived at Halifax and that he was heading *into* Colne with an apparently full pack of goods. He would not, therefore, have known Alison and his unfortunate collapse would have been put down to bad luck in other circumstances. Unfortunately for Alison, and ultimately for the nine other witch trial victims, the locals in the Dog Inn would have taken great delight in convincing John Lawe that he had come up against the daughter of the most infamous witch in the whole of Pendle Forest. The run-of-the-mill dog attack would now become a full-blown bewitching; farm hands, labourers and yeomen alike would prop up the bar in the Dog and the sole item of discussion would have been the frighteningly professional manner in which the devilish Alison Device, of Malkin Tower, had almost dispatched the burly traveller. Lying upstairs on his sick-bed John Lawe would not have been immune from this gossip; the pub customers would revel in the idea of popping their heads around the chamber door and relating to him the fact that he had met with the most evil family in the area and how he had been lucky to escape with his life!

On his arrival, of course, Abraham Lawe would have been furnished with all the gory details of how Alison had set a spirit in the shape of a huge black dog upon his father. The story goes that Abraham was shocked at the appearance of his father, and being readily convinced that he had indeed been bewitched, asked the Inn landlord for the whereabouts of this young demon called Alison Device. On the 29th March Abraham rode over the Colne Edge to Malkin Tower with the intention of bringing Alison to see his father, probably for him to properly identify her and to see what she had to say. Having found the girl, the pair made their way back to Colne where Alison was confronted with the lame chapman. John Lawe proceeded to accuse Alison, in front of a number of people, of bewitching him; according to the Lawe's statements Alison readily accepted that she had done so and begged for his forgiveness. There must have been something about Alison that touched John Lawe as, believing as he did that she had lamed him, he publicly forgave her. This did not appease Lawe junior, however, as the very next day saw him taking the matter to the authorities; by lunchtime he was knocking on the door of Roger Nowell at Read Hall. Also in attendance at Read Hall on that same day were Alison, James and Elizabeth Device. The events that followed were to be the stuff of legend – the Pendle Witches were about to be catapulted into the annals of history.

Taking the fantastic and the downright impossible out the statements of Alison Device we are left with the definite impression of a poor girl, no better nor worse than her fellow forest dwellers, going about her daily business, seizing any small opportunity that might have come her way. Equally, we have in John Lawe a traveller mundanely following his own daily routine; unfortunately there were to be disastrous consequences when their paths happened to cross. Accepting that their ill-fated meeting was nothing other than pure chance, as Potts would have us believe, could well be a mistake as there is a fact to be considered regarding the immediate aftermath. Knowing the lengths to which the local magistrates were prepared to go to bag themselves a witch at this time things might not have been as clear-cut as the prosecution statements would have it.

The town inns of the period were not merely watering-holes for the labouring classes; because Colne was a major local centre for the cloth trade a great deal of business was carried out in the public houses. Business men, manufacturers and workers alike would gather in the tap-rooms to hear the latest news on Halifax woollen prices and find out which wool-pack carrier might have been setting out to Heptonstall and Halifax in the next day or two. The local gentry would also be found knocking-back the porter and sac whilst discussing land deals. Meanwhile, as John Lawe lay crippled in the Dog Inn, Roger Nowell was casting around for inspiration as to how to deal with the thorny situation of the accusations of impropriety being levelled against his junior magistrate son. Barely one month following these accusations someone with Roger Nowell's ear could well have been drinking in the Dog; this is actually quite likely as Nowell's network of authority spread throughout the forest. The forest greaves, constables, servants of the numerous gentry, family, neighbouring landholders, clerks, chaplains, stewards *et al* would have been a part of the magistrate's information-gathering system. This was the only way in which the authorities could keep any semblance of order in the forest and neighbouring towns –

without the aid of telephones or a cheap, fast and reliable postal system, word-of-mouth was a crucial means of keeping the peace.

Someone, then, tipped Nowell the wink – there had been a diabolical case of witchcraft in Colne and, what is more, it took place in broad daylight, as bold as brass! If this were indeed the case it is likely that Nowell had arranged for Abraham Lawe to visit him at Read Hall on the 30th March. He would then have had an official complaint to act upon and, with a bit of luck, he might secure the prosecution and imprisonment of someone on a juicy witchcraft charge, along with all of the attendant good publicity that this would engender for him – not to mention the smokescreen it might throw over his son's small problem. Little would Nowell have realised the extent to which his actions were to influence the area for centuries to come – the smokescreen was to develop into a full-blown forest fire.

It is difficult to ascertain the true depth of guilt that the Device family admitted to at this early stage, the lurid and flowery statements credited to them could have been added to at a later date. It is possible that Nowell would take his lead from Thomas Lister's strident persecution of Jennet Preston; certainly by the time of the Good Friday meeting at Malkin the genie was well and truly out of the bag. The accused were admitting to every heinous crime under the sun, accusing their own families of the most diabolical murders, accusing their neighbours of the same, owning up to having been attacked by exploding hares, having seen flying horses, owned dogs that spoke English and that was all before lunch!

History shows us that John Lawe was to be the real catalyst in the series of events of that spring of 1612. His role did not finish there, however, Roger Nowell had plans for him to appear at the Assizes three months later in a dramatic finale. John and Abraham Lawe were to appear as star witnesses at Lancaster Castle where, in Alison's case, John was wheeled in and his afflictions proudly displayed to the packed courtroom. With half of his body (apparently) awry, and his speech slurred, Law would have made a pitiable sight. Alison was brought forward into the sight of Lawe at which she is said to have thrown herself to her knees in contrition. The statements of both Abraham and John Lawe were read to the court and we see that the son was adamant that Alison had demanded pins of his father whereby John said that she had offered to buy them. Abraham's statement also contained the following line: *'And this Examinate seeing his said Father so tormented with the said Alizon and with one other olde woman, whome this Examinates Father did not know as it seemed.'*

According to Abraham Lawe his father was in a continuous state of bewitchment, Alison and an old woman who John Lawe had never met tormented him. This bolsters the argument for Lawe having been convinced that he had run up against the daughter of a notorious witch in the shape of Demdike. The work of the gossip-mongers can be seen here as neither of the Lawes had heard of Demdike but the son possibly drew her into the matter when he was told of the family's reputation – this is an excellent example of the danger that the accused found themselves facing when their characters were being assessed by the magistrates – give a dog a bad name and it sticks forever. Abraham's statement also said that ever since his father had been struck down he had been unable to travel; it is confusing, then, to see that John Lawe was not only able to make the long and arduous journey, from either Halifax or Colne, to Lancaster, but he had also attended the whole of the court proceedings from the very start, he was also able to appear in court where he gave a dramatic performance.

Another incident occurred which Alison's brother, James, seems only too willing to relate to Roger Nowell on his visit to Read Hall on the 30th march. here, a Henry Bulcock appeared at Alison's door and demanded that she recant the 'spell' that she had cast over his daughter. Yet again we see a contrite Alison falling to her knees and begging for forgiveness after having been accused of bewitching someone. These regular reports of Alison grovelling on her knees were perhaps designed by the prosecution to illustrate the abject depths to which Alison had sunk; showing the perpetrator to be aghast at the crimes they have committed serves to illustrate the enormity of that crime - in other words, even Alison the witch admitted that her crimes were heinous! Alison was not actually accused in court of bewitching the Bulcock child, this was her brother's testimony, but we have to wonder whether Henry Bulcock, as a probable friend of Alison's uncle, Christopher Holgate, had refused to provide a prosecution statement.

There is reason to assume at least an element of truth in James's story, the question is why would Alison bewitch a child? As Alison walked along the dusty track through Roughlee did young Elizabeth Bulcock, as Henry the yeoman's daughter, look down on the somewhat unkempt figure and point the finger of derision *"Oy, Blacka witch, where's yer broomstick?"* or words to that effect? Little wonder, then, that Alison might have reacted to the taunts of the spoilt child; in an attempt to gain respect she might have taken the line that if she was indeed a witch then she would cast a spell on young Elizabeth if she didn't shut up! The child would have run home to her father and told him that that nasty witch-lass from Malkin had put a spell on her; as was to be the case with John Lawe exactly nine months later, Alison was summarily hauled before her alleged victim and fell to her knees. Her pleas for forgiveness hints at the fact that Alison was only too willing to accept the fact that she was in the habit of bewitching people but was equally surprised when there were consequences. In other words, she was not convinced that her own powers of witchcraft had been as dangerous as they now appeared to be!

In respect of the Device children it is worth remembering that the common forest people of that time, especially the youngsters, were extremely naive in comparison to the young people of today. Alison, James and Jennet Device were born into an age where things had changed little since their Iron Age forefathers had lived in the forest area. Only the strongest survived and this can be seen in the high death-rates amongst infants; often every other child within a family would die. The Device children had no official education but they were extremely well aware of their surroundings. They lived according to the seasons, their food was unadulterated by poisons, their spring water as pure as it was possible to be and they could name every bird and animal around them. They knew the names of all the plants and the medicinal uses of each herb and flower, each forest tree was known to them. Their nights were as black as pitch and a billion bright stars, each constellation of which they could name, lighted the ceiling of their world.

The flip-side of the coin was that they were keenly aware of their place within society, this meant that they were frightened of authority and this was the main reason why they appear to have been so willing to accommodate Roger Nowell in his quest for information on the diabolical goings on in the forest. That is not to say that the youngsters were stupid, no doubt they would have been quick to learn, they had to be when they were living largely off their wits – it would be very interesting to see exactly how much information that Nowell and company would have gleaned from them if the cards had been fully laid on the magisterial bench. If the accused had been made fully aware of the consequences of their accusations and 'confessions' just how informative would they have been? If they had known that whole families were to be executed because of their naive fantasies how far along the road to Gallows Hill would the 1612 case have progressed?

Chapter Eleven

The Lawes of Halifax

In 1601, a Richard Lawe of Halifax was granted six closes of land called Chapel Fields in Southwrome and, in 1602, Richard Lawe, a chapman of Halifax, was assigned land at Holbeck, he is also given as a chapman in 1605. A Richard Lawe appears in the Court Rolls on a regular basis, in 1608 Richard Lawe owned land called Hardie Close in the Halifax area and in 1609 he owned land in Halifax abutting on to the lane from the town to King Cross. In 1610 Richard entered into a copyhold agreement with Arthur Ingram for lands in Halifax and in 1611 we meet again with a Richard Lawe of Halifax who is involved in a lawsuit of some kind. Richard Lawe was mentioned in the will of John Hanson of Woodhouse in Rastrick, dated 1621, as having been the husband of John Hanson's daughter Agnes. Through the coming decades Richard is associated with the many lands formerly owned by his father-in-law around the Halifax, Wakefield, Esholt and Bradford areas. In 1658 a Richard Lawe of Over Woodhouse and Rastrick, possibly the son of Richard, and his wife Hester, sold three farms and land in Brighouse worth £50. Whether this family was related to the John and Abraham Lawe of our story is unclear but Abraham, shown to have been a cloth-dyer, was possibly brother to Richard.

In 1587 we might catch a glimpse of John Lawe the chapman when we see a property sale in Dewsbury being witnessed by John Lawe, Edmund Shuttleworth and John Armytage, the son of John Armytage was later (1640) to buy Hartshead Hall, Dewsbury, from Charles Towneley of Towneley Hall in Burnley; this sale was witnessed by Richard Lawe. The Towneleys owned a great deal of land and property in Dewsbury, Heptonstall and Halifax, the Lawe families of that region could well have been related to the Lawe families who were Towneley tenants in Burnley thus providing a direct link between the two regions.

It is possible that the Lawe families of Halifax were related to the many families of that name who farmed the Bradyll estates, served as incumbents at Whalley church and were often indicted on charges of recusancy. This is illustrated in the Exchequer Pipe Rolls of 1581-92 where recusancy convictions for that period are recorded:

Agnes Lawe spinster of Wiswell
John Lawe Goldsmith of Wiswell
Robert Lawe husbandman of Wiswell
Alice Lawe wife of Robert
Sibyl Lawe wife of John Lawe labourer

A more serious case was recorded in 1594-96 when Robert Lawe of Wiswell had his goods and chattels seized for none-attendance at church.

In relation to the links to be found between the Lawes, and the leading gentry of our area who were to play a leading part in the 1612 trials, it is of interest to see that the Lister family of Westby and Horton had dealings with the Lawe family. In 1550-51 John Lister, of Horton, granted lands at Wibsy and Horton to his son Nicholas Lister, William Lawe was a witness to the deed. Wibsy, near Bradford, was an area in which a number of local yeomen settled, branches of the Briercliffe and Parker families of Briercliffe held lands and farmed there, the Parkers of Extwistle Hall were to become the Towneley-Parkers of Cuerden. Furthermore, in

1562 we see a record of a John Lawe suing John Bradyll for entry to a farm called Burnehouse in Newton-in-Bowland (Bowland Forest), it is not clear as to the origins of this John Lawe, he was probably of either the Whalley or the Yorkshire families.

It would be interesting to learn the details of the lawsuit of 1611 in which Richard Lawe of Halifax found himself embroiled. Also, was Richard the brother of the chapman, John Lawe, or was he possibly his son? Was the lawsuit of sufficient severity to have caused the family to raise money in order to fight the case and uphold the good name they would have held?

A tantalising deed of land settlement in Barrowford takes us further along this line of enquiry. The deed shows that in the nineteenth century, some two-hundred years after the 1612 trials, a member of the Lawe family of Halifax owned lands at Whittycroft in Over Barrowford. The document states that William Lawe, gent of Halifax, settled land at Higherford on his attorney, James Wigglesworth of Halifax. Another, related deed shows William Lawe's son, William Lawe of Hebden Bridge, surrendering the Whittycroft land to Thomas Grimshaw of Barrowford. Whittycroft is the area of Higherford between Blacko and Barrowford that once belonged to the Bannister estate of Park Hill and the Blacko estate of Stone Edge. The possibility here is that the Lawe family inherited this land from a family member in the Pendle and Colne locality; they might also have purchased the land at some time. It was not uncommon for people in the Halifax region to do this as Gamaliel Sutcliffe of Stoneshay Gate, near Heptonstall, purchased the Park Hill estate from a man called Yorker in 1813.[1] However, the Park Hill estate records of that period do not mention lands at Whittycroft and this would appear to preclude any link between Sutcliffe and the Lawes. Is it possible, then, that Abraham Lawe was approached by the forest authorities in 1612 to officially report the Colne Field incident and in return the Lawe family were to be rewarded with lands at Whittycroft?

When the Colne Field incident is studied as a whole there is the nagging doubt that all, or part, of the unfortunate chain of events could have been contrived. It is unclear as to the extent of any pre-Commonwealth social unrest that may have existed at the time of the 1612 trials. Certainly there was a deal of unrest and suspicion between the authorities and a large section of the post-Reformation populace. We have seen that in Nicholas Bannister and Roger Nowell that the authorities had reliable and zealous men ready and willing to root out the religiously and socially perfidious elements of the forest. Some twenty years before he helped to prosecute the 1612 accused Nicholas Bannister is recorded as having forcibly removed two-thirds of the property of Edward Chew of Potterford in Billington.[2] This was because Bannister was the king's bailiff, through a Royal Commission from the Exchequer, with a remit to collect the debts of recusant Catholics owing to the Crown. This he appears to have done with uncommon gusto.

Further to the question of social unrest it is worth considering that the early modern period had no less a number of 'ragged-trousered philanthropists' than any other modern period. It is possible that Demdike, Alice Nutter and Chattox, because of their close links with landowners and the gentry, were extremely vociferous in their condemnation of the lingering feudal system pervading society at that time. Having seen the better side of life in their earlier years these matriarchs had possibly become bitter through loss; perhaps they could not accept the extremes of overt wealth and dire poverty that were so obviously on show around them and said so

---

[1] Jesse Blakey, *Annals and Stories of Barrowford.* (SP, Nelson, 1929)
[2] *The Farrar papers*, Manchester Central Library

whenever they could and to whomever would listen. Perhaps we have a parallel here with the modern-day American communist witch-hunt of the McCarthy era?

No doubt there were multiple cognate reasons for the forest witch clearance of 1612, whatever reason drove Roger Nowell to act as he did he was a force to be reckoned with. If we accept that Demdike carried the reputation of being the most astute and dangerous witch within Pendle then she had become, towards the end of her natural days, an obvious early target for Nowell. His long experience as a magistrate would tell him that to tackle the problem of gathering evidence from a canny old bird such as Demdike he would need to get behind her defences. What was the best way to achieve this? The answer was obvious, by concentrating on her weakest spot i.e., her young family, Nowell would soon reach his target. To this end, then, was young Alison Device, as Demdike's somewhat naive granddaughter, set-up from the very beginning; did she walk into a trap on that fateful day in March? Was John Lawe a convincing actor, in the pocket of the authorities and able to reproduce the effects of a stroke?

Before we leave the Colne Field incident there are three more points to consider; these may be incidental to the facts or they may be highly pertinent; whatever the case may be they are worth noting here:

❖ Thomas Lister junior of Westby prosecuted Jennet Preston with the aid of his friend, Roger Nowell. When Thomas Lister's ancestor, another Thomas Lister, married Ann King in 1539 the Lister family became closely associated with the large estates in Halifax of Ann's father, Richard. This provides us with yet more of the network that existed between the people of Halifax and our parish of Whalley.

❖ We have seen the possibility that Anne Whittle had a daughter named Elizabeth Brown; in 1596 Elizabeth married Thomas Ellott whose family were well-established farmers within the area of Colne Field and Carry Bridge. We have, therefore, the intriguing question as to whether the daughter of Old Chattox might have been involved in the Colne Field incident; particularly when we consider that this would have provided the opportunity to harm the old family enemy of the Demdike clan.

❖ Henry Hargreaves was constable of the forest and Roger Nowell's man-about-town; as we shall see, there are two possibilities for our having Henry's marriage on record. One of these dates from the 24th October 1602 where the Colne marriage index shows Henric Hargreaves marrying Elizabetha Lawe. If this was the marriage of Constable Hargreave then it would have been a simple matter for Nowell to coerce his man into involving his family – this raises the interesting possibility that the Lawe family had indeed become embroiled when, in March 1612, Roger Nowell cast his judicial net over the Pendle Forest.

Upon One Good Friday

The Good Friday meeting of witches at Malkin Tower, in 1612, has entered our folklore as a sharp illustration of the fact that the accused were most definitely given to devilment. This event proved to be a watershed within the machinations of the prosecution; in fact the meeting was pivotal in their case. Unfortunately we only have Thomas Potts' lurid account of the events that occurred on that fateful day; an account that was actually based upon the garbled 'evidence' of James and young Jennet Device. If we look behind the smokescreen of diabolical feasts and fanciful plots to blow up Lancaster Castle the Good Friday meeting boils down to one thing – the friends and relatives of the imprisoned Demdike family gathered, quite understandably, to show support and see if there was any way in which they could help their unfortunate family. Relatives of Henry Hargreaves, the forest constable, attended the Malkin meeting and he knew all about it; Roger Nowell would have asked Hargreaves to keep an eye on the comings-and-goings of the families of the accused and so Hargreaves, as a matter of course, reported the gathering to his boss. Nowell, keen to make hay whilst the sun shone, hauled in the Device family and immediately struck gold in the shape of Jennet and James. The following is the testimony said to have been given by James and used by the prosecution against his mother:

The Examination and Euidence of Iames Device Against Elizabeth Device, his Mother

THe said Iames Deuice saith, That on Good-Friday last, about twelue of the clocke in the day time, there dined in this Examinates said mothers house, at Malking-Tower, a number of persons, whereof three were men, with this Examinate, and the rest women; and that they met there for three causes following (as this Examinates said mother told this Examinate) The first was, for the naming of the Spirit, which Alizon Deuice, now prisoner at Lancaster, had: But did not name him, because shee was not there. The second was, for the deliuerie of his said Grandmother, olde Dembdike; this Examinates said sister Allizon; the said Anne Chattox, and her daughter Redferne; killing the Gaoler at Lancaster; and before the next Assises to blow vp the Castle there: and to that end the aforesaid prisoners might by that time make an escape, and get away. All which this Examinate then heard them conferre of.

And he also sayth, That the names of the said Witches as were on Good-Friday at this Examinates said Grandmothers house, and now this Examinates owne mothers, for so many of them as hee did know, were these, viz. The wife of Hugh Hargreiues of Burley; the wife of Christopher Bulcock, of the Mosse end, and Iohn her sonne; the mother of Myles Nutter; Elizabeth, the wife of Christopher Hargreiues, of Thurniholme; Christopher Howgate, and Elizabeth, his wife; Alice Graye of Coulne, and one Mould-heeles wife, of the same: and this Examinate, and his Mother. And this Examinate further sayth, That all the Witches went out of the said House in their owne shapes and likenesses. And they all, by that they were forth of the dores, gotten on Horsebacke, like vnto Foales, some of one colour, some of another; and Prestons wife was the last: and when shee got on Horsebacke, they all presently vanished out of this Examinates sight. And before their said parting away, they all appointed to meete at the said Prestons wiues house that day twelue-moneths; at which time the said Prestons wife promised to make them a great Feast. And if they had occasion to meete in the meane time, then should warning be giuen, that they all should meete vpon Romleyes Moore.

The following is the abridged statement of Jennet Device in relation to the meeting:

The said – Iennet Deuice saith, That vpon Good Friday last there was about twentie persons (whereof onely two were men, to this Examinates remembrance) at her said Grandmothers house, called Malking-Tower aforesaid, about twelue of the clocke: all which persons this Examinates said mother told her, were Witches, and that they came to giue a name to Alizon Deuice Spirit, or Familiar, sister to this Examinate, and now prisoner at Lancaster. And also this Examinate saith, That the persons aforesaid had to their dinners Beefe, Bacon, and roasted Mutton; which Mutton (as this Examinates said brother said) was of a Wether of Christopher Swyers of Barley: which Wether was brought in the night before into this Examinates mothers house by the said Iames Deuice, this Examinates said brother: and in this Examinates sight killed and eaten, as aforesaid.

And shee further saith, That shee knoweth the names of six of the said Witches, viz. the wife of Hugh Hargraues vnder Pendle, Christopher Howgate of Pendle, vnckle to this Examinate, and Elizabeth his wife, and Dicke Miles his wife of the Rough-Lee; Christopher Iackes of Thorny-holme, and his wife: and the names of the residue shee this Examinate doth not know, sauing that this Examinates mother and brother were both there. And lastly, she this Examinate confesseth and saith, That her mother hath taught her two prayers: the one to cure the bewitched, and the other to get drinke; both which particularly appeare.

When James device gave his somewhat garbled evidence to Roger Nowell he stated that, as the Good Friday meeting was dispersing, a pact was made between the people there to meet at Jennet Preston's house in Gisburn *'this day twelve-monthe'* (the Good Friday of 1613) but if they needed to discuss things in the meantime they were all to meet upon *'Romles Moor.'* This has always been taken to mean the Rombalds Moor forming a part of the Ilkley Moor region and some twenty miles away from Malkin. This has never made much sense due to the location and distance of Rombalds Moor from Pendle Forest but things become much clearer when it is realised that Rumleys was a farm upon the lower moorland slopes of Rumleys Moor, below Broadhead in Habergham, and a close neighbour of the Ingham farmsteads in Burnley Wood and Fulledge. This suggests that Demdike's family knew of this area of Burnley, probably through their Ingham connections, and furthers the argument for them having lived within the extended area.

Further to this thread we can take a look at the list of people who Jennet and James Device said were in attendance at the Malkin get-together; Potts stated that a number of others were at the meeting but had managed to escape the district, the truth of the matter is not known although, given Potts' propensity for exaggeration, we can guess that only one or two other people were not named. The following list has been extrapolated from different witness statements as none of them agreed as to exactly who was there, some added in names whilst others left them out:[1]

Elizabeth Device --- James Device --- Jennet Device --- Christopher Holgate --- Elizabeth (Isab.) Holgate --- Jennet Hargreaves, wife of Hugh of Under Pendle Farm --- Alice Nutter --- Christopher Hargreaves alias Jackes alias Thrineyhome (Thorneyholme) --- Elizabeth Hargreaves, wife of Christopher --- John Bulcock of Mosse End Farm --- Jane Bulcock, John's mother --- Alice Gray of Colne --- Katherine Hewett (Mouldheels) of Colne --- Ann Cronckshaw of Marsden --- Grace Hey of Padiham --- Jennet Preston of Gisburn

---

[1] E.Peel & P.Southern, *The Trials of the Lancashire Witches*, (David & Charles, 1969/1972)

Also said to have been present were two women from Burnley whose names Jennet and James did not know but they said that Alice Nutter knew them. There is a strong possibility here that these two women were relations of Demdike on the Ingham side, probably the older-end of the family whom the young Devices had either never met or did not remember. The Hargreaves families would know Christopher Holgate through being farming neighbours, and the Bulcocks of Moss End would know the family through their relations at Roughlee and also from when the Demdikes lived in the western forest.

Hey

One of the people said to have been in attendance at the meeting was Grace Hey of Padiham; Grace was the daughter of Miles Hey and was baptised in 1568. We saw earlier that Christopher Nutter and Hugh Hey held a farm together in Rossendale and it would be no surprise if Hugh Hey were to be related to Christopher Holgate – in fact Demdike's son, who was possibly the son of Christopher Holgate, was also at the Good Friday meeting. Was Hugh Hey's wife, Jennet, actually Christopher Holgate's sister thus making Grace Hey and Christopher Holgate junior cousins? Or was Grace Hey simply a friend of the Demdike family from when they were farming neighbours? Interestingly enough a Lawrence Hey was one of the people accused of being a witch at the 1612 Samlesbury Witch trial.

At the 1425 Ightenhill Halmote Court John del Heye complained that Henry Whitaker had taken from him *'by force and arms' two carts and other farm implements which were at Couyldholme in Ightenhill.'* The plaintiff was awarded 5s: 1d in damages. The 1618/19 Padiham Rentals list shows: *Roger Nowell gent 22 acres at 11s: 1d --- Richard Hey 1 acre 2 roods 3 perches at 12s: 9d and some houses.*

Cronckshaw

Ann Cronckshaw was closely related to the Cronckshaw family of Hollins Farm, in West Close, and would have been a neighbour of the Demdikes in her earlier years within the forest. In fact an area of West Close was called Cronckshaw and this illustrates the length of time in which the family had lived in the forest. They were granted the farm of West Close at a very early stage in the forest development and had long been major landholders in the area. Grace's mother was Agnes Brown and had married her father, Miles, in 1567 – was Agnes related to Chattox whose possible Brown family lineage we explored earlier? A Jennet Cronkshaw was accused of being a witch in the Robinson case of 1633.

1332: *Gilbert de Cronkshawe was a tenant in Burnley*
1423: *John de Cronckshaw collector of the herbage of Blackburnshire from Michaelmas 1422 to same in 1423 and he answers for 3 acres at Blakay*
1425: *John of Cronckshaw fined for unlawfully sending 40 sheep to Burnley commons*
1432: *Lawrence Heys took one rood of land on Cowden Moor (Burnley) near the Stonewell*
1507: *New Hold grant of 30 acres of land called Higham Parrocks at West Close and Hunterholme to the Cronckshaw family*
1510: *Lawrence and Thomas Cronckshaw obstructed a road at Preveryding Stele*
1556: *Leonard Cronckshaw son and heir of John of west Close had lands at Alkincoats from Robert Blakey*

1546:   *Enclosure called Whiteley owned by Nicholas Towneley gent passed in this year to the 1 year-old son Edmund whose uncle George Vaughan of Middlesex was guardian. Dower to Ann Towneley widow of Nicholas £6 6s 8d: they also owned Rowley and Cronckshaw*

1594:   *Georgius Hallstead de Padiham and Jenitta Cronckshey de Westclose in Pendle Nuptuals 20th January vid Padiham*

1607:   *Elizabetha reta Leonardi Cronckshey nup de Westclose in Pendle defuncti 21st Jul (burial at Padiham)*

1609:   *Daniel the spurious son of Daniel Cronckshaw of Carr and Anne Towneley of Pendle baptism at Burnley*

This last record relates to the Towneleys of Carr Hall who appear in our story when James Device was accused of bewitching Ann Towneley, the wife of Henry, following a disagreement. On his daily perambulations throughout the forest James would have called at the back door of Carr Hall to see if the kitchen staff had anything in the shape of food or drink for him. On one occasion Mistress Towneley caught James in the kitchen and ushered him out by giving him a push in the back; James said that he had been accused of stealing turves (peat). This sounds to be a strange thing to have done as turves had very little value and he would have only managed to carry two or three for any distance; these would not have burned for long enough to make the effort worthwhile! It is possible that Anne Towneley, mother of Daniel Cronckshaw who we see in the above baptism, was the daughter of Lawrence Towneley and Margaret Sherburne, and possibly sister to Henry Towneley whose wife, Ann, had the altercation with James Device. This record serves to illustrate the status of the Cronckshaw family whereby they were considered to be worthy of breeding with the Towneley gentry.

Before we leave the Good Friday of 1612 it is worth noting that the gathering at Malkin had been well planned, the attendants had been notified in good time and James Device, like every good host, had pinched a sheep to feed them all! Maybe those who attended were more worried about their own situation than that of the accused; how would the arrest of Demdike and Chattox affect them? Would they be implicated on the *'guilt by association'* principal? Certainly it appears from James's statement that the departing group had agreed to keep a low profile, their next meeting had been scheduled for one year hence. The fact that the meeting took place on Good Friday has attracted numerous theories of covert religious practice, the practising of the Catholic Mass being the most common. The prosecution had ensured that the statements of James and his sister Jennet was littered with references to spirits and familiars along with flying horses and dark mutterings of fatal deeds to be done. Perhaps, however, this meeting was not all that the prosecution had made it out to be; the gathering of people at farm houses on Good Fridays was actually standard practice in the forest as this was the day when tithes were collected; also, farm rents were balanced against output and money was returned to the farmer on this day – in other words Good Friday was party-time! Admittedly, Malkin Tower was not a farm but the tradition of Good Friday family gatherings would still have appertained.

Chapter Twelve

Robinson

Nowell's submission to the Assizes in regard to Jennet's 'evidence' shows that Elizabeth Device was thought to have killed two Robinson brothers by witchcraft. John Robinson (alias Swyre) was bewitched, according to Potts, in the confession that Elizabeth denied making – here it was said that she had killed John Robinson of Barley because he had accused her *'of having an illegitimate child by one Sellers.'* Jennet said that this was three or four years ago thus placing John Robinson's death around 1608/9; the Newchurch burial records do in fact show that a John Robinson was buried at Newchurch in 1609. In Potts' account, Jennet went on to say that her mother also killed John Robinson's brother, James Robinson (alias Swyre) of Barley about a year later – again the Newchurch records show that a James Robinson was buried there in 1610.

The Robinsons of Pendle Forest were as ubiquitous a family as were the Hartleys, Nutters and Hargreaves families. In 1443 a John Robinson was shown as being a tenant of the honour of Clitheroe under the *Old Hold* and in 1546 John Robinson kept an unreasonable way at his farm at Black Moss in Barley and Whiteley Booth. Following the *New Hold* of the forest (post-1507) John Robinson the elder and John Robinson *'thunger'* were tenants in Barley and by the 1650s a Christopher Robinson of Barley bequeathed an ash table, ash trestles and ash forms worth eight shillings.[1]

Henry Robinson of Barley had upset his neighbours for some reason as a Recognizance Roll of the 1633 Easter Assizes at Preston shows that *'Roughlee Booth and Barley. . . Barnard Hartleye, husbandman, John Nowell, husbandman and Henery Bulcock, yeoman, are to keep the peace to Henery Robinsonn.'* As a further illustration of those comparatively lawless times John Robinson, of Foothouseyeate (Foothouse Gate Farm is adjacent to Lower Black Moss reservoir in Barley Booth), was shown in his will as having owned *'a long bow, a staff, one sword, two daggers, a musket and all its furniture.'* At the same farm, in 1664, James Robinson bequeathed; *'a green suit, a grey jerkin and breeches, a brown doublet, a coat with four laps and grey cloth waiting to be made up – this latter to my uncle along with the coat and two of my 'worse' hats.'* It is not unreasonable, then, to assume that the John and James Robinson, allegedly bewitched by Elizabeth Southern, were living at Foothouse Gate Farm at the time.

It is also worth considering that Anne Robinson was the principal witness for the prosecution when Jennet Preston was accused of having killed Thomas Lister at Westby, it would be interesting to know whether Anne was related to the Robinsons of Barley – certainly members of this family acquired lands in the Gisburn area through marriage. As we have already seen, a member of the Robinson family of Wheatley Lane instigated a further witchcraft scare in 1633 when young Edmund started the ball of false accusation rolling and his family joined in with that unfortunate episode (see Chapter Fourteen below).

---

[1] Mary Brigg, *The Early History of the Forest of Pendle*, (Pendle Heritage, 1989)

We know that a branch of the Robinson family owned lands in the Stone Edge area of Blacko and, in the year 1717, it is clear that the extended family were still farming in the forest. Elizabeth Hargreaves, who was the sister of John Hartley of Blacko, left a will in which she named John Robinson of Barley as trustee of her lands and property; . . . *'closes called Upper and Lower Blackoehill and house with a cottage in Barrowford.'*

It is difficult at best to accurately sort any of the old forest families into a true genealogical order; throughout the sixteenth century the Robinsons were farming at New Laund, Over Barrowford, Stone Edge, Reedley Hallows, Firber, Black Moss, Goldshaw, Fence, Higham, Sabden, Roughlee and Barley. John and Christopher Robinson were the sons of a Robinson mother and a Swyer father, given that the name of Swyer was uncommon in the forest it is possible that the brothers were the sons of one Henry Swire, if so this Henry eventually committed to one Elizabeth Whittely whom he married at Newchurch in 1594. It is possible that the Robinson (Swyer) brothers had a half sister in Catherina Swier who, in 1599, married a Robert Bannister at Newchurch. The name crops up again when, in 1538, Robert Swire (the relict or widow of Robert Blakey) was fined one penny for withdrawing his *soke* (custom) from the Kings Mill at Colne.

We have seen enough evidence thus far to show that the minor forest gentry and yeomanry of Hargreaves/Hartley/Robinson/Bannister/Blakey/Nutter were linked by marriage. This is not to say, however, that all of these families actually rubbed along together; in fact the opposite was often the case as the Clitheroe court rolls bear witness. Having seen that there was a family relationship between Demdike and Christopher Robinson of Blacko it is fair to ask why Elizabeth Device held an obvious grudge against the Robinson brothers of Barley? Her son, James device, stole a sheep of Christopher Robinson's of Barley to feed his family and their mates at the infamous Good Friday knees-up and the Robinson brothers were summarily bewitched.

Bulcock

In 1612 Christopher Bulcock was living with his wife, Jane, and son John at Moss End. This is commonly accepted to be Moss End Farm to the south of the village of Newchurch-in-Pendle. This farm, which had become derelict by the middle of the twentieth century, lay between the Dimpenley area of Nether Roughlee and the Nutter's Bull Hole Farm in Goldshaw Booth. There is a possibility, however, that this was not the actual property occupied by the Bulcock family as the present Moss End was formerly known as Moss Nook – the area now occupied by the hamlet of Spen Brook was known as Lower Moss End and an area to the north of this (towards the village of Newchurch) was turbary (peat-land) known as Little Moss Head. These sites were in the same small area, however, and the Bulcocks would have lived in that vicinity. There is a slight caveat here in as much as the 1608/9 Pendle Forest Rental List does not record a Christopher Bulcock within Goldshaw but he does appear in the Whiteley Booth list.[1] Here Christopher Bulcock was paying the sum of £1: 0s: 10d for a farm that would have been in the area stretching from Stang Moor across the Black Moss. It is possible, therefore, that the Moss End property was actually on the Black Moss rather than the Goldshaw Moss; certainly the name of Bulcock was concentrated in the former area. On the other hand we do not see

---

[1] Jonathan Lumby, *The Lancashire Witch Craze*, (Carnegie Publishing, 1995)

Demdike's son, Christopher Holgate, in the rental list and this indicates that both he and Christopher Bulcock were under-tenants within a sub-tenancy.

Both James and Jennet Device accused John Bulcock and his mother, Jane, of having attended the Malkin Tower Good Friday. At the 1612 trial the accused were lined up in an identity parade and young Jennet was asked if she recognised any of the people there. Having failed to name the Bulcocks in her 'evidence' Jennet proceeded to identify Jane Bulcock as having been at Malkin Tower and added that John Bulcock turned the roasting spit for the feast. Both mother and son were accused of *'practising their devilish and wicked art upon the body of Jennet Deane of Newfield Edge in Middop'* so that she was eventually driven mad. It is clear that poor Jennet Dean had psychological problems and the Bulcocks took the blame for this. Yet another illustration of the contrived nature of the statements taken from the accused is provided when the confession of James Device was read to the court: ... *'the said Iohn Bulcock, and Iane his said Mother, did confesse vpon Goode-Friday last at the said Malking Tower, in the hearing of this Examinate, That they had bewitched, at the Newfield Edge in Yorkshire, a woman called Iennet, wife of Iohn Deyne, besides her reason; and the said Woman's name so bewitched he did not heare them speake of.'* James (or at least his so-called statement) was saying that he did not hear the Bulcocks speak the name of Jennet Dean at the same time that he heard them speak her name!

John and his mother protested their innocence vociferously, they denied ever having been at the Good Friday meeting and, as might be expected under those circumstances, they protested (according to Potts) *'even unto the gallows'*. Rather than pricking the conscience of the prosecution into considering that these unfortunates might just have been innocent after all, quite the opposite reaction is apparent; Potts used the fact that they protested as a sign of their belligerence and an illustration of their extreme wickedness!

It is likely that the Moss End family was related to the Bulcock family of Whitehough; this lay not much further to the east along the Pendle Water valley. In 1610 Christopher Bulcock of Whitehough, was granted lands belonging to Randal Holker, gent, of Read. We have already met with this family in their capacity of landowners in Wakefield and close friends of Roger Nowell of Read. Because Christopher Bulcock was a minor these lands (named as *Outhouse* and *Holdall* in Simonstone and Read) were taken into the stewardship of Richard Dawson of Worston. Also granted a part of these lands was John, son of Edmond Robinson of Old Laund.

The wife of Randal Holler's son, John, was the sister of James Hartley of Barley. Christopher Bulcock was probably the son of Christopher who, in turn, was the son and heir of Robert Bulcock of Whitehough. Christopher senior built the earlier part of the extant Whitehough Grange the south porch of which carries an inscription: *'This house was builded by Christofer Bulcocke and Jennet his wife 1593.'* [1] Christopher died in 1640 and left a will showing that he owned forty-seven cattle and four looms, this suggests that he was employing people as weavers. The Bulcocks of Whitehough were successful yeomen as can be seen by the number of leases in which they were involved, in the early part of the seventeenth century the family were involved in at least seven land and farm transactions. The family also became financiers and mortgage brokers.

---

[1] Sarah Pearson, *Rural Houses of the Lancashire Pennines*, (HM Stationery Office, 1985)

Alice Nutter (Alice O'Dick O'Miles)

In 1561 John Hargreaves of Roughlee, William Smith of Roughlee and Nicholas Robinson of Roughlee, at the request of Miles Nutter, his wife Elizabeth and his son Richard surrendered half of a farm property in Roughlee (on rental of £0: 22s: 2d per annum) to the use of John Smith (son of William Smith of Roughlee), John Smith (son of William Smith of Pighole in Briercliffe), James and John Whittaker (sons of Giles Whittaker of Huncote, the brothers of Alice Nutter). The right of John Nutter (son of Miles) was reserved.[1] The intent of the surrender was that the share in the farm was to go to the use of Miles Nutter and Elizabeth his wife and after their deaths a quarter share was to go to *'Alice Nutter, now wife of the said Richard Nutter for life, in the name of her dower.'* The remainder of the property was to go to Richard and his heirs. This was possibly the farm on which John Smith built Roughlee Old Hall.

By 1556 Richard Greenacres was acting as the deputy steward of Blackburnshire and in this capacity he dealt in that year with the transfer of the tenancy of another farm in Roughlee. The farm transfer was at the request of Richard Nutter (husband of Alice Nutter) and his brother, John Nutter. The property in question was in the tenure of Richard and Miles Nutter, the basis of the transfer being that John (Jackes) Hargreaves, William Smith, Nicholas Robinson senior of Roughlee and John Hartley (alias Crook) were to have the right of tenancy. The proviso of the agreement was that the farm should revert to Richard and John Nutter and their mother, Elizabeth, following the death of Miles Nutter.

Alice Nutter played a smaller part within the 1612 drama than any other of her co-accused; the prosecution case hinged upon Jennet Device's statement that Alice had been one of those who attended the Good Friday meeting. Jennet actually picked Alice out from the crowd of accused people in the courtroom, when asked by the judge if she recognised Alice Nutter she went over and took her by the hand. As a ruse to prove that Jennet did indeed recognise Alice from the meeting the judge asked imperiously if she knew a *Joan A'style*; when Jennet replied in the negative the smug prosecution would nod to each other, what a clever judge they had! In actual fact the question was absolutely pointless, the southern judges might have heard *Joan A'style* being used as a metaphor for *Mrs. Bloggs* but Jennet would not have heard this in her life. Were the judge to have enquired whether *Bess O' Bob's* (Robert's daughter, Elizabeth) or some-such was at the meeting he might have received a different answer. It is clear from their 'statements' that neither James nor Jennet could be relied upon to provide the exact truth of the matter. Potts had this to say with regard to Alice Nutter;

ThE ARRAIGNCOENT
and Triall of Alice Nutter, of the Forrest of Pendle, in the Countie of Lancaster,

*T*He two degrees of persons which chiefly practise Witch-craft, are such, as are in great miserie and pouertie, for such the Deuill allures to follow him, by promising great riches, and worldly commoditie; Others, though rich, yet burne in a desperate desire of Reuenge.

*B*ut to attempt this woman in that sort, the Diuel had small meanes: For it is certaine she

---

[1] W. Farrar, *Clitheroe Court Rolls* (1912)

was a rich woman; had a great estate, and children of good hope: in the common opinion of the world, of good temper, free from envy or malice; yet whether by the meanes of the rest of the Witches, or some vnfortunate occasion, shee was drawne to fall to this wicked course of life, I know not: but hither shee is now come to receiue her Triall, both for Murder, and many other vilde and damnable practises.

It is very certaine she was of the Grand-counsell at Malking-Tower vpon Good-Friday, and was there present, which was a very great argument to condemne her.

This Alice Nutter, Prisoner in the Castle at Lancaster: Being brought to the Barre before the Great Seat of Iustice; was there according to the former order and course Indicted and Arraigned, for that she felloniously had practised, exercised, and vsed her diuellish and wicked Arts, called Witchcrafts, Inchantments, Charmes and Sorceries, in and vpon Henry Mitton: and him the said Henry Mitton, by force of the same Witchcrafts, felloniously did kill and murther. Contra formam Statuti, &c. Et Contra Pacem, &c.

To the prosecution the fact that Alice Nutter was *said* to have been at the Malkin Tower gathering was as good an indictment of her previously good character as any. Just to make sure, the prosecution also threw in, almost as an aside, that she also conspired with her friends at Malkin to kill Henry Mitton. These two ridiculous charges, despite Alice's not guilty plea, were enough to convict and execute her. Alice was described as being a rich woman with a great estate and children of good hope and this was designed to mark her out from the rest of the accused. Potts used Alice's position of higher status to show how much more damnable was witch who had fallen from high - the further the fall the more evil was the woman. We have seen in the two farm surrenders that the Nutter family that Alice married into, in 1560/61, was of high standing within the Roughlee area. They had held the same property from at least 1527 through to 1609 when Alice's son Miles was paying rent for it. At the time of the 1612 trials Alice Nutter would have been around seventy years old and her son, Miles, would be forty-seven. Alice would no doubt have known Demdike well, they were roughly the same age and from much the same background – the two were from Catholic/yeoman families and could well have been friends, if so this would be a clue that Alice did actually attend the Good Friday meeting.

Young Jennet referred to Alice in her statement as *Dick O' Miles wife*, Gladys Whittaker suggests that Alice was much younger than her husband, Richard Nutter, and that their marriage had been arranged by her father. Alice had been widowed in her mid-forties and left with five children to bring up, Miles being the eldest at nineteen. Whether the family owned land or not Alice would have struggled to keep things on the straight-and-narrow; in fact she was in a similar situation to that which Elizabeth Device found herself in sixteen years later and would no doubt have sympathised with her.

Who, then, was Alice, wife of Dick O' Miles? The Whitaker family had been in the Padiham area since the thirteenth century and eventually split into three main branches; the Whitakers of Holme-in-Cliviger, the Whitakers of Broadclough and the family of Simonstone. Attached to this latter branch was Gyles Whitaker of Huncoat, he had been constable of Huncoat four times, greave of Huncoat in 1556 and was of sufficient importance to have been only one of two men to have appeared on the Muster Roll. Alice was one of Gyles Whitaker's five children, the others being the eldest, James, John, Agnes and Joan. There is no surprise in the fact that the Roughlee Nutters and the Huncoat Whitakers became related; although some five miles in distance the Simonstone Whitakers were continually trading lands within Pendle Forest. In this capacity they rubbed shoulders with almost all of the landowners hereabouts and when Gyles saw an opportunity to marry his daughter, Alice, off to the ageing Richard Nutter, of Roughlee, he jumped at the chance. Just what Alice might have thought about the matter is another story!

One of the most commonly held beliefs in the Pendle Witch legend is that Alice Nutter found herself being prosecuted because she had been in an acrimonious boundary dispute over Roger Nowell's neighbouring lands. Unfortunately this piece of folklore does not appear to hold water. Many of the local farmers held lands bordering onto Roughlee at one time or another, amongst these was another family named Nowell, from Fence, who were often seen to be involved in land transactions around Roughlee; this was often in their duties as acting forest stewards. That Roger Nowell and the Simonstone Whitakers were often at contretemps with each other over lands in the Read area is well documented; these disputes often ran for generations and it is this link between Alice Nutter and Roger Nowell that might have triggered the folk-memory.

Alice Nutter did not in fact ever live at Roughlee Old Hall (as legend has had it for some 150 years), her home was on the Crowtrees estate some half a mile to the west. [1]Nor did she have the riches and estates that Potts would have us believe, she was wealthier than her companions in the Well Tower dungeon at Lancaster but any real wealth would have stayed with her Whitaker family outside of the forest. It is an integral part of the Alice Nutter legend that her family refused to speak up for her and actively allowed her to be prosecuted in order to gain her estates. It is said that her son, Miles, lived a remorseful life following his mother's demise and in the end he died a lingering, painful death. It is also said that when Miles heard of the Malkin family troubles he enlisted young Jennet to accuse his mother and bring her into the melee. There is a small problem with this because the Nutter estate, under the stewardship of Miles, had actually halved in size and consisted solely of the farmstead of Crow Trees at Roughlee.

Miles had inherited the lion's share of the Nutter properties from his father in any case; the only benefit to Alice's children on her death would have been a small share of a small estate, was this worth bumping off their mother for? What we do have in this story is the idea that Jennet was open to bribery when it came to placing people in the dock. This is of interest as we have seen that Roger Nowell could well have coerced Jennet into making fantastic statements and placing people at the Malkin gathering who were probably never even near the place (i.e. the Bulcocks). We also have the story of Miles Nutter bribing Jennet into saying that his mother had been at Malkin. Being a Seller in a household of Devices might just have caused Jennet to feel isolated within the family; just how close she might have been to the rest of her Malkin kin is open to conjecture. Did she resent her mother, brothers and grandmother? If so it is not impossible that Jennet might gladly have seized the opportunity to drop the rest of the family in the proverbial when the opportunity arose!

As a final word on Alice Nutter, it is clear from Potts' writings that she was decidedly taciturn when being interviewed. She would not make a statement or defend herself in any manner; if she had made any attempt at explanation it is likely that Potts would have reported the content with glee. We have the image of an upright, proud, well-dressed yeoman's wife standing before a courtroom full of accusers, all ready and willing to send her to her maker. One might at least have expected Alice, who would probably have had the education to enable her to speak out for herself, to say something in her own defence. Surely she would have been horrified that the family name was being dragged through the gutter? The common theory that Alice refused to

---

[1] Mary Brigg, *Roughlee Hall - Fact and Fiction* (Marsden Antiquarians, 1982)

speak in order to protect her Catholic friends and family does not really hold water. She was not before the jury on recusancy charges and could easily have denied that she helped to kill her neighbour, Henry Mitton. A single explanation for her recalcitrance stands out above all the rest and that is that the unfortunate Alice Nutter may have suffered from an age-related dementia.

Any one of a number of diseases within this category would cause Alice to lose her short-term memory; if this is indeed the case then the poor woman would have stood before the court in a complete state of bewilderment; this would also have appertained when she had stood before Roger Nowell's bench some weeks previously. She would not be aware of where she was and why she was there; she would know, however, who she was and where she was from and could have unwittingly fooled her accusers into thinking that she was of sound mind. Still we have the nagging question as to why her family did not make a stink about the whole affair; why did Miles Nutter not take the witness stand and speak up voraciously for his mother? Perhaps he did not have the opportunity to do so but we will probably never know!

The Family of Alice Nutter (after Gladys Whittaker)

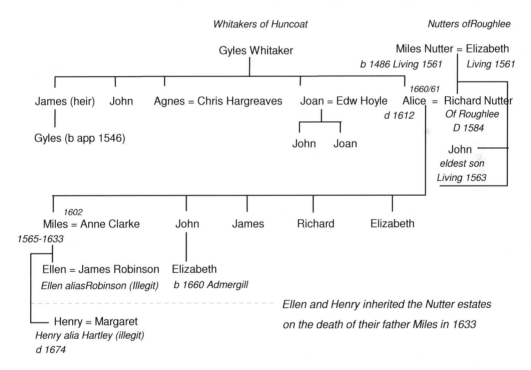

Chapter Thirteen

Chattox, The Nutters and The Coosens

The **Christopher Nutter** named as co-trustee of young Henry Mitton's estate in 1562 was very likely to have been the brother of Robert Nutter of Greenhead and John Nutter of Laund. In 1564 Christopher Nutter and his wife Ellen, of New Laund; *'surrender lands and tenements in Fence to the use of Richard and James Crook for 21 years to the uses created in a pair of indentures made between Christopher and Ellen Nutter and Roger Nowell.'* Richard and James Crook would probably have been close relatives of John Crook who married Margaret Nutter of Greenhead.

1507: *Ellis Nutter devises New Laund to Robert Nutter for £6:13:4 per annum.*

1527: *The New Laund rent was held equally between Ellis Nutter of Waterside (Reedley), John Haliday and John Nowell.*

1530: *Henry Nutter complains that his younger brother touched his title to tenements in New Laund and Reedley Hallows.*

1562: *Christopher Nutter elected fence keeper for Old Laund.*

Robert and John Nutter who were central to the prosecution case against Chattox and her daughter, Anne Redferne. The prosecution in this case used the statement of Christopher's son, John, whereby he said that around *'eighteene or nineteene yeares agoe'* he had been travelling home from Burnley when his brother, Robert, feeling unwell stated that he had been bewitched by Chattox and her daughter, Anne. John's sister, Margaret Crook, took up the story as her testimony shows:

This Examinate, sworne & examined vpon her oath, sayth, That about eighteene or nineteene yeares agoe, this Examinates brother, called Robert Nutter, about Whitsontide the same yeare, meeting with the said Anne Redferne, vpon some speeches betweene them they fell out, as this Examinats said brother told this Examinat: and within some weeke, or fort-night, then next after, this Examinats said brother fell sicke, and so languished vntill about Candlemas then next after, and then died. In which time of his sicknesse, he did a hundred times at the least say, That the said Anne Redferne and her associates had bewitched him to death. And this Examinate further saith, That this Examinates Father, called Christopher Nutter, about Maudlintide next after following fell sicke, and so languished, vntill Michaelmas then next after, and then died: during which time of his sicknesse, hee did sundry times say, That hee was bewitched; but named no bodie that should doe the same.'

Robert Nutter was the retainer of Sir Richard Shuttleworth of Gawthorpe Hall whose daughter, Eleanor Shuttleworth, married Roger Nowell of Read's son, Christopher. Robert accompanied his master, in his capacity as a JP on the Cheshire Justice circuit early in 1593.

Robert had fallen out with Anne Redferne at her home in West Close around May-time of 1592 and he had fallen ill by June. He obviously did not recover from this illness as he was dead by the 2nd of February (Candlemas) 1593. Having died in Cheshire it is likely that his cousin, John Nutter, who was dean of Chester at that time, would have buried Robert there as Robert does not appear to have been buried locally. Christopher Nutter had become ill shortly after brother Robert (by the 22nd of July [Maudlintide] according to Anne Redferne) and by the 29th September (Michaelmas) he was dead. This ties exactly with the record of Christopher Nutter who was buried at Burnley on the 27th of September 1593. In her reply to this Chattox said that Robert Nutter had been to her house at nearby West Close and made a pass at Anne Redfern, when she scorned his advances Nutter rode off in high dudgeon saying that *'If ever the ground came to him she would never dwell upon his land.'* This would have been a source of enmity between the two families but things appeared to get worse. The prosecution reported that:

'this Examinate (Chattox) *further sayth, that Elizabeth Nutter, wife to old Robert Nutter, did request this Examinate, and Loomeshaws wife of Burley, and one Iane Boothman, of the same, who are now both dead, (which time of request, was before that Robert Nutter desired the company of Redfearns wife) to get young Robert Nutter his death, if they could; all being togeather then at that time, to that end, that if Robert were dead, then the Women their Coosens might haue the Land.'*

The insertion of the word 'that' before Robert Nutter often leads to the assumption that Chattox was referring to the Robert Nutter 'killed' by her. In actual fact there is good reason to believe that the Robert in question was uncle to Robert the victim and the son (or step-son) of Elizabeth Nutter the would-be assassin. Robert Nutter's mother, Elizabeth, had once asked Chattox and two other women to kill her son, Robert, so that *'the women their Coosens might have the land.'* Anne Redfern's husband, Thomas, managed to persuade them not to carry out this act and all the thanks he received for this act of humanity was that *Lomashaye's Wife* became intent on killing him! Nicholas Baldwin, the schoolmaster at Colne Grammar School, dissuaded her from this and, to show his gratitude, Thomas Redferne rewarded him with a capon (large chicken).

If it were possible to find the truth behind the accusation against Elizabeth Nutter, of Greenhead, there might be much light shed upon the reason for the enmity between the Nutters and the Chattox family – indeed, there might be an explanation relating to some of the reasons contributing to the cause of the 1612 Pendle Witch round-up. Firstly, it must be said that to the modern mind it is almost unthinkable that a mother (or in this case possibly step-mother) would wish to kill her own son in order to obtain land and property. However, the records of the early modern period, into which our story falls, show a definite thirst for land and property amongst the forest people. This is understandable when it is realised that there was a very fine line between subsistence and abject poverty; those with no land struggled, those people with small areas of land scraped by whilst the tenants of larger holdings had a spiralling need to acquire more land to accommodate the large families that they had in order to work the lands that they already owned! An example of this is where the Chattox family lived in apparent poverty in a hovel upon the lands owned by the huge Gawthorpe estate whose under-tenancy was held by the Nutters of Greenhead. This latter would have been a house of high-status in relation to its neighbours and the Nutter family there were prospering.

Following the initial tenancy confirmation of 1507 (when Pendle was officially deforested) parcels of land changed hands on a regular basis, those with scattered holdings swapped them with the owners of neighbouring lands. In this way the *New Holders* consolidated and their farms expanded; more waste lands were taken into cultivation and this meant that there was more land to be bought, bargained for and swapped. The *Dissolution of the Monasteries* brought about another land grab when glebe lands were portioned out to those who already held land, were wealthy enough to afford to buy into new holdings or had friends in high places. This mindset of land acquisition prevailed throughout the second half of the sixteenth century as the wealthy jostled for position within high society and the yeomanry illustrated their ambitions to climb the social ladder by building their new houses and halls in stone.

It is no surprise, given this state of affairs, that there was a great deal of inter-family rivalry, chicanery and manoeuvring where land and property were concerned. We have seen in Part One the accusation against the trustees of Henry Mitton's estate and this illustrates the matter nicely; many other examples of this type exist and, therefore, we can take a view on the Elizabeth Nutter incident in as much as Chattox's accusation might just contain an element of truth.

'So that the Women their coosens would have the land. . .' In saying this Chattox might have been enforcing her accusation against Elizabeth Nutter by providing a strong motive for her to elicit the death of a member of her own family. The statement can be taken to have different meanings – the women involved in the plot were Elizabeth Nutter, Chattox, Lomashaye's wife and Jane Boothman. If we take this quartet as being *"the women"* then it could be said that their cousins would inherit and therefore these four women were related, however, the third-person intent of Chattox's statement appears to show that she was not included and therefore we are left with Elizabeth Nutter, Jane Boothman and Lomashaye's wife. Alternatively the women could be taken to be the cousins of *'them,'* the connotation being that they were the cousins of the Nutters. Following the death of Demdike in Lancaster Gaol, Chattox began to embroil her deceased foe in all manner of bewitchments; it is significant that Chattox did not accuse Demdike until after her death. In this manner, Chattox said that Demdike had also been involved in the Elizabeth Nutter incident but this can be ruled out with a degree of confidence.

A John Nutter (probably of Goldshaw) married Isabella Hargreaves at Newchurch in 1575 and this is of interest as *Lomashaye's Wife* was one of those who Elizabeth Nutter attempted to enrol into her deadly plan – the Hargreaves family owned the Lomashaye estate, this was the area running to the south of Old Laund from Seedhill (adjoining Nether Barrowford) along Pendle Water to join with New Laund and Reedley Hallows. In 1548 William and Elizabeth Hargreaves were at Rigby Farm, this formed a part of the estate and ran to some 48 acres, three farms, a cottage (in which John Hargreaves, the son of William and Elizabeth lived) and lands in the forest. William Hargreaves' mother was Margery Barcroft of the Lodge in nearby Reedley and she later married John Kippax. By 1594 the Lomashaye estate had been mortgaged to the Bannister family of Park Hill who already owned the neighbouring area of Whitefield.

Taking a closer look at this we find that Old Robert Nutter (husband of Elizabeth) had a cousin Henry who was married to Sybil Hargreaves. This puts another Hargreaves into the equation on the family level of cousin. It is interesting that the Nutter lands were adjacent to the Hargreaves lands of Lomashaye, this meant that the Lomashaye estate would have expanded organically were adjacent Nutter lands to have come their way.

Having said that, it is difficult to see how Elizabeth Nutter and her cousins would have gained from the death of her son when we consider a court record of 1570; this throws a little more light on the family by showing that a John Nutter and Robert Hartley were asked by Robert Nutter and his son and heir, Christopher, to transfer certain lands and tenements, grazing lands, pastures and mosses in New Laund at the queen's rent of £0: 11s: 1¼d. These properties and lands were formerly in the tenure of Robert Nutter and were to be transferred to the tenure of John Nutter, the son of John Nutter and rector of Sefton, and Bernard Hartley of New Laund. The new tenants were to have use of the properties and Robert Nutter was to receive rental for his lifetime and afterwards his son, Christopher, and his offspring were to enjoy the same. [1]

The land surrender record also goes on to provide us with the additional information on the Greenhead family that the offspring of Christopher Nutter's younger brother, James Nutter, were to inherit if Christopher had no issue. If James had no children then the issue of brother Robert were to inherit. Robert was not married at this time (1570) as the phrase *'if he were to marry'* is used. In another, similar land surrender a few years later it is stated that Robert had married Alice. It is apparent from this that, in order to gain any inheritance due to her son Robert, Elizabeth Nutter would have first needed to bump off the eldest son, Christopher, and the middle son, James. The story as related by Chattox, then, becomes ever more senseless. Still, let us press on in the search for viable cousins.

Jane Boothman, according to the Hargreaves cousinhood theory, may well have been a Hargreaves by birth; there are few records pertaining to her other than a baptism and a burial at Burnley:

'Thomas base begotten sonne of Jane Boothman baptised 12th August 1571' and *'A child of Jane Boothman's buried 8th December 1581.'*

The wife of a Christopher Nutter was buried at Burnley in 1586 but it is not known if this was the wife of Christopher of Greenhead. Robert Nutter (Christopher's son) was said to have been married to a Marie and his sister, Margaret Nutter, married a local man, John Crook, at Newchurch in 1590. It is possible that this John was the son of John, Richard or James Crook who appear in the following Court Rolls:

- *In 1531 **John Crook,** Greave of Pendle, surrenders one messuage and appurtenances called Black Moss now in the tenure of John Robinson at £0: 11s: 4d rent to the use of Sir Richard Bannister, chaplain, and Stephen Ellez, clerk.*

- *In 1547 Edmund Towneley aged one year, inherited Towneley and his uncle, George Vaughan esquire, was his guardian. **John Crook** and George Vaughan took custody of all Edmund Towneley's lands and tenements from Ightenhill to Colne until he came of age.*

- *In 1553 the widow of **John Crook,** along with Richard Dobson, servant of Christopher Dickenson, and also **John Nutter** son of **Miles Nutter** were all fined for keeping their beasts on Padiham Moor.[2]*

- *In 1564 Christopher Nutter and wife Ellen, of New Laund, surrender lands and tenements*

[1] W. Farrar, *Clitheroe Court Rolls,* (1912)
[2] John Nutter (son of Miles) was the brother-in-law of Alice Nutter

*in Fence to the use of **Richard** and **James Crook** for twenty-one years to the uses created in a pair of indentures made between Christopher and Ellen Nutter and Roger Nowell, this latter is dated May 1560. This Roger Nowell may have been the father of Roger Nowell, the magistrate, or he could have been of the Fence family.*

• *The Roughlee rentals show that in 1608/9 **John Crook** paid £0: 12s: 0d per year.*

The Crook family was well-established within the forest and Margaret would have made a reasonably good marriage. In 1556 a John Hartley, alias Crook (possibly a son of John, Richard or James Crook), was involved in the transfer of a farm in Roughlee, from the family-to-be of Alice Nutter, to himself and others. Besides the Nutter family cousinhood, between the Roughlee and Greenhead branches, there was also a business relationship between the two by marriage where land tenancy was involved.

The people of Pendle Forest attended the church relevant to their specific locality within the forest; generally speaking the districts of Higham and Heyhouses (Sabden) were within the parish of Padiham whilst the church of St. Peter's in Burnley served the neighbouring areas of West Close, Filly Close and Reedley Hallows. The Barrowford, Admergill and Blacko areas fell within the parish of St. Bartholomew's, Colne, and the rest of the Pendle Forest area used the 'New Kirk' of St. Mary's at Newchurch (fondly known in earlier times as *'The Cross'* and *'The Cathedral of the Forest'*). This is a slight oversimplification as certain parts of the south-western forest areas were extra-parochial being still attached to the castle church of Clitheroe; although marriages had to be carried out there the people mainly attended the Burnley church. It was also common for those who fancied themselves to be of a higher status to attend either the Colne church services or the services at Whalley; a great deal of business would be carried out amongst these 'higher-church' congregations.

There was also another reason why people from the forest and outlying towns used the Whalley parish church. Because the old gentry families were still firmly seated there, and because of the long ecclesiastical history that Whalley held, the congregation still leant towards the old ways. On the 21st December 1616 Elizabeth Marcroft, the wife of the curate of Clitheroe, supplied information to the authorities whereby she accused John Birtwistle of Huncoat, and Dorothy his wife, of being *'Popish recusants and of endeavouring to persuade her to become a Papist.'* The accusation also stated that the Birtwistles harboured seminary priests and the brothers of Mrs. Birtwistle, John and Peter Worthington, were said to have been Jesuits. Also amongst the accused was Peter Ormerod, the vicar of Whalley who was said to have frequented the Birtwistle's house where he conversed for three hours with one of the seminary priests. The Birtwistle family were originally granted lands at *Bridwisell*, near Huncoat, in 1185 when they and the de Legh family took over the post-Conquest holdings of Eudo de Longville. The Birtwistles were yeomen and minor gentry, they built the original Huncoat Hall in the thirteenth century. Ancestors of John Birtwistle were his five-times great-grandfather, Nicholas (1396-1460), who married into the Bannister family of Altham. John's three-time great-grandfather was Oliver Birtwistle (1455-1507) and he married Ann Starkie of Simonstone (later the Huntroyd Hall Family). John's cousin George Birtwistle (1572-1629) farmed at Filly Close and lived at Sabden Fold, George married Elizabeth Lawe in 1598 and we can see, therefore, that the Birtwistle line was somewhat coterminous with the families who played a part in the 1612 witch legend.

Records for the Nutter families are found in the Burnley, Padiham, Colne, Newchurch and Whalley registers but there is no trace of the elusive James Nutter. There is a possibility that

James was Old Robert Nutter's illegitimate son by a woman named Robinson because a James Robinson testified on behalf of the Nutters against Chattox and her daughter – his statement as a witness for the prosecution said that at the time of the death of Robert Nutter junior (1593) he (James) was living with old Robert Nutter at Greenhead. This, of course, does not constitute anything other than a circumstantial clue as to the parentage of James Robinson. Another possibility is that James was the son of Old Robert Nutter's wife, Elizabeth, prior to her marriage to Old Robert. The idea that James Robinson was close to the Nutters is reinforced somewhat by the fact that he was prepared to officially testify in court against the Whittle and Redferne families; in so doing he was throwing his cap firmly into the Nutter ring thus suggesting a strong link between himself and the Nutters of Greenhead.

Returning to the Hargreaves family of Lomeshaye, Chattox stated (1612) that Lomashaye's wife had recently died and we find that the following fits our bill perfectly; the wife of John Hargreaves, alias *Lomatchey,* was buried at Burnley on the 5th March 1611. In the following year John's father, William Hargreaves of Lomatchey was buried. There are two separate records for the marriages of John Hargreaves, one of 1582 tells us that a John Hargreaves married Ellena Robinson and a slightly later entry of 1584 shows a John Hargreaves marrying Margaret Robinson. In all likelihood, then, we have in one of these the record of *Lomashaye's wife* who appears to have been a Robinson. This gives us a lead in as much as we have seen that Elizabeth Nutter could possibly have been a Robinson and we have, therefore, two out of three of the *'women'* sharing the same surname. Just as the neighbouring estates of Lomashaye would have benefited from any addition of Nutter lands, so the New Laund estates of the Robinsons would easily incorporate them. There is every probability that if we have not yet reached our goal in the search for the *'coosins'* then at least we are surely within the right area!

Reading between the lines of Chattox's statement it would appear that Elizabeth Nutter attempted to coerce her into becoming involved in the murderous plot against Nutter's own family. If this was indeed the case, what would have been Chattox's reward for aiding the other conspirators; was she promised security of tenure upon Nutter land?

When the Greenhead estate fell to Christopher Nutter it is possible, as we have seen, that his brother James was actually not a Nutter, therefore Robert senior may not have included him in his will. This would have provided reason enough for Elizabeth to attempt to pervert the natural chain of inheritance. Even so, it is difficult to envisage a situation whereby Robert Nutter would have inherited ahead of his brothers, Christopher and James. To what extent the accusation of Chattox against Elizabeth Nutter holds water is unclear but, given the mindset of the period, there is much here to recommend the supposition that, as Potts quaintly put it, *'there could not be so greate Fire without some Smoake.'*

Moor

*A*nd *further, this Examinate* (Alison Device) *saith, That about two yeares agoe, she, this Examinate, hath heard, That the said Anne Whittle, alias Chattox, was suspected for bewitching the drinke of Iohn Moore of Higham Gentleman: and not long after, shee this Examinate heard the said Chattox say, that she would meet with the said Iohn Moore, or his. Whereupon a child of the said Iohn Moores, called Iohn, fell sick, and languished about halfe a yeare, and then died: during which languishing, this Examinate saw the said Chattox sitting in her owne garden, and a picture of Clay like vnto a child in her Apron; which this Examinate* *espying, the said Anne Chattox would haue hidde with her Apron: and this Examinate declaring the same to her mother, her mother thought it was the picture of the said Iohn Moores childe.*

*A*nd *she this Examinate further saith, That about sixe or seuen yeares agoe, the said Chattox did fall out with one Hugh Moore of Pendle, as aforesaid, about certaine cattell of the said Moores, which the said Moore did charge the said Chattox to haue bewitched: for which the said Chattox did curse and worry the said Moore, and said she would be Reuenged of the said Moore: whereupon the said Moore presently fell sicke, and languished about halfe a yeare, and then died. Which Moore vpon his death-bed said, that the said Chattox had bewitched him to death.*

Here we see yet another example of the apparent enmity between the Demdike and Chattox clans. Accusations between the two flew like feathers in a pillow fight and must have been music to the ears of the magistrates. In the above case, Alison Device stated that Chattox had unceremoniously bumped off young John Moor of Higham and Hugh Moor (possibly uncle to John) of Pendle. Again, as we saw with the Nutters of Greenhead, Chattox was at odds with her yeoman neighbours who, whenever they had the temerity to accuse her of some misdeed, felt the sharp-edge of her tongue. This would have been an almost daily occurrence – as Chattox would have wandered her part of the forest, muttering and grumbling and generally making a nuisance of herself, she would have found herself in many situations where she was not wanted and would have been told in no uncertain terms to 'clear off.' In her usual inimitable fashion Chattox would respond in the only way that she knew how, by the employment of a vitriolic stream of expletives.

In ninety-nine out of one-hundred cases this would have been the end of the matter but, as happened in the Nutter and Moor incidents, young and apparently fit people could be stricken down by disease in a very short time. The dank winter months within the Pendle Forest aided the health of neither man nor beast, pneumonia was a swift and deadly foe but the enemy that everyone feared, rich and poor alike, were the ubiquitous diseases of tuberculosis and smallpox. It is significant that not a single person actually dropped dead on the spot following a tongue-lashing by any of the accused; John Lawe is the only reported case where the accursed suffered an instant and obvious affliction. We have to conclude, therefore, that most of those who died of supposed witchcraft were already ill when they were said to have been cursed; the statements of the accused in relation to this reinforce this argument as the bewitched person would have *'languished half a year'* or *'died presently.'* So, the one-percent of people who were seen to have died as a direct consequence of having crossed a witch would have almost invariably been suffering from TB – having been cursed would, of course, not help their condition, the mindset of the victim would lead to a rapid deterioration and, inevitably, death.

It is apparent that the readiness of the feuding matriarchs to chalk up more assassinations than their opponents led to a 'scatter-gun' approach whereby anyone unfortunate enough to have been within the periphery of their victims would become victims by association. Thus we see that the entirely innocent child of John Moor had allegedly fallen prey to Chattox, this is an identical situation to the 'killing' of Richard Baldwin's child by Demdike. This is indicative of both the apparent willingness of the accused to bolster their reputations and the strength of feeling held by the otherwise down-to-earth forest people towards the existence of malevolent witchcraft.

Alison stated that Hugh Moor died *'about six or seven yeares agoe'* (1605) but in actual fact he was buried at Padiham on 25th November 1602. Hugh Moor was the son of Christopher who had the copyhold of lands in Higham upon which the family home of Dean Farm was built in the 1560s. There is an inscription over the main south-facing window of the property saying; *'This house was builded by Hugh More son of Christopher More eldest brother son and Letice Hugh wife in the year of our Lord God 156-.'* I make the assumption that John Moor senior of Higham was the brother of Hugh as the traditional Christian family names were Christopher, Hugh and John; this is seen within a court record of 1524 when Christopher Moore, John Moore, Hugh Moore and John Moore junior sold a field called *Bronebreak* in Fence. In 1538 Hugh More and John Crook were granted a messuage and land lying in Black Carr within Hunterholme and West Close, *'with 2 partes of le fence in the Forrest of Pennle, surrendered by John Bulcock, bailiff of Pendle.'* The unfortunate demise of young John Moor at the hands of Chattox (in actual fact she was not charged with the killing of the Moors) did not deter the family from raising another child named John as we later meet with John Moor, Overseer of the Poor, of Higham Booth.

The Moor family also appeared in other parts of the forest in their role as minor local gentry; they appear in Foulridge where John Moor, and his wife Ann, built Ball House in 1627. This property is of interest as it boasts a number of features, such as the central entrance via a storied porch, that were of an unusually high-status for such a small house.[1]

The old Nutter property of Greenhead, as we saw earlier, passed into the Moor family upon the marriage of Elizabeth Nutter (b1585) and John Moor, it was almost certainly this family who built the present Greenhead Manor. In 1631 John Moor of Greenhead, along with Miles, the son of Alice Nutter, and others swore an oath stating that lands around the new bridge at Higherford were the inheritance of Ellen Hartley, daughter of Alexander, who was the son of John Hartley of Admergill; the land did not belong to John Robinson of Goldshaw who thought that he held the tenure.

Photograph: Library Stock

Ball House; the Foulridge home of John Moor

[1] Sarah Pearson, *Rural Houses of the Lancashire Pennines,* (HM Stationery Office, 1985)

Chapter Fourteen

The Pendle Witchcraft Trials of 1633

The Pendle Witch Trial of 1633 is often viewed as having been a 'sister case' to the preceding 1612 trials; this is perfectly reasonable – in fact there is every likelihood that the later incident would never have occurred had it not been for the earlier precedent. There are many parallels between the two; again, we had the whole basis of a major prosecution whose pivotal 'evidence' was that of a child. This time the main instigator of events was the ten-year old Edmund Robinson from the tiny hamlet of Wheatley Lane to the north of West Close and New Laund. The case of 1633 had everything that a good trial based upon suspicion and fantasy should have; in fact all of the lurid accounts of diabolical witchcraft present in the 1612 trials were to resurface in young Robinson's story. The only real difference this time was that the presiding magistrates at the Assize trial stopped short of ordering the accused to be executed.

We see a great deal of the style of James Device in the account of young Edmund Robinson whereby many of his neighbours were said to have been given to performing fantastic and supernatural feats in their spare time. The parallel is not surprising given that the two youths had grown up in exactly the same environment, they were both steeped in the local tales of *maleficium* – these were the equivalent of the modern television soap opera. That a lad of ten could furnish such a vivid account of the supernatural deeds of his neighbours bears testimony to the stories he would have heard at his mother's knee. The unfortunate events of 1612 were still fresh in the forest psyche and young Edmund Robinson would certainly have known the names of the surviving families from the earlier period; it even appears that Jennet Device was to play her part in the proceedings.

The source documents for the 1633 Pendle Witch Trials are to be found in private collections. The original confession of Edmund Robinson appears to have been lost but survives as a manuscript copy. Writing in the late eighteenth century Whitaker based the following description of the 1633 case on a copy of the original deposition:

In or about the year of 1633, a number of poor and ignorant people, inhabitants of Pendle forest or the neighbourhood, were apprehended upon the evidence of one Edmund Robinson, a boy, whose deposition taken before two neighbouring magistrates is here subjoined.

The examination of Edmund Robinson, son of Edm. Robinson, of Pendle forest, mason, taken at Padiham before Richard Shuttleworth and John Starkie, 10th February, A.D 1633.

Who informeth upon oath, (beeinge examined concerninge the great meetings of the witches) and faith, that unto all saints day last past , hee, this informer, beeinge with one Henrye Parker, a neare doore neighbour to him in Wheatley-Lane, desyred the said Parker to give him leave to get some bulloes (plums), which hee did. In which tyme of gettinge bulloes, he saw two grehounds, viz. a blacke and a browne one, came running over the next field towards him, he verily thinkinge the one of them to bee Mr. Nutters, and the other to bee Mr. Robinsons, the said Mr. Nutter and Mr. Robinson then havinge such like. And the said greyhounds came to him and fawned on him, they havinge about theire necks either of them a coller, and to either of them which collers was tyde a stringe, which collers as this informer affirmeth did shine like gould, and hee thinkinge that some either of Mr. Nutters or Mr. Robinsons family should have followed them: but seeinge noe body to follow them, he tooke the said greyhounds thinkinge to hunt with them, and presently a hare rise very neare before him, at the sight whereof he cried, loo, loo, but the dogges would not run.

*W*hereupon beeinge very angry, he tooke them, and with the strynges that were at their collers tyed either of them to a little bush on the next hedge, and with a rod that hee had in his hand, hee bett them. And in stede of the blacke greyhound, one Dickinson wife stoode up (a neighbour) whome this informer knoweth, and in the steade of the browne greyhound a little boy whom this informer knoweth not. At which sight this informer beeinge affraid indevoured to run away: but beeinge stayed by the woman, viz. by Dickonson's wife, shee put her hand into her pocket and pulled out a peace of silver much like unto a faire shillinge, and offered to give him to hould hid tongue, and not to tell, whiche hee refused, sayinge, nay thou art a witch; Whereupon shee put her hand into her pocket againe, and pulled out a stringe like unto a bridle that gingled, which she put upon the little boyes heade that stoode up in the browne greyhoundes steade; whereupon the said boy stood up a white horse.

*T*hen immediately the said Dickonson wife tooke this informer before her upon the said horse, and carried him to a new house called Hoarestones, being about a quarter of a mile off, whither, when they were comme, there were divers persons about the doore, and hee saw divers others cominge rydinge upon horses of severall colours towards the said house, which tyed theire hoses to a hedge neare to the sed house; and which persones went into the sed house, to the number of threescore or thereabouts, as this informant thinketh, where they had a fyre and meate roastinge, and some other meate stirringe in the house, whereof a yonge woman whom hee this informant knoweth not, gave him flesh and breade upon a trencher, and drinke in a glasse, which, after the first taste hee refused and would have noe more, and said it was nought. And presently, after seeing diverse of the company goinge to a barn neare adioyneinge, he followed after and there hee saw sixe of them kneelinge, and pullinge at sixe severall roapes which were fastened or tyed to ye toppe of the house; at or with which pulling came then in this informants sight flesh smoakeinge, butter in lumps, and milk as it were syleing from the said roapes, all which fell into basons whiche were placed under the said roapes. And later that the sixe had done, there came other sixe which did likewise, and duringe all the tyme of their so pullinge, they made such foule faces that feared this informer, so as hee was glad to steale out, and run home, whom, when they wanted, some of theire company came runninge after him neare to a place in a high way, called Boggard-hole, where this informer met two horsemen, at the sight whereof the sed persons left followinge him, and the foremost of which persones yt followed him, hee knoweth to bee one Loynd wife, which said wife, together with one Dickonson wife, and one Jennet Davies, he hath seene at severall tymes in a croft or close adioininge to his fathers house, whiche put him in a greate feare.

*A*nd further, this informer saith, upon Thursday after new Yeares day last past, he sawe the sd Loynd wife sittinge upon a crosse peece of wood, beeinge within the chimney of his father's dwelling house, and hee callinge to her, said, come downe thou Loynd wife, and immediately the sd Loynd wife went up out of his sight. And further, this informer saith, yt after hee was comme from her company aforesed to his father's house, beeinge towardes eveninge, his father bid him goe fetch home two kyne (cows) to seale, and in the way, in a field called the Ollers, hee chanced to hap upon a boy, who began to quarrell with him, and they fought soe together till this informer had his eares made very bloody by fightinge, and lokkinge down, he sawe the boy had a cloven foote, at which sight he was affraide, and ran away to seeke the kyne. And in the way hee sawe a light like a lanthorne, toward which he made hast, supposinge yt to bee carried by some of Mr. Robinson's people: But when hee came to the place, hee only founde a woman standynge upon a bridge, whom, when hee sawe her, he knew to bee Loynd wife, and knowinge her he turned back againe, and immediately hee met with ye aforesed boy, from whom he offered to run, whichsaide boy gave him a blowe on the back which caus'd him to crye. And hee farther saith, yt when hee was in the barne, he sawe three women take three pictures from off the beame in which pictures many thornes or such like thinges sticked, and yt Loynd wife tooke one of the said pictures downe but thother two women yt tooke thother two pictures downe hee knoweth not. And beeing further asked, what persons were at ye meetinge aforesaid, he nominated these perones hereafter mentioned, viz. Dickonson wife, Henry Priestley wife and her sonne, Alice Hargreaves widdowe, Jennet Davies, Wm. Davies, uxor. Hen. Jacks and her sone John, James Hargreaves of Marsden, Miles wife of Dicks, James wife, Saunders sicut credit, Lawrence wife of Saunders, Loynd wife, Buys wife of Barrowford, one Holgate and his wife sicut credit, Little Robin wife of Leonard's, of the West Cloase.

*E*dmund Robinson of Pendle, father of ye sd Edmunde Robinson, the aforesaid informer, upon oath saith, that upon All Saint's Day, he sent his sonne, the aforesaid informer, to feth home two kyne to seale, and sayeth yt he thought his sonne stayed longer than he shoulde have done, went to seeke him, and in seeking him, hearde him crye very pittifully, and found him so afraid and distracted, yt hee neither knew his father, nor did hee know where hee was, and soe continued very neare a quarter of an hower before hee came unto himselfe, and hee told this informer; his father, all the pticular passages yt are before declared in the said Edmund Robinson, his sonne's information.

*U*pon such evidence, these poor creatures were committed to Lancaster castle for trial, not greatley to the honor either of the understanding or humanity of the magistrates; for surely the statute of witchcraft did not bind them to commit, upon any evidence, or upon none, or to shut their eyes, against apparent malice and imposture. – On their trails they had the misfortune of falling into the hands of a jury equally ignorant or prejudiced, who found seventeen of them guilty; –the judge, however, whose name I have not learned, very properly reprieved them, and reported the case to the king in council. They were next remitted to the bishop of Chester (Bridgeman), who, certifying his opinion of the case, whatever it was, four of the party, Margaret Johnson, Francis Dicconson, Mary Spencer, and the wife of one of the Hargreaves's, were sent for to London, and examined first by the king's physicians and surgeons, and afterwards by Charles I in person.

A stranger scene can scarcely be conceived, and it is not easy to imagine, whether the untaught manners, rude dialect and uncouth appearance of these poor foresters, would more *astonish the king, or his dignity of person and manners, together with the splendid scene with which they were surrounded, would overwhelm them. – The end, however, of the business was, that strong presumptions appeared of the boy having been suborned to accuse them falsely, and they were accordingly dismissed. – The boy afterwards confessed that he was suborned.* □

James Crossley persuaded his good friend, Harrison Ainsworth, to develop the Pendle Witch story into a novel, Crossley had edited the Chetham Society publication of *The Wonderfull Discoverie of Witches* and in the preface to this volume he wrote of the reasons behind the confessions and fantasies of some of the accused:

'In many cases the confessions were made in the hope, and no doubt with the promise, seldom performed, that a respite from punishment would be eventually granted. In other instances, there is as little doubt, that they were the final results of irritation, agony, and despair. The confessions are generally composed of "such stuff as dreams are made of," and what they report to have occurred, might either proceed, when there was no intention to fabricate, from intertwining the fantastic threads which sometimes stream upon the waking senses from the land of shadows, or be caused by those ocular hallucinations of which medical science has supplied full and satisfactory solution.'

Crossley, in his preface to the Chetham Society publication of Potts' work, states that Whitaker's account of the 1633 story is the most accurate of the three manuscript versions available. We see that young Edmund had placed a Jennet Davies in the case and this is commonly held to have been Jennet, Demdike's granddaughter. Robinson also named others who were known to have been related to the earlier case, for example, *Miles wife of Dicks* was Alice Nutter's daughter-in-law (Miles of Dick's being Richard and Alice Nutter's son). We can take it, then, that further to earlier speculation Jennet Device did indeed carry the name of Davies and she also stayed within the forest following the 1612 trials. Robinson stated that he often saw Jennet in a field in Wheatley Lane and it is not unreasonable to assume that she had lived locally within the Wheatley Lane, Higham and West Close areas. We have seen that Jennet appears to have assumed the surname of Sellers by the time of her death and this suggests that the Sellers family were of the Wheatley Lane area.

From the names bandied around by young Robinson it is clear that he absorbed the details of the local folk-tales relating to 1612; it is to be expected that any close relative of those executed in the earlier case would have been the first on the lad's list. No doubt the names of Nutter, Device, Hargeaves (*Lomashaye*) and Cronckshaw leapt quickly into the formation of a story that was to become another gross miscarriage of justice. Edmund junior eventually admitted that his fantasies had constituted a complete pack of lies but this was not before nineteen people were arraigned on charges of witchcraft, found guilty and almost sentenced to death. It is clear from the lad's statement that he had been playing with his friends instead of bringing the family cow home for milking. Having made up his initial story in an attempt to gain *'respite from punishment,'* we do not know who he first included although we can guess that Jennet Device would be in there. What is almost certain is that the lad's father, Edmund Robinson senior, saw a good opportunity for monetary gain in the fear engendered by the new outbreak of hysteria.

Edmund senior admitted to having attempted to blackmail the husband of one of the accused, Frances Dicconson, because he had refused Robinson credit on the purchase of a cow; no doubt Robinson senior saw fit to include Frances Dicconson in the list as an act of revenge. Others probably fall into this category of unfortunate association with Robinson, it is debatable as to whether the son, acting on his own, would have drawn in the families of Hargreaves of Lomashaye and the Cronckshaws of Marsden *et al.* The eventual tally of local people, of which seventeen were convicted, can be seen as the following:

Jennet Davies aged about 33 (probable daughter of Elizabeth Device)
William Davies (said to have been half-brother to Jennet)
Frances Dicconson of Wheatley Lane
Margaret Johnson (of Marsden Heights)
Alice Higgin
Jennet Loynd (Lund - Loynd wife) of Wheatley Lane
Mary Spencer
John Spencer
Alice Hargreaves
Alice wife of Henry Priestley
Son of Henry Priestley
Wife of Henry Jacks
John Jacks
Ann Nutter (nee Clarke) wife of Alice Nutter's son, Miles
James Hargreaves
Jame's wife (James Hargreaves wife?)
Mr. Holgate (Christopher - uncle to Jennet Device?)
Mrs. Holgate (Isobell - wife of Christopher?)
Buy's wife (Boys)
Wife of Little Robin (son of Leonard) probably Jennet Cronckshaw
Wife of Lawrence (son of Saunders/Sanders)
Jennet Hargreaves (of Chamber Hill)
Marie Shuttleworth
Agnes Rawsterne
Robert Wilkinson
Jennet Wilkinson
Possibly Elizabeth Houghton (of Barrowford)

We have in this list a number of familiar names; Hargreaves of Marsden (Lomashaye), Jacks (alias Hargreaves of Thorneyholme), Higgin (of the family of Coldweather House in Marsden), Spencer (of Spencer's Farm in Wheatley Lane, later Burnley), Holgate, Cronckshaw (of Hollins Farm, West Close), Rawsterne (eventually of Heirs House, Colne), Wilkinsons (of Padiham), Priestley and Shuttleworth. The name of Boys (of Barrowford) is of interest as in 1767 two brothers of this family, by the names of Richard and Thomas Boys, were indicted at York Assizes on charges of highway robbery, the pair were summarily convicted and hanged on the Knavesmire. Another version of the story is that the brothers were convicted of coin-clipping; James Carr (*Annals of Colne)* has it that the brothers were buried in Colne churchyard at the rear end of the church building and this meant that other families did not wish to bury their dead in that area. As a consequence the grave of the brothers was moved in 1856 to a position by the north wall of the Grammar School. The headstone of the Boys brothers carried the following inscription:

> *'Farewell, vain world, I've had enough of thee,*
> *I care not what thou cans't do to me;*
> *My debts are paid, my thoughts are free,*
> *Prepare yourselves to follow me.'*

Returning from that slight digression; Edmund Robinson senior, who was said to have been a mason (builder), took up the embryonic report of witchcraft first garbled to him by his son and ran with it. In what appears to the modern mind as an astonishing act of treachery, the father paraded the lad around the area as a self-proclaimed 'witch finder.' It is probable that anyone willing to offer a bribe to the road-show would have escaped the attentions of the young marvel. Intent only on the money making side of their actions the Robinsons were apparently unmindful of the consequences of their falsified stories; the fact that innocent people's lives were in very real danger appears to have mattered little to them. The dastardly trio of father, son and uncle visited churches in order for the lad to be placed at the front of the congregation from where he would have a good view of any witches therein.

When the Robinson roadshow hit the Cravenshire village of Kildwick they came up against an able adversary in the shape of one John Webster, vicar of that parish. Webster had been an erstwhile chaplain in the army and would later become the master of Clitheroe Grammar School; Webster (with whom we met in Part One) wrote one of the source materials in the 1633 case in *'Displaying of Supposed Witchcraft.'* On the subject of witchcraft Webster tended to err on the side of common-sense and so it was when the Robinsons appeared on the scene. Webster describes the events when young Edmund was ready to strut his stuff:

He . . . was brought into the church at Kildwick where I, being then curate, was preaching in the afternoon, and was set upon a stool to look about him, which moved some little disturbance in the congregation for a little while, After prayers I enquired what the matter was and the people told me it was the boy that discovered witches; upon which I went to the house where he was to stay all night and found him there with two very unlikely persons, that did conduct him and manage the business. I desired to have some proper discourse with the boy in private but that was utterly refused me. Then, in presence of a great many people, I took the boy near to me and said: "Good boy, tell me truly and in earnest, didst thou see and hear such strange things at the meeting of witches as is reported by many thou didst relate?" But the two men, not giving the boy leave to answer, did pluck him up from me and said he had been examined by two able justices of the peace, and they did never ask him such a question.

Richard Shuttleworth and John Starkie esquires were the two magistrates who interviewed young Edmund at Gawthorpe Hall; it would be of interest to know how much truth can be assigned to the statement of Edmund senior that they *'did never ask him such a question.'* If this was indeed the truth then the magistrates must have been more than willing to accept the lad's story; were the magistrates in actual fact unwilling to press too hard in case the Edmund junior's fantastic story were to be proved wrong thus spoiling another good witch-hunt?

Whatever the case may be the accused were hauled before the court and things proceeded much as they had done twenty-one years earlier; absurd stories unfolded and ludicrous tales of the supernatural were spun by the child of ten. Nothing daunted, the case authorities found that, in their learned opinion, the majority of the accused were guilty as charged. However, this case did at least find in the trial judges, Sir George Vernon and Sir Francis Crawley, an element of commonsense. This might have been partly due to a slight thawing in the attitude of authority to the many national accounts of witchcraft that still pervaded the country. At the time of the 1612 trials James Ist, who changed his mind more often than he changed his shirt, considered it as his duty to continually issue the product of his superior intellect to his people. His rantings upon the subjects of witchcraft, homosexuality, tobacco and the Catholic faith were something to behold amongst the common people. The educated classes, however, named him '*The wisest fool in Christendom.*'

James I died in 1625 and it was his successor, Charles Ist, who reigned at the time of the 1633 witch scare. Although the willingness to believe in witchcraft was still as strong in the Forest of Pendle there was at least a willingness amongst the trial judges to seek further counsel upon sentencing. This is exactly what Vernon and Crawley did following their guilty verdict and the Privy Council required that '*the principall and most notorious offenders*' be brought to London for further investigation.

In order to have information on the case-in-hand the Council directed the Bishop of Chester, John Bridgeman, to attend the prisoners in Lancaster Castle before they were moved to the capital. Those of the accused chosen to travel were Margaret Johnson, Alice Higgin, Frances Dicconson, Jennet Loynd, Jennet Hargreaves, Mary Spencer and John Spencer. The Bishop reached Lancaster on the 15th June 1634 and found that Alice Higgin, Jennet Loynd and John Spencer had died in prison whilst Jennet Hargreaves was very ill. On further inspection of the surviving prisoners the Bishop found that Edmund Robinson senior had been involved in bribery and blackmail in the case of Dicconson and that Margaret Johnson's confession did not hold water. Furthermore, Mary Spencer, who had been accused of the ridiculous charge of bewitching a bucket by one Nicholas Cunliffe, was found (in the Bishop's opinion) to have been unjustly accused.

The surviving four women were duly dispatched to London and lodged at the Ship Tavern in Greenwich; here they were examined by William Harvey, the king's physician, and a group of midwives who were charged with the task of finding any obvious physical marks that would set the women apart as witches. No such evidence was forthcoming and this, along with the findings of John Bridgeman, set the finger of suspicion firmly upon young Edmund Robinson. Under rigorous cross-examination (of the type that the Pendle magistrates should have employed in the very first place) Robinson admitted that he had fabricated the whole thing. The case against the accused fell apart and in the meantime Edmund Robinson senior had been arrested on the 28th June 1634; he was packed off to London and placed in the Gate House Prison there. In the July of 1634 Robinson was described as '*A poore distresed prisoner in great want, havinge neither friendes nor money and two hundread miles from home.*'[1]

One might have expected, then, that the case against the women having been proven to be a travesty they would all have been released and lived happily ever-after. Not a bit of it! Johnson, Spencer, Dicconson and Hargreaves were pardoned and then sent packing back up to Lancaster Castle where they were again imprisoned. By the August of 1636 they were still imprisoned along with Marie Shuttleworth, Alice Priestley, Jennet Cronckshaw, Agnes Rawsterne and Robert and Jennet Wilkinson – in 1637 five women, one with a young child, were still being

---

[1] *The Farrington Papers*, (Chetham Society, 1856)

detained at His Majesty's pleasure.[1] It is interesting that there is no mention here of Jennet Device having still been incarcerated and this reinforces the argument for her having been buried at Newchurch in the December of 1635; no doubt the ordeal of prison would have hastened Jennet's demise as had been the case with her grandmother twenty-one years earlier.

The 1633 case became notorious when a play entitled '*The Late Lancashire Witches; a Well Received Comedy, Lately Acted at the Globe on the Banks-Side, by the King's Majesties Actors*', by Thomas Heywood and Richard Bromes, appeared in London in 1634. As a final postscript on the Robinsons, John Webster related in 1677 that young Edmund, now aged around fifty-three, still lived at Wheatley Lane. Known as Ned O' Roughs the young lad of forty-three years past was still dining-out on the tales of his youthful adventures; it has to be wondered if anyone ever pointed out to Robinson that his childish pranks actually caused the deaths of a number of people and caused a great deal of distress to many others?

Margaret Johnson of Marsden, lived, according to the local historian Walter Bennet, in the present area of Marsden Cross (Nelson). Johnson aided the initial accusations made by young Robinson when she fully, and vociferously admitted to having been an active witch. Bennet takes up the story; [2]

Wheatley Lane, 1907

'*Margaret Johnson, a widow, aged sixty and possibly over-excited and mentally weak, made an extraordinary confession that she had sold herself to the devil. In one confession she said she first met Mamilian, as her spirit was called, "on the highway between Burnley and Marsden," but in another confession the meeting place was her own house in Marsden where she was "in great passion of anger and discontent and withall pressed with some want" (hungry and famished); she also confessed to being at a witches' meeting at Pendle Waterside (Quaker Bridge) and at Hoarstones, but not on the occasion when Robinson junior was entertained there. She did not admit to any specific killing, but affirmed that witches met "to consult for the killing and hurting of men and beasts" - Good Friday was always fixed for the annual general meeting to which their devils or spirits could take them "on a rod, dog or anything else" even into any room of a man's house, and the devils could cause "foul weather and storms and so did at their meetings." Mamilian, who had first appeared as a "man apparelled in a suit of black, tied about with silk points (laces)," later usually appeared in the likeness of a cat, sometimes of one colour and sometimes of another.*'

There is a significant difference here in the attitude of the authorities of 1634 to the earlier case of 1612; when we see that Margaret Johnson's statement was accepted to be the ramblings of a confused woman it is difficult not to think what would have been the outcome of the earlier case of 1612 had this attitude then prevailed.

[1] Alison Findlay, *The Lancashire Witches, Histories and Stories*, (R.Poole, Ed, Manchester University Press, 2002)
[2] W. Bennett, *The History of Marsden and Nelson*, (Nelson Corporation, 1957)

Chapter Fifteen

The Mystery of Malkin Tower

Where that same wicked wight - Her dwelling had,
Dark, doleful, dreary, like a greedy grave
That still for carrion carcases doth crave,
On top whereof ay dwelt the ghastly owle,
Shrieking his baleful note, which ever drave
Far from that haunt all other cheerful fowl
And all about it wandering ghosts did wail and howle

The Witch's Mansion

Goldshaw

The people of Pendle Forest have long debated the actual site of Demdike's home, the fabled Malkin Tower. Harrison Ainsworth, following his visit to these parts in the mid-nineteenth century, placed Malkin Tower firmly on the summit of Blacko Hillside, the position now occupied by the Blacko Tower. When I was a child the older people of the Roughlee area, when speaking on the subject of witches (as they often did), tended to be of the general opinion that the Malkin Tower stood either in Blacko or between that village and Roughlee. My own parents, and most of their generation who grew up in Barrowford in the earlier part of the twentieth century, were of a consensus that Blacko Tower was actually Malkin Tower – this common mistake was also adopted by some of the nineteenth century census return officers who confused Blacko Tower with Blacko Tower Farm and Malkin Tower Farm.

However, some of the people of the western forest have always argued that Malkin Tower was located in their area, particularly in the vicinity of the village of Newchurch-in-Pendle. The noted local historian, Walter Bennet, proposed one of the earliest arguments for this.[1] Here, Bennet stated that Malkin Tower stood in Malkin Field, at Saddler's Farm in Newchurch, and this bold statement would seem to show that Bennet accepted the opinion of an earlier writer on the subject, Dr Laycock of Sabden. Dr Laycock claimed to have seen a survey of 1828 that had been prepared for Teesdale's Map of Lancashire; the survey showed three fields at Saddlers Farm carrying the name of *Malkin Fields*.[2] These early maps were often surveyed by privateers, with the aid of military engineers, who would travel around the location to be mapped and gain the required knowledge of the topographical names from the older inhabitants. Thus it was not

---

[1] W. Bennett, *The Pendle Witches,* (First edition, Burnley Libraries & Arts Committee, 1957)
[2] E.Peel & P.Southern, *The Trials of the Lancashire Witches,* (Carnegie Publishing, 1969/1972)

uncommon to see maps of the same area showing completely different names for landscape features; it is highly likely that the Teesdale surveyors would have been informed by the farmer, farm-hand or passing villager, that certain closes of land at Saddlers were then known as Malkin Fields. Teesdale's map, however, did not include this information, nor did any other map to the best of our knowledge. Peel and Southern mention that there had been an old building on the Saddlers Farm land as the foundation stones precluded the use of the plough in that area. It is said that a building existed between Saddlers and Bull Hole and this is shown as the site of a cottage on a sketch map of the area.[1] The deeds to the Saddlers Farm property go back to the seventeenth century and field names are shown on the plans, apparently they do not show any area carrying the name of Malkin, however.

Research has provided a weight of evidence that tips the scales of probability in favour of Malkin Tower having been sited upon the southern slopes of the ancient Blacko Hillside. Having said that, this does not preclude the western Pendle Forest from having an equal share of the 1612 Pendle Witch Trial story – far from it in fact. Most of the forest, as we have seen, had its own input into the legend to some degree; people from many of the older-established areas found themselves involved and this was a result of the close cousinhood between the people of the parish of Whalley. The comings and goings of the people within the 1612 story are concentrated around four main sites, West Close, Malkin, Roughlee and Goldshaw. The village of Newchurch was often central to the machinations of the accused, the church of St. Mary's gave its name to the village (New Kirk) and saw many of the cast within our drama come and go; almost all of the old forest families found themselves, at one time another, within the environs of St. Mary's. The old graves of the Nutter family draw much interest from tourists who, quite rightly, visit the picturesque hillside village of Newchurch in search of the witch legend. None of the graves actually contain the remains of Alice Nutter as convicted witches were not buried within consecrated ground; an early memorial stone does show, however, the Goldshaw line of second cousins of the family of Alice's husband, Richard Nutter.

The early Nutter headstone reads; Ellen Nutter 1651; George Nutter 1657; Issabell Nutter 1658; And Margret Nutter the wife of Richard Nutter.

As we have seen, the hallowed enclosure of St. Mary's also (in all probability) contains the body of Jennet Device who, at the time of her burial in December 1635, had reverted to her father's name of Seller – there is of course no surviving headstone in memory of Jennet. There is a possibility that Jennet's grandmother, Elizabeth Southern, is also interred at Newchurch as she was never convicted of any crime, this seems unlikely as there is no record of the burial and someone would have been required to pay the expenses for the removal of her body from Lancaster to Pendle. Having said that, the parish records are not infallible as can be seen in the above burial of Issabell Nutter, the stone shows the burial in 1658 but the records show no burials for that year.

---

[1] Clifford H Byrne, *Newchurch-in-Pendle - Folklore Fact and Fiction*, (Marsden Antiquarians, Nelson 1982)

The standard procedure of 'best available evidence' has been employed within this text to suggest that Elizabeth Southern and her family, as members of the local Ingham family, would have lived somewhere within the area running south from Goldshaw to Habergham (Burnley). That Demdike would have known the area of West Close and Goldshaw very well is not in doubt, this area forms half of the stage upon which the eventual tragedy of 1612 was played-out. The other half of the stage was Malkin Tower to which Elizabeth Southern appears to have moved in her later years. Around the middle of the last century Jean Walton wrote of her native Newchurch and furnished a picture of the village in the 1890s, this picture evokes the atmosphere of the village and I have no hesitation in showing an extract here:[1]

Kirk Roads

▷ *To country people the roads are something more than highways linking one village with another. The road is an intimate part of their own life and the life of the people who dwell by its side. Those who speed along our country lanes can have no notion of the attachment a countryman has for his roads.*

The roads to Kirk are no main highways; no coach-and-four, no mail coach can be said to have traversed these narrow roads. But they have been used by men of the forest with their pack ponies, by the handloom weavers carrying their piece of finished cloth maybe to Colne or Burnley. Each piece of road has its own special name or perhaps takes the name of the men who have worked them. For instance the road to Burnley starts at Brook Lane, up Nanny Maude, then on't Top O' Hill, down Height Lane, Back Lane to Fence Top, turn left down Greenhead Lane to Pendle Bottom, up the steep Barden Lane and so to Colne Road, Burnley. All the roads leading to Kirk are steep and narrow, as one old worthy remarked, "Tha' needs good bellows (lungs) to get up ta' Kirk."

The cottage door that opens onto the road shares every sight and sound of the road. Strangers to the village are viewed discreetly from curtained windows with pungent sweet-smelling geraniums growing on the window sill to keep the outside world from looking in. Nothing is missed by country people for what goes on in the road is so much part of their lives. All good roads and lanes have names like Christian people, and all roads lead to the church at Kirk.

I was carried down the road to church on my Christening day, and have walked solemnly and proudly in processions on the Sunday School 'Walking Day.' I have jogged along that bit of road with my horse and trap; I have raced down it with my hoop and sledged on my home-made sledge in winter time. Happy childhood days I spent on the Kirk road; it was part of my home. There was no lack of company as you walked, or jogged along in a horse and trap on the road. There was the road-man, tapping with his long-handled hammer, the pieces of limestone to mend the road. There was the farmer slashing his hedgerows or building up a dry wall knocked down by sheep or cows. Travelling the road came the peddler with his wares wrapped in thin black oilcloth to protect them from wind and weather. The postman was friend and confidant of the village folk, even if he did read the postcards - a postman's privilege - he consoled with sorrowful news and shared the joys.

---

[1] Jean Walton, *Pendle Forest Folk*, (SP, Blacko, mid-20th c)

There were men and women going to the mill on the road; there was the local carrier; the farmer's carts; the baker who came to Kirk twice per week with bread and cakes. Well I remember the old wives saying they didn't know what the world was coming to when housewives bought their bread instead of getting some yeast and baking bread at home. My father bought us children a donkey and little cart and each Monday it was our pleasure and duty to go over to Field Top, Fence, where Old Mattock sold barm or yeast. It took us longer with the donkey and cart than it would have done had we walked through the fields for often we had to get out of the cart and push the donkey and cart up steep hills.

Nanny Maude, familiar to all Kirk folk, is a winding steep narrow road. Nanny Maude is supposed to be named after an old woman imbued with the powers of witchcraft who lived in the cottage at the Top O' Hill. Nanny, with her evil eye, would demand foodstuff and fuel from the village folk, and they dare not refuse for fear of her bewitching them.

Brook Loine, which starts and ends who knows where, has its tall banks and hedges that protect the traveller from wind and sun. I have picked sweet wild strawberries in Brook Loine and found lots of birds' nests. My father, Tom O' Quilla's big meadow ran all down one side of Brook Loine. I've brought the cows up that road to the shippon for milking; I've cut the thorn hedge; skipped in it and played in it; it's not just a road to me; it's part of the village, part of its history.

Sandy Lane, leading to Sabden Fold, serves the farms and cottages as it winds along. Sparble Lane, now merely a cow track, was once a well-used road to Wheatley Lane and Nelson. Up t' Bastille, the rocky short cut over to Barley, by Jim O' Beck's field, is lost and overgrown now. Jinny Loine, steep and winding, its hedges thick with blackberries and whinberries, is a direct road to Colne as the crow flies and probably one of the oldest forest roads. Jinny Well, where we used to carry our water from for drinking purposes, is a steep hard climb with two buckets of water; shoulders well braced and a steady walk, you arrived home with great satisfaction, not having spilt one drop of precious water.

So in memory, one travels the roads that lead to T' Kirk, and all the ghosts of the past greet one at each turning; each stile and hedgerow a memory. Customs have changed, people have changed, wars have swept the lands but the old roads remain the same, retaining their own personality; dear familiar roads trodden by the Pendle Forest folk for centuries. ◁

Whilst on the subject of ghosts, before we leave Jean's evocative memories of the western forest I must include a fascinating tale that was related to her in writing by a man (whom she names) who resided, as a child, at Thorneyholme House in the village of Roughlee;

'I was ten years of age, and it was my birthday. My brother, two years older than myself, and I, decided we would get up early on the morning of my birthday and go gathering mushrooms. 'We must start early,' said my brother, for it was a long way to the field where we knew the mushrooms grew. Picture then, two boys full of adventure, creeping down the stairs with our boots in our hands, so as not to wake our parents. It was barely daylight when we crossed the river and into the fields above Roughlee School. I cannot remember how many walls we climbed, how many fields we crossed. We were getting rather tired and very cross with each other, because so far we had found no mushrooms.' Suddenly we both halted, for there came a strange noise which seemed to be in front of us, and then again it might be behind us. We held each other's hands; just two frightened little boys, our spirit of adventure dead with fear and apprehension. The noise came nearer, and a very old woman with a shawl on her head came alongside of us pushing a wheelbarrow. In the wheelbarrow was something

alive, covered with an old sack. The old woman was breathing hard and noisily, and the squeak came from under the sack spasmodically. The old woman went straight on towards the wall, looking neither right nor left. There was no gate, no opening in the wall, but we both saw the woman and wheelbarrow disappear. My brother and I went to the wall; we touched it to make sure. 'She's gone through t' wall' we both said in unison, and two frightened boys turned and ran for home as fast as our legs would carry us. When we arrived home my mother was preparing breakfast. We told our story in a breathless way, our white faces portraying our fear. My father went with us later to the field where we had seen the old woman; there was no gate, no opening, just a blank wall. Well, that's my story; woman, witch or devil, we both saw her go through that wall.'

Goldshaw, within the Forest of Pendle, was an area within the far more ancient British kingdom of the Brigantes. The cast within the story that we have seen played out across the breadth of the parish of Whalley trod on the heels of a truly ancient culture; the early British religious and social practices were still evident within the early modern period of our story. Just as the hard-wired legacy of standing stones and burial mounds, left to us by our ancestors, tell their own tales of another world so did Demdike and Chattox as they called upon their inherited charms of folklore to heal the ailing stock of local farmers. Newchurch has its fair share of extant ancient features as will be seen in the following: [1]

'The moors around Pendle Hill have many hidden stones that are known only to the walker and the sheep farmer. In an article written in 1992 a local field archaeologist, John H Hope, made a number of interesting observations regarding Neolithic stone remains; Mr. Hope studied the area around his home of Newchurch-in-Pendle (SD 823 394) and found a number of standing stones. In the field behind the 'Witches Galore' shop (Up t'Bastille) are a couple of large stones, one taking the form of a stellae (an upright stone bearing ancient inscriptions or figures). If this is a genuinely early example then it is a very rare find within this area. The author also relates a story of the shop owner attempting to drive fence-posts into the ground behind the shop, when driven the posts disappeared into a void beneath the ground, this occurred over a wide enough area for him to postulate the presence of a chambered tomb beneath the field. Given the hillside site, the large amount of extant Neolithic remains in the immediate vicinity and the fact that the local millstone grit does not tend to form large chambers, this theory must hold some water. Around 2700 BC people of a similar culture to the Windmill Hill people of Wiltshire began to arrive in Britain, they brought with them the continental practice of erecting large megalithic structures and chambered tombs. It is pure conjecture, however, to assume that the Newchurch feature could be a consequence of the spread of the Windmill Hill people.

The remains of a double-ring stone circle still exits near to St. Mary's church in Newchurch, this can best be seen from the vantage-point of nearby Green Hill on Saddlers Height. Mr. Hope also identified probable examples of the burial practices of the Neolithic culture. Seven earthen long-barrows appear to be located at Black Bank, behind the woods above the former Lamb Inn (now a Bed-and-Breakfast establishment). At the time of writing his article Mr. Hope had not excavated these mounds but extant parallel ditches, and patches of burnt

---

[1] John A Clayton, *Valley of the Drawn Sword*, (Barrowford Press, 2006)

material brought to the surface by the action of moles, strongly suggests the presence of barrow burials. If these do indeed prove to be long-barrows then they are locally rare and would prove to be of great archaeological interest.'

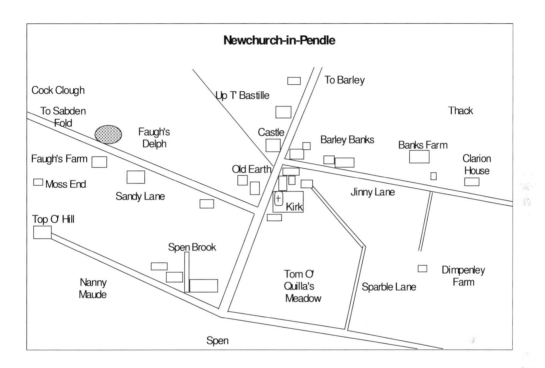

Newchurch-in-Pendle

Blacko

Writing his editorial for the Chetham Society publication of *The Wonderful Discoverie*, James Crossley said that;

'Baines confounds Malking-Tower with Hoar-stones, a place rendered famous by the second case of pretended witchcraft in 1633, but at some distance from the first-named spot, the residence of Mother Demdike, which lies in the township of Barrowford. The witch's mansion— is now, alas! no more. It stood in a field a little elevated, on a brow above the building at present called Malking-Tower. The site of the house or cottage is still distinctly traceable, and fragments of the plaster are yet to be found imbedded in the boundary wall of the field. The old road to Gisburn ran almost close to it. It commanded a most extensive prospect in front, in the direction of Alkincoates, Colne, and the Yorkshire moors; while in another direction the vast range of Pendle, nearly intercepted, gloomed in sullen majesty. At the period when Mother Demdike was in being, Malking-Tower would be at some distance from any other habitation; its occupier, as the vulgar would opine —

'So choosing solitarie to abide Far from all neighbours,
that her devilish deedes,
And hellish arts from people she might hide,
And hurt far off unknown whomever she envide.'

Harrison Ainsworth, in his *Lancashire Witches* of 1849, was responsible for the legend of Malkin Tower beeing seen by many who are only slightly familiar with story to be a brooding, soulless bastion of devilment. Ainsworth takes up his description of the Tower with great relish:

The Legend of Malkin Tower

On the brow of a high hill forming the range of Pendle...stands a stern and solitary tower. Old as the Anglo-Saxons, and built as a stronghold by Wulstan, a Northumbrian Thane, in the time of Edmund or Edred, it is in circular form and very lofty, serves as a landmark for the country around. Placed high up in the building the door was formerly reached by a steep flight of stone steps but these were removed by Mother Demdike, and a ladder, capable of being let down or raised, afforded the only apparent means of entrance. The tower is otherwise inaccessible, the walls of immense thickness, with no window lower than twenty-five feet from the ground.

Internally there are three floors, the lowest being on a level with the door and this apartment is occupied by the hag. In the centre of the room is a trap door opening onto a deep vault which is the basement story of the structure – once a dungeon but now tenanted by a fiend. Round the room runs a gallery in the thickness of the walls, upper chambers accessed by means of a secret staircase. All rooms lighted by narrow loopholes – the fortress is still capable of withstanding a siege.

On the Norman invasion Malkin was still held by Ughtred, a descendant of Wulstan, who kept possession of Pendle Forest and the hills around and resisted the aggressions of the conquerors. His enemies affirmed he was assisted by a demon, whom he had propriated by means of a fearful sacrifice in the tower, Ughtred was very cruel and tortured many in the tower where he kept much treasure obtained by pillage – he was the 'scourge of the Normans'. After the siege of York his destruction was vowed by Ilbert de Lacy who flushed Ughtred and his followers out of hiding in the forest by fire and drove them to Malkin Tower. De Lacy took the tower after much bloodshed and hanged Ughtred from the top of tower.

Blackburn had a liason with Isole de Heton at Whalley Abbey who bore him a daughter who was placed in the care of a peasant's wife at Barrowford. From that child sprung Bess Blackburn mother of Old Demdike.

Blackburn lived at Malkin with De Heton for five years but both were found dead. Thenceforth Malkin became haunted, even though the building was deserted lights were constantly seen and shrieks and groans heard. On stormy nights a huge black cat could be seen on the top of the tower whence it gained its name of Grimalkin, or Malkin tower. The ill-omened pile eventually came in to possession of the Nutter family, but was never tenanted until assigned to Mother Demdike.

Chapter Sixteen

Towers

That there was ever an actual structure worthy of the appellation *'Tower'* in the Malkin area is unclear; there is a suggestion that the description could have been an ironic title referring to the hovel in which Elizabeth Southern and her family lived. Further to this, Thomas Potts and the prosecution in the 1612 trials, made great play on the *'Tower'* description whenever possible in order to give the decidedly biased impression that meetings held at Malkin took place in a dangerous stronghold.–The apparent plot to blow up Lancaster Castle could only have been hatched by dangerous traitors and where else would these people be found other than in a fortified retreat? If this were to prove to be the case then this may well be the end of the search for Malkin Tower. However, evidence put forward in the following text shows that the name possibly applied to a tangible feature after which a neighbouring cottage took its name.

The appellation of *Tower* was often used as description for stone-built houses in the fifteenth and sixteenth centuries. At this time only higher-status building were erected in expensive stonework and even a small farmstead or house might have attracted the grand title of Tower. The larger stately-type houses, such as Houghton Tower, sit comfortably with the grand name and we would not begrudge them their title, especially as they actually expanded from a central defensive tower core. Another fortified gentry house known as Hapton Tower, on the outskirts of Burnley, was once the home of Richard Towneley and his wife, Jane Assheton. When a smaller farmhouse carries the name it is slightly more difficult not to bring to mind the term *'Fir coat and no knickers!'* This is somewhat unfair, however, as there was often a sound reason for the building carrying the name tower; some buildings of the early modern period carried on with the earlier architectural style of placing a circular tower on one gable of the property in order to accommodate an external spiral staircase. This was the case with Hodge House in Marsden and at Bearnshaw Tower Farm near Todmorden. This latter was sited on an old packhorse route on the hillside above Cornholme, a very similar topographical position to that occupied by the Malkin property in Blacko. Unfortunately the local people of Cornholme took it upon themselves to search for the buried treasure said to lie beneath the Bearnshaw stair-tower and the edifice collapsed in 1860.

Pele (Peel) Towers were originally a form of fortified farmhouse built in the northern border areas of England. Designed to repel the frequent Scottish raids of the fourteenth and fifteenth centuries these square structures were usually free-standing but were often extended into large gentry houses as the threat of invasion decreased. Hellifield Pele, near Gisburn, is an excellent local example of this latter practice although the extended buildings were demolished leaving the original ruined tower in situ. In the Pendle Forest a number of smaller houses of the yeomanry were referred to locally as 'Tower' but have now been lost. We have met with Jennet Ingham and Sir John Towneley previously; the offspring of this union was Margaret who married Laurence Habergham around 1562. The son of this marriage, Richard, married Margaret, the daughter of Nicholas Hancock of *Higham Tower* in 1604. This provides us with a tenuous link between Demdike (on the Ingham side) and the property called Higham Tower; although it is a long-shot there is the thought that when Demdike moved to her small Malkin dwelling the local people knew of her distant relationship to the gentry and named her abode *Tower* in an accordingly ironic manner.

Related to the defensive nature of the tower, but intended as more as an early-warning system, was the *watchtower*. The use of this type of structure descends into the mists of time; the Bible has many references to watchtowers being used as posts where lookouts were stationed in order to watch out for the approach of any enemy. Shepherds used watchtowers to oversee their flocks and they often protected large areas of growing crops from thieves. The Tower, then, is easily recognised but what of the origin of *'watch?'* Strong's Concordance shows this word as; *4929; mishmar (mish-mawr'); from 8104; a guard (the man, the post, or the prison); 8104 shamar (shaw-mawr'); a primitive root; properly, to hedge-about (as with thorns), i.e. guard; generally, to protect, attend to, beware, be circumspect, take heed (to self), keep (-er self), mark, look narrowly, observe, preserve, regard, reserve, save (self), sure, (that lay) wait (for), watch (-man).* The archaic translation *mish-mawr* raises the possibility of watch (*mawr - mawr-kin = watch-like*) with *tower* hence *Mawrkin Tower.*

Blacko Tower

There is little wonder that Blacko Tower has often been confused with Malkin Tower. Standing aloft at one-thousand feet on the summit of Blacko Hill (photograph left) the tower appears to have been in its landmark position since the dawn of time. In actual fact the tower was erected by Jonathan Stansfield in 1890 and was usually referred to as *Jonathan's Tower* or *Stansfield's Folly*. Jonathan Stansfield was born in Colne and married a girl named Ellen who was from nearby Nelson; they moved to Barrowford and had a number of children who were all born in the village. The couple lived in Back John Street and ran a grocery and drapery shop in neighbouring David Street. In 1865 Jonathan ran the Old Mill in the Park (Barrowford) along with his brother James but the family lost money on the venture. Nothing daunted, Jonathan started again and re-built his business interests in the village. The Stansfield brothers built a number of the properties in central Barrowford, notably the ones on Gisburn Road surrounding the old Bowling Green and overlooking the park. In later life Jonathan bought Old House Farm and One Tree Farm, the former property is now known as Tower Farm on whose land the Blacko Tower was erected.[1]

When asked why he actually built the tower Jonathan replied that his original intention was for the building to be of sufficient height to enable him to see across White Moor and into the

---

[1] Jesse Blakey, *Annals and Stories of Barrowford*, (SP, Nelson, 1929)

neighbouring Ribblesdale/West Craven district of Yorkshire. The reason for this is often quoted as having been due to Jonathan's wish to see the county in which his wife was born; as we have seen, however, Ellen was a Lancashire lass and this refutes the story somewhat!

The structure of the building was such that the tower reached its optimum safe height before the extended view became possible. Jonathan is quoted as having said *"I've never drunk or smoked in my life, so am making this as my hobby."* It would not be surprising if part of the reason for building the tower was that Jonathan had read Ainsworth's *Lancashire Witches* and, having absorbed the legend of Malkin Tower, wished to provide the area with his own version. There is also the fact that the landmark structure of Blacko Tower has provided a long-lasting memorial to its builder and this would have been intentional. Jonathan's grandson says that his grandfather always maintained that his intention had indeed been to see into Ribblesdale; this information, along with Blakey's primary source information, appears to settle the matter.

Jonathan Stansfield lived to enjoy his tower for four years as, in 1894, he died at the age of seventy-one. Jonathan's friend, the Reverend E. Gough of Barrowford, had a poetical bent and was prone to wax lyrical on almost any subject connected to his adopted village of Barrowford. Never one to miss an opportunity Reverend Gough penned a poem entitled 'Blacko Tower,' of which the following is the first verse:

> *Friend Stansfield pleased his fancies*
> *With Blacko Tower so high,*
> *That draws admiring glances*
> *From every passer by.*
> *E'en if no other token*
> *His lasting fame secures,*
> *His name will be outspoken*
> *Long as that tower endures*

The south-eastern area of Blacko Hillside on which the Malkin area falls is a relatively untouched site, the ancient holly and thorn hedges, boundary ditches and dykes show a continuity of occupation across the whole area that would stretch back at least to the Anglo-Saxon era. There are earthworks, extant medieval holly *ringyard* fences and worked stones in the field walls.[1] Aerial photographs indicate the presence of early circular features within the area and the fact that Malkin rests against two major ancient boundaries lends an atmosphere of antiquity to the place. Ancient earthen banks still survive, often topped with stones or the ubiquitous thorn hedges and when we couple this facet of Malkin with the *shaw-mawr* idea of *'hedged about'* it is worth considering the mystery that is the Malkin Thorn.

There is no doubt that the lone figure cut by the Malkin Thorn immediately attracts the attention; there is also no doubting the fact that the tree is very old. The mystery of the matter is why the tree was originally cultivated in isolation and why it has survived for such a long period of time. The cutting or harming of thorn trees has always been accepted amongst country people as being an invitation to disaster. The *'fairy tree'* as the thorn is sometimes known, had many ethereal uses along with its excellent farm stock-repelling qualities. There is every possibility,

---

[1] *Ringyard* fences were the stock-proof hedges and fences erected to enclose farmsteads or to protect crops from livestock and were a legal requirement

therefore, that the Malkin example once formed part of a network of hedgerows, possibly in the form of the *shaw-mawr;* as the population expanded into the late medieval period it may be the case that these hedges were removed in order to cultivate more crops. When the farm workers were cutting the thorn hedges they would have been aware that they were inviting all kinds of supernatural ills upon themselves and therefore they may have left this solitary tree as a sop to the spirits of nature. In the Fence area of Hoarstones another example of this type of walled-tree

exists, in this case the tree is an ancient holly.

The Malkin Thorn

Further to the *watchtower* theme, following the creation of the Forest of Pendle, it was common practice to station forest *'drivers'* at strategic points around the forest boundaries. The reason for this was so that the deer could be contained within the forest and also the driver would ensure that poachers and the like did not enter from outside. The area of Malkin was one such place, the driver stationed here had the responsibility of policing the north-eastern forest boundary where it came hard against the western Yorkshire boundary. Some forest drivers had the use of timber watchtowers in order to facilitate a wider view of their part of the forest; it is worth asking, therefore, whether there had been such a tower on Blacko Hill from which Malkin acquired its famous descriptive?

Another entirely feasible explanation for the name is that, as we have seen, it is likely that Malkin was glebe land, held of Whalley Abbey via the Colne chapel. Although the chantry priests were almost always unskilled poor people the incumbent priests had a tendency towards the grand. They often gave themselves the appellation of 'Sir' and wished their properties to reflect their assumed stature. It was common, therefore, for their houses to be built, or adapted, to appear of a relatively high-status. To this end the clerics often applied to the authorities for a *'crenulation licence'* in order to add battlements to their houses, the smaller ones were pale imitations of the larger, genuinely fortified houses. Monasteries, churches and granges defended against raids but their buildings were generally the larger residences of a religious community. Bishop's castles and priest's towers were considered as private residences; if a property of this status were to have been located at Malkin then it would not be surprising to hear the local people calling the building a 'tower'. However, given the lack of evidence (both written and archaeological) this is highly unlikely.

The suggestion that there are closes called Malkin Fields at Saddlers Farm in Newchurch is not corroborated by primary source material but there is a field there known as Kiln Field. There is the possibility that m*alt kiln* has changed to *malkin* over the years; many farms had their own malt kiln for the drying of grain and the larger structures often resembled towers. There is no evidence in the Malkin area for the existence of a kiln but there is good evidence for there having been a mill of sorts at the neighbouring Burnt House Farm. Andrew Turner, of

Malkin Tower Farm, says that he recently helped to cover an old wheel-pit under the floor of the Burnt House farmhouse; the stream that flows down Blacko Hillside, from the Black Dyke, runs beneath the farm and it would appear that a former structure on this site would have housed a water-wheel. Historian Stanley Graham, of Barnoldswick, has carried out a good deal of work translating the 1581 White Moor Map and it is clear from this that on the ridge of Blacko Hill, where the Black Dyke meets the old county boundary dyke, there is a point marked as Blacko Mill. Stanley is an authority on water power and together we have inspected the area; that there are water-related groundworks at the end of the Black Dyke there is no doubt but there is no evidence for there having been a water mill on this site. However, this heavily disturbed ground carries the western Black Dyke stream down to Burnt House, the water could also be directed to the east from the Black Dyke and this forms the east Blackbrook, this stream being the eastern Pendle Forest boundary. The Blacko Mill, marked on the 1581 map, could very well relate, therefore, to a tower-like mill structure replaced by the present Burnt House and again we have the faint possibility of the tower appellation being referred to at Malkin – in other words, the presence of a tower in the general area led to that description being tagged on to the other main feature on the Blacko Hill – Mawkin Hole.

Mawken

With regard to the dichotomy of opinion as to exactly where the Malkin Tower was located, Newchurch or Blacko, it is suggested that there is now sufficient evidence to show a strong case for the latter. The first source for this is that of the Clitheroe court rolls;

1508-09: *To this halmote came Christopher Diconson (steward) and surrendered one garden called* **Malkenyerd** *with the appurtenances in Colne to the use of John Hegyn, chantry priest...... granted.*

1564: *John Foulds surrenders part of a garden called* **Mawkynyarde** *lying in the north end of Colne to Christopher Dyconson for a yearly rent.*

The description of this latter property as being *'in the north end of Colne'* relates to the northern edge of the parish, this is the location of Malkin Tower Farm at Blacko and is almost certainly the same property referred to in 1508/9. We have, then, a firm reference to the site that would later become Malkin. The *'yard'* description would not apply to a farm as this would have been given as a *'messuage'*; yard meant enclosure. The fact that the earlier surrender of 1508-09 mentions that the yard called *Malken* had *appurtenances* attached means that the Malken garden enclosure had the rights over neighbouring lands such as peat-digging and water-extraction. We have, then, a record of the smallholding that was Malken being transferred to the use of the Colne incumbent in 1508-09 in order for him to receive the rental income thereof. Christopher Dickinson was the Colne area steward at the time and was therefore acting in his official capacity in the granting of Malken to Higgin. By the time of the later record of 1564 we see that John Foulds, who I take to have been a churchwarden of Colne, transferring the Malken site back to Christopher Dickinson – whether this was the same man who appeared in the earlier surrender is unclear although I would guess that we might be seeing father and son. The later surrender of 1564 is post-*Dissolution of the Monasteries* and post-*Dissolution of the Chantries* and this would suggest that the former church land of Malken is being returned onto the open market. Unfortunately we do not see Malken being mentioned again directly by name until the trials of 1612.

The next piece of evidence relating to the site of Malkin Tower presents itself in the form of an estate map. The deeds of Malkin Tower Farm were only created in the early nineteenth century when the farm property was separated from the extended holdings in the Stone Edge area belonging to the Clitheroe Estates. The estate map of the Malkin area marks the field immediately to the east of Malkin Tower Farm as Mawkin Hole Field.

The Celtic languages of the British continued to be used up to the coming of the Anglo-Saxon peoples whose numbers were made up of Jutes, Angles, Southern Danes and natives of Jutland. Early Indo-European culture spread across Europe and with it came the beginnings of a variety of modern languages. The Germanic language of the Saxons had its roots in the Elbe River region around 3000 years ago, apart from a distant common origin the Celtic and Germanic languages have very little in common. The *Old English* language of the Saxons is ascribed roughly to the period AD500 to the Norman Conquest of AD1066, this language did not assimilate the Celtic language. This is possibly because of racial/ethnic arrogance by the Saxons or perhaps the native Britons were more adept at learning English than the Anglo-Saxons were at learning the indigenous Celtic language. The Old English language gave way to Middle English at the end of the eleventh century and Modern English took centre stage around AD 1500.

The Saxon invaders pushed the *core* of Celtic speaking peoples out of what is now England (although modern genetic tests prove that this was by no means as widespread as once thought) into Scotland, Wales, Cornwall and Ireland, the only one of these regions not to have an extant Celtic language today is Cornwall, the last native speaker having died in 1777. This gradual cut-off in the use of Celtic landscape descriptions provides a useful etymological tool for dating purposes. Although the majority of place, and topographical names, have been left to us from the Saxon, Scandinavian and Norman eras, we do have a small number of Celtic names that can be readily ascribed to the older Welsh language. This method of dating is certainly not foolproof as the etymology of our native languages is extremely complex, the adoption of known languages within a specific timeframe does allow room for the 'educated guess' however. The geography of our area can be seen as a good reason for our local population to have remained insular; the local inhabitants were still largely of an Iron Age culture at the coming of the Saxons and would therefore retain the traditional British descriptions of their environment.

Slightly to the north of Malkin Tower Farm (SD 866 424) is a large hollow feature shown as Heynslack on the 1581 map and Mawkin Hole on the Malkin property deeds; this hollow is large enough to accommodate a small cathedral. The two terms of Heynslack and Mawkin Hole appear to emanate from different periods within our history although they both exactly describe the topography of the site. The hollow is funnel-shaped with the narrow mouth to the east, it is situated hard up against the ancient Lancashire-Yorkshire County boundary along which the Black Dyke stream flows. In the bottom of this hollow, at the northern end, is a natural spring and this has the appearance of having been walled around at some point in the past. The site falls within the very north-eastern-most corner of the Forest of Pendle. The Heynslack name has two derivations; the first is from the Saxon where *'haie'* means *'a hedged place.'* The Norse word *'slack'* is commonly used in our area for a description of *'a hollow – especially on a hillside.'* As a matter of interest there are not many other instances of Heyn Slack within the area (there are many Slacks); one is at Black Lane Ends, Colne and the another at Robin Hood's House (Red Spa Moor) on the slopes of Boulsworth Hill - each of these examples falls immediately adjacent to the Lancashire and Yorkshire boundary. From this it is possible to deduce that the name Heynslack usually refers to a hollow feature on a boundary, the boundary actually being the *'hein'* or fence. This is also reflected in the name of Blacko, the archaic spelling of this was *Blakey* from *black-hey* or *haie* signifying that this area has been a major boundary over a long period. There is also a suggestion that Blacko stems from *black-howe* or *black-hill* and this cannot be ruled out; however, boundary features were often of paramount importance when it came to the naming of sites.

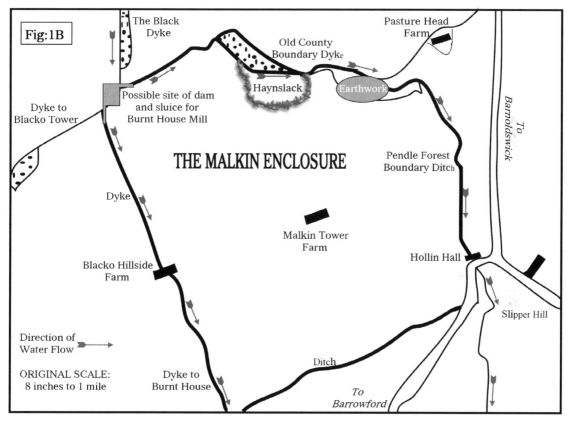

Fig: IB shows the extended area of Malkin as delineated by early (Anglo-Saxon?) boundary/enclosure dykes, ditches and walled-bankings

Aerial photography shows that the outer lip of the large hollow of Heynslack has been 'thrown-up,' in other words it appears to have a man-made banking around the rim. This could very well have supported a wooden paling fence running around the perimetre of the hollow and thus providing an excellent enclosed area in which to hold animals. The fencing could have originated in the Norman period when the forest was a deer-hunting ground; we know that a forest driver was stationed here and it was common practice to provide enclosed areas within the forest parks, with gaps (or leaps) in the fencing, to allow deer to enter the enclosure but not escape. Enclosures for holding livestock were also used from the Neolithic period and this hollow feature, ideal for the purpose, could possibly have had a long continuity of use.

The other *'hay'* or *'heyn'* connotation is from the Scandinavian *'heyne'* meaning *'a body of fresh water.'* This is also interesting as the funnel shape of the hollow would easily hold a large amount of water, a small dam across the mouth would enable the stream running through the hollow to fill the feature to at least a few metres in depth. This would form a shallow lake with enough depth to act as (say) a fishery.

As a matter of passing interest at this point, it is worth mentioning another possible origin of the name Malkin - *Maelecan* is a double diminutive of a Celtic word with the meaning of *'shaven one'* suggested to have been commonly applied to monks. Malkin had an ecclesiastic attachment from at least the fourteenth century but this does not tally with the early etymology; to qualify for the Celtic appellation of *Maelecan* the site would have been a British ecclesiastical site assimilated by the Saxons into their own language, from whence it passed into the later Middle English.

Mawr is a common word in Welsh and is often associated with topographical features such as hills (Bryn Mawr), here it means *'great.'* By the time of the Saxons the word *maw* had replaced the Old English word *'maga'* which had the meaning of *'stomach'* or *'open mouth'* – figuratively this gave a description of *'yawning chasm,'* an extremely apt name for our hollow. Moving into the Middle English we have an explanation for the term *Maw-kin* in *'gaping-like'* and *hole* meant *'a hollow'*, hence we have the accurate topographical description of *'Gaping Hole.'*

There is a suggestion that *maw* could have been the name of a Welsh prince and *'kin'* can be taken as *'of the family'* or *'like.'* The word *'kin'* was also commonly used as a diminutive and would, within the context of *'prince,'* have the meaning of *'little prince'* or *'of a princely family.'* In this case the name of Mawkin would suggest an early memory where the area could have been ruled by a branch of minor local royalty or tribal chieftains. Further to this, Admergill is a settlement at the foot of Blacko Hill and could be named after a prince named *Aed Maw* giving us *Aed Maw's Gill*; this appears to be rather fanciful, however, as there are sound etymological reasons for *Admergill* meaning *Boundary Mound by the Stream.* [1]

The Yorkshire Dales village of Malham has variously been referred to as *Mal-holme, Malk-olme, Mall-home, Mal-um, Maw-lam* and *Mawm* [2] whilst there are boundary stones on the moors between Colne and Haworth carrying the name Maw Stones. Maw was a popular card game imported to England from Ireland in the sixteenth century and in the seventeenth century a *mawkin* was a doll; this was used by parishes in certain southern counties for their May Day festivals. This also crops up in the name of *mawkin* as applied to a scarecrow in the Midlands. The description of *Mawken Yard* is found in other parts of the country along with *Mawkin Hole* and *Mawkin Field*. There is a *Malkin* area in Bury, *Malkin Ees* in Whalley and *Mawkinhurst* in Lathom.

In Scotland the word *Malkin* described an awkward or ungainly girl whilst the English commonly applied it as a derogatory term for a sluttish woman. There is also a medieval meaning of *maukin* that applies to the act of animal breeding, an archaic poem (too flowery to reproduce here) describes the mating practice of the deer and this has connotations of the earlier suggestion that Mawkin Hole was used as an animal coral in the forest – there is here the hint of a deer stock-breeding operation on the Blacko Hillside.

A *malkin* was also the term applied to a bundle of rags tied to the end of a long stick and used

---

[1] John A Clayton, *Valley of the Drawn Sword,* (Barrowford Press, 2006)
[2] T.D. Whitaker, *The History of Craven,* (1885)

to clean out the barrels of ship's cannon or bread ovens. Shakespeare used *malkin* to describe a cat (more commonly *Gray-Malkin*) and in the northern counties *malkin* could describe a hare; *malkin-mad* became *mad-as-a-March-hare*. *Malkin-trash* described a person in dark gloomy clothing. Finally we see yet again a possible link between the word *mawkin* and boundary features as the Old English *mearcian* means 'mark out' or 'mark a boundary.'

The Malkin appellation was certainly not confined to our subject area; in sixteenth century Staffordshire two closes of land were called *Malkin Gorweys* and land in Swinnerton was shown as *The Malkin*. In 1762 Jowett House, in Sheffield, had a four-acre field called *Malkin Croft* and Marshfield, in Gloucester, had a *Malkin Lane*. Betchton, in Cheshire, has a salt-works known as *Malkins Bank* and at Kerdiston, in Norfolk, there was a *Malkin Farm*. Nottingham had a number of examples of the name amongst which were *Malkin Lane,* in Sherwood Forest, *Malkin House,* at Newland and the *Malkin Hills,* at Shelford.

Malkin Mill?

> *Malkin's Tower, a little cottage, where*
> *Reporte makes caitive witches meete to swear*
> *Their homage to ye devil*

The Reverend Richard James, Fellow of Oxford, visited Pendle at the time of the 1633 trials and wrote the above description of Malkin Tower in a first-hand account. He also said *'Whatever the truth may be, those poor wretches find pittie and apologie from manye.'* Within these words there is an accurate contemporary report of the type of dwelling occupied by Demdike and the emotions of the forest people following the 1612 and 1633 trials. Malkin Tower, described by James as having been a little cottage suggests that the dwelling house of the Demdike and Device families was a worker's cottage.

This raises the possibility that Demdike's cottage stood upon the Malken Garden enclosure. Other sites have been suggested; recently the foundations of a large circular stone structure upon a mound were partially excavated in the Admergill area. That particular site, although of great archaeological interest, is outside of the Pendle Forest boundary and this, taken in tandem with the need for Mawken Yard to fall within the parish of Colne, leads to the conviction that the present Malkin Tower Farm will not be very far away from our objective.

Somewhere, then, within the area of Blacko Hillside/Mawken Garden was a structure whose appearance at least afforded the name of *Tower.* We have seen that this appellation could have been applied to a number of types of structure but one that we have not yet considered is the mill. The siting of a mill depended upon a singular necessity and that was the provision of water. On the moors above Blacko Hill is the watershed known as Weets Hill; from its heights this area sends its drainage streams in all four directions of the compass. In the medieval period water from Weets arrived upon Blacko Hillside via White Moor and the Black Dyke and as the farming operations grew around the Malkin area so the water supply to them became ever-more complex. The key to the whole system in this area is the Black Dyke Nook where, as we have seen, the White Moor Map shows that a mill of sorts existed in 1581. The gathering of water at this spot would enable a burst of supply to be sent to any one of the farms of the Stone Edge estate i.e.; the Stone Edge Farmsteads, Beverley, Burnt House, Blacko Hillside, Cross Gates

Farm, Malkin, Hollin Hall, Flaight Moor, Cockpit Hill and Wanless. By a system of sluices at Black Dyke Nook and Burnt House the water could be diverted as and where necessary.

The following court roll is of interest here: 1557: *William Lister of Middop, York, allowed Lawrence Blackey to use water from the field used by John Watson.* The field used by John Watson was the Lister land through which the Black Dyke ran; the Stone Edge estate was being granted rights to divert the Black Dyke water for their own use. This record probably pinpoints the time when the sluice system at the Black Dyke Nook were created and the purpose of this might even have been that Lawrence Blakey was building the Blacko Mill in this area.

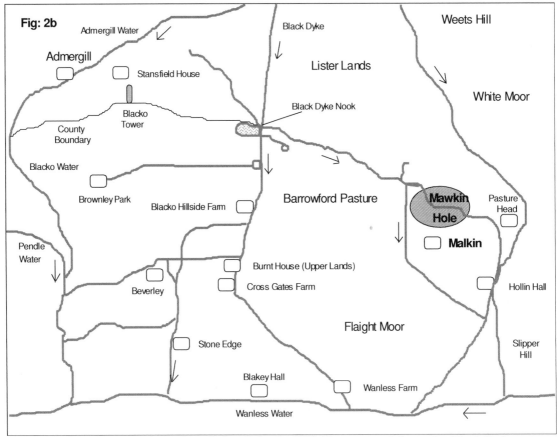

The water supply to the whole of Blacko Hillside stemmed from the Black Dyke

With reference to Figure:2b there are three main points of interest in relation to there having been an important water-related building in the area; these are the Black Dyke Nook, Hollin Hall and Burnt House. We have seen that a site was named as *Blacko Mill* on the 1581 map and a field-study of this site does indeed hint at there having been a structure of sorts here. Directly to the south of this site the main watercourse was directed to Burnt House where we know a wheel-pit existed. To the south-east of the Black Dyke sluice the stream that is the Pendle Forest boundary runs by the present small row of cottages known as Hollin Hall. This site is surrounded by traces of extant medieval stonework within the dry-stone walls and the

274

appellation of 'Hall' does not sit comfortably with the present properties; it is likely therefore that a substantial structure stood here within the medieval period. Furthermore, any building on this site would have had the advantage of the watercourses flowing through it and a study of the modern map shows that the road forms a pronounced *'S'* bend so as to divert around the site; this is a sure sign of there having been an important feature here in antiquity.

To sum up this thread I would suggest that the Malkin *Tower* structure lay within the triangle of possible sites formed by Black Dyke Nook, Hollin Hall and Burnt House; any of these could well have contained a building whose primary use was to dry or grind corn or to full the locally-produced woollen cloth pieces. One of these sites, then, could have provided the *tower* whose description the Mawken Garden cottages adopted – Mawken was a large hole in the ground; the *Tower* would have been a relatively large structure and between them they dominated the whole of the southern Blacko Hillside.

In Nottingham a record of particular interest shows that in 1630 there was *'a close adjoining the mill at Sookholme called Malkin Yard'*; in 1652 this was offered for sale as a cottage and two acre close called Maukin Yard. The fact that Malkin Yard in Sookholme was next to a mill raises the interesting possibility that the term Malkin was, for some reason, applied to mill-related sites; further to this we have the old description whereby a miller was known as a *molendarius*. The Old English word *ing (yng)* was used to describe a meadow and survives in many place-names to this day; coupling *mole* with *ing* would provide us with *'moleing'* for *'mill field'* and this is not far removed phonetically from *mawkin*. Even more apposite to our purpose would be the coupling of *mole* with the word *kin (of/ of the family/like)* thus giving the name *molekin;* we would then have the meaning *'of the mill'* and *Malkin Tower* would be the *Mill Tower*. This brings us back to the water sites proffered above and strengthens the argument for the Malkin Tower having indeed been a type of structure related to the operation of a water-powered mill.

The Blacko Hill actually stood higher than its present one-thousand feet until heavy quarrying operations, in the eighteenth and nineteenth centuries, sliced away the conical summit. The high dry-stone walling that snakes over the ridge of Blacko Hill formed the old Lancashire and Yorkshire county boundary and contains a large amount of worked building stone; many of these stones are too large to have been from a cottage type of structure and it is tempting to suggest that they originated in a substantial building. Furthermore, these stones are located within the immediate vicinity of the site marked as Blacko Mill on the Whitemoor map. This may in fact be the case but there is a major caveat in that the whole length of the walling (hundreds of metres) that incorporates the worked stone is adjacent to the Blacko Hill quarry. No other walls within the extended area contain this type of worked stone and it is possible that it came no further than from the bottom of the quarry; the stones were perhaps originally destined for the building of a local cotton mill but for some reason ended their lives as rejects within the field walls.

The famous mythologist and folklorist, Dr. J. G. Frazer, said that *"I have changed my views repeatedly, and I have resolved to change them again with every change of the evidence."* The researcher must play the chameleon upon the shifting colours of freshly turned-up ground; and so things have proved to be within the search for Malkin Tower. There is no doubt that new evidence will be forthcoming to either bolster the argument for the ruined structure behind Malkin Tower Farm having been Demdike's dwelling or to show equally valid evidence for an alternative site. Until such proof to the contrary is forthcoming I accept this site as being the most likely by far. This allows for the indulgence of standing before the doorway of the ruin and allowing the images of the past to drift into mind; the hustle and bustle of family life, people and animals flit in and out of the scene, children laughing, shouting and (more often) crying. Neighbours calling and lifting the latch of the door that once filled this ruined gap to divulge the latest gossip of the forest. Finally, the last sounds of tragedy as the ominous hoof-beats of authority thundered up to this gap-in-the-wall and escorted the cottage's bewildered inhabitants into the August air. The long-lost door closed for the final time when Elizabeth, Alison and James Device were incarcerated in a stinking dungeon many hostile miles away from their home. Would that door ever close tight on the laughter and tears of a family ever again?

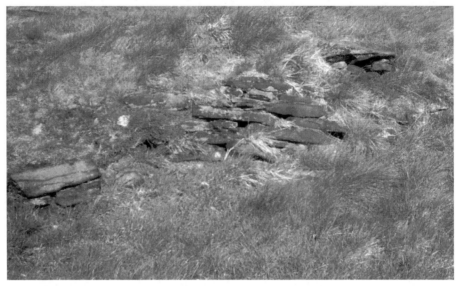

Demdike's Dwelling?
The remains of the possible cottage structure immediately to the rear of Malkin Tower Farm

The oldest part of the farm complex at Malkin is the farmhouse, probably erected by the Towneley family in the early eighteenth century. A barn was added to the house at a later date and, in the first part of the nineteenth century, John Hargreaves built the western barn onto the end of that intermediate structure in 1860. This later building contains a great deal of reclaimed building stone and it would be of great interest to know where this came from originally; the stone would no doubt have come from a demolition site within a reasonably local area. There is the germ of an idea here that the stone might have originated in the Malkin Tower and, if this indeed proved to be the case, the quality of the worked stone suggests that the donor building was of a higher-status than we might expect in a lowly cottage or half-timbered barn.

Continuing the search in the Malkin area we see that on the brow of the hill, above the farm, is a length of worked stone incorporated into the dry-stone field wall. This part of the field wall is far higher than the rest and the stone is of better quality than the surrounding walling-stone. Traces of lime mortar can still be seen within the stonework; the site would certainly have lent itself to a building as this is a level area on the otherwise sloping hillside. There is the possibility that the site could have contained a small out-barn or field-barn for the use of Malkin Farm lower down the slope. However, having said all that there is no doubt that this length of wall is not an extant gable from a demolished building, the random construction and lack of any perpendicular quoins suggests that the 'gable' was erected simply as a free standing wall. Further to this John Holt, who owned Malkin Tower Farm in the later nineteenth century, was said to have erected this length of wall in memory of the Malkin Tower legend.

The Malkin 'Gable'

This, however, does not preclude there ever having been a building on this part of the Malkin lands, far from it in fact. The worked stones that have been incorporated into the gable came from somewhere and, as people did not carry stone very far when building walls, the source of this stone is likely to have been a demolished local building. Another clue here is that traces still remain of a flagged footpath to this site, this path ran from the top of Slipper Hill Lane via Hollin Hall and up through the Mawkin Hole Field straight to the gable. Below the gable, in the Heynslack/Mawkin Hole hollow, is another site of interest, here a levelled area on the hillside was served by a metalled trackway, part of which still survives. Again, this is suggestive of a lost building but yet again, because this site is just on the Yorkshire side of the old county boundary, we are not looking at a building within Pendle Forest. This particular area, in the hollow of Mawkin Hole, was a place into which the local farmers would not venture; Stanley Graham relates that he once worked on the farm to which the Yorkshire part of the hollow belonged and none of the farm staff, including the farmer, would go down into the hollow. This was also the case with other farmers within the area, the hollow held a definite influence over local people.

A short distance to the east of the gable is another feature of great interest, this is a large earthen mound with all the appearance of having been man-made although there is the possibility that the mound is an extant glacial drumlin; whatever the origins of this mound might be the fact remains that the top has been levelled. The mound describes a perfect semi-circle when seen from the air; the northern edge drops steeply into the stream forming the Pendle Forest boundary and would have been highly defensive. Over this stream, long-buried beneath centuries of undergrowth, can be found the stone footings of an old bridge, this once carried a track over the stream and onto the centre of the levelled mound platform. There was obviously a reason for this and it is highly possible that a building of some description stood on this elevated site. This site has all the hallmarks of having been the site of a raised defensive/warning feature and the notion of a watchtower, as discussed earlier, springs to mind. This mound is located in Mawkin Hole Field and is within the boundary of the Pendle Forest.

The levelled mound in Mawkin Hole Field

When it comes to the location of Demdike's dwelling, however, by far the most interesting is situated where one might have expected it to be in the first place, at Malkin Tower Farm. On a levelled plateau immediately to the rear of the original farm building we find the tantalising ruins of what appears to have been a cottage. Only the bottom metre or so of the original stonework has survived and this has been almost buried by the down-shift of soil from the hillside above; there is, however, enough evidence to provide the outline of the building. This building would in all probability have been a thatched cottage whose lower walls were of semi-worked stone. Of single-storied construction the cottage would have contained at least one bed-chamber, a working/cooking area and a living area containing a fire-hearth. When Bessie Whittle was accused of stealing from Malkin Tower she was said to have broken *'into the firehouse,'* this term was used in order to separate the living quarters of a house from the working areas and it was also commonly applied to a dwelling set amongst other farm or commercial buildings; in other words the dwelling would have been described as the *firehouse* in order to distinguish the property from a nearby barn, shippon, mill or loom-shop.

The impression gleaned from reading the statements accorded to James Device is that he appears to separate his own dwelling from that of his grandmother, Demdike. There is no good reason to assume that this was not the case, there was perhaps more than one property on the Malkin site. There could well have been a barn structure on the levelled site that now contains the Malkin Tower Farm property as recent structural work within the farmhouse has revealed a number of roofing beams that were taken from an earlier structure. This was common practice when timber building were being replaced by stone buildings, any reclaimable timbers were used in order to save on the cost, and short-supply, of new ones. Incorporated into the door and window lintels at Malkin are timbers that could well have been part of the original fifteenth-century buildings and it does not take a huge leap of faith to imagine Elizabeth Southern, sitting beneath these timbers, huddled over the fire on a howling winter's night! The following is taken from James Device's statement and is relevant to the Malkin site:

The sayd Examinate Iames Deuice sayth, that about a month agoe, as this Examinate was comming towards his Mothers house, and at day-gate of the same night, this Examinate mette a browne Dogge comming from his Graund-mothers house, about tenne Roodes distant from

278

the same house: and about two or three nights after, that this Examinate heard a voyce of a great number of Children screiking and crying pittifully, about day-light gate; and likewise, about ten Roodes distant of this Examinates sayd Graund-mothers house. And about fiue nights then next following, presently after daylight, within 20. Roodes of the sayd Elizabeth Sowtherns house, he heard a foule yelling like vnto a great number of Cattes: but what they were, this Examinate cannot tell. And he further sayth, that about three nights after that, about midnight of the same, there came a thing, and lay vpon him very heauily about an houre, and went then from him out of his Chamber window, coloured blacke, and about the bignesse of a Hare or Catte.

We see from this that James made a distinction between his *Mother's house* and his *Graund-mother's house;* reading between the lines the dwellings, if indeed James does refer to two separate properties, must have been in the same area as James relates the *foul yelling* to both his Grandmother's house and the house in which he slept. The descriptions that James gave of children skreiking (an archaic term still used today) and the fowl yelling of a great number of cats is not as fanciful or ridiculous as it might at first appear. The awful noise reported by young Device was within *20 roodes* of Elizabeth Southern's house and this distance tallies exactly with the distance from Malkin Farm to the massive hollow of Mawkin Hole. This place would have been an ideal breeding area for feral cats due to its secluded and sheltered situation. The evening, or *daylight-gate,* would have been particularly noisy when a colony of wild cats began to exercise their tonsils, especially as Mawkin Hole is a superb natural amphitheatre with the ability to amplify sound. Furthermore, it is interesting to learn that there are still wild cats breeding in the immediate area of Malkin although today they have the luxury of large cattle sheds in which to live instead of the Mawkin Hole; did an ancestor of one these modern feral felines, in search of warmth, once leap onto James Device whilst he slept in his bedchamber at Malkin?

The salient fact relating to James's report of screeching and fowl noises is that the county folk of that time often spoke of a supernatural sound known as the *Gabriel Ratchets*. This term was used in association with exactly the sound heard by James Device, the child-like howling of cats, the distant screeching of a family of barn owls, the wind howling through a grove of trees; these were the sounds of restless spirits and the term *Gabriel Ratchets* described them all. An interesting contemporary description of this is where, in the reign of Charles II, strange lights were reported above the town of Bolton, Lancashire. For two consecutive nights the 'strange flaming' in the sky was so bright that *'one could not see clearly on the ground and it shone in at the windows.'* Accompanying this phenomenon was *'a strange noise in the air heard in many parts this winter, they are called Gabriel Ratchets by country people . . . another strange noise is heard in the air and these are called night-whistlers, which make a whizzing, as if a piece of timber that arrives with violence through the air.'* [1]

No doubt the jury of 1612 would have seen James's *'foul yelling'* as a direct reference to the supernatural.

---

[1] *The Diary of Rev.Oliver Heywood,* (Bolton, 1664)

Chapter Seventeen

The Final Days

Thomas Potts concludes his *'Wonderfull Discoverie of Witchcraft,'* by recording the verdicts and the final judgement of Sir Edward Bromley:

There the Iurie of Life and Death hauing spent the most part of the day in due consideration of their offences, returned into the Court to deliuer up their Verdict against them, as followeth.

The Verdict of Life and Death

Who vpon their Oathes found Iohn Bulcock and Iane Bulcock his mother, not guiltie of the Felonie by Witch-craft, contained in the Indictment against them. (This was actually an error in Potts' account - the Bulcocks were found guilty and executed).

Alizon Deuice conuicted vpon her owne Confession.

Whereupon Master Couel was commaunded by the Court to take away the Prisoners conuicted, and to bring forth Margaret Pearson, and Isabell Robey, Prisoners in the Castle at Lancaster, to receiue their Triall. Who were brought to their Arraignement and Trialls, as hereafter followeth, viz.

The Prisoners being brought to the Barre

The Court commanded three solemne Proclamations for silence, vntill Iudgement for Life and Death were giuen. Whereupon I presented to his lordship the names of the Prisoners in order, which were now to receiue their Iudgement.

The names of the Prisoners at the Barre to receiue their Judgement of Life and Death.

Anne Whittle; Elizabeth Deuice; James Deuice; Anne Redferne; Alice Nutter; Katherine Hewet; John Bulcock; Jane Bulcock; Alizon Deuice; Isabel Robey

The Judgement of Sir Edward Bromley, Knight, one of his Maiesties Iustices of Assize at Lancaster vpon the Witches conuicted, as followeth.

There is no man aliue more vnwilling to pronounce this wofull and heauy Iudgement against you, then my selfe: and if it were possible, I would to God this cup might passe from me. But since it is otherwise prouided, that after all proceedings of the Law, there must be a Iudgement; and the Execution of that Iudgement must succeed and follow in due time: I pray you haue patience to receiue that which the Law doth lay vpon you. You of all people haue the least cause to complaine: since in the Triall of your liues there hath beene great care and paines taken, and much time spent: and very few or none of you, but stand conuicted vpon your owne voluntarie confessions and Examinations, Ex ore proprio. Few Witnesses examined against you, but such as were present, and parties in your Assemblies. Nay I may further affirme, What persons of your nature and condition, euer were Arraigned and Tried with more solemnitie, had more libertie giuen to pleade or answere to euerie particular point of Euidence against you?

In conclusion such hath beene the generall care of all, that had to deale with you, that you haue neither cause to be offended in the proceedings of the Iustices, that first tooke paines in these businesses, nor with the Court that hath had great care to giue nothing in euidence against you, but matter of fact; Sufficient matter vpon Record, and not to induce or leade the Iurie to finde any one of you guiltie vpon matter of suspition or presumption, nor with the witnesses who haue beene tried, as it were in the fire: Nay, you cannot denie but must confesse what extraordinarie meanes hath beene vsed to make triall of their euidence, and to discouer the least intended practice in any one of them, to touch your liues vniustly.

As you stand simply (your offences and bloudie practises not considered) your fall would rather moue compassion, then exasperate any man. For whom would not the ruine of so many poore creatures at one time, touch, as in apparance simple, and of little vnderstanding?

But the bloud of those innocent children, and others his Maiesties Subiects, whom cruelly and barbarously you haue murdered, and cut off, with all the rest of your offences, hath cryed out vnto the Lord against you, and sollicited for satisfaction and reuenge, and that hath brought this heauie iudgement vpon you at this time.

It is therefore now time no longer wilfully to striue, both against the prouidence of God, and the Iustice of the Land: the more you labour to acquit your selues, the more euident and apparant you make your offences to the World. And vnpossible it is that they shall either prosper or continue in this World, or receiue reward in the next, that are stained with so much innocent bloud.

The worst then I wish to you, standing at the Barre conuicted, to receiue your Iudgement, is, Remorse, and true Repentance, for the safegard of your Soules, and after, an humble, penitent, and heartie acknowledgement of your grieuous sinnes and offences committed both against God *and Man.*

First, yeeld humble and heartie thankes to Almightie God for taking hold of you in your beginning, and making stay of your intended bloudie practises (although God knowes there is too much done alreadie) which would in time have cast so great a weight of Iudgement vpon your Soules.

Then praise God that it pleased him not to surprize or strike you suddenly, euen in the execution of your bloudie Murthers, and in the middest of your wicked practises, but hath giuen you time, and takes you away by a iudiciall course and triall of the Law.

Last of all, craue pardon of the World, and especially of all such as you haue iustly offended, either by tormenting themselues, children, or friends, murder of their kinsfolks, or losse of any their goods.

And for leauing to future times the president of so many barbarous and bloudie murders, with such meetings, practises, consultations, and meanes to execute reuenge, being the greatest part of your comfort in all your actions, which may instruct others to hold the like course, or fall in the like sort:

It only remaines I pronounce the Iudgement of the Court against you by the Kings authoritie, which is;

You shall all goe from hence to the Castle, from whence you came; from thence you shall bee carried to the place of Execution for this Countie: where your bodies shall bee hanged vntill you be dead; And God Have Mercie Vpon Yovr Sovles; For your comfort in this world I shall commend a learned and worthie Preacher to instruct you, and prepare you, for an other World: All I can doe for you is to pray for your Repentance in this World, for the satisfaction of many; And forgiuenesse in the next world, for sauing of your Soules. And God graunt you may make good vse of the time you haue in this world, to his glorie and your owne comfort.

Margaret Pearson

The Iudgement of the Court against you, is, You shall stand vpon the Pillarie in open Market, at Clitheroe, Paddiham, Whalley, and Lancaster, foure Market dayes, with a Paper vpon your head, in great Letters, declaring your offence, and there you shall confesse your offence, and after to remaine in Prison for one yeare without Baile, and after to be bound with good Sureties, to be of the good behauiour.

And so ten people (eight women and two men) were judged to have been worthy of being summarily removed from the face of the earth. Elizabeth Southern would have brought the total number of executions to eleven but her demise in the stinking Lancaster Well Tower dungeon had spared her the rope. We must not forget also that Jennet Preston had been hanged at York a few days earlier (on the 29th of July). The wording of the death sentence passed by Sir Edward Bromley was designed to reflect his professional position, a need to rid the country of such damnable creatures was balanced by contrition; that the poor souls should have had the temerity to be poor in the first place was a source of great sadness to him!

History does not inform us as to how many people of the forest area attended the Lancaster Assizes. There is no doubt that the affair would have caused a massive stir both locally and in the wider northern region, the court rooms were packed to bursting point and within a day of the trials beginning, on Monday the 17th August, the broadsheet sellers and street-ballad singers were proffering their wares in all of the major towns of the North West.

In the afternoon of the 18th August Judge Bromley had heard the opening of the witch trials where Chattox, Elizabeth Device and James Device were found guilty; Ann Redfern was tried and acquitted. The following day Ann Redfern was tried on a second charge of witchcraft and convicted, the Samlesbury Witches were tried and acquitted whilst Alice Nutter and Katherine Hewit were tried and found guilty. In the afternoon John Bulcock and his mother, Jane Bulcock, Alison Device, Margaret Pearson and Isabel Roby were all tried and found guilty. This was followed by all of the convicted prisoners being brought before the judge who then passed the death sentence. On Thursday the 20th August Sir Edward Bromley confirmed the sentence of death by hanging upon the nine condemned prisoners and sentenced Margaret Pearson to the pillory to be followed by a period of incarceration.

Large crowds of onlookers would have attended the mass execution in Lancaster on that later-summer day in 1612. Many lined the streets as the cart passed with its sad load of condemned prisoners; pathetic, starved and shivering with fear this once-proud group of Pendle Forest people sat with their backs to the horses. Surrounded by their own makeshift wooden coffins the prisoners stared blankly at the baying crowds as the un-sprung 'dungeon-cart' rattled, bumped and swayed along the bone-shaking road to Gallows Hill. Having left the Castle gates behind the pitiful procession would have passed along Moor Lane and Moor Gate before making a stop at the newly built Golden Lion Inn; the prisoners would have been allowed a final drink at the inn along with their friends and relatives. A more heart-rending sight than this can hardly be imagined, mothers and daughters, mothers and sons, all on their way to certain death were spending a last few precious minutes with their loved ones whilst surrounded by drunken, rowdy revellers out for the day's 'entertainment.'

The nine condemned forest-folk were hanged together upon Gallows Hill; this was an area of moorland close to Williamson Park. As the sad group breathed out their last it is possible that their family and friends would have grabbed their legs and pulled as they dangled from the heavy wooden gallows, this hastened the process of strangulation and was seen as an act of mercy. Finally, having been pronounced dead by both the Lancaster coroner, Thomas Covell, and the prison surgeon, the nine rough coffins would have been unceremoniously piled into an open pit on the present site of Nightingale Hall Farm, now a Quaker graveyard. Within the execution area stands St. Martin's College and, within a short distance, an ancient row of cottages carries the emotive name of *Golgotha*. This translates from the Hebrew as *Place of the Skulls* and this surely reflects the grisly history of the area.

Such then is the end of our story. We are left only with reflections of an age by which many of us are fascinated but most would not care to visit. An age of strict codes of conduct within and between the social classes; unfortunately this conduct did not often filter down the ladder of a society in which the 1612 Witch trials could take place. We have seen that there is good reason to believe that the Old Demdike of folklore was actually of a decent yeoman family, circumstances conspired against the young woman and she was probably married-off by her family. This brought her into the Pendle Forest area where her husband died leaving her with a daughter and a son from a previous relationship; if Elizabeth Southern had not already dabbled in the healing and herbal practices so prevalent in the forest she soon learned to do so following the death of her husband. The coppers and farm-produce she would earn from curing a sick beast here and there, or supplying a love-potion to some young farm lad with his eye on a dairy maid, would have meant the difference between real hardship and survivable poverty.

Here, in the West Close and Goldshaw areas of Pendle Forest, Demdike honed her natural skills and a legend was born; the legend would gain legs and run as time passed and the family of the newly widowed Demdike arranged for her to live in the far corner of the forest in a tiny cottage called Mawken Yard. Demdike's daughter, Elizabeth Device, lost her husband John in the year 1600 and it was possibly this event led to her following her mother across the forest to Mawken along with her three children, one of whom was a newborn baby; no doubt grandmother would look after the child in order for Elizabeth Device to earn a living of sorts.

For the next twelve years the extended family listened to Demdik'es fantastic stories of Familiars and spells, stories designed to increase the old woman's standing in the community and to enable her to gain work as a mid-wife, herbalist and healer. Little would any of them have realised what the dreadful consequences of these beliefs were going to be. The older generation, such as Demdike and Chattox, were instilled with the Catholic doctrines as many generations of their forefathers had been; they had the old ways coursing through their veins. The new Protestant/Puritan faction were in great fear of a Catholic revival and did everything within their power to prevent this; the Catholic prayers were now referred to as charms and the practice of blessing with beads and bells had now become sorcery or conjuring.

When Anne Whittle used the following lines in order to cure sour ale she was recanting an old prayer that invoked the Holy Trinity against the ill-will, curses and evil-eye of the witch:

> *Three Biters hast thou bitten,*
> *The hart, ill eye, ill Tonge;*
> *Three bitter shall be thy Boote*
> *father, Sonne and Holy Ghost*
> *a God's name.*
> *Five Pater-nosters, five Avies,*
> *and a Creede,*
> *In worship of five wounds*
> *Of Our Lord.*

The pre-Reformation beliefs, then, were writ-large within the poor forest communities; the very spells and incantations that they used in their every-day lives had been accepted a generation earlier as the norm; within living memory their usage had been taken as a sign of someone who had been brought up to be a decent God-fearing Christian. Unfortunately, 'another man's meat is another man's poison' and the pent-up angst of a new generation would ensure that the old practices, however innocently or naively intended, would be stamped upon with great force.

Demdike was all-but blind and obviously very frail in her later years, there is no doubt, however, that she was still the matriarch of the Malkin brood; when her daughter required someone to fight her battles, to stand up to the insults of Richard Baldwin, the frail figure of Old Demdike stepped into the fray. Because of her demise within the Well Tower dungeon we will never know how Elizabeth Southern might have reacted in the courtroom to the trial of her family; would she have begged for mercy for them as Old Chattox did? Would she have vociferously protested her innocence in the manner of the Bulcocks? Perhaps she would have cut a dignified figure, composed and resigned to her fate as we are led to believe was the case with her friend Alice Nutter.

John Bulcock and his mother, Jane, paid the ultimate price for having lived a poor life in the forest, they protested their innocence loud and long, to the bitter end in fact. It is difficult at this distance not to accept the fact that they had been framed and to imagine the depth of despair that would have caused to them and their family. Chattox pleaded for her daughter's life whilst the daughter of Elizabeth Device threw her mother's life away. Little is known about the character of Elizabeth Southern beyond the standard caricature of the old hag furnished by Thomas Potts.

The Malkin *firehouse* in which Elizabeth Southern lived was probably a small two or three roomed half-timbered cottage, built around the end of the fifteenth century, or early in the sixteenth century, for the workers on the Mawken Yard garden. This garden could well have been a specialised arable enclosure and had been cultivated and taken from the rough grazing and semi-waste of the southern Blacko Hillside. The rent from the sub-tenant of this property went to the incumbent of the parish of Colne until the *Dissolution of the Chantries* saw this property being re-let. The small size of Mawken Yard meant that it would become increasingly untenable; population growth in the sixteenth century led to ever-larger areas being developed and Mawken reverted back into being a tiny part of the Stone Edge/Park Hill estates. Elizabeth Southern's sister-in-law was related to Christopher Robinson of Stone Edge and through this link with the estate Elizabeth was allowed the use of the cottage property at Mawken, possibly around 1580-90. By this time the property could have been empty for some time and was of little value. Christopher Holgate, John Device and perhaps members of the Ingham family helped Elizabeth to improve the dilapidated cottage; following a clean-out, a couple of new windows, a new door and two cartloads of bracken from nearby Admergill Banks to repair the roof, the cottage would once again be reasonably habitable.

Demdike, possibly still only in her forties when she arrived at Malkin, would have settled in well to her new home. She continued to bumble about her business in the forest, still tripping around the lanes and leaping the hedges of her old stamping grounds in West Close and Goldshaw; a flippant wave of a sprig of bog-myrtle here, a bit of a curse there, a pull of the face in some churchwarden's direction and a two-fingered salute to Richard Baldwin whenever she happened upon him – all this was part of a normal day at the office for Old Ma Demdike. In 1590 her first grandchild was born and named James after his mother's cousin, James Blackburn. Three years later baby Alicea arrived and the proud grandmother spent much of her time at her daughter's household, helping with the children wherever she could. In 1595, the Device family was blessed with another child, a boy named Henry, again after his Mother's cousin; unfortunately young Henry was not destined to live long as, in 1599, he died at the age of four. This hit Demdike hard, she was now approaching the age of sixty and the hard forest life was beginning to take its toll, she was becoming hunched with the continuous cold and damp of the forest and, above all, she was developing cataracts, her sight was rapidly beginning to fail.

The death of young Henry possibly affected Demdike to the extent that she became mentally unstable for some eight weeks; on the other hand there could have been a nasty bout of pneumonia or influenza in the forest and Demdike caught it, she might have passed this to young Henry and the resulting infection carried the unfortunate child off.

Things did not improve in the following year as Demdike's son-in-law, John Device, died and to cap it all Elizabeth Device bore another child in this year, allegedly to a man named Seller. The death of her husband might have seen Elizabeth Device and her young family being evicted from their home within the western forest but fortunately there was a property available next-door to Demdike's cottage at Mawken. This timber-framed building, again in need of repair but a potential home nevertheless, may have been a small barn and root-store. This stood on the very spot on which the original farmhouse at Malkin Tower Farm now stands, a few yards down the hill from the Mawken cottage. The Device family quickly moved into the building and made it into a home as best they could; this was to become James Device's *'Mother's house'* whilst the neighbouring Mawken cottage was his *'Grandmother's house'* and the *'Firehouse'*, following the death of Demdike this too became his *'Mother's house.'*

Photograph courtesy of A. Turner and Mrs. Hartley-Sutcliffe

The Malkin Tower farmhouse around 1900; the above photograph shows members of the Hartley-Sutcliffe family whose ancestors had farmed at Malkin for generations. The farmhouse was probably built by Richard Towneley (died 1727) in the early eighteenth century whilst the outshut porch building to the left was added at a later date. This structure, now demolished, was known as a 'shop' and would have been used in the delaine weaving trade so prevalent in the nineteenth century upon the Blacko Hillside.

Blacko Tower, Blacko Hillside and Black Dyke Nook; looking westward from Mawkin Hole

The writings of Potts have been examined and criticised within this text and the dangers of inter-age assumptions have been acknowledged; in the final analysis, however we ourselves might judge the echoes of the past by pondering upon the fact that if Master Potts had not responded to the wishes of his Patron (Lord Knyvett) and written up the prosecution evidence we would never have had the invaluable record of the events of 1612 in which we are so fortunate.

It is time, then, to conclude the search for the ethereal Malkin Tower. The research for Demdike's dwelling has led through forest and file, book and bog, ream and stream, publication and pub – ultimately the evidence exists to enable us to at least say that we have a viable site for the lost buildings of legend.

One abiding mystery remains when we consider the life and times of Elizabeth Southern. How did she acquire the surname of Southern? No records to date have been able to furnish an explanation for this. Did she take up with a man of that name in later life? Did she adopt the name in order to protect her extended Blackburn and Ingham families when it became apparent that she would be in the public gaze. Or did her landowning relatives make it a condition of her being allowed to live at Mawken Garden that she would change her name from Ingham? If so this would indicate that Demdike had earned a reputation for herself within the forest long before she arrived at Mawken.

Whatever the case may, be a lady is entitled to keep a secret here and there!

Demdike's Lament

Such power have I, of seasoned renown
to bring the memory crashing down,
And visit ill the house of Read,
by bitter winds I would succeed;

But this I trow will serve no man,
Stilled be my spirit and stayed be my hand.

Gabriel's door stands wide undone,
washed bright with my children's blood,
The hand of man has finally done,
nor seventy winters could.

The rats and the mice, the fleas and the lice
dance to Hell's dungeon tune,
Mocking chains and rattling lungs,
rasp out their rhythmic drone,
And. . .
Drifting now in my final hour
through the sweet high meadows of home.

What would I ne'er give as I close my eyes,
to be that young maid again?
Who ran along with the morning song
of the meadowlark and wren.

Aye! all would I give in this life-dusk hour,
to see daylight-rise over Malkin's Tower.

Still now she lies in careworn rags,
Once proud in her Green Wood home,
Known by her memory as witch, crone and hag,
Her blindness and burden now gone.

The long, sharp road to Old Malkin's Tower,
the ways of man unknown,
The weight of age decays forest flower,
but sweet Bella Donna still grows!

J A Clayton

Appendix I

The Cousinhood of Gentry

A deed of covenant in 1579 saw the lands of Edward Bradyll of Whalley transfer to Ralph Assheton, John Nowell of Read (uncle to Roger) and John Crombock of Whalley. The Assheton and Nowell families we have met with but not the Crombocks – we shall see later that they were related to the Nutters of Greenhead of whom Old Chattox and her family may have been sub-tenants. The lands granted by Bradyll were formerly the property of Whalley Abbey and stretched from Simonstone (near Read) to Blackburn. Some interesting names crop up as tenants on these lands and farmsteads: Henry Hargreaves, the forest constable who played a significant part in the detention of the 1612 accused, was of the Higham/Sabden branch of the family and appears to have rented land at Simonstone. Robert Bulcock was another tenant and was related to the Hartleys of New Laund who were related to the families of Alice Nutter (1612 accused) and Henry Mitton (1612 victim). William Blackburn was a tenant in Billington whilst his brother George Blackburn, and Thomas Holker, tenanted farms in Dinkeley, both in the Blackburn area. Blackburn is a surname that we have an interest in relating to the possible origins of Elizabeth Southern and this will increase in relevance as our story unfolds.

The powerful Houghton family take their place in the story when Henry Houghton of Pendleton marries Katherine in 1453. Their son William had a son John Houghton who married Katherine, daughter of Ralph Catterall of Mitton, she was the widow of Henry Shuttleworth of Hacking Hall in Great Mitton. John and Katherine had a son Roger Houghton who, in 1516 married Elizabeth the daughter of William Lister of Middop whose family were involved in the 1612 prosecution of Jennet Preston for witchcraft. Roger and Elizabeth had a son, William Houghton, who married Margaret the daughter of Sir John Towneley of Towneley Hall in 1537. John and Katherine had another son, Henry Houghton, who married Jane, their son John married Agnes Ashmole, their daughter Katherine married Thomas Houghton (brother of Sir Richard of Houghton Tower) and they in turn had a daughter Anne Houghton who married Symon Blakey the owner of a large part of the lands around Malkin in Blacko.

The sister of Sir Richard Houghton married Sir Thomas Gerard who was the brother of John Gerard *'the most wanted priest in England.'* John Gerard it was who was fundamental in the organisation of the Gunpowder Plot and his brother, Sir Richard, eschewed his Catholic background to become a convert to the Protestant faith (on the face of things at least). Along with his brother-in-law, Sir Richard Houghton, Gerard made a show of his new-found loyalty to the king in 1611 by being the first baronet to fund the Protestant movement in Ulster. Further to this their display of loyalty also included a marked involvement in the hunt for poor none-conformists to serve up to the authorities as witches in 1612.

A daughter of John and Katherine, Jane Houghton, married Richard Greenacres in 1517, their son, John Greenacres (MP, of Worston - died 1608/9), married Ann and their son Richard Greenacres (died 1618) married Jane Sherburne of Little Mitton. John and Ann also had a daughter, Jane Greenacres who married Thomas Lister of Arnoldsbiggin in 1572 – this was Thomas Lister senior who was reputedly bewitched to death by Jennet Preston. The niece of Jane (nee Greenacres) was Frances Greenacres who married Nicholas Assheton son and heir of Richard Assheton of Downham.

Further to the above Asshton relationship we bring into the fray the family of de Legh. John Legh married Cecilia de Towneley in 1321 and their son, Gilbert Legh (possessor of the

Towneley estate) married Alice Vernon and their son, also Gilbert Legh, married Katherine the daughter of Sir Richard Balderston. It is worth noting at this stage that Balderston was the maiden name of Jennet Preston; in the fifteenth century there were two prominent members of the Balderston family – Richard de Balderston esquire shows up in the Towneley family records as having been involved in land ownership at Ribchester. In 1441 Richard Balderston and Richard Towneley evict the tenant, Elias de Coke, from a farm at Ribchester and Richard Balderston and the rector of Ribchester, John Etheliswick, take the property to themselves. Thomas de Harrington, son of Sir James Harrington, confirmed this transaction. Later, in 1496, one William Balderston (probably the son of Richard) clerk, and Edward Whitehead, chaplain, made Miles Kippax and James Marsden their attorneys of land around Malkin *lying next to Blackhowe within the forrest of Penhill.'*

The Legh family were closely involved in the abbey at Stanlaw before it relocated to Whalley where they became as closely involved in the new enterprise, according to Whitaker they were amongst the first to supply monks to the new abbey. Another daughter of Sir Richard Balderston, Hellen, married into the leading family of Radcliffe when she married Richard of Clitheroe. In the fourteenth century one of this family was outlawed for burning down the Pudsey family's manor house at Bolton-by-Bowland and the abbot of Whalley seized his lands. Richard, the son of Hellen and Richard Radcliffe, was the Master Forester of Blackburnshire and died in 1522 but not before he had a son, Thomas Radcliffe, who married Alice Gerard of the family of Sir Thomas the crypto-Catholic and his bother John, the Catholic outlaw.

Thomas and Alice Radcliffe had a daughter, Cicely, who married Thomas Farrington, this family were important landowners and in the nineteenth century would assume ownership, mainly by marriage, of large tracts of land within the Pendle district. They owned much of the area of Nether Barrowford at this time and continued to do so well into the twentieth century. Cicely was widowed and remarried to Edward Radcliffe who had previously been married to Matilda, the daughter of Roger Nowell of Read. By Edward Radcliffe, Cicely had a daughter, Johanna who married Ralph Assheton of Lever. They had a son, Richard, who married Margaret Hutton and acquired the Downham estate by gift of his great-uncle, Richard was supposedly bewitched to death by Elizabeth Southern in 1597. We have already made the acquaintance of Nicholas (born 1590 - died 1625), the other son of Richard and Margaret, when he married Frances Greenacres, the niece of Jane and Thomas Lister. Dorothy, the only sister of Nicholas and Richard married Richard Sherburne, the younger son of Sir Richard Sherburne of Stoneyhurst. . . . And that is just the tip of the iceberg of local gentry cousinhood!

Appendix II

The Smallholder's Plight

Early in the reign of James I the Crown decided to contest the land tenure of the forest area and this caused a great deal of anguish and upheaval amongst the lesser landowners. The king's bare-faced cheek was rewarded by a compromised settlement whereby the tenants made a one-off payment to the Crown. Things quietened down for a while but by 1611 the king was up to his old tricks. He commissioned another enquiry as to the 'doubtful' land-holdings and new lands taken from wastes. The Crown commissioners appointed to oversee the new legalised robbery were none other than Sir Richard Mollyneux and Sir Ralph Ashton, to whom John Nutter of

Greenhead was servant. The commissioners stated that they would only recognise copyholds if they were purchased from the king for £0: 9s: 4d per acre (twenty-eight years rent at four pence per acre). A carrot was offered here in as much as any tenant wishing to pay this sum was offered extra waste land, the ordinary people were understandably unhappy with this state of affairs and said so. The gentry, however, were quick to spot an opportunity to acquire yet more land, this put them at variance with their smaller neighbours. Again, the Crown won the case and the copyholders of the Manor of Ightenhill paid a settlement of £2,141: 10s: 10d – this ensured that the remaining waste lands were divided amongst them at a rental of six pence per acre. However, this incident would have caused much unrest and ill feeling on behalf of the poorer classes against the local gentry; furthermore one of the local yeomanry, in the shape of John Nutter, would have been firmly on the side of the Crown; this would surely have reflected badly on Nutter and his family whose standing within the local community would have been somewhat tainted.

The steward's deputies were despatched into the forest with their customary heavy-handed approach and demanded equal payment regardless of whether the inhabitants were struggling or prospering. It is perfectly reasonable, then, to assume that the poor would oppose the government authorities on the new tenancy order; to what extent, however, did the rich landowners see an opportunity to evict the smallholders adjoining their own lands and thus gain them for themselves? Was the date of 1611, in which the Crown acted, of any significance to the roundup of the poor in 1612? We have seen that Jennet Preston, Anne Whittle and Elizabeth Southern lived in dwellings upon larger estates – in the all of these cases their families may have previously held the tenancies of holdings upon these estates. Alice Nutter had, by reason of her dower, a veto on the sale of Roughlee properties. If a part of the ultimate objective was for particular members of the gentry to gain/regain certain tenements and closes by evicting them through accusations of witchcraft then their devious machinations worked a treat!

Appendix III

The Device Name in Parish Records

One of the most common problems encountered in palaeography is the minim, or downstroke of the pen. In cursive handwriting some words can appear to be nothing other than a row of minims as illustrated here; *minimimum* In cases such as this it is worth remembering that the letter **i** is a single minim, **n** or **u** are made up of two minims and the letter **m** has three. By counting the number of minims, and placing the awkward word within context of the sentence, it is usually possible to arrive at the correct meaning.

With direct relevance to the *Denis–Device* transcription from the original records the following extract is from *'The Voices of Morebath'*, Eamon Duffy, Yale University Press, 2001;

P18; The translation of Tudor (1549) records kept by the priest of Morebath in Devon reads; *'Sent Davys downe ys campe'* – in the nineteenth century this was translated as *'Sent Denys downe his campe.'* This gives a clear example of the palaeographic difficulty encountered within the *Denys, Dennis, Denis, Devis* and *Device* transcription of the surname *Davies*.

Bibliography

Ainsworth, W. H	The Lancashire Witches - a Romance of Pendle Forest 1854
Bannister, F	The Annals of Trawden Forest 1922
Bennet, W	The History of Burnley - Vols 1 and 2 1946
Bennet, W	The History of Marsden and Nelson 1957
Bennet, W	The Pendle Witches 1957
Blakey, J	Annals of Barrowford 1929
Brigg, M	The Early History of the Forest of Pendle
Brigg, M	The Forest of Pendle in the Seventeenth Century; Part Two (paper) 1963
Byrne, C H	Newchurch-in-Pendle – Folklore fact and Fiction 1982
Camden, W	Britannia - 1695 reprint of 1586 original
Carr, J	Annals and Stories of Colne 1878
Chetham Soc.	Wonderfull Discoverie of Witches in the Countie of Lancaster - written by Thomas Potts 1613 and republished 1845
Clayton, J. A	Valley of the Drawn Sword - History of Burnley, Pendle & Craven 2006
Conroy, M. P	Backcloth to Gawthorpe 1971
Crowther, D	Various unpublished genealogies
Dyffy, E	The Voices of Morebath 2001 Yale University Press
Farrar, W	Clitheroe Court Rolls - Vols 1, 2 and 3 1912
Fell, J	Window on Whalley
Harland & Wilkinson	Lancashire Legends 1873
Harrison, D	The History of Colne (Pendle Heritage) 1998
Hopwood, E	The Lancashire Weaver's Story - Amalgamated Weavers Assoc. 1969
Kenyon, D	The Origins of Lancashire 1991
Lambert, Ven. C H	Whalley Abbey – Yesterday and Today
Lancashire Parish Register Soc.	Indexes and Registers of Newchurch-in-Pendle 2002
Lumby, J	The Lancashire Witch Craze 1995
Macvicar, J. R	Colne Parish Church 1944
Moncrief, A. R. H	Classic Myth and Legend - Gresham
Moorhouse, C	The Birth of a Lancashire Village (Sabden) 1975
Mullett & Warren	Martyrs of the Diocese of Lancaster 1987
Pearson, S	Rural Houses of the Lancashire Pennines 1985
Peel & Southern	The Trials of the Lancashire Witches 1969
Poole, R	The Lancashire Witches - Histories and Stories 2002
Smith, R	Blackburnshire - occasional paper of 1961
Snape, A. W	English Martyrs Whalley 2000
Spencer, K. G	An Outline History of Habergham Eaves 1989
Starkey, D	The Monarchy of England - Vol 1 2004
Whitaker, T. D	The History of Whalley - 1st edition 1881
Whitaker, T. D	The History of Craven 1885
Walton, J	Pendle Forest Folk 1950
Welch, M	Anglo-Saxon England (English Heritage) 1992
Whittaker, G	Roughlee Hall - Fact and Fiction 1980
Williams, E	Walks and Talks with Fellman 1951

Illustrations and Plates

Whittle/ Redfern Family (proposed)

All Newchurch St. Mary unless otherwise stated

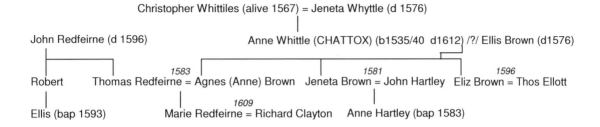

Christopher Whittiles (alive 1567) = Jeneta Whyttle (d 1576)

John Redfeirne (d 1596)   Anne Whittle (CHATTOX) (b1535/40 d1612) /?/ Ellis Brown (d1576)

Robert   Thomas Redfeirne = Agnes (Anne) Brown   Jeneta Brown = John Hartley   Eliz Brown = Thos Ellott
1583   1581   1596

Ellis (bap 1593)   Marie Redfeirne = Richard Clayton   Anne Hartley (bap 1583)
1609

The Early Blackburn Family (proposed)

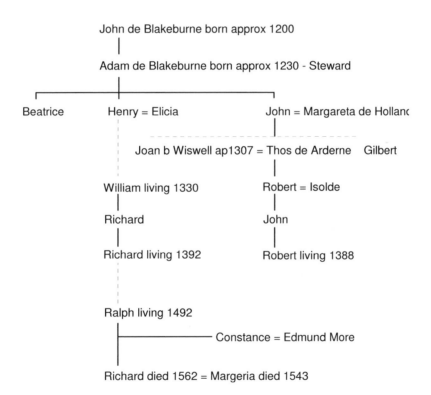

John de Blakeburne born approx 1200

Adam de Blakeburne born approx 1230 - Steward

Beatrice   Henry = Elicia   John = Margareta de Holland

Joan b Wiswell ap1307 = Thos de Arderne   Gilbert

William living 1330   Robert = Isolde

Richard   John

Richard living 1392   Robert living 1388

Ralph living 1492

Constance = Edmund More

Richard died 1562 = Margeria died 1543

The early Blackburn genealogy shows the proposed family of Elizabeth Southern prior to the extended family tree on page 209.

The Nutter Family (proposed)

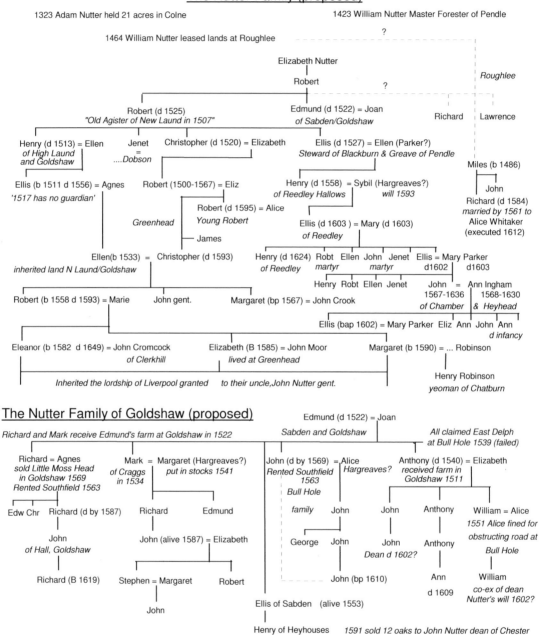

1323 Adam Nutter held 21 acres in Colne   1423 William Nutter Master Forester of Pendle

1464 William Nutter leased lands at Roughlee   ?

Elizabeth Nutter

Robert   ?   *Roughlee*

Robert (d 1525)   Edmund (d 1522) = Joan   Richard | Lawrence
"Old Agister of New Laund in 1507"   *of Sabden/Goldshaw*

Henry (d 1513) = Ellen   Jenet   Christopher (d 1520) = Elizabeth   Ellis (d 1527) = Ellen (Parker?)
of High Laund   =   *Steward of Blackburn & Greave of Pendle*
and Goldshaw   *....Dobson*

Miles (b 1486)

Ellis (b 1511 d 1556) = Agnes   Robert (1500-1567) = Eliz   Henry (d 1558) = Sybil (Hargreaves?)   John
'1517 has no guardian'   *of Reedley Hallows   will 1593*   Richard (d 1584)
        Robert (d 1595) = Alice   *married by 1561 to*
    Greenhead   Young Robert   Ellis (d 1603) = Mary (d 1603)   *Alice Whitaker*
        James   *of Reedley*   *(executed 1612)*

Ellen(b 1533) = Christopher (d 1593)   Henry (d 1624) Robt Ellen John Jenet Ellis = Mary Parker
inherited land N Laund/Goldshaw   *of Reedley martyr   martyr*   d1602 | d1603
        Henry Robt Ellen Jenet   John = Ann Ingham
            1567-1636 | 1568-1630
Robert (b 1558 d 1593) = Marie   John gent.   Margaret (bp 1567) = John Crook   *of Chamber | & Heyhead*

        Ellis (bap 1602) = Mary Parker Eliz Ann John Ann
                d infancy

Eleanor (b 1582 d 1649) = John Cromcock   Elizabeth (B 1585) = John Moor   Margaret (b 1590) = ... Robinson
        of Clerkhill   *lived at Greenhead*
        Henry Robinson
    Inherited the lordship of Liverpool granted   to their uncle, John Nutter gent.   *yeoman of Chatburn*

The Nutter Family of Goldshaw (proposed)

        Edmund (d 1522) = Joan
Richard and Mark receive Edmund's farm at Goldshaw in 1522   *Sabden and Goldshaw*   *All claimed East Delph*
        at Bull Hole 1539 (failed)

Richard = Agnes   Mark = Margaret (Hargreaves?)   John (d by 1569) = Alice   Anthony (d 1540) = Elizabeth
sold Little Moss Head   *of Craggs put in stocks 1541*   *Rented Southfield Hargreaves?*   *received farm in*
in Goldshaw 1569   1534   1563   *Goldshaw 1511*
Rented Southfield 1563   *Bull Hole*

Edw Chr Richard (d by 1587)   Richard   Edmund   *family* John   John   Anthony   William = Alice
        1551 Alice fined for
John   George   John   John   Anthony   *obstructing road at*
of Hall, Goldshaw   John (alive 1587) = Elizabeth   *Dean d 1602?*   *Bull Hole*

Richard (B 1619)   Stephen = Margaret   Robert   John (bp 1610)   Ann   William
                d 1609   *co-ex of dean*
        John   *Nutter's will 1602?*

        Ellis of Sabden   (alive 1553)

        Henry of Heyhouses   *1591 sold 12 oaks to John Nutter dean of Chester*

Map of Blackburnshire at the time of the De Lacy inquest of 1611

Index